DENIS MONIÈRE is a member of the Department of Political Science at l'Université dc Montréal.

In the years since 1960, Quebec has been transformed by the momentum of the Quiet Revolution and the social and economic impact of modernization. Historians, social scientists, and other commentators have been prompted to take a fresh look at the question of Quebec's future as a society – and to attempt a scientific response. The last two decades have seen unprecedented development in the social sciences in the province.

   Professor Monière brings a focus to Quebec's evolution by studying its ideologies. He locates them in their dynamic economic and historical contexts from the French regime to the present. In so doing, he reveals their relationships to social classes. With few exceptions, the history of ideologies is the history of the ideas of the ruling class. Monière stresses material on the labour movement in order to compensate for this tendency, but takes care not to identify any particular ideology with the whole of Québécois society. His choice of time periods and themes, and of the men and movements by which ideas were spread, highlights the economic and political liberation of Quebec labour at work throughout Quebec's history, as well as the ways in which this class has been blocked.

   This book brings scholarship on ideologies to the fore, opening up the collective memory and putting today's problems in perspective. It is a provocative presentation offering an important insight into how the radical strain views itself and the future of Quebec and the country. It is of particular interest to political scientists and to all interested in the evolution of Canadian society.

DENIS MONIÈRE

Ideologies in Quebec
The historical development

translated by Richard Howard

UNIVERSITY OF TORONTO PRESS

Toronto Buffalo London

© University of Toronto Press 1981
Toronto Buffalo London
Printed in Canada

ISBN 0-8020-5452-8 (cloth)
ISBN 0-8020-6358-6 (paper)

Canadian Cataloguing in Publication Data

Monière, Denis, 1947–

Ideologies in Quebec
Translation of: Le développement des idéologies au
Québec.
Bibliography: p.
ISBN 0-8020-5452-8 (bound). – ISBN 0-8020-6358-6 (pbk.)

1. Quebec (Province) – History. 2. Quebec (Province) –
Politics and government. I. Title.
FC2911.M6613   971.4   C81-094336-0
F1052.95.M6613

This translation was funded by the Canada Council and made by Richard
Howard. It, and the French original, were published with the help of a grant
from the Social Science Federation of Canada, using funds provided by the
Social Sciences and Humanities Research Council of Canada.

To the original work, *Le Développement des idéologies au Québec: des
origines à nos jours* (Montreal: Editions Québec/Amérique, 1977), was
appended the author's reflections, 'The PQ and the Test of Power,' and to
this edition a second essay, 'On the Referendum of May 1980.' Publication
of the translation was also assisted by a grant from the Publications Fund of the
University of Toronto Press.

Contents

Preface to the English Edition

Whatever the future may hold for relations between the two nationalities that form present-day Canada, the reality of the one can never be expunged from the collective consciousness of the other. This country's history has been profoundly influenced by the uneasy coexistence of the two national communities. All too often, this dialectic of conflict has proceeded in an atmosphere of misunderstanding and mutual incomprehension of the social realities of the English-Canadian and Québécois peoples.

Up to now, perception of the Quebec question has been distorted by the ruling ideology and those who preach it. They take advantage of the absence of complete data, and project their prejudices and simplistic explanations of Québécois political behaviour. The politicians tend to reduce the national question to its linguistic and cultural aspects, glossing over the socio-economic basis of the struggle for political power. This pretence is harmful to both Quebec and Canada, for it stands in the way of a mutually advantageous settlement of the constitutional crisis. As they persistently refuse to change the power structure, and as persistently relegate francophone identity to one of culture, the Canadian political élites are acting against the best interests of the English-Canadian as well as the Québécois people. They are simply not addressing the causes of the conflicts that have always impeded the functioning of the Canadian political system. They intend to begin the process again instead of moving towards a new and mutually acceptable agreement.

I hope that English-language publication of this synthesis of historical ideologies in Quebec will contribute to a better understanding of Québécois demands, and encourage the search for a solution that will result in harmonious relations between Quebec and Canada. Knowledge of the economic, social, and ideological evolution of Quebec is an indispensable part of this process, for with it we can isolate the constants in the life of the Québécois community, and dismiss the delusions of the politicos. The Québécois response to the referendum and the current plan for constitutional reform will solve nothing. We must give urgent consideration to our respective futures, working from a historical awareness of our two situations. Knowing where we have come from will help us realize where we are going.

DENIS MONIÈRE
Dunham, November 1980

Preface

The years since 1960 in Quebec have seen an unprecedented surge of development in the social sciences. The momentum of the Quiet Revolution and the socio-economic impact of modernization have prompted historians, social scientists, and other commentators to take a fresh look and attempt a scientific response to the burning question of Quebec's future as a society. Some have merely sifted the past through new conceptual grids, while others have tried to detach the evidence needed for change now, or develop proposals for change to come.

This process has generated a substantial literature. Most research has been highly specialized, or confined to specific periods. At this point, we have little by way of synthesis or comparative study to help bring into focus the general picture of Quebec's evolution. True, its general drift is not impossible to discern for anyone with the time and patience to devote to the task. The basic data exist, although not easily accessible, tucked away in unpublished dissertations and specialist periodicals. Moreover, the variety of approach in these materials is such as to discourage even the most persistent seeker; in the area of ideological studies alone I have counted over a thousand titles.[1]

Hence my decision to attempt a synthesis of the accumulated research on ideologies in Quebec. In doing so, I make no claim to exhaustiveness or originality. I do not pretend to have explained in any conclusive way how economic, social, and political philosophies arose in Quebec. My contribution has been simply to reread the literature, extracting and arranging what seemed to me to be the relevant data, pausing from time to time to hypothesize and point out some basic conflicts. It has also been my aim to locate the various ideologies which have influenced

Quebec society in their dynamic contexts, economic as well as more broadly historical. And I have tried as far as possible to reveal the relationships between these ideologies and the social classes of Quebec. Here my own objectives have not always been those of the studies on which I was drawing, and I have thus been forced to offer hypotheses that are not based on actual research.

With few exceptions, the history of ideologies has so far been the history of the ideas of the ruling class. Unfortunately, I have not been able to steer clear of this bias. I have had to depend on sources where it is present, and the ordinary Québécois and the working class might as well not have existed. Whenever possible, I have tried to compensate for this built-in élitism by stressing what we do have on the labour movement and not identifying any particular ideology with the whole of Québécois society. At the same time, I have not tried to hide my own philosophical preference. The line between ideology and the scholar's analysis is a thin one; there is no study that is not conditioned by a particular aim formed in a particular context. The choice of time periods and themes in this book and the choice of men and movements by which ideas were spread reflect my own desire to highlight the progressive forces that have been at work throughout our history for the economic and political liberation of Quebec labour, as well as the ways in which this class has been blocked, and thus bring out the ideological class struggle of Quebec.

I have not aimed to please everyone. Some will disagree with my basic theory and purpose, while others will criticize me for the passages and interpretations I have chosen, or for any omissions and elliptical reasoning, and will no doubt find other shortcomings as well. The important thing for me, however, is to have brought the scholarship on Quebec ideologies to a wide public, opening up our collective memory and perhaps also putting today's problems in their proper perspective. Without making the past our master, we can usefully make its acquaintance, and recognize the various forces that have given texture to the time in which we live. Understanding where we have come from will make us better able to assess the possibilities before us.

Introduction

A Theory of Ideologies

The concept of ideology is one whose history is strewn with definitions that are vulnerable to particular ideological environments. My purpose here, however, is not to open up debate on how strictly scientific the concept may or may not be, or to explore its academic connections, but simply to define it in such a way that the reader understands my basic subject-matter in what follows, and what I am looking for in the historical movement of ideas in Quebec.

An ideology, then, is a complete and more or less narrowly defined system of concepts, images, myths, and representations which, in a given society, supports a specific hierarchy of values and certain patterns of individual and collective behaviour. This system leads back sociologically to an economically, politically, ethnically, or otherwise limited group, whose more or less consciously realized interests it expresses and rationalizes. It prompts a channelling of human action in accordance with a particular array of value judgments.

An ideology can be defined further in terms of four main functions. First, it presents a particular world view as universal, attempts to 'eternalize' specific values, and is in this sense ahistorical. Second, it acts as an apologetic, defending certain class structures and the domination of a particular class. An ideology is also a vehicle of mystification, for it is a more or less conscious distortion of the reality of a given situation. Finally, it is action oriented, mobilizing the individual and collective energies of a society. It operates on reality and serves as a guide to action.

On its own, my definition is inadequate to explain the ideological phenomenon. It needs to be complemented by an analysis of the process by which ideologies are generated. And here I turn to the tradition of Marx and historical materialism, according to which ideological analysis must go beyond mere recitals of what politicians and parties, pressure groups, and the mass media are thinking and saying, to expose their reasons for making one pronouncement instead of another at one point in time instead of another – to lay bare, in fact, the relation between discourse and material concerns, and to examine this relation critically. If we are to end up with explanations that are plausible, it is essential to set out with a theoretical framework which can satisfy us as to the nature, origins, and development of ideologies, as well as their active roles and functions.

The Marxist background

Marx and Engels addressed the problem of ideology in several works, notably *The German Ideology*, *Theses on Feuerbach*, *The 18th Brumaire*, and *Capital*. In none of these, however, are we given a synthesis definition of the concept. Rather, Marx portrays the ideology at work in a social structure. Hence, the term *ideology* can have various meanings in Marxist theory, and if we are to understand its full significance, we must take it back to the context of historical materialism.

The essence of the materialist idea of history is contained in the postulate that man's consciousness is determined by his social being. The following précis of his approach occurs in Marx's *Contribution to the Critique of Political Economy*:

In the social production of their existence, men inevitably enter into definite relations, which are independent of their will, namely relations of production appropriate to a given stage in the development of their material forces of production. The totality of these relations of production constitutes the economic structure of society, the real foundation, on which arises a legal and political superstructure and to which correspond definite forms of social consciousness. The mode of production of material life conditions the general process of social, political, and intellectual life. It is not the consciousness of men that determines their existence, but their social existence that determines their consciousness.[1]

Marx criticized the thinkers and philosophers who had gone before him for ignoring men's concrete action as a determining factor in history. He saw history as the result, not of God's will or the play of ideas, but of the actual doings of mankind.

Marx and Engels developed their historical materialism in *The German Ideology* in a move to break with that country's idealism and examine it critically. For Marx, German philosophy was idealist in holding that concepts were the determining factors in history, and that to change reality one had only to change one's ideas. In his contrary view, it was not ideas that determined reality, but reality that generated the world of ideas; it was men who made history, by their acts and their labour. They did not make it independently, however, or of their own free will; they were conditioned by their material situation, the state of development of the forces of production. Marx exposed the close connection between all forms of thought and the social reality in which they are generated.

The human reality, he argued, was one of movement. All social realities were seen as transitory. By their actions, men altered their material conditions, changing society and thus changing themselves. Men, then, were made by what they did; they were the products of their products. Since history was the product of acts and not of philosophies, it followed in Marx's thinking that no idea or theoretical system or mode of thought had autonomous existence, and that these could be understood only in relation to the passing social-historical conditions which were the environments of the men who produced them. Anyone wanting to understand and explain the ideas men had of themselves and their societies must relate these ideas to what the men did, the mode of production by which they sustained their material existence.

In addition to this thesis of the indivisibility of thought from action, Marx developed the concept of the collective or transindividual subject. Men made history not as individuals or geniuses – the 'great men' – but as classes. This is not to deny that greater roles were assigned to some; they played their roles, however, not as individuals but as representatives of a class. The ideas of the great men are not their own creations, but rather the dominant ideas generated by the ruling mode of man-nature and man-man relations. The concrete man, for Marx, was the social man. The essence of man, in his teaching, is the aggregate of the social relations in which individual members of the human group are involved.

The central idea I have been developing up to this point is that historical materialism sees human consciousness – what men think about the world and about themselves – as determined by the social being. From this viewpoint, ideology emerges as a social product: to grasp the nature and process of an ideology, we must turn to the concrete manner by which men produce their own existence.

The production of ideas, of conceptions, of consciousness, is at first directly interwoven with the material activity and the material intercourse of men, the language of real life. Conceiving, thinking, the mental intercourse of men, appear at this stage as the direct efflux of their material behaviour. The same applies to mental production as expressed in the language of politics, laws, morality, religion, metaphysics, etc., of a people. Men are the producers of their conceptions, ideas, etc. – real, active men, as they are conditioned by a definite development of their productive forces and of the intercourse corresponding to these, up to its furthest forms.[2]

The determining factor in the thought of an era, Marx insisted, was not divine will, or, as the ideologues had it, the material make-up of the brain and the nervous system, or even, as Feuerbach had it, what men were eating. Here, he was casting out the theories of the metaphysicians, idealists, and coarse materialists. One could not conduct the analysis of ideologies in isolation, reasoning only from what men told themselves or imagined. If their representations were to be understood and explained, men must first be seen in their concrete acts. For Marx, ideas as ideas had no history, no autonomous development, for they were by-products of material action and the social relations of production. Ideologies were invariably linked to and distributed by social classes that used them to try to stabilize their own historical dominant phases, passing them off as universal, transhistorical, and impregnable: 'For each new class which puts itself in the place of the one ruling before it is compelled, merely in order to carry out its aim, to represent its interest as the common interest of all the members of society, that is, expressed in ideal form: it has to give its ideas the form of universality, and represent them as the only rational, universally valid ones.'[3]

In this first sense, then, ideology was for Marx a social product, historically specific and expressing the special conditions affecting the production of material existence. Ideologies arose because of the division of manual and intellectual labour, and the resultant layering of society into classes. Possessing the means of production, the ruling class would generate a value system that portrayed its position as universal and necessary – a natural domination. It then used the system to try to stabilize the rules and behavioural norms of the whole society, so that its position would go unchallenged.

The ideas of the ruling class are in every epoch the ruling ideas: i.e., the class which is the ruling *material* force of society, is at the same time its ruling *intellectual* force. The class which has the means of material production at its disposal, has control at the same time over the means of mental production, so that thereby, generally speaking, the ideas of those who lack the means of mental production are subject to it.[4]

Ideology is essentially, then, a product of the class interaction that constitutes society, and expresses the special conditions for the production of material and social existence that it is designed to promote as universal.

There is another sense, proceeding from the first, in which ideology is a false perception, a delusion. Its dishonest vision of the world does injustice to the reality; it conceals the true situation of the classes of society. It misleads not only the dominant group ambitious for universality but also the dominated classes, who fail to perceive their own true interests or the exploitation, alienation, and domination that afflict them. Seen in a wider perspective, ideology is a false reading of history, false because it is billboarded as universal, autonomous of what is actually happening in a society. For Marx, let us not forget, philosophy and law, religion and morality, art and learning, were autonomous in appearance only.

Thus it is that ideology generates mystification. Offering a value model, it aims to fix answers, not to elicit questions. By presenting a simplified picture of social reality, it limits the range of possibilities. All ideological messages contain blanks: there is what is said, and there is what is not said. No ideology is truly false, since each arises from an at least partial view of reality, but the entire reality eludes an ideology because of the peculiar and specific conditions that engendered it in the first place. None is exempt from delusion because all substitute for the true whole one that is abstract and limited to the ruling class, expressing concerns peculiar to that class. Ideologies, then, bear no record of the connection with their praxis or of the material conditions in which they developed. If they fool the subject classes they also, according to Marx, fool the members of the ruling class in a process of self-deception by which a group of this kind appears spontaneously to blind itself to its true situation, interests, and goals. The process can in many cases be explained by the weight of tradition, of the past: 'Men make their own history, but they do not make it just as they please; they do not make it under circumstances directly encountered, given and transmitted from the past. The tradition of all the dead generations weighs like a nightmare on the brain of the living.'[5] Thus does Marx qualify the role of the economic structure in determining the ideological superstructure. In other words, the dominant mode of production does not necessarily or automatically dictate the accompanying structures of law, politics, and ideology. The mode of production is not the sole determining factor in the elaboration of society and ideology; past ideologies also weigh in the relation of infrastructure to superstructure. So I shall insist again on the dialectical nature of relations between ideology and mode of production; although the former is indeed a mirror of material conditions, it exerts influence in turn on the human actions that create these conditions, and reflects a dialectic that swings from the imagined to the real, the real to the imagined.

In a letter to Bloch in 1890, Engels expanded:

According to the materialist conception of history, the *ultimately* determining element in history is the production and reproduction of real life. More than this neither Marx nor I has ever asserted. Hence if somebody twists this into saying that the economic element is the *only* determining one, he transforms that proposition into a meaningless, abstract, senseless phrase. The economic situation is the basis, but the various elements of the superstructure ... also exercise their influence upon the course of the historical struggles and in many cases preponderate in determining their *form*. There is an interaction of all these elements in which ... the economic movement finally asserts itself as necessary.[6]

Of course, as Lucien Goldmann has noted, Marx's entire output was a critique of political economy. In this sense, the predominance of economic considerations was historically determined; it was certainly not a transhistorical absolute.[7]

The 18th of Brumaire brought important clarification to Marx's idea of ideology, for there he stresses that although it offers a distorted view of reality, and is false and illusory, ideology still has genuine power, and is always active and productive. Ideologies mediate between act and thought. Entering reality, they direct men's actions; providing a rationalization for belief, attitudes, and behaviour, they abet action. They screen reality through special values, and then return to reality with rules and inhibitions. This position has some significant theoretical results: the fact that men conduct and organize their labour and their lives consciously, imagining the product of their action in advance, and attempting to make idea and deed correspond, confers on ideology a degree of productive force, liberating it from the superstructure so that it can be present at all levels, lending them consistency and pulling them together. Thus seen, ideology is not merely an expression; it takes on material qualities in its association with the organization of labour, the apparatus of production, in social and political institutions, and in the machines of law, education, the state, and so on.

In conclusion, then, we can say that the dominant mode of production in any social structure is the chief determinant of the ruling ideology, but that variation can occur because of the ancillary force of superstructural elements typical of that structure, and/or the appearance in the ideological sector of a given society of superstructural elements lent or prescribed by interaction between societies in which the modes of production differ. In this way, I believe, historical materialism can act as an explanatory framework for the dynamic of the ideological process, in which ideologies, while being by-products of structures, also bear the mark of superstructures in and between societies and are involved in the process of social reproduction.

Colonial background[8]

The basic element of Marxist ideological theory is that the emergence of ideas and concepts is conditioned by men's concrete acts, by which they generate their means of existence and the consequent social relations. This alone, however, is not enough to explain the ideological dimension of a society or its developmental process, since there are other factors involved. The dialectic by which ideologies are generated is not only a vertical process but also a horizontal one. In our analyses of modes of production and social formations, we must avoid falling into a simple linear approach and keep in mind that several interrelated modes may exist in a given society.

For instance, a dominant capitalist mode of production can, at least for a time, coexist quite peacefully with surviving elements of modes of production associated with feudalism or slavery, even though the process will lead eventually to the elimination of these elements in favour of generalized capitalism. Depending on the ways in which these modes are interrelated, then, one can expect the superstructure of a dominant mode of production, particularly in periods of transition, to contain traces of the previously dominant mode. Nor can we assume that this coexistence is mutually exclusive, something Marx himself recognized when he referred to the 'weight of tradition'[9] in explaining possible discontinuities between structural and superstructural elements. Thus, elements of a past ideological configuration may be encountered in a current superstructural system.

Moreover, as I have stressed, a society is not to be seen as a sealed system. We must consider its interrelations with other societies using other modes of production. Ideologies, like goods, and often in tandem with these, move around and can significantly influence the plans and ideas of classes in conflict. When we do encounter borrowed ideological elements in a given society, however, they have been revised and adapted according to the material situation of the borrowers. It is in this light that we begin to unravel the process of ideological development in colonized societies.

Before making this beginning, however, and testing whether the process takes a truly special form in colonized societies, I must outline the general principles of ideological change. I will not concentrate here on the problem of the origin of ideologies, or on the psychological factors that are the individual aspect of ideological change; rather, I want to stress the basic factors that can explain this change in terms of history and societies.

Historical materialism sees ideological change in a given society as due chiefly to change in the conditions of the production of material existence, and the social relations that follow from these.

Does it require deep intuition to comprehend that man's ideas, views and conceptions, in one word, man's consciousness, changes with every change in the conditions of his material existence, in his social relations and in his social life?

What else does the history of ideas prove, than that intellectual production changes its character in proportion as material production is changed? The ruling ideas of each age have ever been the ideas of the ruling class.[10]

Analysis of ideological change must therefore start with analysis of these relations of production and society which, out of their inherent tensions, generate various representations or views of the world, so that in the end changes in ideology are brought about by class struggle.

The change here referred to is that occurring in the ruling ideology. It must not be thought, however, that the process unfurls mechanically, by the interplay of structures and the momentum of events. Engels was clear on this point in a January 1894 letter to Heinz Starkenburg:

Political, juridical, philosophical, religious, literary, artistic, etc. development is based on economic development. But all these react upon one another and also upon the economic basis. It is not that the economic situation is *cause, solely active*, while everything else is only passive effect. There is, rather, interaction on the basis of economic necessity, which *ultimately* always asserts itself.[11]

The causality yielded by this approach is multiple, yet ordered hierarchically and dialectically.

Other variables enter the historical dialectic of ideology. In the class struggle, the existing political and ideological apparatus plays an active part and can impede ideological development. The dominant ideology is not without its effect on the growth of ideology among the dominated, since its avowed purpose is to distract these classes from awareness of their subordinate status. In them, one encounters the influence of the ruling group and its ideology.

History, then, is not a well-oiled machine that proceeds with the inexorability of the laws of physics. It emerges from conditions set by practice, the action of collective subjects. The practice is itself conditioned by the weight of structures and the experience of past generations, but it is also influenced by a plan, by the awareness of what is possible and how one might proceed beyond. The routes of change are not laid down *a priori*. Subjective and contingent factors are not excluded, but rather integrated with the overall social process. Such particularities are to be looked at, as well as the whole, in any comprehensive analysis. The advantage of this approach is to allow us to see the various parts within the overall pattern of ideological change.

In the end, the mode of production of material existence determines historical change in ideologies. 'In the end' merely means, however, that when all other determining factors have been considered, we return to the basic element of existence – the production of the means of exist-

ence and the social relations of production. There is no question here
of trying to explain everything by economic factors alone, but simply of realizing that in the final analysis these form the basis of concrete existence and the social whole; and that as a result of this, ideological development occurs in the wake of the development of the relations of production in a given society; that the ideas cannot generate their own change,
but are formed and developed out of practice.

These, then, are the main theoretical signposts which I will use to explore the specificity of ideological development in colonial situations.

Up to now, I have concentrated on the growth of ideology within
social formations. We cannot stop there, however, for with rare exceptions societies are not closed, self-sufficient systems, at least not since
the spread of commercial exchange. We have to analyse the development of capitalism, and look at ideological development in relation to the
interaction among societies with different modes of production.

Historically, the development of capitalism has occurred in non-
capitalist environments. It is a mode of production typified by the need to
expand. Of necessity, the accumulation and regeneration of capital require new markets to absorb surpluses, new sources of raw material and
manpower, new outlets for capital; they work towards the generalization of capitalist relations of production. The result is penetration and conquest of new non-capitalist areas, and the ruin or change of the non-
capitalist social structures encountered in the process of expansion.

My purpose, then, is to discover how this process affects ideological
development in non-capitalist social formations. In doing so, I will use the
dialectical principle noted by Mao Tse-Tung: 'External causes are the
condition of change ... internal causes are its basis, and ... the external
causes work through the internal ones.'[12] This implies that the superstructural effects of capitalist penetration will vary according to the specific
conditions of each non-capitalist society. I will not attempt to record all
possible combinations, but merely outline the general way in which the
process works.

In societies of the centre, the capitalist mode of production tends to be
exclusive, eliminating other modes of production. Hence the social structure tends to polarize into two basic classes, though this does not rule
out the possibility of other social strata formed on a political and ideological basis. In peripheral societies, however, the capitalist mode is introduced from the outside, and its development is conditioned by the outside
market. Thus, it tends only to dominate.

Depending on the time of penetration and the characteristics of the mode of production at the centre as well as the specific conditions obtaining at the periphery, we encounter various hybrids in which dominant capitalism coexists with such precapitalist modes as the tributary, simple merchant, feudal, or slave-owning. These modes are made part of a system, and subject to the goals of capitalism: for example, a peasant works within his old mode of production, but his products are made for export to the centre. Production is therefore carried out primarily for the outside market, and only secondarily to regenerate the internal forces of production. While exchanges are regulated on the basis of capitalism, the production of goods occurs on a non-capitalist basis. 'The form of the peripheral formations will depend finally on both the nature of the precapitalist formations under attack and the types of external aggression.'[13]

This will give rise to a differentiated development in ideology and social structure. The peripheral society will tend to be heterogeneous and not polarized, as in the centre. The peripheral social structure is incomplete, and can be understood only when it is viewed as an element in the world society. The history of Latin America offers a good illustration of this process.

American societies differ from Asiatic or African formations in that the settlers were emigrants who arrived before capitalism triumphed at the centre and either pushed out or exterminated the indigenous peoples. According to Samir Amin:

It was during this mercantilist period that Latin America acquired the main structures that characterize it to this day. These were based on agrarian capitalism of the latifundia type, the labour force of which was supplied by peasants of degraded status (peons and former slaves). To this was added a local merchant bourgeoisie of the comprador type, when the monopoly of the mother country became overstretched.[14]

The process would give power to the landowners and local comprador bourgeoisie, stimulate the growth of a limited proletariat, and reduce the peasant class to poverty. Thus, peripheral societies do not develop on the models of social formations of the centre. And the same is true of their ideological development.

Whereas the standard-bearers of liberal ideology in nineteenth-century Europe were the bourgeois of industry, in Latin America they have been landowners and tradespeople and this has generated all kinds of distortions. I turn to the case of Brazil, so admirably described by Roberto Schwarz, to whom a reading of his country's literature revealed the rift between the liberal values it expresses and the objective reality of human subjection. In Europe, he argues, the concepts of freedom of labour, universalism, and equality before the law did mask the basic truth, that of the exploitation of the workers, but they were still consistent with appearances. In Brazil, they were spurious in quite a different way.

It was inevitable that bourgeois economic philosophy – the priority of profit and its social corollaries – should affect Brazil to the extent that it dominated the international trade which oriented our own economy; and the constant practice of commercial dealings educated, at least in this sense, a limited but not insignificant body of people. Moreover, only a few years previously, we had won our independence in the name of French, English, and American ideas, liberal ideas in varying degrees which thus became part of our national identity. And with the same inevitability, this ideological ensemble would clash with slavery and its supporters – worse, coexist with them.[15]

In ideological terms, the effect of the arrival of the capitalist mode of production in a precapitalist society is to accentuate the rift from the real. Liberal ideology in Brazil accommodated itself to the practice of chattel slavery when it ought in principle to have been its critic. It found itself in contradiction; it became absurd, lost all credibility and real influence. Thus, its function in a colonial setting was not to legitimize the situation by concealing it, but rather to cloak the dominant class with social prestige, allow it to identify itself with the great, modern European world. The reason for its class existence was supplied by external markets. Internally, it was ineffectual. 'As we have seen, the ideas of the bourgeoisie, whose measured grandeur went back to the public-minded and rationalist spirit of the Enlightenment, here took on the functions of ornaments and badges of rank; they certified and celebrated adherence to an august world, that of a Europe ... that was becoming industrialized.'[16] In this dependent environment, ideological development is completely out of step with the real situation. It is a case of ideology's total autonomy from the internal economic base. However, this autonomy expresses nothing more than domination by the external economic base – in other words, dependence on the expansion of the capitalist mode of production at the centre.

To sum up, in our periodicals, our social customs, in our houses, national symbols, revolutionary statement and theory, we encounter the same pied outfit: contradiction between the concept and what examination tells us is its context in reality.

So it is that a latifundia watched largely undisturbed the passage of baroque, neoclassical, romantic, naturalistic, modernist and other styles that in Europe accompanied and expressed immense changes in the social order.[17]

In a dependent society, the reverse is true: change in the dominant ideology is accompanied by inertia in social relations. Thus, this ideology – liberalism in our example – is thrown off balance from its European function, and invariably takes on a false meaning. The distortion is explained historically by the relations of production and of parasitism in the country, by the economic domination and intellectual hegemony of Europe.

In order to understand the specific quality of ideological development in colonized social formations, we have to refocus our approach in terms of the worldwide process of colonization, looking at the distinct modes of production that preceded capitalism, modes that might have been destroyed, marginalized, or preserved, depending on the type of colonization process that took place. We must realize as well that each process of colonization differs according to the state of development of the colonizing power and the specific conditions in the place where penetration occurs. Here, then, we cannot draw on a simple model that would accommodate all possible variants. All one can do is offer a few general proposals that can guide our investigations.

We must first recognize the structural peculiarities of these colonized societies. In the first place, the process of colonization involves the penetration of a social formation by a social force, whose technical power and normative system enable it to subject the indigenous peoples, and impose on them a socio-economic order that expresses an outside rationality and external goals. The articulation of modes of production does not occur in symbiotic relation, as, for instance, capitalism developed within the feudal mode. Capitalism's penetration on the periphery results in coexistence of modes of production, and thus hybrid combinations, not found at the centre, which express one specificity. One could even say that the modes of production are disconnected, or in other words that the exported mode has no historical relation to the penetrated mode. Thus, there is a break in development following the act of colonization. Depending on colonial phases that are determined by the colonizer's economic and political imperatives, the results of penetration may be the maintenance, marginalization, or the ruin of the indigenous relations of production.

Colonial expansion also involves the creation of a double, superimposed class structure. Clearly, this duality can apply only in situations where the colonized people have not been virtually exterminated, as they were in Australia, the United States, and, to a lesser extent, Canada beginning in the nineteenth century. There arises, then, a double system of authorities, institutions, norms, and behaviour – that of the colonizer, applying, in law that is, to all elements of the social formation, and by which the new legitimacy is imposed, and that of the colonized, applying only to the subordinate class structure. Obviously, the two will never be completely sealed off from one another: the two systems can exert a mutual influence, but most of the time this influence will be felt on the superstructures of the dominated mode of production. As a force of domination, the colonizer's ideology is at work in the very process of colonization, taking an active and direct part in the acculturation of the colonized. The long-term result of this is the destructuring of the colonized social system, and the reduction of its culture to mere folklore. In colonial societies, then, we encounter two types of ideological development: that of the colonizing social structure and that of the colonized social structure. It is worth underlining here that ideological analysis can proceed only from previous knowledge of the material conditions of existence, and especially from their differences.

As far as political and ideological superstructures are concerned, colonization brings with it institutions, rules, behaviour, and values that were formed by metropolitan social experiences, and which, supplanting or overlaying the indigenous superstructures, try to legitimize the privileges claimed by the conqueror. Yet what exactly is transferred? Is the exported ideology identical with the dominant metropolitan ideology? In my opinion, this is not necessarily the case. A comprehensive approach must take account of the state of social relations in the colonizing country, and understand colonization as the product of the contradictions in these relations. As a general rule, the colonial process is carried out by an expanding commercial middle class which tries to entrench its economic power by getting a kingly state to underwrite this crucial phase in the generalization of goods and exchanges. The other classes of society have no objective interest in colonial adventures. The colonizing motive can finally be understood only in terms of the spirit of accumulation. To be persuaded of the truth of this, one has only to remember the theme of the early explorers from Europe – the road to the riches of the East.

Since the colonizing society is in a transitional phase, with capitalism trying to push out feudalism, it may be supposed that, in ideological terms, the colonizers will show an ambivalence that reflects this structural change, while still strongly under the influence of the capitalist class on the way up. This supposition depends on the scene and especially on the phase of colonization in each case. It may be plausible in the cases of American colonial societies of the seventeenth and early eighteenth centuries, but it is far less so for African colonial societies, or in the industrial phase of capitalism, when those who went to the colonies were frequently members of classes that were declining in the mother country, going out to maintain their existence in places where second-rateness and pliancy were the rule. Here, the ideology of the colonizers would be made up of the most backward elements of the dominant ideology in their own countries.

At all events, these metropolitan ideologies were not reproduced in the colonies. Colonial practice required special attitudes and special thinking. Moreover, contacting the colonized society and wanting to suit itself to the new circumstances of colonial domination, the exported ideology will shift away from its metropolitan origins. This shift tells us, not that a new economic base is emerging in the colony, but simply that the growth of the capitalist mode of production is accelerating in an environment where the social forces in opposition are, at least at the outset, external, belong to another kind of society, and thus offer less resistance than at home. Here, the accumulation of capital can dispense with class conflict, although in fact it may generate classes and opposing relations in society. Nor does the ideological shift involve a radical break, a qualitative change. The disparities are expressed above all in symbols and matters of form. The world views of the related classes in colony and mother country, that is the bourgeoisie, remain the same. Both are seeking happiness through property and the individual accumulation of wealth. In the colonial situation, it is not so much the ideology in itself that is specific, but rather the development of ideology, subject to pressure from several dialectics: colony-homeland relations, colonizer-colonized relations, and relations between social forces in the colonizing class structure.

As for the ideological system of the colonized people, its development is checked and thrown off track. The colonizing process, based essentially on military conquest and violence, brings about a bipolarization in the economic system: there is subsistence production as in hunting and gathering, tillage, and cottage industry, and there is production for trade, where we see the relation of dependence that in the long term will have repercussions on subsistence production. Corresponding to this bipolarization with different modes of production, there comes a split in the colonized social structure, where two distinct powers emerge. There are the traditional authorities directing internal life, and then there is the new power installed by the process – that of the 'intermediaries,' the people in touch with the colonizer. These mediators derive their authority from submission to foreign masters, whom they offer the co-operation and obedience of the colonized. It goes without saying that I am applying these terms to functions, and not to all the people who exercised them.

Thus, the colonized people live split lives. There is one range of symbols and social relations for communicating internally and another, a borrowed one, for their relations with the world outside. The development of ideologies is wrenched outwards, and loses its internal consistency, for if it is to survive, the colonized social formation must take in some elements of the colonizer's ideological system. The carriers of this system are the members of the mediator group, who tend to assimilate and identify with the behaviour, culture, and world view of the colonizer, imitating in their daily lives the details of his way of life.[18] And, in fact, skill in using the foreign symbolism and reference field is the condition of their continued authority. These 'homegrown foreigners' will try to spread 'their' bastardized ideology throughout the colonized structure, and in order to do this they must denounce their ancestral customs and traditions, forswear the ideological system that is related to the traditional mode of production. The result is a conflict between the value system brought in from outside and that of the indigenous people, doomed to a future of folklore. We begin to see a sociocultural type who has moved into a world of social fantasy and symbolic acts, pretended solutions to the problems the community cannot effectively solve, but which assuage his sense of powerlessness. For many of these societies, religion is the bolt-hole from colonial oppression, affording a glimpse of liberation in the hereafter. Thus, the ideology of religion occupies a central position in the dominant ideology of the colonized.[19] Quebec is an excellent example of this.

The effects of the colonizing process on ideological development are many, then, and they vary according to a person's social position in the colonial society. In the colonialist social structure, the ideology of the dominant class breaks away gradually from the dominant ideology of the mother country, and develops special characteristics that are the result of its colonial situation. The dominated classes of the colonialist structure, even though they are subordinated and exploited, still get a share of domination, and they are more tightly bound to the dominant ideology than their metropolitan counterparts. These classes accept their subordination more easily, and offer less resistance to ideological mystification.

In the colonized social structure, the process of colonization dams up the internal dynamic of ideological development, cuts down the status of the dominant social group, limiting the world view of this class to the internal life of the colonized community, bringing about its degeneration, reducing it to folklore. A parallel development sees the emergence of another social group or another type of authority, that of the mediators who copy and attempt to generalize the ideology of the colonizer. Thus, ideological development receives an outward wrench that brings about the acculturation of the colonized society.

The above typology does not take all specificities into account and does not fit perfectly in every concrete situation. It can be useful to the extent that it serves as our guide as we seek out the special qualities of each colonial situation. It will direct implicitly my own analysis of the development of ideologies in Quebec.

The originality of Quebec's case

Any examination of a society's ideologies must depend in a general way on an understanding of the process by which that society was built: its historical origins, the material conditions of its growth, its situation in the world economic order including the relation between centre and periphery, its class structure, and the conflicts among its various component parts. Combining these different elements, we can see the interconnection of the main lines of force that define the chief phases, and show the specific qualities, of that society's ideological development.

When we are considering colonial societies, special attention must be paid to the relations of forces and ideological conflicts occurring in the mother country, for to a certain extent, and at least for a certain time, these social formations are dependent in socio-economic and ideological terms. Obviously, this outside domination is not total. Its weight is mediated and made relative by the internal characteristics of the colonial society, characteristics that give it relative autonomy in economic and social development, expressed also in a specific development of ideologies.

We have seen that colonialism generated a double dialectic of ideological development – one for the colonizers and the other for the colonized – and that these are most often differentiated by their respective modes of production. Whereas the first dialectic has a chance, because of the particularity of the colonial situation, to become autonomous of the mother country, the second has its internal dynamic shut off, is made dependent, and, given the dominance of the colonizing socio-economic structure, its ideological development is turned outwards. Nor is winning political independence enough to turn this process around.

The originality of Quebec's case lies in the fact that the two situations are combined: the colonizer was in turn colonized. Quebec's social structure has successively encountered the two situations inherent in the colonizing process. Before it could achieve automony as a colonizing element, at a time when it was still dependent on the mother country, Quebec was conquered and placed under the domination of another country and another social structure with an appreciably similar economic base. Here, however, it must be emphasized that a progressive change in that base would appear, as far as the colonized society was concerned, in the wake of military, political, and economic domination, and that this change would be characterized by the emergence of a peculiar mode of production – that of the petty producers, to be defined in my first chapter.

Quebec's dominated society, then, was cut off from its centre, from which it received no further ideological messages. The process of the differentiation and separation of the two ideologies was halted; ideological development in the colony became subject to the dialectic arising from the formation of a double class structure, separated on the basis of nationality as well as conditions of existence. This superimposition of two social structures was not the only result of the conquest, for the change of imperium also meant changes in class relations in the society that had been the colonizers. In fact, one can observe the old rising class, in the wake of structural change occasioned by the change of imperium, slowly lose its hegemonic grasp to the declining class; this latter class, in order to secure its position and counter the threat that had formerly been represented by the rising class, allies itself with the foreign ruling class. One is then left with an overall hegemonic class – the Canadian bourgeoisie that dominates the social relations of production – and a partial hegemonic class, the petty bourgeoisie, dominant in the colonized social structure which differs in nationality from the colonizing social structure.

In ideological terms, this double social structure, differentiated by nationality as well as by mode of production, is expressed for the dominated collectivity by a ruling ideology that is blocked, determined as it is by the interests of an apathetic, backward class that takes advantage of the new colonial situation to impose a value system from dead history. This means a widening rift between the ideology of the dominated social structure and the real, concrete situation in which this group finds itself.

The hegemonic class that is subordinated in this society with the double class structure will have control over the development of ideological elements counter to its own interests, and oppose the penetration of ideological influences from outside. It will allow the ideologies of the backward classes in other societies to filter through, along with the ideology of the overall hegemonic class, whenever it perceives no danger to its partial hegemonic position. This clampdown on the part of Quebec's petty bourgeoisie was made possible by certain mechanisms of structural and cultural control, and it would be especially effective in the years between the collapse of 1837–38 and the Second World War – years in which the dominant ideology of Québécois society was Catholic and rural in its focus.

These few theoretical indicators will condition my exploration in the following chapters of the development of ideologies in Quebec. I will be refining them as I go along, to take into account the special vectors and phases of this development. I will be using this conceptualization as a focus for my analysis, and as a guide in choosing and organizing the ideological material.

1

Nouvelle-France

No really thorough research exists on the ideologies of this first era of Quebec society. The historical investigation of ideologies requires source material; in researching the past, we must obviously refer to the written records of that past. For some periods, however, such documentation is so rare as to be virtually nonexistent, and even where some does exist, it is not always reliable, thus leaving ideological analysis open to question.

In Quebec's case, our source problem is a serious one when we begin to research political and social philosophies under French colonial rule. This inadequacy of sources explains the absence of genuine ideological work for the period. We must remember that the printing press was not seen in Canada until 1764.

If we are to gain an understanding of the thought of that era, therefore, we must, in addition to analysing its socio-economic context, turn to indirect sources in the ideological climate of metropolitan France. We can also pick up clues from direct accounts of the conflicts and problems of the age, though sources here are suspect in that they reflect the particular interests of the participants who left them. Since the colony's intellectual output was slender, we have to be satisfied with administrators' reports and the narratives of personal notes of the protagonists of the day.

I will attempt, then, to pull together the assorted research elements we do have and map out a general outline of the political and social thought of the era, taking into account the specific conditions – material, economic, and social – current in New France, and advancing some hypotheses concerning ideological development in the colonial context. This approach will also mean relying to some extent on the general ideological background of the age as seen in the main forces moulding the society of metropolitan France, since it may plausibly be assumed that the ideological direction of New France reflected with fair accuracy the world views of those social groups coming to settle the new lands of America.

Here, we must be wary of the bias of certain historians, more Catholic than scientific, who have a tendency to idealize the French past, holding up the pioneer settlers as models of virtue sprung from Zeus's brow, pious and respectful of authority. It would be naïve to imagine that social research is completely free of the influence of the society in which it is carried out; in this sense, we must view this idealizing tendency in context – the colonial context of Quebec society. Analyst and research target are interrelated, and the values of the dominant culture are also those of the analysts of that culture.

Finally, though we began in Quebec by importing the elements of our ideology, it is by no means certain that the goods received were tailored perfectly to the official norms of the age. There was undoubtedly an attempt to reproduce in New France the socio-economic structure of Old France. All transplanting, however, involves adapting; and it may be assumed, despite the will of French colonial policy and those who implemented it, that any reflection we do find will not be without its variations and novelties.

The ideology of seventeenth-century France

What were the thoughts of the first settlers taking ship for New France? What social and political notions can have made up their world view? To find answers we have to work by analogy and deduction. There are very few relevant documents to help us describe in a direct way the ideology of the residents of New France. In order to understand their ideological universe, we must isolate the dominant value system of the time, and, on the basis of the social and economic realities in France, distinguish the motives and concerns that prompted these people to emigrate.

The seventeenth century was a time of crises arising out of contradictions between the feudal mode of production and emerging capitalism. The social and political structure of feudalism no longer responded to the needs of an expanding mercantile economy. Powerful businessmen, bankers, and manufacturers employing wage labour came together to form a capitalist class.

This new class was in conflict with the craft guilds and the institution of serfdom that impeded its expansion. The capitalists allied themselves with the monarchy, which would impose order on anarchy and the patchwork of feudalism, thus creating the necessary conditions for the spread of mercantile exchange.

The century was marked first by economic crises: decline in the value of money, inflation, famine, peasant revolt. Indeed, in its first half, popular uprisings were endemic in France. Violence broke out in Caen, Lyons, and Angers in 1630, and in Lyons and Provence in 1631. The years following saw uprisings in the Poitou and Limousin regions. In 1639, armed peasants led by Jean-va-nu-pieds and Bras-nu ruled the countryside. In 1641, four thousand men seized Arvenches.

The rise of capitalism also meant conflict among the main European nations in the process of extending Europe's domination over the rest of the world. The Thirty Years' War raged from 1618 to 1648. This was also a century of political crisis: the problems of the regency of Marie de Medici, widow of Henri IV; the summoning of the Estates-General in 1614, the Fronde in 1648–53. Finally, with the revocation of the Edict of Nantes and the repression of the Huguenots, it was a century of crisis in religion.

This was also a time of far-reaching change in the relations of the classes of French society. Though the feudal nobility, or 'nobility of the sword,' played a role in the domestic upheavals of the France of this period, the collapse of the Fronde spelled the beginning of its decline. Noblemen were living miserably on the meagre incomes of their lands. For the maintenance of their standing, they were dependent on the goodwill or pleasure of the king, who had church benefices in his gift as well as the appointments in royal households, the court, the army, and the diplomatic service.

The urban middle class existed in layers. Its ranks included the printers, booksellers, doctors, lawyers, and notaries as well as the shipowners, businessmen, and bankers. These bourgeois owned the capital, financed the monarchy, bought themselves lands and titles, and aspired, most of them, to live as noblemen, thus weakening the feudal socio-economic order from within.

The vast majority of the population were peasants. They suffered greatly from the troubles, civil wars, and foreign wars. They lived badly on overdivided and poorly cultivated lands. In the towns, ordinary people lived under the thumb of the nobility and middle class.

From this brief outline of socio-economic France in the seventeenth century, one might conclude that those liable to be interested in colonial ventures could be either out-of-favour noblemen with no royal preferences at home, members of the ruined rural élite anxious to refurbish their escutcheons, or else the businessmen and shipowners of France's ports. On the whole, it can be said that the colonies would hold no great attraction for the peasantry, the town dwellers, and members of the liberal professions, for their crisis would find its cure beginning at mid-century, with Louis xiv's accession to the throne.[1] Those who would come from the lower classes, on forced or volunteer military service, were all young and single, with little in the way of schooling or qualifications; often, departure was the great solution for them. They were poor, but not paupers, for the act of self-exile points to qualities of decisiveness and seriousness.

In general, these immigrants came from the west of France, chiefly from areas near the ports. According to an estimate made by Marcel Trudel, the immigrant contingents were made up of some 2,900 craftsmen, 3,500 military recruits, 1,100 marriageable women, and 1,000 transported convicts. Most of the newcomers, then, would have to improvise and innovate if they were to survive.

Finally, I must take note of one further social phenomenon – the Catholic renaissance accompanied by the proliferation of religious communities. The first half of the seventeenth century was the era of the Catholic Counter-Reformation against the influence of Protestantism. Numerous communities were founded or reformed to bring back religious fervour and the spirit of charity, austerity, and piety. Reformed in 1609, the Abbey of Port-Royal would be the base for Jansenism. The Carmelite and Ursuline orders were introduced into France. The Jesuits opened colleges for the education of the young nobility and bourgeoisie.

These new communities devoted themselves to education and assistance to the poor and the sick. The religious revival would give rise to heated theological-cum-political controversies, and of particular note here were the contests between Jansenists and Jesuits who opposed one another on the question of grace: the Jansenists drew close to the followers of Calvin with the assertion that man's state was utterly dependent on the will of God, while according to the Jesuits, it fell to man by his own free will to secure salvation. The Jansenists denounced all compromise between the requirements of religion and the necessities of life in the world and of the temporal power. They rejected the alliance between Catholicism and worldly power. Their severe morality upset the Jesuits, who readily accepted these compromises, and the society arranged for its opponents to be condemned by the pope and the king. Mysticism, austerity, and proselytism were the hallmarks of the Jansenist movement, which would attempt a foothold in New France.

These, then, were the classes and the general context of rapid change in which we discover a dominant ideology expressed in three main isms: absolutism, Gallicanism, and mercantilism. To begin with the first of these, we are looking at a century, the seventeenth, that marks the conceptual zenith of the doctrine of absolutism institutionalized by the reign of Louis xiv.* Though founding kingly legitimacy on divine right, this doctrine in fact began the progressive secularization of the temporal power. As far as Louis was concerned, the essential principle was the total power of the monarch, who could be accountable to no one. There must be no limit to the royal authority.

Reinforcing the doctrine of kingly absolutism was the theory of 'raison d'état,' the immunity of government. According to this theory, individuals have no rights against the state, so that tyrannical and arbitrary acts become legitimate. It was held that in affairs of state, the king could override the normal rules of justice. Even though the principle could result in abuses, these endangered only individuals – something that could be disregarded since, as Richelieu told us: 'The loss of individuals cannot be compared with the public safety, and the blow can fall on a few individuals only, whereas the public receives the benefit and advantage.'[2] This doctrine became especially influential in the wake of the shattering experience of the Wars of Religion, and also because of the intensifying class struggle between the nobility and the Third Estate. Absolute monarchy was seen then as a bulwark against anarchy. People were weary of the troubles that had racked France since the mid-sixteenth century, and saw only security in the strengthening of the royal power.

The Estates General of 1614 heard no protest against royal absolutism.

---

* The dominance of this doctrine would provoke critical reactions that passed through the dialectical process to surface in the liberal and democratic theories of the following century. The writings of Claude Joly as well as the *Mazarinades* that came out of the Fronde are indications of the existence of an embryonic liberalism in the century of absolutism. Openly maintained in opposition writings of the period were the principles of popular sovereignty and the social contract; the *parlement*'s role was seen as limiting and controlling the royal power.

There were voices, however, calling for a restrained monarchy that would respect the opinions of the *parlement* and the Estates. Among other issues, that of taxing powers provoked the sharpest challenges, with the Estates calling for recognition of their right to intervene when the king wanted to create new taxes. Public opinion wanted reforms: abolition of the sale of offices, cuts in pensions, reduced tax. Yet doubt was never cast on the king's complete power; his sovereignty was sacred.

Absolutism in France was a matter of both learned treatises and popular feeling. There was an abundance of political tracts to celebrate the prince and exalt the state. Their main themes were the superiority of the hereditary monarchy, the divine origin of powers, the duties of the prince as father and protector of his people, and finally, the monarch's absolute power, for the state had its reasons and the sovereign was God on earth. The state's interests took precedence, and the clergy must be at the king's service. The problem of church-state relations lay at the heart of the political and social thought of the age, and the aim of most political discussion was to define the role of the church within the state.

Thus Richelieu, in his *Testament politique*, attempted to reconcile Christian morality and *raison d'état* by clothing the latter in the mantle of the former. Another theoretician of absolute monarchy, this time under Louis xiv, was Bossuet, who wrote in 1679: 'The interests of the state must go first. Keeping the state in view, one works for himself. The good of the one is the glory of the other.'[3] For Bossuet, history was wrought by Providence, and monarchy was the most universal, ancient, and natural governmental form. He stressed particularly the necessity of order and the legitimacy of established power. He was not especially concerned with legitimizing a particular government.[4] Nothing, according to Bossuet, was more opposed to genuine Christianity than the spirit of revolt; the themes of obedience and submission dominate his work. It was to be used widely a century later to justify the post-conquest policy of the Canadian clergy. Our bishops found their inspiration and their policy in Bossuet.

Bossuet was also a Gallican. He held that by God's order, in temporal matters kings were not subject to ecclesiastical power, that their peoples could not be exempted from the obedience they owed their monarchs, and that this doctrine was essential for public peace and beneficial for both church and state; it must then be adhered to as sacred, a teaching in accordance with the word of God and the tradition of the

Fathers of the Church. The temporal and spiritual powers must lend one another support instead of falling into envy and conflict. 'So much has the Church laboured for the authority of kings, she certainly deserves that they become the protectors of her own.'[5]

As the absolutist doctrine gained ground, so did the Gallican doctrine. The aim was to secure the independence of France's royal authority against the Holy See; in other words, to check theocratic impulses. As the seventeenth century began, the passionately debated issue of relations between the temporal and spiritual powers set Gallicans against Ultramontanists, with the latter group trying, under Cardinal Bellarmin, to prove the pope's supremacy over princes. The Ultramontanist doctrine can be reduced to the following principle: his spiritual mission gave the pope the right and even the duty to intervene in the temporal business of sovereigns. It followed from this concept that tolerance for heretics must be forbidden to Catholic princes, who were to curb the heresy, act as God's soldiers in placing the temporal power at the church's service.

An associated belief of the Ultramontanists was that the clergy must be independent of the royal power. Like the Gallicans, the Ultramontanists accepted the principle of the divine source of royal power, but they did not believe that kings held their political authority directly from God; this authority had to command popular support. 'It is the people's consent,' Bellarmin wrote, 'that makes kings, consuls, or any other governments.'[6] Since the royal power was a human institution and not directly divine, men could exchange the monarchical regime for another. Thus, two essential theories emerged from the Ultramontanist doctrine: the supremacy of the spiritual over the temporal, and the principle of popular sovereignty.

The Gallicans attacked them both. They proclaimed the total independence of the temporal from the spiritual power, asserting at the same time that nothing stood between God and the prince, who held his authority directly without popular sovereignty as mediator. According to the three basic rules of Gallican doctrine: popes could not command in temporal matters in the kingdom of France; in France, even in spiritual matters, the pope's power was not absolute, but restricted by the rules and canons of the former councils; and kings had the responsibility for carrying the canons into effect. As kings were sacred beings, they had jurisdiction over the church of France and its clergy. In other words, the king was the sovereign master of the Gallican church, with God alone as his superior. Thus, he had the power to appoint bishops and levy taxes on the clergy.

In the Middle Ages, because of the fragmentation of states and struggles among feudal lords, the church was the only structured and widespread organization, and for that reason it confused temporal and spiritual power; then, with and in reaction to the absolute power of the popes, the absolute power of kings arose to repel the church's temporal claims and, later, interfere in the spiritual and temporal affairs of the church itself. The Gallican movement brought about the creation of 'national' churches, subject to royal authority.

The seventeenth century is thus distinguished by a vigorous movement of emancipation from the church and from medieval concepts of the primacy of the spiritual. In opposition to these concepts, a world view arose that exalted wealth on the one hand, and the absolute value of the monarchical state on the other.

We have already noted how the seventeenth century was characterized by the growth of trade and manufacturing, developments made possible by an increase in the productive forces. At the same time, in the world of ideas, a new doctrine, mercantilism, rationalized this new situation. The mercantilist doctrine rested on two main contentions: one, the state gains power by facilitating the enrichment of its citizens, and two, a country's wealth depends on its stocks of gold and silver.

The writers supporting this thesis are apt to be merchants, financiers, and manufacturers. At first glance, their chief concern appears to be the power of the state. Most of them, however, are rising in defence of the state because they think the commercial success of a nation is tied closely to the growth of the sovereign's political power and the triumph of his military campaigns, on land but especially at sea. Thus, we move from the concept of the state as the supreme end of human life to the idea of wealth as its supreme value.[7]

One of the French mercantilist theorists, Montchrestien, argued in his *Traité de l'économie politique* for the thesis of happiness through wealth, and laid down the principle of the primacy of the economic activities of production and distribution in such a way that the state's main task became the stimulation of production and exchange. The state's wealth gathering, then, depends on that of the businessmen and manufacturers.

From this viewpoint, the state must promote the development of domestic production and trade as well as protect new industries against foreign competition. Mercantilism was nationalist and protectionist. Thus, for Colbert, the trading companies founded by the state were the king's armies, the factories, and the state's reserves; trade itself was a war fought with money.

The accumulation of wealth based on trade, however, calls for more money in circulation, a stable currency, and a steady buying power. The mercantilists worked out a monetary theory according to which the power of the state was a function of the extent of its monetary reserves. The way to increase this power was to bring into the country the precious metals from the new worlds. 'We must have silver,' wrote Montchrestien, 'and having none of our own, we must get it from the foreigners,' by war against other states, or by conquest of new lands, or by the expansion of exports.

The doctrine was backed by the cause of evangelism. Montchrestien added as one of his arguments that the aim of colonization was 'to make known the name of God, our Creator, to so many barbarous peoples, peoples deprived of all civilization, who call to us, who hold out their arms to us, and are ready to submit to us so that, by holy teaching and good example, we may set them on the road to salvation.'[8]

It is in this economic context and against this ideological backdrop that we must see the beginnings of New France. Anyone doubting this has only to recall the mirage of riches on the banks of the St Lawrence that gulled Jacques Cartier, who reported having found 'an excellent mine of the best iron in the world ... certain leaves of a pure gold as thick as a fingernail ... a good quality stone that we think is diamond ...'

Cartier's dreams failed to come true. The initial disenchantment was gradually eased by the discovery of the wealth of the American lands – their fur. The French colonial expeditions to North America would act out mercantilist ideas that expressed in ideological terms the economic requirements of a young capitalism.

The society and economy of New France[9]

When we look at any analysis of the society of New France, we find that what the historians and sociologists are doing most of the time is describing the colony's social structures (those of the seigniorial system), political system (absolutism), and economic activities (the fur trade and farming), while its complex social makeup is reduced for the Quebec school to feudalism, and, for the Montreal school, to an emerging economy of the capitalist type. Both these historiographical schools take as given the existence in metropolitan France of a relatively simple social structure, that of a devolving feudal society under pressure from developing capitalism.

On the one hand, it seems to me, these writers have oversimplified the metropolitan economy, while on the other hand they have spared themselves a thorough investigation, based on analogy, of the colony's mode and forces of production. I believe that the concept of the 'petty producers' mode of production' can be usefully applied to the study of New France, setting in a more relevant light the special qualities of the colony's political economy. This concept could give us fresh understanding of the forming of Quebec society and the development of capitalism.

My aim here is to review briefly the problem of this transition, then isolate the qualities of the petty producers' mode, assess how it can be seen as corresponding to the situation of New France, and, finally, see how this new approach affects the traditional interpretation of the growth of social classes in Quebec. I am not claiming to venture beyond the stage of the exploratory hypothesis; I will limit myself to the presentation of a few theoretical criteria that might make it possible for me, in further research, to identify this particular mode of production and, through some empirical examples, emphasize its relevance.

Failure to recognize a problem of transition – apart from preventing us from distinguishing in theory a number of maladjustments between infra- and super-structure, as, at certain times, the primacy of the politician and his characteristic interventions – results in misinterpretation and spurious problems.[10]

This same reproach could be addressed to the historiography of the French and British regimes in Canada. Most of our historians are committed to a formal thinking that requires successive modes of production, and thus manage all too often to ignore the complexity of the reality. They seem irritated by any lack of proper adjustment, timing, or symmetry. Some set out to find a dominant capitalism under the French regime; for others, this regime belongs to the age of feudalism and reaction, and capitalism emerged only after the conquest, under the happy influence of the English businessmen who were chiefly responsible for progress in this country.

Modes of production are not erased mechanically; nor do they follow in single file like the carriages of a train. Rather, they are interconnected in terms of the dialectical relations of conservation, subordination, and disintegration. Capitalist forms are not pure in their development. To understand them, we must seek them out in the context of the transition where they are dislodging, adapting, and on occasion even maintaining the previous forms of the relations of production. The phases in the development of a socio-economic entity cannot be sliced cleanly apart. The process by which a form establishes domination is a long one, characterized by lopsided developments, which implies the possible coexistence of a number of modes of production. Understanding the transition involves understanding the way in which the modes of production are interconnected, and this is possible only if we reject the idea of unity or homogeneity in so far as the way of producing existence is concerned. It is not because of the absence in a society at any given time of a liberal state, a bourgeoisie in the strict sense of this term, or even of a capitalist ethic, that the capitalist mode of production does not hold sway – unless, that is, we assume a perfect agreement between the economic structure and the political and ideological superstructures, something that seems highly unlikely in historical terms.

Continuing in this vein, we can join Poulantzas in seeing the state as relatively autonomous under the French crown in the seventeenth century:

The great majority of historians agree that the shift from the feudal to the capitalist state does not occur at the moment of the appearance of the state that reflects the consolidation of political dominance by the middle class, of which the state that emerged from the French Revolution would be the typical example, but in fact at the moment when we see the 'absolutist state.'[11]

In the same way, the bourgeoisie can be seen as integrated with the feudal system, and not forever frozen in antagonism to the nobility:

For the nature of the middle class in the *ancien régime* was complex. Amassing capital, it turned into a monopolist of ground rents, creditor to the state, profiteer on colonies, and its supreme ambition was to penetrate the system of the state by buying offices and the nobility by buying judgeships or letters patent; for a long time, it worked in co-operation with the nobility under the sceptre of the arbiter-king. The middle class was part of the feudal system just as truly as it undermined it.[12]

At a preliminary stage, then, the bourgeoisie needed the feudal order if it was to grow. Afterwards, the existence of a powerful, even a dominant, middle class was not incompatible with the temporary retention of feudal social structures. This is in fact what occurred in seventeenth-century England, where bourgeoisie and landowning aristocracy functioned in symbiosis.

Although for the purposes of our investigation, if, to understand and explain the development of social entities, we must see them in terms of the problem of transition and the coexistence of modes of production, and also distinguish the power relations between dominant and dominated classes, this does not mean that we are obliged to reason with only two factors. Fights are not invariably one to one. Feudalism and capitalism will not necessarily account for the whole of social reality.

It was Marx who sensed the possible presence of a third factor, an obscure mode of production that escaped general notice and tended to be cast as history's victim. He made several references to it without ever giving it a specific name, and it has been in a sense the chameleon of history. The main difficulty with this odd mode of production is that it grafts itself so easily on to other modes – capitalism, for example. In capitalism, the petty producer displays a double personality; in addition to being his own wage-earner, he is easily turned into a small capitalist. 'Here,' says Marx, 'we encounter a peculiarity characteristic of a society in which a specific mode of production dominates, though not all elements of production are yet subject to it.'[13]

Guy Dhoquois has tried to further pinpoint this peculiarity, and outlines in these terms the main characteristics of this mode of production:

The petty producers' mode of production is made up of workers who are at the same time individual owners of their means of production and exploit not at all, or very little, the work of others. In numerous instances this mode emerges as a small-scale merchant economy ... In this mode of production, there are no social classes in the strict sense, since there are no opposing classes ... Yet Marx attached to it a dreadful word. Its very absence of social antagonism condemned it to 'mediocrity.' It was always covered over by other modes of production, modes with opposing classes, more dynamic, more aggressive.[14]

Though this mode cannot dominate, it cannot be eliminated either, for it is endlessly renewed through the many changes that occur in societies, and is found in the slave-owning and feudal as well as the capitalist

mode of production. Though it is 'mediocre,' this does not make it unimportant; it can enter the historical process and play an active role that
might at least account for the asymmetrical development of the various elements of the social whole.

The following factors predominate in this type of economy. The worker
owns his own tools of production. He himself produces all that is required for his production and social reproduction. Producers exist on
terms of equality with one another, in a condition of near autarchy or self-
sufficiency. There can be production of surplus value but there is no direct
extortion of surplus. The transition, when it occurs, takes the form of
an exchange for use value rather than monetary value. Since production is
not done for the market, there is little accumulation of capital. Finally,
this mode of production cannot have its own superstructure. The economic agent that typifies this mode of production is the artisan or peasant
farmer. According to Guy Dhoquois, the petty producers' mode emerged
in France in the wake of the disintegration of feudalism, and is in this
sense an unexpected result of the growth of capitalism. And contrary
to what one might imagine, it was strengthened by the French Revolution,
which gave legislative approval for small, independent landholdings.

We must move beyond the simple listing of criteria, however, to outline
the main factors defining the special qualities of this mode of production in terms of trading relations, social relations of production, technical
relations of production, and, finally, relations with the dominant mode
of production.

Various types of production can be noted in a rural society. There is
production for personal consumption and then there is craft production of
articles ordered by other country people for their own consumption.
This type of exchange pattern is not capitalist in the sense that it is not
generalized; the products are not made for unknown, undifferentiated
consumers. These artisans or petty producers have, to pick up Lenin's
term, direct contact with the market; they produce articles ordered directly from them by their customer for his own use. The chief result of
their productive activity is simply the reproduction of their means of subsistence. They are not subject to the process of alienation which results
from market relations, even if they do produce an exchange value. They
have a personal relation with the product they create. They are concerned
about the quality of the product and take personal satisfaction in their
work. The value of use is what chiefly determines the producer's activity.

In the towns especially can we note a more advanced version of the petty producers' mode, one having stronger connections with the capitalist mode of production. This version is simple trading production which occurs when the petty producer hires workers who generate a surplus value that allows an accumulation of capital. This accumulation is then expressed in the expansion of the unit of production, in terms of both quantity of work and the means of production employed. At this stage of development, exchange value is predominant over use value; the chief aim of productive activity is the generation of profit, and not now the product itself. A 'distancing' has occurred in the producer-consumer relation.

With respect to the social relations of production in the petty producers' mode, their chief expression is a personal dependence of a paternalistic variety. The apprentice depends on the master craftsman for shelter, food, and clothing. As an artisan, the apprentice is customarily a member of the family to whom the father passes on his knowledge and means of production. Under the system of simple commodity production, the apprentices have not for the most part the same family ties with the master; they are more numerous and achieve journeyman status more rapidly. Here, the apprentice is not yet a wage-earner in the strict sense, for he receives a share of the profits and can on occasion, on down time, use the means of production for his own direct benefit. Moreover he hopes one day, when he has absorbed the necessary skill, to set up shop as an independent.

As for the technical relations, the petty producer carries out all the stages of production. He selects the raw material, sometimes actually producing it himself, and controls the production process, deciding when and how he will work, what tools he will use, and how he is going to use them. He needs no one to tell him what to do or how to do it. In the basic artisan system, the division of labour is unimportant, whereas in the simple commodity system it tends to assume more importance and foster relations of subordination.

In the transition period brought about by the Industrial Revolution in Europe, the growth of capitalism meant the disintegration of the petty producers' mode. Most petty producers became either small capitalists or proletarians. None the less, there survived a residual craft sector limited to certain very specific activities.

In colonies or other export oriented economies, the situation was quite other. In the articulation to the dominant mode of production, one notes more conservation than disintegration: its effect was to slow down the process of proletarianization in the society, confer a special role on the lower middle class, direct the general thinking to family, religious, and ethnic ties, and also impede the development of class consciousness. In such economies, such low-profit sectors as services and consumer goods are generally left to the independent petty producers, which allows the capitalists a free hand to maximize profit in the more interesting sectors. Although the capitalist mode of production does not eliminate the petty producers' mode, it does subordinate the less aggressive mode.

In my opinion, the inclusion of this persistent mode in an examination of Quebec's social development will afford a more accurate view of our history and allow for the revision of certain theses concerning it. Marcel Rioux and his co-workers are alone, as far as I am aware, in adopting it, and they have applied it only to the period from the conquest to Confederation. In their words:

The Québécois remained outside the socio-economic system of the English colonizers; in the rural areas where the vast majority of them lived, they participated in a mode of production that was neither feudal nor capitalist ... In Quebec, there arose a temporary mode of production which, due to the dominator-dominated, colonizer-colonized antagonism, continued for several decades and exerted a powerful influence on this social development. It was the mode of production for which Guy Dhoquois suggests the name 'petty producers' mode.'[15]

Unfortunately, Rioux and his colleagues do not give this theory a particularly vigorous push. We are left on a research trail that, while promising, remains to be cleared. One notes also that the problem of the effects of the conquest underlies their hypothesis.

Personally, I tend to think that the petty producers' mode was not restricted to the British regime, but rather arose under the French regime as a mode of production underlying the commercial phase of the development of capitalism; and that the specific effect of the conquest in terms of the articulation of modes of production was to generalize the petty producers' mode and establish it as dominant at the base of the social structure of French Canada.

It would be appropriate in my view to inject a certain relativism into the theory of the changelessness of the French colony's internal economic structure. Seen in this way, the effect of the conquest would have been to strengthen a mode of production that was present but not dominant in the society of New France. Obviously, this hypothesis is arguable only if we extricate ourselves from the mechanistic approach that takes feudalism and capitalism to be mutually exclusive.

Obviously, too, the hypothesis involves a new look at the economic bases of New France, which, while moving towards capitalism, was distinguished by a combination of commercial capitalism and a petty producers' mode with a wash of feudalism. This interpretation has already been advanced by Larry MacDonald, according to whom: 'The history of Quebec, until Confederation at least, seems to belong, structurally, to the more universal category of a petty-bourgeois economy hosting emergent capitalist profiles.'[16]

I shall attempt to offer a few observations to support the plausibility of this hypothesis. Until now, our historians have been focusing on superstructure in their attempts to understand the society of New France. From this point of view, discussion has revolved around identifying the colony's élite or ruling class. On the one hand, there are those, including Cameron Nish, who argue that New France was a dynamic society dominated by a reactionary nobility and an absolutist state. Neither group, in attempting to find out who the members of the élite were and what its characteristics were, has taken into account the basis of class development, the relations of production.

The line taken by Jean Hamelin is significant in this context: he finds his evidence for the absence of a colonial middle class in New France's state of economic development, and the telling factors are inadequate numbers of specialized, well-heeled immigrants, difficulties in building a supply of specialized, native-born manpower, a commercial system favouring metropolitan France at the expense of the local bourgeoisie, and the inability to direct capital into other economic sectors and, in general, diversify the economy. One has the impression that these historians have looked for the results of the development process at its beginning; they have begun with the hallmarks of an evolved and dominant capitalism and then presumed that these must have been present when the process started. Similarly, according to Fernand Ouellet, for a capitalist mode and a middle class to exist, there must also exist a typically bourgeois way of thinking, a liberal ideology. What these writers are doing is telescoping the historical process. In their analyses, Ouellet and Hamelin explain the existence of the classes by the classes' own ideas about themselves, instead of beginning by looking at the places they occupy in the production process.

Relevant though it may be, Cameron Nish's analysis does not entirely escape this defect of reasoning, and like the others, he avoids examining the social relations of production. Taking a functionalist stance, he sets out to show that the period 1729–48 in New France reveals the existence of occupations that are those of a genuine middle class. He notes that the traditional distinction between nobility and bourgeoisie fails to correspond to reality in New France, where we encounter what might be described as a composite historical bloc: 'We can conclude, then, that the colony's military, civil, and judicial administration was dominated by a few families. These families were not part of a military aristocracy, but formed a seigniorial, military, commercial, and administrative elite.'[17] In Nish's view, this élite bears comparison with the ruling class of the British colonies. It is a view that relativizes the weight of the ideological factors in historical interpretation: with or without the Protestant ethic and capitalist mentality, one finds notably similar class structures. Nish employs three criteria – trading monopoly, monopoly on political power, and social cohesiveness – to prove that in general, New France and New England were comparable in their economic structures; that as a result, the differences in ideology were not significant, and, finally, that there is solid evidence for the existence in New France of a bourgeoisie, coalescing as a class in the transition from feudalism to capitalism.

We may observe that the underlying criterion in all these readings is the ability to accumulate wealth. In the view of Hamelin and Ouellet, the colony's economic activity went to enrich the mother country and not to build prosperity for New France and its middle class; Michel Brunet and Cameron Nish have attempted to prove the contrary. At the centre of this debate is really a struggle for historical legitimacy involving two elements of the French-Canadian ruling class. Hamelin and Ouellet are backing the ideology and practice of the French-Canadian élite's co-operation with the British colonizing power: Brunet, Nish, and others highlight the negative effects of British conquest and rule, thus vindicating an autonomist ideology and practice aimed at re-establishing a national bourgeoisie by and within an independent state.

This historiography gives one the impression that only one actor trod the stage of time; that up to now, Quebec's history has simply been the story of its ruling class and the struggles between factions of that class. On the one hand, the argument has been that serfdom did not exist because capitalism was on the rise; on the other, it is advanced that there was no proletariat in New France because the system was feudal. Ultimately, if we lumped all these various readings together, we would have an absolutely classless society – no bourgeoisie, no nobility, no serfs, and no proletarians.

A historical paradox? A gap in our historiography? I would tend to opt for the second of these possibilities. And to fill that gap, I think we can usefully turn to the concept of the petty producers' mode, which I find better suited to describe a transitional situation. It offers the added advantage of taking into account a factor that is crucial to understanding the nature of a society: the process of the division of labour and its relation to the means of production.

It is not my intention here to embark on a full-scale examination of New France. I will simply raise a few considerations that seem to indicate the usefulness of the petty producers' mode concept in understanding New France's social development as well as the effects of the conquest, with the hope that these will suggest new avenues of research.

We can assume that in general, the state of development of productive and social relations in New France depended on the state of these same relations in the mother country, and that this period may be described as the pre-industrial phase of capitalism, one in which wealth is accumulated much more through trade than through production. However, there can have been no exact mirror image: the colonizing effort responded to specific requirements from certain sectors of the society of Old France, and it encountered specific local conditions that required certain adjustments. The socio-economic system of New France can be understood only as a projection of French society with alterations from the original model. The interpretation according to which there was a total transfer of the feudal social order from the Old World to the New is untenable. I find this view more arguable: the synchronistic asymmetry of the colony's social and economic organization in relation to that of the mother country was a function of France's economic and political needs as conditioned by the internal circumstances of the colony.

'With her own hands,' Sigmund Diamond writes, 'France created in Canada a social base for disobedience, a social context in which departures became the only means of surviving or making a profit.'[18] This pattern occurred in relation not only to feudalism, but also to capitalism as it was developing in Europe through the process of proletarianization, for before it becomes a system of accumulation, capitalism is a system of exploitation of workers producing surplus value. For capitalism to exist, therefore, there must be more than a commercial bourgeoisie; there must also be a proletariat, wherein the producer does not own and control his tools of production. This separation is the necessary condition for the growth of a market economy and it could not be achieved in New France. We cannot, as Larry MacDonald tells us, consider the Indians as proletarians: 'The French were not purchasing native labour-power, they must be understood as purchasing the product of native labour, that is, furs.'[19] The Indians depended for their existence on the forest, and not on the French, who were merchants and not, except in rare cases, employers.

It was the conditions of colonial exploitation that imposed these variations in the articulation of the modes of production in the first Quebec society: they called forth the petty producers' mode in New France. And as it expanded, commercial capitalism used the petty producers' mode in confronting the particular conditions in the conquered lands and the particular circumstances of the exchanges between the colony and the mother country. On the frontier, then, to ensure the reproduction of the exploiting forces – in other words, to ensure the colonizers' subsistence and pare down the expense of carrying on the fur trade – the producer had to be left with his means of production: a degree of self-sufficiency was necessary even for the growth of capitalism. Non-specialization was a condition of the colony's survival, as was the maintenance of an agrarian economy that was independent of the capitalist mode of production.

The fact is that colonial policy was subject to contradictory imperatives. The only profitable colony was a colony of exploitation; the trading monopoly could not, however, be upheld without settlement, and a colony of settlement meant a noticeable cut in profit margins. The settlement of America by farmer-soldiers was necessary to police the fur trading monopoly with the Indians, making it possible to give military support to the Montagnais, Algonquins, and Hurons in their fights against the Iroquois. This policy of alliances was intended to increase the French zone of influence and check disturbances in the flow of furs. Rivalry with the English for control of these new sources of wealth could be advanced as another reaon for its existence. Simple trading posts were inadequate as a system for bringing the Indians into the French colonial circle and resisting England's monopolist claims. We may conclude, then, that France's colonial strategy was subject to the exploitation-profitability-settlement dialectic that, seen from this point of view, is no more than an alibi, a prop for the basic aim of commercial exploitation.

In order to reduce the colony's operating expenses, the absolutist state tried to diversify production and achieve self-sufficiency. But to do so, the state had to guarantee the inhabitants free access to the means of production and subsistence: 'In New France, the necessity of establishing production, in the absence of economic or physical compulsion on labour to produce more than was necessary for its own subsistence, required the establishment and maintenance of conditions guaranteeing the freedom of labour from just such compulsion.'[20] Sigmund Diamond has this to add:

In French Canada ... the use of forced labour and indigenous Indians met with failure, and it was necessary to turn to voluntary workers. They needed persuasion and good offers to get them to sign up and go to work. The concessions granted to French workers were so substantial that their position became completely different, not only from the one they had in the Old World, but also from what the planners had in mind for them ... For North America, the need to recruit manpower was the source of all freedoms.[21]

New France did not experience the process of dispossession of the means of production as Europe did in the transition from feudalism to capitalism. There was no expropriation of lands to create a floating work force, an essential factor in capitalism's development: quite the reverse occurred in Canada, where immigrants were escaping from this very process of proletarianization, the separation of the worker from his means of production. Nor, however, did New France have serfdom. The farmer owned his plot of land and he was sole master of his work and production. Free access to the land was not so much the consequence of enormous space as of concessions made by colonial administrators. We must also note that 'the allotment of rural lands was carried out on an equal basis,'[22] and that parcels were not broken up.

Unlike the French or English peasant, the Canadian was not obliged to sell his labour to live. He was an independent worker producing for his own subsistence and that of his family. And he was not unaware of this novelty in his objective situation. The first Canadians wanting to be seen as distinct from those paying feudal rents insisted on being called 'habitants,' which meant that they were free men, owners of land, settled permanently in the colony.

Although the seigneur enjoyed a certain prestige and pre-eminence socially in terms of production, the farmer was not his dependent. The seigneur's income came more from his activity as a businessman – which he could carry on here without social embarrassment – than from rents or appropriations of habitant production. As a general rule, he was re-luctant to develop his seigniory and preferred to pursue the fur trade, thus leaving the peasants a great deal of freedom. In Canada, the seigneurs were for the most part not of noble origin, and their socio-economic status was not bound up with their titles. The seigniories were granted to a developing bourgeoisie made up of landowners, merchants, soldiers, and administrators, with the same individual often involved in all these ac-tivities. 'They intermarried; they lived, not humbly on a farm, but right in the towns of the colony.'[23]

This peculiarity of infrastructure is also observable in terms of the col-ony's social relations and the institutions that expressed them. Let us recall briefly the novel aspects of Canada's seigniorial system, as Jean-Pierre Wallot sums them up: 'The seigniorial system produced a new social type whose interests were united in it: the independent habitant, exempt from personal taxes, owning his land, highly mobile because of the fur trade and the abundance of land, released from seigniorial sta-tute labour, and on a footing with the seigneur in community relations.'[24] I believe that the seigniorial system in Canada was no more than a feudal crust over the petty producers' mode of production, and that it dif-fered fundamentally from the French seigniorial system in letting certain seigniorial rights fall into relative disuse, in its novel family structure and system of inheritance, in the flexibility of Canadian social distinctions, in the seigneurs' relative lack of interest in the income from their es-tates, and, finally, in the absence of the attributes of legal and political sovereignty among the seigneur class.

Moreover, virtually no production was expropriated in New France. The tithe represented 4 per cent of production, and the seigniorial rent – when it was collected – 11 per cent, whereas for the French peasantry these extortions totalled 30 per cent. The habitant was also free to increase his production to ensure self-sufficiency; thus, he could avoid the labour market, and his standard of living compared favourably with that of free peasants in France. Immigration to New France was a guarantee of social mobility.

When the seigneurs and the clergy demanded payment of the rents and tithes, or when they wanted to raise them, the habitants resisted and fiercely refused to pay. 'A number of individuals,' Duchesneau reported in 1677, 'in open disobedience and contempt for the Church, are not only refusing to be tithed, but even run to violence.'[25] Longueuil saw a two-day armed rising of the people to challenge the government's demand for statute labour. The habitants did not collapse in the face of the royal power, but tended rather to be undisciplined. On several occasions, the people imposed their will and forced the administration to pull back. Individualism and a spirit of independence certainly seem to have been two dominant elements in the Canadian mentality under French rule. And the spirit of freedom was accompanied, some commentators tell us, by a sense of social equality: 'Here, everyone is *monsieur* or *madame*, peasant as well as gentleman, countrywoman as well as the greatest lady.'[26] This statement, though it contains more than a touch of the idyllic, reveals the peculiar nature of social relations in New France.

In the classic feudal system, moreover, by their control of justice, the seigneurs had the power to exact obedience. 'The almost unrestricted use of the courts placed in the seigneurs' hands,' as Marc Bloch writes, 'an incredibly formidable instrument of economic exploitation. The right to judge had been the surest basis for the right to command.'[27] No such judicial institution existed in Canada. No seigneur could exact submission from a habitant. It was from among the habitants, and not the seigneurs, that militia captains were chosen, and the post of militia captain was one involving the exercise of civil as well as military authority.

Granted, institutional New France existed as a branch of absolutism, but the governors found it extremely difficult to obtain respect for the law. Insubordination and disobedience were widespread in the colony. The government's retaliatory power was weakened by distance, a poor communications system, and the scattered nature of settlement. For these reasons it is dangerous to suggest, as some have done, that because of its absolutist cast, state power in New France was tyrannical, authoritarian, and paternalistic. Because of local circumstances and the peculiarities of the colonial situation, absolutism did not achieve expression as a state of despotism and mass enslavement.

In this connection, we must beware of the poisonous propaganda from the British victors as it has infected the thinking of certain historians who claim, with Lord Durham, that 'the French institutions in the era of Canada's settlement were, perhaps more than those of any other European nation, formed with the purpose of repressing the freedom and intelligence of the masses.'[28]

Though we should be on our guard against the colonizer's ideology in our reading of history, we cannot allow ourselves to react idealistically, and imagine New France to have been a kind of paradise on earth. What we have to do is assess the material conditions of existence, understand how these affected the superstructures of Canadian society, and by this route arrive at hypotheses that are plausible, recognizing the specific circumstances and possibilities of distortion.

The habitant of New France, then, spun out his existence in a feudal-type structure taken from the mother country, but which in the colonial context obeyed new imperatives in the form of development of capitalism in its commercial phase, and took on a specific character – serfdom is nonexistent, the worker is not cleaved off from his means of production, the habitant enjoys independence with relation to the seigneur, there is non-specialization in labour, there is self-sufficiency except for luxury goods, and market production assumes a secondary role.

This last proposition is borne out by some of Louise Déchêne's observations.[29] From her analysis of the ledgers of Alexis Monière, she asserts that the exchange relations between merchants and habitants were secondary in terms of the overall trading figures of the former group; that the merchant took little or no profit from these transactions; that craft production took place entirely outside the merchant's control; and finally, that the absence of contact between commercial capital and local production prompts the reflection that, for this sector, use value surpassed monetary value, and production developed at some distance from the market economy.

These are qualities that indicate the presence, beneath the feudal crust, of the petty producers' mode. I should emphasize that this economic model was not in competition with growing capitalism. Rather, it supported the latter and aided the first-stage accumulation of wealth. It occupied approximately 75 per cent of the colony's manpower, the rest being employed in commerce or administration or some combination of the two. We can thus conclude that in the articulation of the modes of production in New France, feudalism was merely symbolic, and capitalism filled the leading role, giving meaning to the colony's existence; and that in this, capitalism was supported by the petty producers' mode that furnished the existential base for commercial activity and kept alive the capacity for trade exchange and the fur trade.

Economic development under the aegis of capitalism, however, because of the imperatives of the concentration of capital and the generalization of goods, leads inevitably to the decay of the petty producers' mode and the appearance of a proletariat. The petty producer has no historical future, for sooner or later his sphere of action will be taken over by the laws of trade. Without class antagonism, the petty producers' mode lacks the necessary elements to drive a society. Its existence is invariably conditioned by the domination of another range of relations of man with man and man with nature – in terms of our discussion on New France, capitalism in its commercial phase. It must none the less be pointed out that this process of dissolution was delayed or temporarily blocked in Canada. From being a subordinate current under French rule, the petty producers' mode became dominant in the post-conquest social structure of French Canada, a circumstance that made possible the rule of the petty bourgeoisie class and ideology.

This rapid survey affords some indication that the petty producers' mode concept can be applied to New France and greatly aid our understanding of its development. In my view, it allows us to improve our knowledge of the economic underpinnings of this society by focusing attention on the complexity of the process of transition from feudalism to capitalism and the specific qualities of the colonizing process. The petty producers' mode concept lends a fresh perspective to our understanding of the effects of the conquest, qualifying the thesis that denies change in the colony's internal economic structure.

In this connection, the theory of the ruin of the Canadian colonial middle class and its replacement by an English class becomes inadequate as the sole explanation for the country's social development after 1760. As a theory, it describes more effectively than it explains. Clearly, capitalism continued its development in terms of the exploitation of the same basic product, and there emerged here a double class structure with a superimposition of nationalities. However, what modes of production underlay these class systems? The current historiography seems to imagine that the capitalist mode of production is the only one, and concludes that there exists a bourgeois nation and a proletarian nation, within which we find a dominant class, in fee bound to the bourgeois nation, and dominated classes.

Would it not be appropriate to take another look at the economic basis of the structure of subject classes, and for this make use of the concept of the petty producers' mode? It is a hypothesis that would enable us to better understand the influence of the petty bourgeoisie in the historical development of Quebec society.

Ideology in New France

It is not possible, given the shortage of documentation and research, to offer a coherent summary of ideologies in the period of French rule. All one can do is look for the broad lines of the colony's systems of values and ideas in the events and personal records of the time. I am not in a position to evaluate the various ideological elements in terms of their relative importance, to make a hierarchical ladder of the era's social and political ideas, and by this means identify movements in ideology in relation to the state of the colonial society. I am still at the exploratory hypothesis stage. Yet it does seem that in an environment in which family units were scattered, isolated, and self-sufficient, in contact with the forest and its aboriginal peoples, the Canadians were highly individualistic, and that their reaction to authority, whether civil, military, or religious, was typified by insubordination.

Despite some well-established preconceptions to the contrary, the average habitant was not avidly religious. Jean-Pierre Wallot tells us that the image of a Quebec mothered and dominated by an ubiquitous and all-powerful Catholic hierarchy is an invention of the clerical historians: their devout, submissive, pastoral populations, bracketed solidly by family and parish, was sheer myth until we reach the second half of the nineteenth century.[30] The likelihood would seem to be that the clergy had no ideological hegemony over the society of New France, and that their influence on Canadian thoughts and habits was not even particularly strong. As Louise Déchêne has asked:

How are we to know from the outside how much individual support there was for the Christian ideal? If we look at the family setting, evidence is rare. Of 46 inventories taken after the deaths of officers and businessmen, one third contain some tangible signs of piety – four crucifixes, three basins for holy water, and a few religious pictures. Where a small library did exist, Christian works are more heavily represented than any other, but among the majority, who read nothing at all, we do not even find a catechism.[31]

She adds a quote from Intendant De Meulles: 'Three quarters of the residents of Canada do not hear Mass four times in a year, and they often die without the last rites. They are no better educated in our religion than the Indians are.'[32] Finally, it seems that Canadians had a natural antipathy for the religious calling. Their response to recruitment was feeble, forcing the church to rely heavily on imports. It was otherwise with the women.

As a small landowner, the Canadian habitant put his own interests ahead of the church. He refused to pay the tithe. Before 1663, according to R.-L. Séguin, he was supposed to pay one minot of grain for every twelve harvested. Public resistance, however, forced Msgr Laval to cut this back to one in twenty. The habitants found this reform inadequate, and in 1691 the Bishop of Quebec had to issue a threatening reminder that the tithe was an obligation under natural, divine, canon, and civil law: non-compliance would be tantamount to theft and punishable by excommunication. The habitants do not appear to have been frightened, since 'whatever the taxing formula might be, the habitant always had to be badgered to get his grain to the presbytery.'[33]

There was also unruliness in religious observance. The habitants kept neither the Lenten fast nor the Sabbath day of rest. In fact, it may have been by sheer force of circumstance that there was not much church attendance: priests were not conspicuously present in the habitants' daily lives. At the beginning of the eighteenth century, many Canadian parishes had no church buildings, or else had churches but no priests in charge. In 1730, only 20 of 100 parishes had curates. In 1712, the clergy represented 1.6 per cent of the colony population, and it must be remembered that of its 312 members at that time, 196 were nuns. Priests were rare: the rural districts went virtually untouched by direct clergy influence, although this was more substantial in the towns.

From the complaints of Bishop St Vallier, we learn that these Canadians cursed when they pleased, rarely went to Mass, and when they did, stepped out for a smoke or a drink during the sermon; they even brawled in church, and paid their priests scant respect. It would seem, still

according to the prelate, that the habitants had tendencies to loose living –
if, that is, we take as our point of reference the catechism's formal bans
on dancing, theatre-going, and open fraternization with members of
the opposite sex. Nor were Canadian women shy about displaying their
charms: their deep décolletés gave the bishop much pause. Shameful
debauchery, he claimed, was universal.[34] Although he may well have had
his own instructional reasons for blackening the situation, the conduct
he describes does seem consistent with the general morality of the age,
not yet enamoured of strictness. Finally, ecclesiastical thunderbolts would
also fail to stem the practice of interest lending, immensely popular in
the eighteenth-century colony.

I am not attempting to deny that the church had any influence at all
on the habitants of New France. I do believe, however, that most historians' readings overestimate church power. Reasoning regressively, they
transpose to the French colonial era the qualities of French-Canadian
society at another time in its history. I am proposing another tack on the
issue of the clergy's ideological ascendancy in the society of New France,
one that begins by analysing the relations between church and state.

It must be remembered that in the seventeenth and eighteenth centuries, the church's omnipotence in matters temporal was in the process
of disintegration. The royal state emerged as a pole of authority to compete with the church. Church-state conflicts clearly affected religion's
influence among the habitants. Indeed, their mutinous mood may have
been a result of this antagonism, which was especially evident in the
feuds between Count Frontenac and the bishops, Laval and St-Vallier.

According to Canon Groulx, the years before 1663 had seen what
amounted to a theocracy in Canada. Louis xiv's accession marked the
end of that regime, and the beginning of political and religious Gallicanism.[35] There is evidence of the continued hold of this philosophy in a
January 1728 ordinance from Intendant Dupuy:

The church existing within the state, and not the state within the church, being
part of the state without which it cannot subsist; and the clergy being so powerless to resist even momentarily the justice of the prince, that His Majesty can
charge his magistrates by the laws of the kingdom to compel their attendance
for the distraint of their temporal revenues; the only thing needed to persuade the
whole population of this colony, inviolably attached to the worship due to God
and obedience to the king according to God's express command, being our pres-

ent announcement of the public declaration made by the bishops of France
assembled at the head of the clergy on March 19 of the year 1682: which declaration states in appropriate terms that St Peter and his successors, vicars of Christ,
as well as the whole church, were given power by God only over things spiritual
concerning salvation, and not over things temporal and civil; Jesus Christ having
taught us himself that his kingdom is not of this world, and in another place,
that we must render unto Caesar that which is Caesar's, and following the pre-
cept from St Paul the Apostle that all persons are subject to the power of kings,
for there is no power that does not come from God; in consequence of this,
continues the aforementioned declaration of the clergy, we state that kings
are not subject to any ecclesiastical power in accordance with God's own
command in matters concerning the temporal sphere.[36]

Moreover in Canada, clerical claims to political hegemony were challenged by the merchant class. They complained of the disastrous results
of missionary interference with the sale of liquor.

It was Frontenac who emerged as the most uncompromising partisan
of the royal Gallican policy. He had the missionaries watched in their
comings and goings. He tried to block the founding of new religious
communities and sow discord among the existing ones. Gradually, state
supremacy became a fact. Significantly, in the torrent of correspondence
over church-state relations, Rome was never mentioned. The church
of New France looked only to Versailles, giving proof of its Gallican loyalties. And according to Guy Frégault, the competing strain of Jansenism
made few inroads in Canadian society.[37]

How did the habitants view these tensions? What impact did they have
on popular awareness? In Frégault's opinion, issues of theology raised
not a ripple in the colony: more than anything else, it was money questions that started the bickering.[38] The picture one comes away with,
then, is a popular attitude towards the church that was typically independent and not, as would later be the case, one of blind obedience.[39] As
for the clergy of Canada, their social and political philosophy began with
devotion to their own hierarchy and the joys of submission, moving on
to rigid moralism and rejection of such immediate human pleasures as
music and alcohol.

The average Canadian's approach to religion finds some echoes in
his attitude to civil authority. Although the habitants often disobeyed the
laws, they were not challenging royal absolutism or the political and

social institutions by which it was represented. State power was absolute in New France as in the homeland, but it was so more in theory than in practice. The difficult communications and sparse settlement of the new world reduced its repressive effectiveness. Thus, in this sector as well, the habitants showed a sense of independence. They did not obey the fur trade ordinances. They went off to roam the forests without waiting for an official blessing, even though there was a death penalty for doing so. They smuggled. They objected to statute labour, rents, and other feudal obligations. In 1704 and 1705, the people of Montreal demonstrated against inflation. In 1733, Longueuil had an armed uprising that lasted two days. Finding great difficulty in law enforcement, the governors asked Versailles for troops. New France may have been absolutist in its institutions, but this did not necessarily mean mass enslavement for its people. Cracks were opened in the system by local conditions and the special quality of the colonial process.

Frégault argues that the absolute monarchy was not an instrument of oppression. In New France, the royal institutions were more paternalistic than absolutist. For instance, the king enjoined colonial administrators to treat the Canadians 'gently and with kindness ... involving yourselves in their needs, helping them settle, and preventing the powerful habitant from harassing the little man.'[40] To be emphasized as well is the fact that the colony's bureaucratic machine was a small and simple one. Its people did not have to put up with the level of meddling and provocation that occurs when the state parasites form a large, powerful, and well-organized class. It is not surprising that the birth of a prince, or news of the royal good health, prompted general celebration in the colony.

The common people took no part in political life. Until 1728, however, the leading citizens could influence the administration through the sovereign and superior councils. The year 1717 saw the appearance of a representative institution when the Quebec and Montreal business communities obtained royal permission to meet daily and discuss their affairs. They were also authorized to elect two delegates as lobbyists for trade. The two merchant assemblies would come to represent not only their corporate interests but also, on occasion, those of the townsfolk. On a broader basis, habitants in various parts of the colony were often called together to discuss questions of general interest. The government received numerous grievances, demands, and remonstrances. All the evidence indicates, then, that the Canadians, far from prostrating

themselves before the royal authority, tended to be unruly and disobe-
dient. On several occasions, the people actually forced the administration
to pull back.

Individualism and an independent spirit seem to have been two of the
dominant elements in Canadian thinking under French rule. Some ob-
servers have noted the emergence of national consciousness as well.
One can glimpse this embryonic nationalism in the clergy feuds and obedience problems encountered by non-Canadian governors and intendants.
Bishop St-Vallier complained to the colonial ministry in 1715 that Canadian
priests were being disagreeable to the ones from Europe: this indicates
rivalry between the locals and the French members of the hierarchy.
And of hostility between French and Canadian officers, Bougainville commented: 'It is as if we are a different, even an enemy, nation.'[41]

If we look at the colony's cultural life, however limited this may have
been, we find that it was not out of step with the homeland in intellectual
development, and that the clergy's best efforts could not stop the flow
of ideas from France. In 1720, Father Charlevoix was charmed by the
society of New France: 'Past politics are canvassed, with conjectures for
the future: the arts and sciences have their turn, and conversation does
not lag. The Canadians, that is to say the Creoles of Canada, are born
to an air of freedom that makes them most agreeable in human intercourse; and nowhere is our language spoken with greater purity. One detects no trace of an accent.'[42] Antoine Roy contends that Canadians
read a good deal, estimating that there were sixty thousand books in the
colony at the time of the conquest. Louise Déchêne points out that
the habitants had a reasonably high literacy rate for the time: the marriage
register was signed by 38.4 per cent of the men and 31.7 per cent of
the women.[43] Yet the question remains: who did the reading? It is hard to
imagine pioneer farmers, woodsmen, or soldiers giving it much of their
time, and in any case the average habitant did not even possess a catechism.

The literary consumers seem to have been the élite – nobility, clergy,
and merchants. In the town of Quebec, the Jesuits and the seminary
lent out books. Some private libraries were impressive for the time.
Monsieur Cugnet had three thousand volumes and Monsieur Verrier four
thousand, including all the noted sixteenth- and seventeenth-century
authors with the single exception of Ronsard. Verrier had Montesquieu's
Esprit des lois and Buffon's *Discours sur les arts et les sciences*; ra-

tionalism was represented on his shelves by the works of Montaigne, Charron, Fontenelle, Voltaire, Locke, and Bayle. According to Antoine Roy: 'The Canadians of the eighteenth century were acquainted with the chief authors and Montesquieu and Voltaire and Rousseau. The best that France produced arrived in the colony without an overlong delay.'[44] Over clergy protest, the theatre was part of New France's intellectual life too, mounting productions of Racine and Molière.

While stressing its limited influence, Marcel Trudel has shown that Voltairean thought had repercussions in New France: 'The French society of Canada came into fairly early contact with the spirit of Voltaire – even, so to speak, before Voltaire himself was in existence.' The contact came through Baron de la Hontan, who spent ten years in the colony. 'Here was an author of the Régence, an Encyclopedist,' Trudel writes, 'He attacked Revelation, monks, clerical celibacy; he called for freedom of thought, wanted to change judicial procedures, and criticized the customary law.'[45] The range of this philosopher's influence seems to have been limited to a small circle of friends.

Intendant Bigot, and army officers arriving at the close of French rule, were the chief mediators of Voltaire himself. Trudel tells us: 'Most of these officers landed with Montcalm at Quebec. Lévis, Bourlamaque and Bougainville are the best-known names. They came from a France that was already saturated with Voltaireanism. They brought the *Encyclopédie* with them and read it. They maintained the gaiety, tastes and way of thinking of their homeland.'[46] Still, according to Trudel, the pre-1760 influence of Voltaire surfaced first in libertinism and frivolity. The shrilly complaining Bishop Pontbriand is our witness: 'These vices, formerly so rare in the colony: licentious talk; impudently reading dangerous works and listening to talk of godlessness and irreligion – does not libertinism stalk among us with its head high?'[47]

It is clearly difficult to assess the true influence of these new ideas in the colony and yet it seems to me that for political as well as polemical reasons, Trudel tended to minimize their reach among the élite and ordinary people of New France. If he is correct, why the ill-judged reaction on the part of the church authorities? Is this not an example of ideological conflict within the ruling class, in which a rising commercial bourgeoisie made common cause with the oligarchy of the administration against church power and hegemonic claims? For the moment, we have only scattered indications that allow us to advance this particular hypothesis.

In concluding this analysis of the economic, social, and ideological structures of New France, two well-established preconceptions seem in need of qualification. These are the ideological ascendancy of church and clergy and the intrinsically despotic nature of political absolutism. Both are belied by the individualism, independent spirit, and unruliness towards authority that emerge as the salient characteristics of habitants' attitudes and system of values. Behind these characteristics lie the material conditions of life in New France: low population density, remoteness, forest wanderings, contacts with the Amerindian way of life, intimacy with nature, and the need for adaptability and innovation in this environment. The habitant was not a biddable character, harnessed into a feudal social structure. He was undisciplined and disputatious in religious, civil, and military business. Since he normally owned his means of production, he tended to put his material interests ahead of the interests of the spirit. He seems not to have been a zealous and devout supporter of religious practices. He displayed a fondness for libertinism and frivolity, at least when he was a member of the dominant class. The values of the church came into conflict with new values that arose with the rise of commerical activity: loans with interest, and the desire for quick profit. The values preached by the clergy were out of joint with the requirements of economic practice.

In social and political terms, the habitant's spirit of independence did not involve an ideological defiance of absolutism. In fact, absolutism was more form than substance in New France. Some have noted an additional factor in the emergence of national consciousness, as evidenced by the civil, military, and religious confrontations of Canadian and European. Finally, the colony seems to have followed the broad lines of French intellectual life. Cultural currents and new ideas were moving between mother country and colony. There was no clampdown or ideological freeze as yet.

It is clear that New France, as a society in the process of acquiring a structure, cannot be qualified as an original society developing under its own power. Even given its dependence, however, we have been able to distinguish original forms of economic and social organization that could have served as the basis for a process leading to autonomy. The circumstances prevented this structural development from gaining impetus and expressing its own special qualities.

2

Under British Rule
1760–1791

To the extent that events in history help mould the structures of economic, political, and social life, the conquest is a factor of immense importance in the examination of French Canada's evolving political and social thought. The broad currents of ideology follow from specific practice, the concrete experience of collectivities. The phased colonization process brought about by the conquest and the shock waves it produced in Canadian society meant that the environment in which political and social ideas developed could not be the same as in societies where development occurred in a relatively stable continuum, and whose community life was not jeopardized by the military, economic, social, and political domination of another society.

It is from this viewpoint that Michel Brunet has characterized French Canada's political thought as short-term, existential, 'incomplete, often childish, ... dogging foreign example or seeking refuge in barren isolationism; powerless to grasp and unable to define the complex problems of its environment; inclined to feed on delusions and grand ratiocinations that have nothing to do with the reality of every day, and displaying all the features of retarded development.'[1] There is nothing innate about these qualities. They are not part of the genetic inheritance of the French Canadians. They are products of history and society: a people is shaped by the behaviour of its classes in certain historical conditions. We have no native vocation for spirituality, romanticism, or inferiority in economic, scientific, artistic, and political pursuits. Our basic nature is not unlike other people's. We must explain ourselves to ourselves by examining the material conditions of our collective existence, and to do this, we have to understand the effects of the conquest on Canada's economic and social structures.

Economy and society

Interpretation of the conquest's consequences for Canadian society
has become a focus of ideological controversy. The event is more than a
label for a chapter in our ideological development. It has become an
ideological phenomenon in itself, cited variously in debate, whether on
the possible existence of a national – or colonial – bourgeoisie under French
rule or on its own meaning for the evolution of the French-speaking collectivity.

Traditional historiography, reflecting the official line, has attempted to
play down the effects of the conquest, generally presenting it as a blessing
for the Canadians and, by encouraging the belief that it brought with it
freedom and prosperity, veiling the reality of British colonial rule and the
domination of the clerical-middle-class élite. Military operations are invariably followed by ideological operations whose purpose is to make the
victory complete and permanent by getting the vanquished to accept
their subject status. The historiography of the clergy has in this sense often
acted as spokesman for the ideology of the dominant class.

Fernand Ouellet's interpretation also has a colonialist slant. Though
he took his sights from a different system of values, he too failed to break
clear of the stifling dominant ideology. He replaced the official line of
the French-Canadian ruling class with that of the dominant colonizing class.
Thus, Ouellet and Jean Hamelin have argued that because it was impossible in New France to accumulate capital and open up new sectors of
production, there was no native-born middle class in the colony. Given as
the chief reasons for this are the control of trade by European-French
merchants, the absence of a capitalist ethic, and the domination of the nobility. For those who hold this view, the conquest, rather than putting
paid to a local bourgeoisie, simply opened the way for the insertion of a
British bourgeois group in an unoccupied part of the social structure,
hence for impetus in Canada's economic development. In fact the Quebec
City school, in seeing the conquest as a bearer of progress and freedom
because it gave rise to a middle class in Canada, comes very close to
the traditional interpretation.

There are three main arguments against this interpretation. In the
first place, the existence of a bourgeoisie is not proved on the basis of psychological criteria: it is identified, not by its ideas, attitudes, or religious beliefs, but by the position it occupies in the productive process. Second,
these writers do not establish that the nobility were actually dominant in

New France. And finally, one can attack their argument that structural weaknesses in the economy of New France, expressed in a lack of diversification and traceable to the attitude of the colony's inhabitants, meant that there was no middle class: 'How in fact, given this view, do we explain why the Anglo-Saxon middle class that was supposed to be better equipped intellectually did not significantly reorganize the economy after the conquest? On the contrary, it kept functioning in the same way. This seems to prove that the basic impulse came from the economic and not from the ideological structure.'[2] The commercial middle class from Britain would no more succeed in diversifying the economy than had the commercial middle class of New France.

Another group of historians, led by Maurice Séguin, Michel Brunet, and, with a somewhat different optic, Gilles Bourque, distinguish a genuine colonial bourgeoisie before the conquest, a class that arose in opposition to the clergy and nobility, used the state to advance its interests, and tried unsuccessfully to round out the colonizing enterprise. 'This group of men,' Bourque has observed, 'whose economic force depended on a single product and highly regimented military rule, displayed obvious signs of weakness.'[3]

Most historians agree that the conquest brought no change to the colony's internal economic structure. The economy was still built on the same generative product, furs, and the same secondary products of grain and fish. The dominant mode of production remained the same. The political system, a monarchy expressed locally through military, authoritarian government, was unaltered.

The differences in interpretation appear when historians look at the effects of the conquest in terms of external structure. For the Quebec school, assuming the separation of economic growth and class struggle, it is a simple matter: since there was no middle class before 1760, the change of imperium had no significant consequences. For those who reject the mechanistic approach and argue for the existence of a bourgeoisie, however, the conquest brought about an upheaval in the external structure that had repercussions on the class structure of the colony; the change of imperium struck at the economic underpinnings of the colonial middle class, and Canada lost its dynamic leader group. Brunet has placed special emphasis on the slide of disintegration that blocked the economic development of the Canadian middle class and ensured its eventual ruin: 'Substantially affected by the collapse of France's treasury, unable to get hold of merchandise ordered before the war's end, and cut off from their former suppliers, Canadian businessmen were utterly helpless. The conquest had closed the old markets, along with the credit and trading goods they needed.'[4]

The conquest prompted the departure of some 1,200 wealthier citizens who realized that it would be impossible for them to carry on a profitable trade in the new colonial circumstances. Those who stayed were less well off: 'They were not in the circle of big businessmen, monopolists, and war profiteers. Most of them came from the second rank of the Canadian capitalist bourgeoisie of the last years of French rule, the class of small entrepreneurs with modest incomes and ambitions.'[5] This class had not profited from official favour. Its members were dissatisfied with the Bigot administration and envious of the shameful successes of their big competitors, patronized and protected by government. There had been conflict, then, between the two strata of the middle class: the second group looked to profit from the destruction of French rule, and were bewitched by the ideology of free competition and trade – in fact they were gulled, for they misread the economic, social, and political meaning of the conquest. Britain had not made war merely to run her flag up in place of the French one. Her goal was to seize the rich commercial empire of the St Lawrence, Great Lakes, and Mississippi basin, and to eliminate the French rivals.

Lacking capital and reliable distributors and suppliers in Britain, the Canadian businessmen lost control of the fur trade and became mere agents selling to the British merchants of the colony. Relegated to the fringe of trading activity, they vacated the rich fields to others, and made do with leavings as purveyors of raw material. Gradually, too, they lost the internal colony business in such articles as wine and brandy. Their storehouses were empty, the orders sent to France could not be filled, and, without credit or correspondents in Britain, they could not restock. Turning to local British middlemen for those supplies, the Canadians sank to agent status even in domestic trade.[6] Finally, they lost their hold on the state apparatus of Canada, which, as mediated by the buyers for the military, played an active and important role in the colony's economic life.

The conquest, then, meant the shift of economic and political power to a group that came from outside the colony's class structure. The monopolies in government contracts and fur concessions passed to this new clique of British businessmen. Even the trade practices they imported with them worked to the disadvantage of Canadians as, for instance, systems of measurement were changed to facilitate dealings with the new mother country. The result of all this was a shrinking trade horizon for the Canadians, who took to the rural communities for survival, abandoning the richest fields of commerce to the new masters.

Structurally, the conquest brought change in the interrelation of modes of production. The capitalist mode maintained its momentum, certainly, but at the same time the changes in the colony's external economic structure that caused the emergence of a double, nationally superimposed class stucture also produced a countermovement in the economy: the reinforcement of the petty producers' mode of production, already described at some length in chapter 1. Canadian people would have to fall back on their own resources and rely for subsistence on farming, cottage industries, and local trade. The years following the conquest saw the emergence of a double class structure whose classes were not identified with the same mode of production. The two were differentiated not solely by nationality but also by their economic bases, one the capitalist and the other the petty producers' mode. Changes in Canada's external economic structure were rebounding on the internal structure to foster the coexistence of these two modes, the one focusing on commerce, the other on subsistence.

We have seen, then, how structural change in the Canadian economy was accompanied by comparable change in society, expressed in the double, nationally oriented structure and new class relations within the French group. At the top, a new hegemonic group emerged. 'Having caused the disappearance of the bourgeoisie,' according to Bourque,[7] 'the conquest would hand power to a conservative class that soon turned reactionary.' This new class, especially in the early decades of the new regime, was made up of civil and military administrators, associated on occasion with some of the British merchant group. The social origins of the bureaucrats in the hegemonic class were generally aristocratic, whereas the members of the commercial wing tended to be commoners from the American provinces.

These contrasts in group interests and social status lay at the root of conflict within the new ruling class. Rapidly dominant in the economy, the Anglo-Saxon commercial middle class was none the less somewhat excluded from political life. Its radical faction challenged the ideologically aristocratic government on the issue of a representative assembly, calling repeatedly for the establishment of the system used in the other provinces of the British Crown. In addition to this class struggle for political power, there were differences as to the appropriate attitude of victors to vanquished. The aristocrats in the dominant class favoured an ideology of conciliation and alliance with the aristocratic class of the conquered society. Their political aim was to reorganize the colony and entrench the new rule, while avoiding conflicts and radical measures that might goad the Canadians and cast doubt on the wisdom of setting these new 'jewels' in the crown of Great Britain:

As in any occupying or colonizing enterprise, they felt the need to base their power on co-operation from an element in the occupied or conquered society, a need that was accentuated by the conquerors' numerical weakness in relation to the conquered, and the threat from the Thirteen Colonies, which launched an invasion of the newly acquired territory on the eve of their own independence.[8]

In 1761, 99.7 per cent of the population was French Canadian. Their weight of numbers made an unvarnished colonizing drive impossible, especially as the British administrators were concerned about the possibility of another French invasion. Accordingly, governors Murray and Carleton, assuming that the province of Quebec would always be French and that the loyalty of these new subjects had to be won, preached a policy of conciliation. The success of such a policy required co-operation from the conquered, and hence the building of a class alliance between the two national groups.

Their own class interests left Canada's seigneurs no choice but to get themselves on the conquerors' payroll. Turned out of the colony trade at the same time as the Canadian businessmen, they had to fall back on the extortion of seigniorial rents and dues. The possibility that the British presence might jeopardize the system of land tenure was a direct threat to their class existence. Moreover, since their income came in part from royal patronage of various kinds, the seigneurs could not live divorced from political power. Added to commercial activity, the conquest took from them the appointments and ancillary revenues associated with it. The new colonial regime used this as a stick to force compliance from the local aristocracy. Noblemen were handed second-rate offices and a limited role in public and military business in return for their commitment to the new regime, subservience, and work as propagandists and intermediaries through whom the dominant class hoped to extend its hegemony and win popular acceptance. Carleton used this tactic with some skill,[9] and if his hopes were dashed, this was not due to resistance from the nobles, but rather to their lack of influence among a population which had already shown them scant respect or obedience under French rule. The passiveness of the Canadian people in the face of American invasion would signal the failure of this colonial policy as well as the falseness of the absolutist image British leaders had of the society of New France.[10]

As landowners in the church, the Canadian clergy found themselves in the same economic jeopardy as the seigneurs, and their status was made still more uncertain by the informality of British guarantees for freedom of religion. In the wake of conquest, these two groups joined together as the official dominant class in the social structure of the colonized community, and offered willing co-operation in order to retain their basic economic grasp: seigniorial tenure and the tithe, as well as episcopal control of the church and clergy independence. With the disintegration of the old ruling class of New France, its members either ruined or returned to the homeland, the clergy-seigneur alliance offered the conquerors its services as intermediary, palming its own class interests off as the interests of all Canadians. Thus, the conquest turned a declining class – and it is worth remembering that the church, particularly since the end of the seventeenth century, had not played so important a role[11] – into a dominant class in the colonized society. The conqest altered the class structure of Canadian society and assigned the church an adjutant rank that would not be exercised with real effectiveness until after the collapse of the rebellion of 1837–38.

Thus the Canadian clergy and aristocracy made common cause to protect their class interests, aiming for official recognition of their language, religion, and the French laws and customary practices that would ensure the maintenance of the seigniorial system of tenure as well as the continued availability of offices in the civil and military administration of the province. In return, they offered the people's loyalty and fidelity to the new colonial domination. Their ideology was one of co-operation based on assumptions of the occupying power's goodness and generosity and of the divine necessity of obedience.[12]

Shorn of economic power, reduced to mere middlemen for British merchants, the Canadian traders, most of them small businessmen who had not prospered under French rule, were hoaxed by the official line and allied themselves with the 'clerical aristocracy.' There were some mavericks who attempted to forge ties with the British merchants, but the experiment turned out to be unprofitable. Little by little, they were pushed back into the fringes of commerce, most moving out into rural areas as agents for British business interests. They lost all power as a force in society, and the unnatural alliance with the clerical aristocracy hastened their decline. Their interests were neither understood nor defended by an élite that took a dim view of all trade, an 'antidemocratic, antiparliamentary' group that stood in opposition to 'the capitalist middle class and the rise of commercial capitalism.'[13] Thus, the conquest changed a rising middle class into a petty bourgeoisie, limiting it to small business and pushing it into the service sector.

The conquest would clearly not change much in the situation of the masses in Canadian society, though it did intensify the general withdrawal into agriculture, increasing overall dependence on this sector of the economy. Under French rule, Canadians showed no special fondness for this type of production, taking it up to meet their basic needs but setting it aside whenever they had a chance to get into the woods. However: 'Towards the end of the period 1760 to 1792 the numbers engaged in the farm sector may be reckoned at about 80 per cent of the French-Canadian population. The agricultural vocation of French Canada appears then to be a product of the conquest. Later, it became an object of veneration for the élites.'[14] The products of the soil became the main source of income for Canadians, a shift that brought about the generalization of the petty producers' mode at the base of society. Another effect of the conquest was to widen the gap between aristocracy and farm population, and indeed mass reaction to the event may be said to have been typified by passive resistance, and distrust of the clerical aristocracy's collaboration.

In social terms, then, the results of the conquest were the removal of Canada's ruling class and the creation of the environment for two major changes to follow: the emergence of a double class structure in which the classes were differentiated by nationality and mode of production, and the co-option of a decaying group, characterized by a reactionary ideology and an uncreative economic situation, to which the conquerors entrusted the leadership of Canadian society. Although this clerical aristocracy failed to win popular acceptance as a political power and was moreover challenged by another class, the petty bourgeoisie, the French-Canadian social structure would none the less bear the marks of the situation arising from the conquest: its subjection, in distinction to most other societies, to the partial hegemony of the lower middle class.

Ideologies

Conciliation

Unacquainted as they were with Canada's true situation, the conquerors initiated a programme of full colonization. The author of the 1763 royal proclamation decreed the law and land tenure of England, as well as a house of assembly and the submission of the Catholic church to the king's will. The proclamation also imposed the oath of the Test Act, by which Roman Catholic Canadians wishing to take public office or government jobs would have to renounce their faith. In fact, however, this much-protested act of infamy affected none but the local noblemen.

James Murray, the first governor, was persuaded by the Canadian census figures, unrest in the colonies to the south, and the ever present possibility of the return of the French fleet that the law was unrealistic, its colonizing aims impossible to carry out. He and Carleton turned to argue a policy of conciliation, not to please the Canadians, but to better protect the Crown's interests in North America. Carleton became a master of the art of the carrot and the stick, and wrote:

Therefore must we use all our energies and address, sparing no expense, to uproot faction and party, to secure the tranquillity of these provinces and maintain their firm attachment to His Majesty's government. It is therefore equally essential to preserve that sentiment of security and strength that will keep in obedience and fear those who are not yet wholly aware of the duties that go with the titles of loyal subject and honest citizen.[15]

To achieve these objectives, they would seek allies in the conquered society. Sons of the British upper classes themselves, they quite naturally based their strategy on an alliance with the seigneurs and the church, assuming, as their feudal concept of society would suggest, that they would find in this class the natural leaders of Canadian society.

Their strategy ran counter to the royal proclamation that undermined the economic power of clergy and nobility. Pragmatically, the two governors tried to softpedal the law and preserve the seigniorial system to win the seigneurs over to the new regime. In terms of the special situation in the colony, they gradually put together a programme that preserved French civil law, the compulsory tithe, seignorial land tenure, and government offices for the nobility. To entrench the subordinate status of vanquished to victor, however, they were careful not to sanction these privileges in law: when at last this was done, it was done under pressure from outside events in the form of the secession movement in the Thirteen Colonies.

Before anything else, conciliation served the imperial interests of Great Britain. Canadians had become no more than pawns on a chessboard. They had lost all autonomy and power of initiative. The governors' policy must also be seen in the context of class struggle between the British aristocracy and rising British middle class in Canada, a struggle that produced criticism of conciliation from within the conqueror group.

Assimilation

British businessmen opposed conciliation with a programme of total assimilation for French Canadians. They produced two approaches, differing not so much on assimilation as on the colony's political system. Their radical wing wanted parliamentary government, and clamoured for an assembly on the same basis as in the American colonies from which most of them had come. The moderate wing saw the plan as premature and risky for it might hand too much power to the conquered people and endanger the new hegemony. How, they asked, can we justify a representative assembly that shuts out 99 per cent of the population? Given equal rights, the French would control the assembly; an assembly without the French might annoy the people.

This dilemma dogged the political planning of the British merchant class. To make Canada a British colony of settlement, there must be encouragement for massive immigration: but how were they to give those who came the rights they enjoyed in the mother country while at the same time withholding these rights from the local population? The assimilation of the Canadians by English-speaking settlement meant that civil rights in the conquered colony had to be equivalent to those in the other colonies. Conferring these rights meant handing power back to the majority Canadians. Colonialism was in conflict with democracy. As Brunet has noted:

Conquerors are not in the habit of entrusting the conquered with the administration of occupied territory ... By refusing to endow the new colony with a government comparable to those of the other American colonies, the mother country greatly disappointed the British settlers who had already arrived in the conquered lands, and gave no encouragement to prospective immigrants.[16]

Colonial policy, then, faced conflicting objectives. One constant may be noted here in British colonial policy for the French Canadians: democratic rights were conceded only in inverse proportion to their power and strength of numbers – the Loyalists arrived and in 1791 there was an assembly without responsibility, and in 1848, with an English-speaking majority, there was responsible government.

The suggestion of the moderate merchant wing was to delay plans for an assembly and promote a rapid assimilation of the French Canadians. Francis Masères, representing this faction, advocated the fusion of the two races, by which he meant absorption of the French by the British through the penetration of English law, the English language, and the Protestant religion. Murray, no great admirer of democracy, took advantage of the split in the commercial middle class to entrench the system of centralized political control, confirm the trust of the Canadian élite, and in so doing, strengthen the aristocratic position in the fight with the bourgeoisie.

This fight expressed a conflict between two ranges of economic interest. Landowners faced businessmen who wanted political power in order to create the environment needed for commercial growth. Their claims were supported by the clause in the 1763 proclamation calling for the establishment of assemblies, and they used it against the ideologically militaristic government, making this demand of the king in 1765: 'Your petitioners pray ... Your Majesty ... to send us a governor imbued with principles of government other than military principles ... to order the establishment of a House of representatives in this Province, as in all Your Majesty's other provinces ... The new subjects could be authorized to elect Protestants if Your Majesty so wishes.'[17] Only British residents or Protestants would sit in this assembly. Catholic French Canadians would have only the right to vote. The merchants also requested such English laws as habeas corpus and jury trial, but above all they were eager for laws on bankruptcy, registration, and other matters that would promote their trading interests.

Here we may glimpse one of the first consequences of conquest in terms of the development of ideology. Widespread economic and social changes were brought about by British domination, such as the disappearance of a dynamic, native-born middle class, the rise of a reactionary class, and the formation of a new and foreign bourgeoisie. New ideas would henceforth flow from a dynamic that was foreign to the social structure of French Canada, and these ideas would be associated with groups unfriendly to the national existence of the French Canadians. Ideological innovation coming from another society would not always correspond to the material circumstances of the classes of the French-Canadian social structure. Embraced on occasion by the petty bourgeoisie of the professions, such innovations assumed a special significance; with the failure of this group, French-Canadian society beneath its clerical umbrella would prove resistant to liberal ideology.

Similarly, within the dominant social structure the growth of this liberal ideology would be prejudiced by the specificity of the colonial situation, which obliged the British commercial middle class to downplay its liberalism in order not to lose its ascendancy. In other words, the colonial situation hampered the development of liberal ideology and bourgeois democracy in both the colonial and the colonized social structures, and it reinforced the dominant ideology's autonomy from the socio-economic conditions that formed the basis of the two societies.

Collaboration

The colonial administration's desire for conciliation was matched by a desire on the part of the seigneurs and churchmen for co-operation. The aim of these Canadians was to protect their economic bases in the seignorial system and the privileges – tithes, episcopal status, and clerical independence – traditional to the church. Relations between the two groups were abetted by common class origins. Their community of interests, political as well as economic, was obvious. Their goal was official recognition of French laws and customs that would mean the maintaining of seigniorial tenure, the tithe, and access to public preferments. The three main themes were our language, our rights, and our religion. It was an essentially defensive ideology, seeking to maintain the privileges of a single class by presenting them as the cause of the entire French-Canadian nation. By its summons to national solidarity, it attempted to obscure the class differences in French-Canadian society and stem the flow of new ideas. In attempting to deliver up that society's loyal submission in return for recognition of its triad, this emerging dominant class opposed British merchant claims, supported the colony administration, and reinforced the monarchical, militaristic character of the colonial state.

Brunet has observed of the Canadian churchmen of the time that 'their powerlessness and state of mind moved them quite naturally to wish an understanding with the conqueror. A co-operative policy cost them nothing and could bring them some advantages.'[18] (The comment would apply equally to the small businessmen of Canada, relegated to the retail trade on the edge of money-making activity.) Of the men of the church, Bishop Briand was one of the warmest supporters of collaboration, a stance suggested to him by his concept of the social order as well as his political philosophy. Defeat and military conquest had descended as the will of God. As it was the part of divine Providence to exchange one monarch for another, the British king must now receive his fealty. He addressed these words to a British officer: 'I beg you, Sir, to continue your protection of the Church; I would almost dare say that you are obliged to do so, as is the Church to give you honour.'[19] The temporal power must give support to religion, and the spiritual power must see that the masses pay the respect and obedience they owe their princes and superiors.

In his mandamus for the celebration of a Te Deum on the signing of the Treaty of Paris, Bishop Briand asked the faithful for perfect submission to the decisions of blessed Providence which, according to the prelate, was all the more merciful when it coincided less with our own wishes and pandered less to our own inclinations. Thus did he define a philosophy of resignation. Canada must submit to the new king, George, for he was good-natured and generous. Briand concluded: 'Nothing can excuse you from perfect obedience, scrupulous fidelity, and sincere affection for our new monarch and the cause of the nation to which we have just been added.'[20] The colonial administration made skilful use of the Catholic religion, and the episcopate's goodwill, as an opiate for the people. A reason Murray gave for his policy of religious toleration was that 'the Catholic religion is the best in the world, because it gives us good subjects.'[21] And so long as it retained its status in an environment of toleration, the church of Quebec attached no importance to the change of imperium, a straightforward transfer of monarchical allegiance. What God has wrought, man cannot undo: kings come and go, but Holy Church remains ...

Although the hierarchy sought to convey an impression of unruffled continuity, I think it worth while to examine the role of the conquest in the Canadian church's ideological development. I believe that it forced the church to repress its Gallican tendencies and advertise a return to Ultramontanist principles. The main issue as far as the colonial authorities were concerned, in fact, was to divorce the church from the old homeland and the Gallican practice of the royal appointment of bishops. The episcopal question had to be solved before they could proceed to eliminate French influence by Canadianizing the colony church. British Crown interference was to be side-stepped by making the bishop's appointment a papal rather than a royal prerogative. Rome, understanding the new stakes of the game, accepted the co-option of church authority and let Bishop Briand choose his own successor. Despite the delicacy of the situation, then, the way was clear for the reassertion of papal control in the church of Canada, and the rise of Ultramontanism.

The Quebec Act of 1774 was a triumph, not for the Canadian people, but for the alliance of colonial administration and clerical aristocracy. The act gave legal expression to the ideology of conciliation and co-operation. To understand its nature and scope, we must view it in a context far broader than the demands of the churchmen and nobles, for it 'gave the colony an aristocratic regime such as it had never really had before.'[22] It was primarily a response to the strategic requirements of British imperial policy, echoed in Carleton's efforts to preserve order in the colony and secure it as a base for possible military action against the seditious American provinces. There was also the matter of blocking the democratic agitation of the English-speaking businessmen. Class interest prompted the nobility to oppose a representative system, and Carleton himself saw popular assemblies as poles of resistance to imperial government, encouraging insolence and insubordination among the common people, and undermining the king's authority. According to the governor, assemblies were behind the current unrest in the American colonies. If Britain desired to keep her empire on this continent, the democratic movement must be thwarted. Canada also needed a system of government, in which its cultural distinctness was recognized, that could bind the

Canadian élite to the cause of empire and make it a bulwark against American ambitions.

Superseding the 1763 proclamation, the Quebec Act provided for the maintenance of French civil law and the abolition of the test oath, thus satisfying the seigniorial desires for access to preferments and official status in society. Rather than a representative assembly as demanded by the British commercial middle class, the act created a legislative council in which one third of the places were reserved for the seigneurs. It authorized the extortion of seigniorial rents and tithes, restoring their traditional economic security to church and nobility. It opened the way to religious toleration by its silence on episcopal appointments. The Quebec Act also restored the colony's former boundaries, gratifying the expansionist ambitions of the merchant community and containing the growth of the American colonies. Marcel Trudel has summed up the act admirably as 'an extremely smooth scheme to set Canadian and American against one another.'[23]

Canadian discussion on the new constitution revealed conflicts in political and social philosophy. The seigniorial class supported Carleton's project. It opposed the representative system, fearing the consequences of democratic innovation. The vote would mean political freedom for the common people, and the potential challenge to seigniorial status and power of political influence in the hands of men of another social class. Conscious of their dependence on the conqueror, the seigneurs approved the plan for a legislative council in which they would be represented.

There were Canadians, however, who were not against the idea of a representative assembly. In the summer of 1773, a group calling themselves the True Patriot Canadians drew up an 'Address by the inhabitants of the Province of Quebec to His Majesty and the Commons' that broached a general outline of parliamentary democracy. The group rejected the paternalism of the governor and the British bourgeoisie, pronounced English criminal law acceptable, and disputed the plan for a legislative council, declaring its preference for an assembly elected without discrimination as to national origin. If London refused them the assembly, they would accept the council idea. In its boldness as well as in content, this group was conspicuously different from the conservative elements of the clerical-aristocratic élite who gave unconditional support to the governor. Its existence proves that the churchmen and seigneurs did not have a true ideological monolithism and political hegemony in the immediate post-conquest era. What power that élite did possess came much more from its submission to the colonizers than from influence on the people.

Mass ideology

How did ordinary Canadians in the town and rural areas react to the changes in their society brought about by the conquest? What was their reaction to the new rulers and the new role of the clerical élite? In attempting an answer, we can turn to some indications that emerged at the time of the American Revolution and the subsequent invasion of Canada.

In the early years of British rule, though the clerical-aristocratic élite was advocating a policy of unconditional obedience and co-operation, the people of Canada failed to display overwhelming enthusiasm for the conquerors and the new colonial situation. Rarely, in any case, is there a great welling of spontaneous popular affection for yesterday's enemy metamorphosed suddenly into today's chief magistrate. The Canadians were no exception to this general rule. They were unconvinced of the providential blessings of conquest. Brunet tells us that zealous obedience was more typical of the ruling minority than of the mass of the people, whose reaction tended to take the form of passive resistance. In fact they went so far as to label as treasonable the attitude of the new ruling group, and showed distrust of both priest and seigneur:

The people viewed the members of the colony's ruling class as no better than slavish collaborators of the victors. It was a rift between the Canadians and those who claimed to be their spokesmen that had a considerable and unfortunate influence on the evolution of political thinking in French Canada, bursting out every time the conquerors asked the Canadian leaders to summon their fellow-countrymen for a collective action in the service, chiefly, of British interests ... The Canadians lived in a permanent state of passive resistance.[24]

The people of the Montreal region, for example, systematically neglected to pay the rents they owed their seigneurs; the militia captains of Trois-Rivières failed to show up for a meeting called by Lieutenant Governor Burton; a number of families sheltered prisoners or British deserters; and Canadian businessmen advised the Tête de Boule Natives not to sell their furs at Montreal. These varieties of sabotage indicate a climate of insubordination and uncertainty among the people. There is further evidence of passive resistance. At the time of the Pontiac uprising, the governors attempted with church support to raise five companies of Canadian volunteers. One objective of the operation was to show the Natives that they must look for no more help from the French, who accepted British authority. Yet 'the mass of the people saw this military expedition against the rebelling Indians as a move to strengthen the conqueror's position,'[25] and when Governor Haldimand's generous offers had been met with refusal from the Canadians, he threatened to impound all their hunting guns. The governor discovered that more than half the Canadians, of all degrees, did not accept the peace as conclusive.

Also to be noted, without straying into unwarranted generalization, is the persistence of an irreligious strain which indicates that the leadership claims of the new ruling group were baseless, recognized only by the colonialists. In 1769, the residents of Repentigny refused to rebuild their church; similarly, the people of Saint-Thomas withheld contributions for a new edifice. Bishop Briand himself commented:

There is all too much evidence of intractability, stubbornness, rebelliousness, and ill will towards the faith and the Lord's worship, of scant respect for priests and inattention to their teachings and opinions; and I can no longer pretend otherwise than that a very large number of you, though still professing the faith, attending service and taking the sacraments – though, in a word, still seeming to hold to the faith – do so only on the outside, and so as not to appear separate from the others.[26]

The prelate was well aware of the habitants' disrespect for the spiritual and temporal power of the clergy. Brunet interprets this behaviour as that of a population contemptuous of its former ruling classes when they have lost a war and submitted to the authority of the conqueror, offering him their co-operation.

The American invasion was another occasion when the people of Canada openly disobeyed the new imperium and the clerical-aristocratic élite. Moreover, the revolution began the spread of democratic ideas in the colony, and was in a sense a prelude to the Canadian's own revolution, which borrowed certain ideological elements from it. American propaganda was a political education for the people of Canada, explaining their rights as citizens, outlining the principles of popular representation and

democratic taxation, and introducing the concepts of personal freedom
and political equality. Since the ideological influence of European France
had been contained and diluted, innovation would now come from another cultural world. The Canadians' political awareness would bear the
mark of American liberalism.

American democracy

The elements of the revolutionary ideology of the rebelling colonists
can be found in the various appeals sent by the Continental Congress and
some American politicians, urging the Canadians to join the movement
and, later, explaining their reasons for invading the country. The first
letter of congress outlined its political theory as well as the rights claimed
by the Americans, beginning with the fundamental tenet of democracy:

There is in all human societies a force that tends constantly to endow one part with
the heights of power and happiness and reduce the other to the uttermost degree
of weakness and misery. The intention of good laws is to oppose this force
and spread their influence *equally and universally.*

All history demonstrates the truth of the simple proposition that to exist at
the pleasure of one or of several men brings misery to all. It is upon this principle
that the English have raised the house of their government to resist tyranny
and injustice, and it is for this reason the peoples of the colonies possess their own
governments.[27]

The first right the Americans were calling for was that by which the people took part in their own government by electing those who would
represent them and make the decisions. As a result, they would be governed by laws they had approved, and not by edicts or decrees from men
over whom the people had no power. This right was presented primarily as a bulwark in defence of private property: the person who had
amassed wealth by his work and 'honest industry' could not have it taken
away without his free and full consent. It followed that the people could
refuse money supplies to leaders who oppressed them. The Patriotes
later took up this argument in the struggle for control of the public purse,
to challenge the governor's power and get responsible government. In
the American colonies at the time of revolution, this particular demand reflected the cause of a rising middle class that wanted control of politi-

cal power to eliminate the external obstacles – the colonial restrictions – hampering its development. In Canada, it was used by the lower middle class of the professions and against a dominant middle-class group, the British commercial bourgeoisie whose strategy for economic development depended on exploiting the rural population in the context of colonial domination. The obvious variation in use is accounted for by the presence in Canada of a double class structure, in which the national groups were superimposed and further differentiated in terms of their modes of production.

The letter from the American congress went on to condemn the Quebec Act and attempt to prove that it gave Canadians nothing: 'Liberty of conscience and religion is a mess of pottage: they give you nothing: it is a hoax, for these come from God and not from London.' There was no assurance that French laws would be restored: this was left to the discretion of the governor and his council. Nor would there be any liberty at all without a division of powers.[28] The Quebec Act left all power to the administration: in the absence of a representative assembly, Canadians had no protection against despotism or taxes.

The second basic right described by the congress was that of jury trial: 'This provides that a citizen cannot lose his life, liberty, or goods unless sentence has been passed against him by twelve of his peers, fellow-countrymen of irreproachable reputation, under oath, and resident in his vicinity.' The third was that of personal freedom under habeas corpus, which gave people the right to a judicial hearing if they were detained by the authorities, and the fourth was freedom from statute labour as imposed by the seigniorial system, with small rents to be conceded. Finally, the congress called for freedom of the press, and to give the argument more weight with francophones, the authors invoked a famous Frenchman: 'What would your countryman, the immortal Montesquieu, have said of the plan of government that has just been drawn up for you?' In the Americans' view, the Quebec Act reduced Canadians to slavery.

The letter concluded with an invitation to join with the other colonies. Canadians were to hold meetings, elect representatives, and form a provincial congress to send members to the Continental Congress in Philadelphia.[29] The issue of independence did not arise in this first communication. Americans were merely organizing to oppose the British parliament and its arbitrary repressive measures, and not to break with the Crown.

This letter, of which two thousand copies were printed in French, was followed by others that took up the same themes. On 7 September 1775, General Washington exhorted Canadians:

I pledge myself not only for your safety and security, but for ample compensation. Let no man desert his habitation – Let no one flee as before an enemy. The cause of America, and of liberty, is the cause of every virtuous American citizen; whatever may be his religion or his descent, the United Colonies know no distinction but such as slavery, corruption and arbitrary domination may create.[30]

Washington made his plan clearer in his instructions to Benedict Arnold. If the Canadians fought the invasion or refused to collaborate, Arnold was to withdraw; any ill treatment of or damage to Canadians was to be severely punished; the troops were to respect those Canadians who opposed the invasion and pay full price for everything they bought; they were not to ridicule Catholicism, but make every effort to ensure the free practice of religion.

The invasion that began on 10 May 1775 found the Canadian people in a mood of passive resistance to the British authorities and the colony élite. The events that followed showed the weakness of this clerical-aristocratic group's hold, political and ideological, on the common folk. When Montreal military headquarters asked seigneurs to enrol their tenants in militia companies, the Canadians and Natives refused to co-operate, wringing this complaint from Governor Carleton:

The handful of troops in the province were mobilized at once and ordered to assemble at or near Saint-Jean. The noblemen of the vicinity were requested to gather their habitants for self-defence. Though the gentlemen acted with great alacrity, the people were unmoved both by their entreaties and by their example.

The spirit of obedience seems to have disappeared entirely, and the people are poisoned by the hypocrisy and lies spread with such effect in the other provinces, whose friends and emissaries have been retailing them everywhere with much craft and energy.[31]

The American Revolution brought Canada's class conflicts into the light of day. The élite, well aware of their class interests, lined up on the British side and flaunted their loyalty. The people, for their part, showed their lack of conviction as to the benefits of the Quebec Act; they chose a neutrality that approached goodwill to the revolutionaries, and they were not unreceptive to the political ideas of their southern neighbours.

Carleton's loyal ally Bishop Briand was a fervent propagandist for the doctrine of fidelity to the crown and 'legitimate' authority. In 1768, he had already issued a pastoral letter to dampen expectations of a French comeback, and now, on 22 May 1775, a mandamus reminded the flock that the church taught obedience to established power, that the invaders were in rebellion against their rightful sovereign 'who is ours as well.' The prelate offered indulgences to all who bore arms in defence of the British colony. He exhorted Canadians to remember the government's kindnesses as well as the recent favours enshrined in the Quebec Act.[32] The mandamus met criticism all over the province.

In a draft sermon, Superior de Mongolfier of the Montreal Sulpician house outlined four arguments that may represent the clergy position. First, as patriots, Canadians were bound to defend their country against invasion: neutrality was equivalent to taking the enemy's side. Second, as duly sworn subjects, citizens could not disobey orders without withholding the justice and fidelity due the king. Furthermore, as Catholics, Canadians were bound to prove that the religion which taught them to obey God taught them also to obey their king. Finally, Canadians were bound by gratitude to the monarch who had treated them well and the governor who had so warmly espoused their cause. The churchmen acted like any other ruling class in portraying their interests as those of society in general; and they wanted the Canadian population to share their slavish reaction to the sympathy which the British authorities had shown their claims. At this time, however, the clergy were a ruling class only in the eyes of the British authorities. The people of Canada, not yet sharing this view, refused to obey their summons.

In fact, the bishop's open support for the government's militia callup won him accusations of having donned a general's uniform. Resistance to the callup was, as I have noted, strong in the rural areas; and even when seigneurs managed to enrol militiamen, they refused to march. On 17 September, the habitants of Saint-Mathias, Saint-Charles, and Saint-Denis seized a presbytery where two of Carleton's emissaries lay hidden. They manhandled the parish priest, made the emissaries prisoner, and then spread out to plunder the local manors. These would be among the most belligerent parishes in the later insurrection of 1837; but over seventy in the province showed more or less active resistance when church and imperial authorities attempted to mobilize them. A habitant in Saint-Michel de Bellechasse broke into the sermon and reprimanded the priest for preaching for 'les Anglais.' The feeling was the same in Saint-Thomas de Montmagny, as residents addressed Fr Maisonbasse: 'You are an Englishman, and you want to make Englishmen of us by forcing us to obey.' In some places, this resistance developed into an actual uprising against the church.

Some Canadians were not satisfied with neutrality and moved into open revolt against the government. All the southern parishes welcomed the 'Bostonnais,' who put local men on sentry duty. 'The Canadians of Pointe-Olivier,' according to Gustave Lanctôt, 'were totally committed to the rebel cause.'[33] An estimated five hundred Canadians were to fight on the American side, while others became their provisioners, guides, and spies, even in the face of Bishop Briand's order to excommunicate anyone with rebel ideas. And there was not a village in all the St Lawrence and Richelieu valleys that co-operated with the authorities. Only in the bigger towns was there some evidence of loyalism; not a hundred Canadians outside the magic circle of the élite were prepared to do battle for the king. It was a massive rejection of church power: 'The country's leaders, including Monsignor Briand and Carleton, had presumed much too much on the Canadian's "absolute obedience" to the call of the church. They were forgetting that the individualist, independent-minded temperament, to which the New World experience had added a measure of indiscipline and love of freedom, of the average Catholic had been freed from his old inhibitions by British rule.'[34] These people were not listening to the seigneurs any more, Lanctôt explains, for, 'apart from the conditions of his tenancy, the tenant had in fact and, given the occasion, actually demonstrated total independence of the manor. He did not accept the seigneur's authority in society or his claim to dictate opinions. Under French rule, this militiaman took orders, not from the seigneur, but from officers who were his social equals: the seigneurs had no influence, and could not call up a single militiaman.'[35]

In this generalized resistance, the people of Quebec were not unaware of their own interests. They realized that the Quebec Act did nothing for them, but benefited the church élite. Official blessing for the traditions of tithing and seigniorial rents meant heavier taxes. Those who went over to the American rebels called for the abolition of both, a call that was echoed by the patriots of 1837.

Moreover, the British were militarily weak with only 750 regular troops in the province. Had they rallied round, the habitants would have borne the brunt of the colony's defence. And they were not stupid: it was up to the king, and not the conquered, to defend his prize. The Canadians had nothing to gain by enlisting, and they had everything to lose. Finally, the rumour of the presence of French troops with the Americans seems to have stimulated the sympathizers and awakened vague hopes in the general population.

To sum up, we may say that the mass of the people displayed a friendly neutrality towards the Americans. There was a pro-rebel minority that took direct action, either against the clerical aristocracy or, with the Americans, against their British overlords. On the whole, the people showed awareness of their class interests, and interest in the democratic ideas of the American propagandists. Although the invasion forces were defeated in the spring of 1776, following the arrival of British reinforcements and the erosion of rebel effectiveness by such problems as illness, lack of supplies, and the expiry of soldiers' contracts, the Canadian experience of the American War for Independence was an important one in our history. It caused a far-reaching political crisis in Quebec, and it opened a channel for democratic ideas. America's revolution was the first external influence, in the wake of the conquest, on the development of ideologies in our society.

Other outside influences

A survey of the reading matter available in the Canada of these years reveals the influence of outside ideas and discredits the old myth maintained by historians and sociologists that the people of the colony, living on the fringe of the great ideological movements of the age, were introverted as a community and impervious to the new philosophies rocking the western world. The truth, according to Jean-Pierre Wallot and John Hare, was that 'the foreign ideologies circulated in an élite group and then percolated slowly but surely through to the masses.'[36] Such developments were aided by the printing press, first introduced by William Brown in 1764 for The Quebec Gazette, which emerged as a vehicle for liberal Protestantism and the philosophy of Voltaire. So it was that, as Gilles Bourque has noted, the Enlightenment reached the French Canadians in the English language: 'We know that cultural relations with the old motherland were outlawed for many years. The conqueror even refused admittance to French books, with the result that Voltaire was read in translation.'[37] It was on Voltaire's authority that the *Gazette* denounced religious intolerance, the temporal power of the pope, the practice of excommunication, and the harmful effect on the conduct of business of the existence of too many religious feast days and holidays. Ideologically, British influence was expressed in ideas that suited the needs and interests of the commercial middle class: the balance of powers, individual independence, the need for schooling, a certain material wealth as a qualification for lawmaking, and liberty through and under the general social system.

Another printer, Fleury Mesplet, stayed after the American occupation and published *The Montreal Gazette* in the years 1785 to 1793. His influence was small, attracting a handful of democrats recruited for the most part from the French-Canadian petty bourgeoisie. Mesplet was an admirer of representative assemblies, and wanted one to control taxes and public spending in the colony. He and his circle were followers of the French Encyclopedists, preaching religious toleration, anticlericalism, the reign of reason, equality before the law, and freedom of thought and speech; they welcomed the revolution in France.

Wallot and Hare sum up in these words:

Well before the American and French revolutions, the Canadian elite were acquainted with the eighteenth-century philosophes, Voltaire and the Encyclopedists in particular. These literary influences, with American and then French propaganda, the short-lived activism of the 'democrat' cell around Mesplet and *The Montreal Gazette* that was a vehicle of ideological commitment from 1785 to 1793, and the gradual penetration of philosophe ideals on government, all were factors of unquestionable influence on certain social strata.[38]

It is hard, however, given the state of research in this area, to form any clear idea of how extensive these influences were overall, or in the different classes of Quebec society.

We may turn to the revolution in France to help measure the impact of outside influences on the growth of ideologies in Quebec, and also to arrive at some assessment of popular attitudes. According to Michel

Brunet, Canadians were much excited by the French Revolution, and the lower classes believed that its success would mean their liberation from the English. Certainly, there were echoes of conflict on the shores of the St Lawrence, as the revolutionary propagandist Citizen Genet called Canadians to arms in a pamphlet *From the Free French to their Canadian Brothers.* Known popularly as 'The Catechism,' it argued that although the colonials had been sold out and oppressed by their old despotic rulers, the liberated French could now be their avengers, making Canada as free and independent as France or the United States: 'Canadians! Follow their example and ours; the way is clear; a magnanimous revolution can lift you from the abject state into which you have fallen.'[39] Men were born free: it was the ignorance of some and the perfidy of others that forged their chains. Revolution was a necessity, 'insurrection ... your most sacred duty.' The reasons were many: British cruelty, obstacles to trade, monopolies, the English hold on the fur traffic, the poor constitution, corruption at the top. 'Canadians! You possess in yourselves all that is needed for your happiness ... Men have the right to govern themselves; laws must express their will as declared by the voice of their representatives; no one has the right to oppose their enforcement.'[40] Through their representatives, the people were sovereign. For Canadians, the special benefits of liberation were listed as follows: (1) the country would be a free and independent state; (2) it could make alliances with France and the United States; (3) Canadians would choose their own government, selecting the members of the legislature themselves; (4) the governor's veto would be abolished; (5) all Canadian citizens would have access to civil service posts; (6) there would be no more statute labour; (7) trade would be free; (8) monopolies and privileges in the fur trade would be abolished; (9) the seigniorial system would be annulled; (10) there would be freedom of religion, and (11) there would be no more tithe.

According to Brunet, enthusiasm for the French cause found expression in grass-roots movements in various parishes. For example, some Laprairie citizens responded to Genet's appeal by declaring their readiness to join with the French in liberating the colony. In the years 1794 to 1796 there were generalized small outbursts against the established order and the laws on militia and road service; Bishop Hubert commented on the 'surprising excitement aroused in the minds of the people by the revolution in France.'[41] The clergy weighed in once more on the side of obedience and fidelity to the British Crown, and launched an intense propaganda campaign against France, that lapsed daughter of the church, and her revolution. Hubert told them that 'the ties that bound them [the Canadians] to France are completely broken, and all the fidelity and obedience they used to owe the King of France are now owed to His Britannic Majesty. It is their duty to repel the French from this province.'[42] As for the French-Canadian dominant class, it saw the ideas of the revolution as a direct threat. In order to protect its privileged situation and ascendancy, it paid homage to the British colonial domination that made these possible.

In 1799, following the French defeat at Aboukir Bay, Bishop Plessis called for rejoicing: 'Anything that weakens France tends to put her farther from us. Anything that puts France farther from us means security for our lives, our liberty, our peace of mind, our property, our religion, and our happiness.'[43] Here are the seeds of messianism and the French-Canadian mission of the spirit. The sins of atheistic France had to be redeemed, the torch of French Catholicism carried high. One may, however, be sceptical of the response to this clerical appeal among the common people of the late eighteenth century. It was not until the second half of the nineteenth that this mysticism had a real impact on mass awareness.

As well as providing assurance to the dominant class that the break with France was final, the French Revolution brought clerical reinforcements in the persons of fifty or so priests in full flight. Reinforced at the same time was the level of French culture in Canada. The clergymen came with books and works of art to a country that had been cut off almost entirely from its cultural sources since the conquest. The priests also brought fresh impetus to Quebec education, opening the schools and colleges that trained the lower middle class of the professions.

Despite this new blood, however, the situation of the Canadian church remained shaky. There was a chronic shortage of priests. Those in the colony had poor theological and pastoral training, and many were still immature at ordination. The church's legal status was fraught with uncertainty. The unhealthy condition of the church had far-reaching effects on the relations between clergy and lay people, who generally rejected clerical leadership. Traditional habitant independence continued vigorous and was even abetted by the difficulties of the church, as Jean-Pierre Wallot has noted: 'but a serious shortage of priests at a time of rapid population increase could only be a great handicap to the spread of doctrine and morality.'[44] The conquest found 170 clerics serving sixty thousand Canadians; by 1805, a diocese over two hundred thousand souls strong could count only 186. Already by the close of the eighteenth century, seventy-five Quebec parishes lacked curates. 'There was clearly no church triumphant, strong and wealthy,' Wallot has concluded, 'any more than there was a clergy of great influence and dominance. Even less was there a theo-cracy.'[45]

If we put any faith in the notes Bishop Plessis kept on his parish visits, the people of Canada were less than zealous for their religion and less than eager for instruction in it. What they did have, however, was a lot of vainglory, conceit, and resistance as well as disobedience to authority. Their chief sins were drunkenness, disorderly and shocking public be-haviour, dancing, adultery, incest, and other varieties of fornication. At-tendance at holy services was for them much more a social than a spiritual thing. Above all, it gave them a chance to see their neighbours, discuss harvests and politics. Their Catholicism was only a veneer, without the political and social dimensions that were the conditions for ideological and political hegemony by the clergy. It is clearly necessary to rethink the traditional reading of post-conquest Canadian society as withdrawn, conservative, dominated by the church and the clergy, and closed to the progressive ideas of the age.

Conclusion

The conquest, then, affected the ideological development of Canadian society by eliminating its dynamic class layer, breaking the rhythm of its development, removing it from the intellectual sources that were na-tural to it, and allowing a reactionary, regressive ideology to become first entrenched and later dominant. This ideology was essentially defensive, a vehicle for the continuance in privilege and economic power of the clerical-aristocratic class who were its sponsors. Their eyes were fixed on the past, and their inspiration was the feudal hierarchy that placed them at the social summit. The ideal they quested after was out of tune with the new socio-economic situation. Their economic situation rendered them uncreative as a class, and, as a result of this, incapable of promoting original ideological elements that expressed the specificity of the organiza-tion of the modes of production. The only innovations they could allow themselves were submission and survival based on resignation and co-operation. They attempted an ideological blockade that let in none but the most backward-looking ideological materials from other societies. Without being dogmatic, we have to recognize that a break occurred: to say the least, the flow of new ideas from the old motherland was choked off, and there was a new field of ideological influence from Britain and her American colonies.

On another level, the conquest wrecked the development of democratic awareness in Canada by imposing intermediaries who were foreign to the country's society. The ideological consequences of conquest touched not only the Canadians, by eliminating the class that could have sponsored progressive ideas, but also the British businessmen who formed the new dynamic class, and became embroiled in the paradox of colonialist democracy. Aspiring to political and ideological hegemony, this new group needed democratic political institutions to better control the state apparatus and round off its economic dominance. The employment of these democratic principles, however, in a society with a double class structure in which the classes were distinguished by nationality as well as by mode of production, involved the loss of economic and political power. As long as the British formed a minority, their dual objectives – political control and parliamentary democracy as the means to achieve this control – remained in conflict. In this sense, it can be said that colonialism blighted the flowering of bourgeois democracy. As colonizers, the English-speaking middle class alone could not hope to seize political power; it had to be left in the hands of another group with different class origins.

The effect of the conquest was to confuse ideological development in the ruling minority nationality and to confer a dominant position on two backward-looking social classes that were ideologically reactionary. Within the class structure of the dominated majority nationality, the conquest brought about the emergence of a new social group that became predominant – the petty bourgeoisie of the professions that was based on a specific mode of production, the mode of the petty producer. The democratic ideology was salvaged and used against both the British aristocracy and the clergy, as well as the commercial middle class. This colonial situation lent a special quality to Canadian liberalism, which deviated from its European and American models in uniting political democracy with an anti-capitalist bias.

Finally, it is interesting to note that a goodly number of Canadians seem not to have been bewildered or terrified by the new ideological points of view that came with American propaganda. Their receptivity to the democratic claims of American and French revolutionaries leads one to suppose that they were not fooled by the clerical élite's ideology of collaboration, and moreover that French rule had not blocked the emergence of a mass awarenes that was individualistic and democratic; that the intellectual climate of that era had not been one of classic feudalism, but rather that New France, like other societies of the time, offered fertile ground for the growth of capitalism, liberalism, and democracy. Had it not been for the conquest, Canadian society would probably have evolved ideologically much as its mother country and the other American colonies had evolved.

3

Under British Rule
1791–1840

The salient economic features of this period were the decline of the fur
trade, the crisis in agriculture, the rise of the timber trade, and the
improvement of the colony's transportation networks. All these developments affected class relations in Québécois society.

In the fur trade, the new century brought shrinking markets and falling prices. To make things worse, there was renewed competition to
hasten the trade's decline. In 1770, furs had accounted for 76 per cent of
the value of our exports; by 1810, the share had dropped to 9.2 per cent,
and timber, accounting for 74 per cent of exports, had taken over. Move-
over, the profit margins of the fur trade went down as costs went up.
Beaver was growing scarcer, and the journeys to harvest it longer and more
expensive. All these conditions brought about the disappearance of the
North-West Company for the Bay Company's benefit. They also spelled
the end of the fur trade as a generative product in the economy.

The closing decade of the eighteenth century was a prosperous one for
farmers. Rapid urbanization and population growth in England meant
that that country could not meet its own food requirements. Canadian
foodstuffs were in demand. Beginning in 1803, however, there was a softening of external markets. From that year to 1812, farm exports dropped by 27 per cent. The situation was aggravated by poor harvests: farming
techniques were archaic, the lands worn out, and various attempts to
diversify farm production came to grief.

The crisis in agriculture reached its plateau between 1816 and 1836.
The effects of factors already cited were exacerbated by crowding on
the land. The colonial government was refusing to grant new seigniories,
and French Canadians were excluded from the townships opened up

for British settlers. The seriousness of the situation is indicated by the fact that in the years 1784 to 1831, there was a 234 per cent rise in population on the seigniorial lands, while the acreage in cultivation grew by only 138 per cent.

The French Canadians could no longer find subsistence within the petty producers' mode of production, confined as it was by the dominant commercial capitalism and colonial policy. As this mode failed to ensure their social reproduction – continuity in the basic elements of their society – farm people began emigrating to the towns and the United States. By now, Lower Canada was unable to meet its own food requirements. It began to be dependent on wheat from the upper province and the United States. Butter imports went up thirty-three times, lard seventeen times; pork and beef purchases trebled.[1] The rural masses were turned into paupers. And in addition to spreading discontent among these people, the economic disaster attacked the economic base of the petty bourgeoisie of the professions, who could not sell their services.

Furs were giving way to timber as the prime force in Quebec's economy. The years from 1815 saw a dramatic increase in exports of square timber, owing to the imperial protectionist policy that placed heavy duties on the north European competition. English capital flowed into Quebec for investment in forest industries. There was bitter conflict between two merchant groups in the mother country, one associated with the North American timber trade and the other with the traditional Baltic trade. The latter, finding itself at a disadvantage because of the high tariff, launched a violent free-trade campaign. The Canadian bourgeoisie was alarmed, for with agriculture in disarray and the fur trade in decline, timber was Quebec's last resource. Failure to protect the trade would jeopardize the imperial tie.

The free traders lost. The timber trade expanded rapidly. It procured the necessary credit for the import of manufactures and other commodities; it generated for the capitalists profits to be reinvested; it supplied the government with revenue needed for public works; and it gave jobs to the rural proletariat that was idled by the crisis in agriculture. It is to be stressed that French Canadians were absent from the management of the large enterprises in this economic sector. Only the mercantile bourgeoisie had access to the commercial channels of the mother country. The French-Canadian role was to supply cheap manpower and generate wealth for others.

The surge of forest development brought about a veritable economic

revolution in Quebec. Furs and grain had always been the poles of economic growth. The early nineteenth century completely changed this picture. Primitive commercial capitalism gave way to a form of industrial
capitalism which, while leaving the dependent colonial relation untouched,
greatly changed the interrelation of the modes of production by its partial
proletarianization of the agricultural petty producers, and launched a
revolution in transportation and commercial practice. The need for state
support for the building of roads and canals was behind a class struggle
between the petty bourgeoisie of the professions and the English capitalists for the reins of the state apparatus, for the Lower Canadian assembly controlled by the petty bourgeoisie was against massive state
investment in the economic infrastructure. Mediated by the two classes,
two social structures and two economic philosophies came into confrontation. It can be said that the timber economy, hastening French-
Canadian withdrawal into the unprofitable economic sectors, put the
finishing touch to what the conquest had begun. With the vanquished cast
as mere hewers of wood, the English merchant bourgeoisie was responsible for the timber trade.

Changes in the economy were accompanied by changes in Quebec's
social structure. The period saw the emergence of a class of big capitalists and a petty bourgeoisie of the professions. The great landowning
class declined and an abject rural proletariat made its appearance. All these
changes brought about a realignment of all alliances and power balances
that I shall explore in more detail farther on. At this point, I want to concentrate on the newcomers, the petty bourgeoisie of the professions.

The rise of this class to leadership in French-Canadian society is an indication of the originality of our social formation. It expresses also, and
tellingly, the effects peculiar to the double colonizing process resulting
from the conquest. Unlike most societies, Quebec would be dominated
by a class, the petty bourgeoisie, that was disintegrating everywhere
else, and which certainly never developed enough cohesiveness to be able
to impose its political and ideological hegemony. The overblown historical
role played by this class in Quebec was a consequence of the incompleteness of the French-Canadian social structure, the subordination of this
structure to one differing from it in nationality, and the persistent presence at the colonized society's base of the petty producers' mode of
production, a mode that made the interests of our petty bourgeoisie compatible with those of the peasant class.

The membership of this new élite was drawn from the masses. Indeed, its rural origins can partly account for its power and prestige. These were farmers' sons sent to school and classical college. Education and politics were the avenues of social advancement open to them; all other sectors were out of bounds. And so they headed for the liberal professions; they became notaries, doctors, and lawyers. Others were from the entrepreneurial world: some 432 tradesmen and innkeepers were enumerated in 1792.

In the period from 1791 to 1799, the number of professionals in Lower Canada rose by 15 per cent.[2] The increase in the same group over the years 1800 to 1815 was 58 per cent as compared to 32 per cent in the overall population. What we are seeing is overproduction. In 1836, for instance, the province had 373 notaries and 208 lawyers, people educated to exaggerated expectations that would not be gratified. Canadian society could not accommodate these expectations when all the places in administration and engineering, the army and the navy, were monopolized by the élite of the colonizing social structure. Given this colonial situation, the process that would otherwise have distanced petty bourgeois from peasant could not take place. The two classes had to support one another in order to protect their economic bases.

Their career hopes dashed, their pocketbooks threatened by the glut in the service sector and the agricultural crisis that was impoverishing their customers, these young professionals soon realized where their interests lay and found an outlet in politics, where they used their talents, assumed leadership, and imposed their world view, which at that moment suited the interests of the habitant. This petty bourgeoisie opposed the existing regime and the clerical aristocracy, which it was to supplant as the dominant class in French-Canadian society. Being democratic, it attempted to seize political power with the electoral support of the people. This class stood against the English commercial middle class and fathered French-Canadian nationalism. In addition to running the assembly, it won political supremacy by developing journalism as a political and ideological weapon. More than anything else, it was the 1791 Constitutional Act that opened the way for its ascendancy, as witness these words from MLA John Black:

The house of assembly of Lower Canada is composed of 50 members, and notwithstanding the government and commerce of the colony are in the hands of the English, still at the general elections British influence can never get more than twelve members returned who have to contend with the passions and prejudices of 38 French, the majority of whom are by no means the most respectable of the King's subjects ...[3]

Smouldering as it is with ethnic chauvinism, this analysis leaves a false impression. In fact, the Lower Canada assembly was not split entirely along national lines. It was split along social lines as well: the French-Canadian seigneurs sided with the English, while some English elements made common cause with the professional petty bourgeoisie. For instance, John Neilson, the Scottish publisher of the *Quebec Gazette*, joined the French middle-class bloc because he was ideologically opposed to commercial capitalism, and he remained with them until the 1830s. Others, such as the country doctor Wolfred Nelson, were drawn into the French group by a common economic situation. And a number of Irish MLAS were pro-Patriote because they were anti-British. The question of nationality, then, cannot be isolated from the class struggle.

This dialectic is evident in the two principal features of the petty-bourgeois ideology, nationalism and political liberalism. In this context, the latter took on a special meaning. Given the fact of superimposed nationalities and the specific qualities of the colonial social structure, the French-Canadian petty bourgeoisie stalled the English commercial middle class with the very political tools the English group had clamoured for. Yet in so doing, the French separated political liberalism from the economic reason for its existence, the spread of trade. This meant an ideological superstructure that did not grow out of the economic base. The professionals took up the political ideology of the bourgeoisie, but could not ally themselves with this class and accept its hegemony because of the colonial situation. They cast their lot with the people, since it was the people who supplied them with their economic base. The farmers were the customers for the notary, lawyer, doctor, and small tradesman. They really had no option but to defend the farmers' cause.

As far as French-Canadian MLAS were concerned, therefore, political power must be used for the benefit of agriculture; just as for the English-speaking capitalists, it was there to benefit trade. The class conflict in this period was thus a conflict of nationalities as well, and all the fights in the legislature bore the imprint of this antagonism. It was the battleground of two social structures:

The first, the English, was made up of two 'ruling' classes, one economic – the commercial bourgeoisie – and the other political – the administrators and civil

servants, but neither could draw on adequate supplies of farm manpower or proletarians; the second, the French, was made up of a normal population and two
'ruling' classes, the clerical aristocracy and the petty bourgeoisie, both of which
lacked significant economic strength as well as the political strength that would
have made it possible for them to wield power effectively.[4]

The antagonism made itself felt at various levels. Two economic
practices came into confrontation, one based on agriculture and confined
to Quebec, the other based on commercial capitalism and embracing
all of Canada. In politics, the opposing forces occupied different bases, the
English Canadians in the executive and legislative councils, the French
Canadians in the assembly. Ideologically, the churches and educational
systems of the two societies were in competition. The French Canadians
were anti-imperial and wanted independence; the English Canadians
depended on the mother country and wanted to keep the colonial tie.
Finally, the French Canadians opposed immigration in order to check the
demographic progress of the English, while the English wanted immigrants in order to swamp and assimilate the French. Up to 1837, the Lower
Canada assembly was a recognized theatre of conflict.

Change in the social structure of the dominated nationality – the replacement of the clerical aristocracy, opposition to the policy of co-operation, the petty-bourgeois hegemony and confrontation politics – was
echoed by change in the social structure of the dominant nationality – notably, a tapering off in the feud between the colonial administration and
the commercial middle class. The aristocracy of the bureaucrats could
no longer rely on its alliance with the seigneurs; and the English bourgeoisie, deprived of the assembly as a vehicle for its class interests, had to
pass the sponge over its old campaign for democracy and get hold of the
state apparatus by means of the council, where bourgeois replaced
seigneur. This reversal of alliances put paid to the policy of conciliation and
led straight to the confrontation of two antagonistic social structures.

The Constitution of 1791

Canada's political system, under French as under English rule, had always been one of overlapping competencies. With the American invasion
and the arrival of democratic ideas, the emergence of an English commercial middle class augmented by Loyalist immigration, pressure
mounted for parliamentary institutions.

The political position of the commercial middle class, which had been fighting since the conquest of Canada for political institutions that would benefit commercial capitalism, was reinforced by the inflow of Loyalists fleeing the revolution in the Thirteen Colonies. The newcomers dotted themselves along the north shores of Lakes Erie and Ontario, and in the Eastern Townships. In return for their loyalism, they insisted that they be exempt from French civil law and seigniorial tenure. It was their aim to have the same political rights as their contemporaries in America and Great Britain: access to public administration and a representative assembly. Opposing the American democratic ideal, they preferred the political institutions of the mother country.

The influx came, then, as an ideological reinforcement for British liberalism and British-style democracy, as against the republicanism of the rebel colonies. As Fernand Ouellet tells us: 'Admiration for British institutions as opposed to the American democratic spirit now was given a prominence hitherto unknown. American democracy appeared as a force that might corrupt men's minds and find converts. American independence and Loyalist immigration had the effect of bringing the habitants of the St Lawrence Valley closer to the empire.'[5] Controlling 90 per cent of the colonial economy, the English merchants had been after the political power to complement their economic power for a long time. They demanded a house of assembly, but without a division of the province that would cut them off from most of the Loyalists and perpetuate their minority status. As for the French Canadians, they had realized even before the American War for Independence that a representative assembly could be useful to their cause and rescue them from their inferior position. Meanwhile, the clergy and seigneurs of French Canada opposed any change in the constitution, for the mere existence of a democratically elected assembly, along with the distribution of Crown land to free tenants, would undermine their economic, social, and political position.

It was to appease all these contradictory elements that a compromise was made conferring representative institutions on a province divided into two, Upper and Lower Canada. The arrangement met the requirements both of the Loyalists and of the French clerical aristocracy. The Constitutional Act gave as little as possible to the merchants, and was first and foremost an attempt to solve the problem of Loyalist immigrants who campaigned for British institutions: 'English law and tenure, British justice and the parliamentary system, were their main criteria.'[6] The Act accepted the principle of popular representation. Its qualification of an annual income of two pounds gave the vote to virtually every landowner. The farm vote became crucially important, and Quebec farmers made massive use of their new right.

In fact, the new constitution was a compromise that threw together the monarchical, aristocratic, and democratic philosophies of political power. With it came a system of counterweights under which the power of elected representatives was balanced by executive power. The Act of 1791 did not recognize the principle of responsible government, for executive appointments were to be made independently of the elected assembly. These appointees could remain in office even if the majority of assemblymen withheld their support. The peak of the political system was occupied by a London-appointed governor general whose fief was all of Britain's North American colonies. Heading each province was a lieutenant governor backed by executive and legislative councils whose members were appointed for life. All these people were chosen by the imperial government.

Giving Canada representative but not responsible government, the 1791 constitution opened the way for conflict. As soon as it came into force, it was the scene of French-English confrontation. The first Lower Canada assembly included seigneurs, lawyers, notaries, businessmen, and a few habitants, and yet of a total fifty MLAS, sixteen were English-speaking at a time when the British accounted for only ten thousand in a population of 156,000. Moreover the French Canadians were the minority in the non-elected areas of government, accounting for seven of the sixteen legislative councillors and four of the nine members of executive council. Conflict erupted at the opening of the first assembly session over the election of a speaker and the language of debate. Bitter discussion resulted in the choice of a French Canadian, Jean-Antoine Panet, as speaker, and the acceptance of both languages in the house. The political struggle between house and executive surfaced over the issue of supply. It ended with the 1837–38 rebellion.

These, then, are the main avenues to an understanding of the ideological array and the power lines that gave definition to this crucial period in our development. It is useful to know something not only of the source but also of the nature of the nationalism in French Canada that came into focus during this time.

Before the nineteenth century, French-Canadian nationalism was episodic and embryonic. In order to grow, this ideology needed a sponsoring social class that would act as its spokesman in the political and ideological apparatus. This did not come until the early decades of the nineteenth century, when one saw the emergence of petty bourgeoisie along with awareness of class interest, class cohesiveness, and access to a political institution in the form of the legislative assembly as well as access to newspapers – *Le Canadien* and later *La Minerve*.

It should be remembered that the nineteenth century saw numerous national liberation movements in Europe and America, movements that rode the momentum of the revolution in France and proclaimed the right of self-determination. In the years 1804 to 1830, this right was in high fashion, and it became part of the liberal creed. The Serbs, Greeks, and Belgians gained their independence; attempts in Italy and Poland were unsuccessful. In South America, where the forces of national liberation faced the great landowners and the commercial middle class, Portuguese Brazil became independent in 1822, Spanish Bolivia and Uruguay in 1825 and 1828. In Canada, Patriote thinking was influenced by these movements. 'Are we to keep standing still,' Papineau demanded, 'when the democratic principle is spreading over the whole face of Europe?'[7] For the Patriote leader, the association of self-determination and democracy was axiomatic.

Here, the national struggle expressed itself in parliamentary conflict. Representative government was seen as a means of disloding the oligarchic power of governor and executive council and checking the favouritism of the so-called 'Château Clique' in such matters as speculation in Crown lands. The other features of this period were quarrels between governor and assembly, religious disputes over the appointment of curates and the Jesuit estates, a certain amount of toying with the idea of assimilation, the arrival of new immigrants, and the union proposal of 1822. Amid these conflicts, the Patriote group forged a dynamic nationalist ideology. Their political and economic thinking proceeded from the basic tenet that a nation must be self-governing. Gradually, from the political battles that expressed the material interests of classes in conflict, a national consciousness was seen to emerge.

The first issue in the new century to be the focus of a national skirmish was the proposed Royal Institution for the Advancement of Learning. This first salvo in a campaign to make Englishmen of the French Canadians was to be run by a committee made up of the governor and lieutenant governor, the Anglican bishop, and the Speaker of the House. Its purpose was to set up free elementary and secondary schools. The result would have been to give the British authorities control of the provincial school system. In the words of the governor's secretary, the institution would be 'a most effective means of increasing the executive power and modifying by degrees the political and religious sentiments of the French Canadians.'[8] The bill was passed by the assembly with a few amendments to protect the autonomy of private confessional schools and make the founding of parish schools conditional on approval by the majority of the people. Although the project never became active, it must be recognized as part of an organized effort supported by the English merchants, the Château Clique, and the Anglican clergy to assimilate the French-Canadians.

The constitutional fight between executive and elected assembly really got under way with the issue of the upkeep of public institutions. In 1805, there was need for a new tax to build prisons in Quebec. The assembly faced the alternatives of taxing trade or taxing property. In line with its class interest, the English commercial middle class favoured a property tax that would shift the burden on to the habitant. Defending the farmers' cause, the petty bourgeois wanted the money to come from the business community in the form of a tax on the rum used in the fur trade. With the majority in the House, the French Canadians made their views prevail, deploying their political power to undercut the economic interests of the commercial middle class.

With the founding in 1806 of the newspaper *Le Canadien*, the rising petty bourgeoisie acquired a necessary ideological weapon, a medium for the stating of its positions. The founders were four MLAS: Pierre Bédard, Jean-Thomas Taschereau, and Joseph-Louis Borgia, all lawyers, and the doctor François Blanchet. It was an irritant to assembly-executive tension, and these words from the 27 October 1806 number of the *Quebec Mercury* may sum up the anti-French reaction from the government aristocracy: 'This province is already much too French for a British colony. To degallicize it as much as possible, if I may use that expression, must be our prime objective.' On 23 November, another columnist took up the same theme: 'What remains to be done? Withdraw these privileges which are represented as being too few but are in reality too many, and which the conquered enjoy too liberally, and take measures to ensure that the administration of public business takes place in English and by Englishmen, or men with English principles. This would be the first and most efficacious step towards the Anglicization of the province.'[9]

What we learn from these words is that the ideology of conciliation was a thing of the past, and that there was a new alignment of social forces among the conqueror group. The British commercial middle class had abandoned its hopes of controlling the assembly, and was trying to forge an alliance with the aristocracy of government. At the same time, this latter class had been obliged to revise its strategy, and in particular, its alliance with the French clerical aristocracy, which had failed to live up to the conquerors' expectations and revealed its powerlessness with the people at the time of the American invasion. Seigneurs and clergy were forced to yield to the advance of the petty bourgeoisie as it assumed real leadership in the rural districts and formed the political opposition to the colonial power.

The policies of Governor James Craig, appointed in 1807, bore out this new trend in class alliances and sharpened animosities between executive and assembly. Craig was a career officer whose ideas on colonial government came from the previous century; he championed the royal prerogative against the vague stirrings of independence and responsibility in the House. In its campaign against patronage, favouritism, and corruption in the province, this body asserted the principle of the separation of powers – specifically, the impropriety of being a judge and an MLA at the same time. It drove the magistrates from its ranks by passing a bill that made them ineligible. The bill was promptly vetoed by the legislative council, controlled by the British oligarchy. When the assembly banished its judges again in 1809, Craig fell back on his power of dissolution and prorogued the legislature. The fall elections returned the same faces to the Lower Canada House, and in the feud that ensued, the government aristocrats batted the assembly back at the voters, who batted their same representatives back at the government. As the House continued obstinate, supported by the people, Craig turned to terrorism. Summarily, he seized the *Canadien* printing press and jailed its printer, Pierre Bédard. Arbitrarily, he filled the streets with soldiers and suspended the postal service. Lower Canadians were unmoved, and gave renewed support to their MLAS in the fight against arbitrary government, favouritism, and discrimination on the basis of nationality. It was the first skirmish in the long, drawn-out campaign for responsible government.

The conflict between executive and assembly was an expression, not only of resistance to national oppression, but also, and above all, of class struggle between the commercial bourgeoisie and the petty bourgeoisie of the professions. In addition to the issue of taxing for prisons, three other problems of this period may serve to illustrate the dialectics of the social and national struggle: immigration, money for transportation development, and the proposal for uniting the two Canadas.

The assembly was fierce in its opposition to immigration, essentially British and American, because it was seen as a long-term assimilation plot. In the years from 1830 to 1837, some 217,185 people from the British Isles came to Canada. Given an annual average of 31,041 arrivals, 1832 stands out as a bumper year with 51,746.[10] Most of these immigrants were Irish, pushed out by famine in their own country. They landed in a deplorable state, often carrying diseases which, like the cholera that ravaged Lower Canada in 1832, afflicted the communities receiving them. The Montreal merchants encouraged this influx, hoping to spread settlements through the Eastern Townships and Upper Canada, develop a pool of cheap manpower for the ambitious canal projects, and offset the demographic and political preponderance of the French Canadians. Realizing the assimilative purpose of this strategy, the House refused to accept the new townships as part of Lower Canada, withheld funds for a road system in the area, and objected to its people being represented in the legislature.

In the early 1820s, with the completion of the Champlain and then the Erie canal, the Montreal business community saw its economic hegemony slipping away to the American capitalists. It became a matter of urgency to develop communications with Upper Canada and create a pan-Canadian commercial unity. In particular, the merchants needed canals along the St Lawrence. They counted on government support, but they ran into opposition on the drift of economic development from French-Canadian members of the House. French members were reluctant to loose the public pursestrings for the canal project: 'Their attitude was all the more annoying for the commercial middle class since Upper Canada was beginning work on its section of the canal. Still, given the more or less contumacious mood of the French-Canadian assembly, supported by London, which for strategic reasons preferred the Rideau, the work had to be stopped.'[11] Thus, the professional petty bourgeoisie opposed the rise of commercial capitalism and refused to pay for public works that would benefit the commercial middle class.

Its class interests frustrated, this British bourgeoisie, supported by the government aristocracy that was weary of contumacious assemblies, suggested the union of the two Canadian provinces. They lobbied for the

Westminster parliament to abandon the 1791 constitution and replace it with the Union Bill presented to imperial legislators by Edward Ellice, backed by such representatives of the Montreal business community as Richardson, Grant, and Molson. At this point the colonial administration was virtually bankrupt, starved of revenue by a hostile assembly. Union was welcomed as a means of breaking this political log jam, as well as of solving the customs feud between the Canadas, funding the canal network required for commercial development, rescuing Upper Canadians from the influence of the United States, and, last but not least, swamping and thus more quickly anglicizing the French Canadians. This, at least, was the aim expressed by a group of English-speaking citizens: 'Union's influence in favour of the Anglicization of Lower Canada has been the chief argument used by the French Canadians to oppose its adoption, and, by false pretentions, they have been trying to exaggerate the disadvantages for them of the change in their language, customs, and habits. No one can doubt the benefits that would come from this change, even for the French Canadians themselves.'[12] The petition is a fine example of colonialist paternalism. Its authors went on to assert that in the absence of union, the French Canadians would form a separate state, a French nation, 'or, as they call it, the Canadian nation.' Under this proposed union, English would be the official language. There would be a combined legislative council and one assembly, to which Upper Canada would send forty members and Lower Canada fifty members. Proportional representation was to be distorted in order to secure an English majority. There would also have been an increase in the money qualification for assembly candidates to £500, another measure discriminating against French Canadians. Finally, the appointment of curates would become subject to viceregal approval.

Here, then, was a 'radically conservative and antidemocratic proposal'[13] aimed directly at the political ambitions of the French-Canadian petty bourgeoisie. The news of it raised a tumult in Quebec City. An antiunionist petition collected sixty thousand signatures, and was sent to Westminster with Papineau and Nelson. The imperial parliament took up some of its trade recommendations while leaving the constitutional system unchanged.

The triumph of the commercial middle class was only deferred until 1840. The petty bourgeoisie of Quebec was committed to a political course leading, through the fight over supply to the establishment of agriculture as the base of the province's economic development, to the triumph of the French-Canadian nation. If this course was to succeed, and if its sponsoring class was finally to attain the dominant position in its own society, there had to be an end to the superimposition of nationalities and the colonial tie with Great Britain.

Impasse

In the battle over supply, governors and their councillors demanded approval of a round sum for the monarch's lifetime, while the assembly majority fought to control public expenditure by voting supply each year on the basis of detailed estimates. Their campaign of vigilance led to such acts as their insistence in 1824 on a 25 per cent cut in the salaries of civil servants. While the Act of 1791 did not oblige the executive to report financially to the people's representatives, it did give them the exclusive power to vote new taxes. Underlying the money question was a more basic issue of competing interests. The majority French-Canadian assembly was intent on wresting control of the state apparatus and the distribution of lucrative appointments away from the Château Clique, which budgeted according to its own dreams of wealth and mismanaged public funds in favour of the English minority. Gilles Bourque has cited the case of John Caldwell as an example of what, and whom, the assemblymen were getting at:

This receiver-general used the public treasury to underwrite his commercial ventures. In 1822, he had to declare bankruptcy, and could not reimburse the government. The assembly demanded that state revenue and expenditure be placed under its control. The government could take countermeasures and dispense with a vote in the assembly, but it was in a difficult financial situation. The colony's revenue sources were split in two: the government had access to one part, but for the other it needed the assembly's approval.[14]

At the executive's disposal were the imperial revenues from services and land transfers plus the income from fines, licences, and customs duties. As early as 1794, these proved inadequate, and the government turned to new taxing instruments for which it had to have assembly backing. At first, MLAs were agreeable, but it soon dawned on them that their interests lay in controlling new income sources themselves. By

1810, the assembly was refusing supply without control of expenditure. Craig dissolved it, and was encouraged by Westminster to govern without the people's representatives by getting his funds direct from the imperial treasury. It was an unhappy expedient. In 1817, the Lower Canada government ran up a £120,000 deficit, while the assembly, through the taxes it collected, had a substantial accumulated surplus. Since Britain was no longer prepared to cover the deficits, the assembly became the governor's creditor. In return for its loans, it insisted on detailed annual control over the outflow, not only for public works but also for the civil list, the government salary bill, a move that threatened the economic base of the bureaucratic aristocracy.

By 1836 there had been fourteen sessions of the assembly without approval of supply. The colony administration was in grim straits: 'From 1822 to 1836, the legislative council of Lower Canada rejected 234 bills passed by the assembly, while in a period of about ten years, approximately three hundred bills met the same fate in Upper Canada ... In both cases, the issue was to establish the supremacy of the elected representatives over the appointed administrators, an essential element in any bourgeois-democratic revolution.'[15] Powerless to resolve the impasse, the imperial government turned to force. The governor was told to cover his deficit by seizing the assembly's unused income and to draw up a civil list to be paid automatically, by-passing the assembly. That body would not submit and the governor dissolved it, thus causing the rebellion.

The fight over supply revealed the aspirations to political democracy of the petty bourgeoisie of the professions, which agitated its own interests in the name of responsible government and claimed to be the only class able to restore peace in Canada. In 1832, Etienne Parent told the readers of Le Canadien: 'Never can we hope for peace and harmony in the government as long as the constitution does not put men around the king's representatives who are responsible for all the acts of administration and have the confidence of the House, as in any well-organized representative government.'[16] Even though Parent represented the moderate Patriote group, it should be noted that responsible government was initially seen as occurring within the colonial relationship. The notion of independence was not yet – not explicitly, at least – part of the package. The threat came into somewhat clearer focus with the Ninety-two Resolutions, which attracted wide popular support. In 1834, the Patriote party received a total vote of 483,639, while its opponents got only 28,278.[17] The claims of the petty bourgeois politicians were listened to, for the Canadian people were angry about immigration, which had produced a cholera epidemic, and about the granting of 850,000 acres in the Eastern Townships to the British American Land Company, a speculative enterprise.[18] Furthermore, the economic situation was disastrous and sinking into a depression. Finally, popular discontent was fanned by the arbitrary dissolutions of the assembly, the violation of freedom of the press by the imprisonment of Duvernay and Tracy, and the bloody repression by the army in the election of 1832. The assembly's determined and aggressive resistance symbolized for the people of Quebec the national fight against colonial oppression and for national and social legitimacy, as expressed in the Ninety-two Resolutions supported by eighty thousand signatures.

In drawing up its political manifesto, the Patriote party may have been modelling itself on the file of grievances, and the meeting of the States General, that preceded the French Revolution. Its principal authors were Papineau, Morin, and Bédard. They set in relief the two main features of Patriote ideology – nationalism and democracy. The resolutions amounted to a declaration of principle that can be compared to those of the French and American revolutions.

The eight first rubrics were an act of faith in Britain, but they were later qualified by numbers 50 and 86, which contain the threats of secession if the reforms required by the Canadians were not carried out. The essence of what was being demanded was the democratization of the state apparatus and the respect for the national rights of French Canada. These words were used to describe that nationalism: 'Most of the country's inhabitants have no intention of repudiating any of the benefits of their origin and descent from the French nation, which, given the progress it has contributed to civilization in the arts, letters, and sciences, has never lagged behind the Britannic nation, and is today, in the cause of liberty and the science of government, its worthy rival.'[19] By this resolution, the Patriotes were doing more than rejecting cultural colonialism. They were also, in opposition to the clergy, asserting their ties to revolutionary France. Moreover, in Resolution 88, the authors brought out the parallels between the Irish and Canadian situations, and in numbers 41 to 50, concluded their declaration of sympathy for the political system of the United States with a threat that they would demand separation from the empire if the mother country was unresponsive to their cause.

Tyranny on the part of executive and legislative councils forms the subject of about one third of the ninety-two. Number 34 rages against the plurality of places and the muddling of competencies. Number 75 rebels against discrimination against French Canadians in the civil service, where they then occupied forty-seven of a total 194 positions. In numbers 64 to 74, the Patriotes insisted that the legislative council be made elective, and that the assembly be given budgetary control, the right of inquiry, and, in a development of the right to parliamentary immunity claimed in Resolution 49, the power to decide its own rights and privileges. In numbers 79 to 83, the writers demanded recognition for the democratic principle of proportional representation. Resolution 21 invoked the right of the king's Canadian subjects to alter their own constitution. Thus, as Stanley Ryerson has written: 'The Patriotes were simply defining their conception of a popular assembly, which was to become the decision centre for the nation, and be completed by a legislative council responsible to it and amounting in fact to no more than a committee instructed to execute the assembly's decisions.'[20] The manifesto of the Ninety-two Resolutions reaffirms Patriote opposition to the aristocratic system then in force and their goal of self-determination through parliamentary democracy. The resolutions passed the House by fifty-six votes to twenty-three before being sent to the imperial parliament. The strong support of the habitants is attested by the fact that in the 1834 general election none of the French-Canadian moderates who had opposed them was returned.

If the Patriote platform was essentially political, this is because the resolutions expressed the special nature of the colonial situation, in which national and social domination was ensured by the vehicle of the state. Actually, the democratizing of the province's political institutions was intended to overturn the economic power of the commercial middle class and its ally, the bureaucratic aristocracy, and build towards a Canadian nation state under the leadership of the professional petty bourgeoisie.

In fact, the Patriotes did round out this political programme with an economic challenge. In the seventh resolution passed at their St-Ours meeting of 7 May 1837, they called for a boycott on British imports: 'We will prefer products manufactured in our own country; we will greet as one well deserving of his country any who sets up factories for silk, cloth, sugar, liquor, and so on.'[21] Canadians were urged to relinquish wines and rum, tea and coffee, sugar and tobacco and fabrics from outside, so that the public purse would be chastened by the lack of customs revenue from these imports, as well as to encourage local development. The Patriotes also laid seige to the very bastion of the commercial bourgeoisie: they advised Canadians to stage a massive withdrawal of their money from the banks under English control. The response was the creation of the Banque du Peuple which competed with the Bank of Montreal controlled by John Molson and Peter McGill. No further proof is needed that the national conflict was crowned by class struggle for economic power.

The political thought of Louis-Joseph Papineau

Louis-Joseph Papineau's maiden speech contained this summary of the political principles by which he had been guided:

I have found the good political doctrines of modern times explained and revealed for the love and regeneration of the peoples in a few lines of the Declaration of Independence of 1776 and the Declaration of the rights of men and citizens of 1789 ...

The real social doctrine of modern times is summed up in a few words. Recognize that in the temporal and political order the only legitimate authority is that which is consented to by the majority of the nation; the only wise and benevolent constitutions are those in whose adoption all concerned were consulted and free majority consent obtained: that all human institutions are subject to successive change, and that the endless perfectibility of man in society gives him.the right and the duty to call for improvements suited to fresh circumstances and new needs in the community where he lives and moves ...[23]

Though he began his career admiring British political institutions, and even accepting the colonial tie as a benefit for French Canadians, Papineau would become radical in his positions as a result of the political and social struggle against the commercial middle class and the government aristocracy. Papineau worked out a political platform that aimed at petty-bourgeois control of the state apparatus, and he realized that the imperial connection was incompatible with the existence of a democracy that served the interests of French Canada. From 1827, he was a republican, and drew increasingly on the United States model of democracy. 'Of all governments,' he wrote, 'that which has borne the most incomparably happy fruit is the pure, or very slightly modified, republicanism of the confederate states of New England.'[24]

The petty bourgeois ideology may have been ambiguous and changeable before 1830, but as of that date it grew more precise through radicalization. It was a change of direction that produced schism in the Lower Canada assembly, where a minority group of MLAs led by John Neilson wanted to limit the programme to administrative reforms. In 1833, Etienne Parent came out in support of this policy of co-operation, tending to 'define French-Canadian society culturally, rather than in political-economic terms. The French Canadian was distinguished by his culture; he participated in the Canadian economic and political structures, which were seen as non-national. Parent would oppose the Patriotes root and branch.'[25] The majority of MLAs, however, with Papineau as their leader, clamoured for constitutional change and planned an autonomous French-Canadian republic.

Papineau's programme for political reform has been summed up in these words by Fernand Ouellet: '[He] developed a democratic platform on the American model. He called for reform at all levels: an independent judiciary, an elected legislative council, a responsible executive, the end of patronage, and administrative and governmental decentralization through new systems functioning at the county and municipal levels.'[26] His political liberalism and his nationalism were inseparable. For Papineau, parliamentary government meant possible French-Canadian control of the province's political institutions, and a secure environment for the growth of French-Canadian society. His view was centred on Lower Canada: the Patriote leader never imagined a Canada embracing all the British North American colonies, and he opposed the inclusive vision of the commercial middle class.

Like the nationalism of the Patriotes in general, Papineau's was not only political but economic as well. Percolating through the nationalist language of the period was the desire to create a French-Canadian economic order that would serve primarily the interests of the people of Lower Canada. Economic development was to be anchored to the sole resource that was accessible to French Canadians – agriculture. This could be achieved only by putting an end to the ascendancy of commercial capitalism, by its very structure a source of social injustice and, combined with colonialism, a system that kept the French Canadians in a position of dependence and inferiority. In the campaign to boycott British imports and encourage local production, Papineau had these words to explain his economic policy:

Some of you will say – but this means the ruin of trade! I will reply first that if trade were inseparable from the triumph of our oppressors, inseparable from our own degradation, trade would have to be destroyed. But this is not the case. By our efforts, we can set trade on a new and better course. Increase your flocks to give more wool, your herds for food and to improve the land, to tan more leather and have more craftsmen producing more articles; sow more flax to have more cloth and keep our industrious and charming female compatriots busy in the long winters as well as helping us emancipate our country.[27]

Reviving a version of Talon's old programme, he defined economic growth built around French Canadians, and exploiting the wealth of the land, as an objective of the national struggle. Papineau opted for an economic system based on the small peasant landholding and on petty production geared to the people's basic needs. He accepted commerce and industry to the degree that they served the interests of a farming society, a distinction that has drawn this comment from Gilles Bourque:

The petty bourgeois was no farmer. He did not set agriculture up against capitalism. He opposed a commercial capitalism that eluded him and made the French Canadians a group of second-class citizens. He attempted to implant a new economic perspective, focused on the development of Lower Canada. He turned to the only resource – agriculture – still controlled by the French Canadians. His plan for the economy was to encourage a capitalist, industrially inclined development coming from the farming sectors itself.[28]

Papineau believed that an egalitarian and democratic society could flourish in the traditional economic structure. His opposition to the banks, record offices, canal building, immigration, and the abolition of seigniorial tenure was an expression of his nationalist viewpoint on economic issues. It also spoke eloquently of the specific effect of the colonial situation on the interrelation of the modes of production. In my opinion, Papineau's economics do not indicate – as such scholars as Fernand Ouellet and Fernand Dumont claim – a feudal model. Rather, they come from the world of the petty producers' mode of production, in which work is largely unspecialized, production is geared to subsistence, exchanges are limited, and there is little accumulation. Given the two nationalities and the colonial structure, relations between this mode and capitalism became antagonistic, whereas in normal societies the two coexist symbiotically. The capitalist development rejected by the Patriotes was that serving the economic interests of the mother country and the colony bourgeoisie.

The sagging economy and the constitutional impasse that was built into Lower Canada's colonial society caused the Patriotes to turn to the possibility of independence and revolution as a means of carrying out their political and economic programme: 'Beginning in 1830, the notion of revolution took root among the members of the Patriote republican party. The Parisian rising of that year had come as a stimulus to Patriote hopes for Lower Canadian independence. Crises, epidemics, social and racial conflicts and political struggles made revolution appear as the only solution for these problems.'[29] The Patriotes were particularly receptive to the idea after the 1834 election, in which they faced a brutal campaign of violence organized by the established power and the dominant class. In response to the demands of the Ninety-two Resolutions, the military opened fire on a peaceable meeting in Montreal's Champ de Mars and paraded afterwards through the streets. Not satisfied with this show of force, the English merchants invoked anti-republicanism and imperial loyalism to organize their own armed vigilante groups – the British Legion and the Doric Club. Amid threats and terrorism from the established order, Papineau asked the people to hold themselves in readiness to defend their cause by all possible means. The British oligarchy had made nonsense of constitutional legality.

Although the ideology of Papineau and the petty bourgeoisie was based on the defence of the French-Canadian nation, it was not without its opponents in the French-Canadian social structure. This nationalism did not pass the sponge over class conflict; it bore the deep imprint of antagonism between its sponsoring class and the clerical aristocracy. One way this antagonism found expression was in the anticlerical, secularist stance of Papineau, who saw French-Canadian society in lay terms, and called for the separation of church and state. He condemned clergy interference in politics, and called for government operation of such services as schools and hospitals. Anticlerical though he was, Papineau also believed in freedom of thought and religious toleration; in this sense, he was not denying the basis of the existence of Catholicism.

According to Stanley Ryerson, the democratic, secularist side of Patriote ideology came from the philosophers of eighteenth-century France:

As a student at the Quebec Seminary, Papineau read a great many of the then banned writings of the French materialist revolutionaries – the Encylopedists, Holbach, Diderot, Voltaire, and so on – as well as the English materialists. The French Revolution was a powerful influence on his early years, and until the end of his life, he remained deeply affected by its democratic, revolutionary philosophy, joined by the national, democratic spirit of a French Canada fighting for its survival.[30]

Fernand Ouellet has given this description of the secular thought of the period:

The secular spirit kept gaining ground among the petty bourgeoisie. One began to see anticlericalism and unbelief. Secular ambitions grew. The idea of a neutral state, protector of individual rights, made its appearance, as did the concept of a neutral school system. There was a growing view that schools and hospitals were government services. Gradually, through criticism levelled at the clergy and aristocracy, there emerged the concept of a liberal state and a secular society.[31]

Here were two essential preconditions for the social ascendancy of the petty bourgeoisie.

For Papineau, the state's role was to protect and encourage the flowering of individual liberties. Without being paternalistic, it was to supply the collectivity with those services required to ensure universal access to justice. In the economy, the state should avoid taking any measures on behalf of trade. Papineau opposed protectionism, advocating free trade and the development of trading relations with the United States.

His thinking can be summed up as republican, democratic, anticlerical, secularist, and nationalist. He was not, however, the most radical of the Patriotes. The events of 1837 to 1838 found him outstripped by his own left wing. At the eleventh hour, Papineau was still advising against violence. It was his belief that the confrontation must remain a constitutional one. His political strategy was not without its inconsistencies, as in this statement made from his United States sanctuary: 'My opposition was constitutional and never otherwise ... We were not conspiring to overturn the government by force; our desire was to give it a regimen to make it healthy.'[32] The most extreme political measures he would support were smuggling and the boycott of British products. The rejoinder of Dr Nelson, who also disagreed with Papineau about the abolition of the seigniorial system, was that 'the time has come to melt our plates and spoons down into bullets.' The Sons of Freedom too grasped the necessity of shifting to active resistance. The opponent of armed insurrection was overtaken by events. Papineau would not lead the revolution. With the first salvo, he took the advice of his intimates and sought refuge in the United States.

The moment of revolt found the Canadian people pushed to the limit by economic debacle, inflation, unemployment, epidemics and poor harvests, and a political situation that had become terminal. The special legislative session of 1836 lasted twelve days and achieved nothing. The impasse was total. The next year brought Lord John Russell's Ten Resolutions to goad the Patriotes to fury. They dismissed demands for responsible government and an elected legislative council. The governor was to be given free rein on the budget and the key to the assembly strongbox. The Russell resolutions confirmed the legal title of the British American Land Company It was an intolerable oligarchic counterstroke, and pushed the French Canadians towards open revolt.

The immediate Patriote response was to call public meetings in the towns and villages of the province. Twelve hundred people gathered in St-Ours to condemn imperial oppression in twelve resolutions. The earl of Gosford's ban on such meetings only made them more numerous. People streamed out of their churches that summer when the priests began the Te Deum in honour of Victoria's accession. In August, Gosford dissolved the assembly. The young Patriotes banded together as the Sons of Freedom.

The revolutionary party encouraged the forming of shadow institutions. Their committee in Deux-Montagnes decided to elect its own judges. At St-Charles on 23 October, a crowd of five thousand invited the citizens of the six Richelieu counties to choose their own magistrates and militia captains. They proclaimed the right of a people to change its own form of government. The radicals were assuming the leadership. Dr Côté, MLA for L'Acadie, told the crowd: 'The time for talk is past: what we have to send our enemies now is lead.'[33] In Montreal, the Sons of Freedom swore allegiance to their native land and committed themselves to victory or death. Their manifesto proclaimed the group's resolve 'to emancipate our land from all human authority but that of democracy.'[34] On 6 November, they fought the Doric Club in the streets. The English vigilantes sacked the *Vindicator* printing shop and attacked Papineau's home. November 12 brought an official ban on all public demonstrations. On the 16th, treason warrants were issued against twenty-six of the Patriotes.

On 22 November, the 500 Men of Gore faced some 700 habitants armed with a hundred or so hunting guns. The English were put to rout in the victory of St-Denis. Papineau's flight came swiftly to wound the movement. On 24 November at St-Charles, badly led and organized, barely armed and without a military strategy, the Patriotes were crushed. The imperial troops spread a reign of terror, pillaging and burning up and down the valley of the Richelieu. December 14 brought another Patriote defeat, at St-Eustache. It was a spur-of-the-moment insurrection with indecisive generalship.

On 10 February 1838, the imperial parliament suspended the Canadian constitution and appointed Lord Durham the new governor-general. On 28 February the Patriotes who had taken refuge in the United States under Robert Nelson's leadership proclaimed the Republic of Lower Canada. The animating principles of this new republic were political independence, the separation of church and state, the abolition of the tithe and seigniorial dues, freedom of the press, universal male suffrage that would include Native men, the secret ballot, nationalization of Crown lands and the landholdings of the British American concern, the election of a constituent assembly, and official status for both French and English languages in all public business. Nelson was the president of the provisional government of Lower Canada and, with Côté, organized a liberation force called the Hunters' Lodge, which met secretly in the border states to prepare an invasion of Canada.

The forces of the establishment were regrouping too. On 4 November 1838, they declared martial law and suspended habeas corpus. On 8 and 9 November, a six-thousand-man army led by John Colborne routed a Patriote force of one thousand that could muster only one firearm for every fourth man. The general took 753 prisoners. They appeared before a court martial with no Canadian lawyer to defend them. Ninety-nine of them were sentenced to death. Under pressure from English papers out for blood, the authorities hanged twelve of them in Pied-du-Courant jail at the corner of Notre-Dame and Delorimier streets. Another fifty-eight were deported to Tasmania; two more were sent into exile, and twenty-seven were finally freed on bail. None of the leaders of the insurrection was executed, since for the most part they had fled the country.

According to Bourque,[35] the events of 1837 to 1838 can be seen both as a civil war among social classes in the context of a colonial state and as a national war between two conflicting social structures of differing nationality, each attempting to assert political hegemony. The finale would be victory for the English-Canadian society, a victory whose monument was the Act of Union.

Clerical and popular reaction

Two great principles confronted the established order in the nineteenth century: the sovereignty of the people, under which republics replaced monarchs ruling by divine right, and the separation of church and state, which challenged the temporal power of religious institutions. These principles formed the basis of the liberal ideology of the Quebec petty bourgeoisie as it faced the clerical aristocracy and the commercial bourgeoisie. The secular ambitions of the petty bourgeoisie had already put the clergy's social power to the test in the education acts of 1824 and 1829 and the vote on the law concerning parish schools. In the first case, the church monopoly in education was disputed by assemblymen who wanted to expand the government's role and set up a school system that would be accessible to ordinary people and less geared to dogma and moral instruction. In the second, the local lay élites used the schools act to get control over church income and property.

The essence of clerical reaction to the Patriote movement can be found in the mandamus from Bishop Lartigue that was issued on 24 October 1837, the day after the mass meeting in St-Charles. Permeated with royalist reactionism, the episcopal letter amounts to an anti-liberal manifesto. Monsignor Lartigue turned for his inspiration to Gregory xvi's 1832 encyclical *Mirari vos*, which denounced the Polish patriots and supported the czar of Russia as their lawful sovereign. 'This mandamus represents an important turning point in the evolution of ideas in nineteenth-century Canada,' Ouellet has written: 'It signals a conclusive break between the liberals and the clergy whom they would cast as the mouthpieces of the English oligarchy.'[36] The document's loyalism, returning to the same fears and themes that were conjured up at the time of the American invasion of the 1770s, indicated that there was still life in the ideology of co-operation.

Bishop Lartigue reiterated his belief in the divinely sanctioned rule of kings. No state could harbour more than one supreme authority, and the power of that authority came not from the people but from God. As a result of this, any revolt against the monarch and the temporal power was equally a revolt against God's will. 'Let yourselves not be led astray,' the prelate wrote, 'if anyone attempts to win your support for the rebellion against the established government, on the pretext that you are of the "sovereign people".'[37] Lartigue passed sentence on the insurrection because 'the Church is an enemy of revolution,' and also because all power was in the gift of God. On 11 December, Monsignor Signay, Lartigue's Quebec City counterpart, used similar terms to denounce the turn to violence: 'The use of legal and constitutional means to attempt to rectify wrongs believed to exist is a right we would claim to deny no one; to seek remedy by insurrection, however, is to use a means [that is] criminal in the sight of God and Holy Church.'[38] In Bishop Lartigue's opinion, a Catholic's duty to the established civil power was a matter of religion and not of politics. Therefore, the Catholic's duty was to obey. He indicted the Patriotes as would-be despotic bandits. On 8 January 1838, to prove his loyalty and wean the people from the taste for rebellion, he ordered the clergy of the Montreal diocese to refuse the sacraments and Christian burial to all revolutionaries. Lartigue and Signay had their priests sign a petition to queen and parliament proclaiming their own loyalty and denouncing the uprising.

The Patriotes fought back by condemning clergy treason and their collusion with the state. In Papineau's words: 'Nothing disgusted me more than the sight of the ministers of religion serving as the tyrant's runners in times of crisis and revolution by which the people desired to claim their due rights, and sacrificing their own flocks in alliance with the malefactors against the faithful, damning them to eternal torment in another world if they resisted the torments of bondage in this one.'[39] Church meddling brought an angry reaction. There were popular demonstrations, and anticlerical pieces in the Patriote press. Twelve hundred demonstrated in front of Montreal's St James's Cathedral. 'Down with the mandamus' was heard when readings were attempted in the churches, along with 'Vive Papineau!' and snatches of the Marseillaise. Popular feeling grew so intense that Lartigue offered his notice to the Vatican and thought of shutting himself away from it all in the seminary at Quebec. Some priests had their property vandalized, while there were Patriotes who wanted to take the parish strongboxes for purchasing arms.

The Patriotes would not accept the mandamus as dogma. The church had no authority in matters political. There was no question of submission, or even of excommunication. In the view of these liberals, the church, when it mismatched doctrine with politics, was using its spiritual power to shore up the temporal. The rejoinder of *Le Libéral* ran along these lines: 'It would have been far better for the priests to collect their tithes, along with the innumerable added contributions levied on popular ignorance, quietly, than it was for them to enter directly into political debate – silent as their private interests always keep them on such questions ... The day cannot be far off when the bishops will regret having meddled in what is none of their business.'[40] In the liberal opinion, any Catholic could challenge the dogmatic significance of the Lartigue mandamus without being considered a heretic. It was a theological controversy in which British might championed the church.

Strictly speaking, no rift between senior and junior clergy occurred over the rebellion. Compared to the solidarity of the more highly placed clerics in support of the government, however, the range of opinion was wider at the bottom. Their closeness to the habitant did not cause the country priests to see the Patriote programme as anything but a threat to their local authority and material position. Since the century began, they had become used to criticism from the new local élites on the excessiveness of sumptuary expenditures in the building of churches and presbyteries, and the rigidly religious content of church-run education. These priests were not irresistibly drawn to liberalism and nationalism. It is no surprise to find, then, that the attitudes of those priests who did show some sympathy for the Patriote cause were frequently ambiguous and opportunistic; at all events none of this small number, according to Richard Chabot, 'supported the revolutionary movement unreservedly.'[41] Their passive resistance and criticism of the mandamus flowed from their knowledge of popular opinion: it was too blatant in making the connection between the palaces of prelate and governor.[42] And their moral support for the rebels was soon succeeded by their scramble to smear them.

The only cleric to line up actively with the Patriotes, and express views that were frankly liberal, was Fr Chartier de St-Benoît, a former lawyer.

As principal of the classical college at Ste-Anne de la Pocatière, he carried out far-reaching reforms: corporal punishment was abolished, confession and weekly attendance at mass ceased to be obligatory, and there was even a student-teacher committee to examine unruly boys. St-Benoît's friendships included such Patriote leaders as Papineau and Chénier. He wanted laymen to have more power in parish management. He was critical of episcopal authoritarianism and the lifetime tenure of curates. In the fall of 1837, his sermons incited parishioners to rise in defence of their rights. In Chabot's words: 'He challenged the traditional church ideology on obedience to the civil power, the temporal power of popes, and the divine right of kings.'[43] St-Benoît was a glaring exception in his calling.

Most priests were openly hostile to the revolutionary movement, and their loyalism was decisive for those who were hesitant about defending their reform convictions with firepower. In many villages, especially in the Nicolet, Trois-Rivières, Joliette, Quebec City, and lower St Lawrence districts, revolution was paralysed from the pulpit. The priests, failing secular leadership and revolutionary committees in these places, stemmed the tide of insurrection. Chabot tells us that they played an essential role as mediators for the hierarchy's call to obedience:

To what extent were the clergy responsible for the collapse of rebellion? We may be sure that its influence among the illiterate masses was considerable. The religious sanctions levelled at the Patriotes persuaded some habitants not to join their movement. However, we must not overestimate the importance of the priests. In the face of church censure, rebellion still drew five thousand farmers in 1837 and more in 1838. This massive participation seems to suggest a fundamental opposition between the people and the church.[44]

At the very least, rural Quebec society in 1837 was not a scene of unopposed loyalism. The people had a rooted will to resist that was more or less general in the various regions of Lower Canada.

One way of assessing this is by the massive support the habitants gave their elected representatives throughout this stormy period. There was a sort of symbiosis between the petty bourgeois élite and the people. Even though the political struggles in the legislature were waged chiefly in the petty bourgeois interest, the issues happened to coincide with the defence of the material situation and objective interests of the peasantry, for the two classes were involved in the same mode of production.

We cannot know with any certainty the true effect of the liberal democratic ideals spread by Patriotes in the rural areas of Quebec. We do,
however, have some indications of the Canadian people's state of mind.
In an environment of economic and political collapse, the habitant became aware of the effects of colonial domination, and receptive to the
patriotic appeals of the new élite whose fate was bound up with his own.
He was naturally sympathetic to the Patriote cause, and he showed
up at the meetings held across the province. At those meetings, he could
listen to long excerpts from the patriotic prose of *La Minerve*, and *The
Vindicator*. Unquestionably a supporter of the national cause, he consistently voted for radicals opposing British oligarchy. The habitants' politicization by local revolutionary organizers was seen also in confrontations with the clergy on parish management. Competition with the priests
for local leadership from the notary, doctor, lawyer, and tradesman
meant constant challenge for the clerical credo of obedience to the established order. The curate's social standing was not now automatic. His
luxury living and sumptuary expenditures were viewed as scandalous.

The parish-council controversy occasioned violent debate about democratic management of church assets. Agricultural crisis made the
habitants even tougher about the tithe and seigniorial obligations. They
wanted these cut out altogether. The democratic principle of the
sovereignty of the people seems to have won a warm response from
the mass of small landowners: they realized that political power put
them in a better posture for the defence of their economic interests. For
the farmers, democracy and control over public taxing and spending
went together. They saw political liberalism as a means of preserving their
way of life and their nationality, and of developing in accordance with
their own needs and means. It is not surprising then that the Patriote
party, confronting the bureaucratic aristocracy, the commercial middle
class, and the clerical aristocracy, could rely on broad popular support,
which included general agreement with its national democratic ideals.

This support and agreement was not universal. The social authority
of the church was not dominant, but weakened as it was, it still counted
for something. The rate of religious attendance had never been lower.
Priests were less and less numerous in relation to the general population:
in 1810 the proportion had been one to 1,375 and by the crisis of 1830 it
was one to 1,834 habitants. Durham recognized this situation when he
wrote that 'the serious decline in the district of Montreal of the influence
of the clergy ... concur(s) in rendering it absolutely impossible for the

Government to produce any better state of feeling among the French population.'[45]

As Durham indicated, the rift between clergy and people was not the same everywhere. Clerical influence, social and ideological, seems to have been stronger in the Quebec City district. An organizer there was sufficiently stung to write to the editors of *La Minerve*: 'It enrages me to see public meetings all through the Montreal area, and at Quebec ... nothing! Ah, poor Quebec, will you always be deaf and uncaring?'[46] The church was not the only factor accounting for the low patriotic temperature of the capital district. The presence of the colonial power was more immediate there, the economic activity, including the timber trade and shipbuilding, was more diversified, softening the blow of agricultural collapse.

In the mêlée of 1837–38, there was a leadership vacuum without clear messages from the Patriote leaders, who were forced into hiding by military repression. The distressed habitant, hesitating as to whether he should take up arms, heard only one command. It was the command of the church: loyalty, obedience, and resignation. Although the hierarchy took advantage of the confusion to reinstate its influence, the most significant things are that in the circumstances a large habitant group supported a hazardous attempt at rebellion, and that in the main, there was popular support for the nationalist, democratic philosophy of the petty bourgeoisie.

The Durham Report

Following a relatively brief five-month visit, the earl of Durham reported to London on the situation in Canada and the measures he thought should be taken to correct it. His report is important not only because it contains a preliminary sketch of the next Canadian constitution, but also because the ideological construction it placed on what had happened in Canada would be tremendously influential later on. We should look, then, at the man, his interpretation, and his solutions.

Durham was a British diplomat and parliamentarian from a traditionally liberal and radical family. In the Westminster parliament, he had defended the disinherited classes and the reform principles that became law in 1832. He was dropped from the cabinet because of his radicalism, and sent abroad on a variety of diplomatic missions. It was with this background that Durham arrived in Quebec City with the title of governor-general and the power and money he needed to carry out his inquiry. His first impressions of Canada came largely from the London representatives of the Montreal business community, Messrs Ellice, Moffatt, and Badley, veteran advocates of the federation of Britain's North American colonies.

Their legislative union had as its primary objective to submerge the French-Canadian population in an English sea, thus removing the obstacles to the growth of capitalist interests. In his short stay, Durham talked mainly with this English merchant group. Few of the French Canadians came to his office, and the earl made no special effort to seek them out. This did not, however, prevent Etienne Parent, representing the moderate wing of the petty bourgeoisie, from greeting him as 'a new Messiah coming ... to erase a new original sin.'

Reading the report, one soon detects Durham's ideology. The document reveals the paradoxical mentality of a radical aristocrat, as expressed in a mélange of colonialist, racist, and liberal attitudes. He was a colonialist in considering that Canadian problems were to be resolved primarily in terms of the interests of the mother country: 'The country which has founded and maintained these Colonies at a vast expense of blood and treasure, may justly expect its compensation in turning their unappropriated resources to the account of its own redundant population, the ample appanage which God and Nature have set aside in the New World for those whose lot has assigned them but insufficient portions in the Old.'[47] Durham saw the economic exploitation of colonies by the mother country as a divine and natural right. He reconciled the local reproduction of the inconsistencies of British capitalism in his own mind by viewing the colonies as a part of the capitalist system to be kept in a state of permanent economic dependence.

The racist earl thought that British stock was superior, and that assimilation was the Canadians' only chance at civilization:

And is this French Canadian nationality one which, for the good merely of that people, we ought to strive to perpetuate, even if it were possible? I know of no national distinctions marking and continuing a more hopeless inferiority ... It is to elevate them from that inferiority that I desire to give to the Canadians our English character. ... They are a people with no history, and no literature ... their nationality operates to deprive them of the enjoyments and the civilizing influence of the arts.[48]

Like any other colonialist convinced of his own superiority, the earl assumed that the French Canadians could resolve their problem of inferiority only by turning into Englishmen. His racism blinded him to the real causes of the political situation in Lower Canada. For him, Canada's troubles were the expression, not of a basic confrontation arising from divergent class interests, but of race conflict. Rejecting the social and historical dimensions of this conflict, Durham saw two races in opposition, one progressive and dynamic and the other, responsible for the troubles, reactionary, backward, and static.

In sharp contrast to this, a writer for *Le Canadien* attacked the ideological swindle of colonialism and offered a much more lucid analysis of the situation:

Here, then, is our position. The government does all it can to frustrate our industry and then tells us: you are not industrious. It seizes assets intended for the schools, discourages education, and then tells us: you are ignorant. It refuses us the posts of honour and profit and then says: you have no wealth, no status. The press it controls, along with all who benefit from this state of affairs, take up the chorus: you are lazy, you know nothing, your are poor, you are unimportant. Injustice has all too unfortunately bred this very result, which they now seize upon to humiliate us. We stand convicted of lack of industry and want of knowledge, as if the crime and shame were not upon them who are their cause.[49]

Durham saw his countrymen somewhat differently: 'Our happy immunity from any feelings of national hostility, renders it difficult for us to comprehend the intensity of the hatred which the difference of language, of laws, and of manners, creates between those who inhabit the same village, and are citizens of the same state.' Here is a fine example of the self-delusion inherent in colonialist ideology: the others become inferiors, incapable of raising themselves up save through the domination of the colonialist, with his qualities of progress and civilization. Concluded Durham: 'I entertain no doubts as to the national character which must be given to Lower Canada; it must be that of the British Empire; that of the majority of the population of British America; that of the great race which must, in the lapse of no long period of time, be predominant over the whole North American Continent.'[50] His very liberalism was shot through with racist feeling. True liberalism was a British monopoly, and French Canadians were tainted by a hereditary incapacity for real democracy: 'the French appear to have used their democratic arms for conservative purposes, rather than those of liberal and enlightened movement; and the sympathies of the friends of reform are naturally enlisted on the side of sound amelioration which the English minority in vain attempted to introduce into the antiquated laws of the Province.'[51] The true supporters of democratic reform, then, were those who had been stalling political change for twenty years in order to maintain their privileges as the colonizing, exploitive minority. The liberalism of the Patriotes was a false liberalism because it came as a challenge to colonial domination and the dominant class that benefited from it.

The democratic colonialist's analysis of the Canadian situation led him to condemn the Patriotes for using the institutions of democracy to cripple the growth of British capitalism and promote their own 'unworthy' interests. He was also critical of their lack of the capitalist urge to exploit and accumulate:

It may be said, that, if the French are not so civilized, so energetic, or so money-making a race as that by which they are surrounded, they are an amiable, a virtuous, and a contented people, possessing all the essentials of material comfort, and not to be despised or ill-used, because they seek to enjoy what they have, without emulating the spirit of accumulation, which influences their neighbours.[52]

Without following through on the idea, Durham realized that the 1837–38 rebellion had featured two competing modes of production, with agents of each trying to seize the power of the state and use it to facilitate the type of development that would best serve their own interests. As a supporter of one of these modes – capitalist accumulation – Durham reasoned that in the face of the commercial imperatives of the mercantile bourgeoisie, the French Canadians must abandon their claim to national and political hegemony, and fall in with the 'irreversible' march of capitalism by providing taxes and labour to the English bourgeoisie: 'The pretensions of the French Canadians to the exclusive possession of Lower Canada, would debar the yet larger English population of Upper Canada and the Townships from access to the great natural channel of that trade which they alone have created, and now carry on.'[53] 'They alone have created': at a stroke, the memory of the conquest and the elimination of the French fur traders is erased. Before the colonialist, the deluge: he had begun from scratch.

Thus, over the ignorant, uncultured, jealous, inert, and conservative French, the civilized and progressive English were to be given control of the state apparatus, so that trade and industry could grow in Britain's own interest. Moreover, this apparatus was to be more powerful, and not less. In sketching his solution to the constitutional, political, and administrative problems of all the North American colonies, Durham suggested that Britain scrap one of the chief ideological bases of her colonial policy and concede the system of responsible government. Putting internal policy in the hands of the colonials would in the long run relieve the mother country of the financial dead weight of these colonies, as well as promote imperial unity and trade relations. Britain would retain the exclusive powers of controlling the colonial constitution, land grants, external trade and international relations, and the military.

What the earl was proposing was in fact a colonialism of local autonomy, an early version of what we now call neo-colonialism. For the specific problems of Lower Canada, he had a short-term solution, the legislative union of Upper and Lower Canada, which would lead to his long-term solution: assimilation of the French. Legislative union would not only place the French Canadians in a minority position, and confer responsible government on a colony so rearranged, but it would also have the effect of encouraging French integration into a Canadian whole. Britain should respect the law of the majority, wrote the earl, and make sure that the majority was English, altering the demographic and political map if necessary by shipping in immigrants.

The assimilation of the French Canadians was not to be accomplished by force, but by the natural train of events, that is, by a conscious policy of minority containment, slow but ineluctable: 'Without effecting the change so rapidly or so roughly as to shock the feelings and trample on the welfare of the existing generation, it must henceforth be the first and steady purpose of the British Government to establish an English population, with English laws and language, in this Province, and to trust its government to none but a decidedly English legislature.'[54] In this policy, Britain was to be guided by the example of Louisiana. Apparent equality of rights would camouflage a truth of inequality. The myth of local autonomy would cover actual absence of power. There would be judicial near equality for the two languages, but massive immigration. National divisions would be encouraged by the interplay of political parties, deliberate creation of political minorities, and the law of social and economic self-interest that would cause the élites to give up their defence of the popular interest, of the French language and nationality. The policy would not achieve the desired result of assimilation; it would, however, defuse the French Canadians' tendencies towards anti-colonial struggle and national liberation for a period of time.

Durham saw various other advantages in the plan for legislative union. In addition to making the French a minority and promoting their assimilation, the union would resolve the disputes over revenue sharing in customs duties; it would wipe out Upper Canada's deficit with the surplus funds of Lower Canada; it would lend impetus to the canal building that was essential to the prosperity of Montreal's commercial middle class; and it would save public funds by making the colonial administration more efficient. In the earl's opinion, this legislative union of the Canadas should soon be extended to include all the British North American provinces.

Given Durham's radical reputation, the government at Westminster, hesitated for some time before bringing his report into the House. His diagnosis was only partially accepted; his proposals were not taken as interrelated. Parliament approved the union plan but threw out Durham's recommendations on ministerial responsibility and representation by population. His assimilatory measures were the only ones to attract the favour of the colonialists. The mother country was not ready to change the ideological base of her colonial policy by the concession of responsible government.

The earl's plans for placing the French in a position of demographic and political minority were greeted with pleasure by the colonial bureaucrats of the Château Clique and Family Compact. Those gentlemen refused, however, to see constitutional change accompanied by a change in political structure that would remove their executive power. They were against responsible government that handed control of budgets and preferments to the assembly, even if that assembly were to be English. And for the time being, they had the ear of the British government.

Upper Canadian reformers and Montreal merchants were delighted with the Durham Report, which met their main demands: an end to the French-Canadian problem, legislative union, and the system of responsible government by which they hoped to take over the political apparatus and administration of the country. They would have a few years to wait, however, before their joy was complete.

For French Canadians, the report was a total disaster. It spelled the end for their plans of political and national hegemony. With Msgr Lartigue as spokesman, the clergy came out openly against it. Durham's proposals were an indirect threat to their own position in society, for if French-Canadian society was doomed to assimilation, their own theocratic ambitions went with it. From the petty bourgeoisie, in the circumstances, the only voice to be heard was that of the moderate wing whose spokesmen – Parent, Lafontaine, and Cartier – joined the church in denouncing the policy of assimilation. Some, however, including Etienne Parent, grew despondent enough to suggest abandoning the defence of their nationality and accept the all-Canadian melting pot.[55]

Thus, the collapse of rebellion led to the union of the two Canadas and hastened the process of inferiorization in French-Canadian society. The dynamic and liberating movement of resistance that had tried to build a politically independent, economically self-centred French society on the St Lawrence was succeeded by a defensive, conservative resistance and the ideology of survival. In the colonized nation, the classes of society were realigned by clerical thunderbolt. New alliances developed, and the petty bourgeoisie of the professions, led by its moderate wing, built a new strategy that was essentially based on self-preservation through willing service.

Conclusion

The collapse of the rebellion brought about new relations among the social forces of Lower Canada. First and foremost, it meant victory for the commercial middle class over the petty bourgeoisie of the professions. The Patriote movement came as a threat to the economic base of the commercial bourgeoisie, and deprived it of the political power it required for its development. Now, the political apparatus would give free rein to the economic interests of commercial capitalism. Hegemony was handed to the commercial bourgeoisie; the favourite child of the new constitutional arrangement, this class could emerge as spokesman for the democratic ideal. As far as it was concerned, the obstacle had been removed to the installation of responsible government in the United Province of Canada. The fate of the Patriotes made it possible to resolve the conflict between bourgeois liberal ambition and the bourgeois role in colonial domination.

For the nation conquered in 1760, the defeat of 1837–38 held grave consequences. It marked the end of a century of development for the French-Canadian nation. Only after 1838 did the defeat of 1760 assume its full significance for the future of French Canada. The new defeat drove home all the implications of the colonial situation imposed by force of arms in the earlier era.

What happened in 1837–38 was an attempted bourgeois revolution in a colonial state, where, given its peculiar class structure, it was the petty bourgeoisie of the professions that related social and national objectives and became the driving force of change and not, as had been the case in England, the United States, and France, the bourgeoisie as a whole. To carry out this task, the Quebec petty bourgeoisie had to mobilize the common people, confront the ruling oligarchy and its ally the clerical aristocracy, and then overthrow the colonial power, declare independence, and entrench its own position as hegemonic class at the helm of the state. It did succeed in mobilizing the people and putting itself at the head of the colonized social structure; what it could not do was finish what it had begun. It lacked the necessary economic power to do so. The pathetic state of the Patriotes' armament is evidence of this. To bridge this financial gap, the petty bourgeois leaders had counted on help from the American bourgeoisie. In this, they were deceived.

For this group, defeat meant the loss of its hegemony in French-Canadian society. No longer could it assume the responsibility for leading that society on its own. It was forced to cede the role to another segment of the élite, and be satisfied with a secondary part of support and co-operation. Anyone who was still interested in politics would have to abandon his radicalism and submit to the clergy and the colonial power. The moderate elements of the petty bourgeoisie accepted church tutelage and a new system of alliances in which they lost all possibility of initiative. They became clients of English-Canadian capital, peddling their political support for honorary appointments and a few marginal dividends. Obedience procured for them a new economic base in the public service, which made it possible for them to drop their old alliance with the people. They put aside their traditional defence of the people's interests, and accommodated themselves to myriad compromises and a course of lucrative pragmatism.

The collapse of the rebellion, then, brought about a rift between the élite and the masses of French Canada, and overturned the old alliances. The petty bourgeoisie cast its lot with the spread of capitalism, abandoning the idea it had had of autonomous economic development based on agriculture, the small landholding, petty production. The events of 1837–38 also left a deep impression on the popular mind. The habitants were profoundly disenchanted. They felt betrayed. They withdrew into their own world, resigned to their fate as colonized people, diminished men. They would be receptive as they had not been before to the blandishments of the ideology of resignation, obedience, and collaboration with the conqueror.

This ideology of collaboration was ready to rise again. It was presented as the only possible means of French-Canadian survival. A dynamic and progressive nationalism became defensive and conservative. Opening the way for clerical power in the society of French Canada, 1837–38 cast the fixations of the clerical élite in the role of the dominant ideological system. The failure of the rebellion can be seen as a victory for the clergy: its enemy, the radical and anticlerical petty bourgeoisie, was neutralized; it received the support of the moderate elements of that class, and it was left free to install a backward-looking value system whose main themes would be agriculturism, messianism, and anti-statism. From now on, the dominant ideology in Quebec would reflect the clergy's world view and interests, as well as the sources of its power. It was the beginning of a century of obscurantism.

4

The Path to Confederation
1840–1867

The years of the united province were ones of sweeping change in the economic situation of the colonies. They saw the imperial system dismantled, and economic ties strengthened with the United States. The economy of Lower Canada (Canada East) went into decline, while Canada West, freed for development, laid claim to the economic ascendancy conferred by the Act of Union. The era closed with the establishment of an intercolonial common market.

Before looking at the internal forces that moved the economic currents of the times, we should bear in mind two especially noteworthy factors that were external. By degrees, Great Britain was abolishing her tariff preferences for Canada's timber and wheat. To the south, the growth of their railway system put American capitalists in an even better position to compete with their Canadian counterparts, still tied to a canal-based communications network.

It was a time of fundamental crisis in European capitalism that culminated in the events of 1848. Britain's free traders found in economic hardship fresh impetus for their lobby to lower the costs of staples by discarding preferential tariffs. The free trade policy that emerged in 1842 led to the repeal of the Corn Laws in 1846. Losing their protection in British markets, Canada's natural products had to compete with foreign ones. Free trade helped British capital open European markets to manufactures. As in all imperial situations, the interests of the mother country came before those of the colony.

The overhaul of trade agreements meant change in colonial policy. Unable now to guarantee home markets, Britain had to acknowledge a degree of Canadian autonomy. Canada's capitalists had to have a free rein in their search for new customers. In this sense, we can say that the changes in the trading pattern of the mother country pushed the Canadian economy towards that of the United States, and, little by little, British imperialism was replaced by American imperialism. Canadian business turned south to avoid disaster.

For a time, it was believed that talk of annexation by the United States would get Britain to pull back from her free trade course. When their pressure tactics failed, however, Canada's traders decided to back the negotiations that produced the Reciprocity Treaty of 1854. This trade agreement was their solution to the problem of outlets for their natural products. With the forests of New England depleted, Canadian capitalists found ready takers for the timber they could no longer sell to Britain; and in exchange, Americans could move into the Canadian food market. What is more, this alteration in the external economic framework of the colony brought important advances for the timber trade and accelerated the process of industrialization: the American market required, not square timber, but planks, and the result was the proliferation of that great novelty of the time, the sawmill.

All these changes had their effects on the internal economic structure of the united province, and increased the economic dependence of Canada East, where a stagnating agricultural sector was no longer capable of feeding the population. Lower Canadians depended on Canada West and the United States for their food supply. As the period opened, the timber trade was the mainstay of their economy. With the collapse of the imperial market, however, Lower Canadian hegemony in the trade was lost to western Canada, nearer the United States midwest where demand was strong.

So it was that from 1840, with the roadblock of French-Canadian nationalism removed, Canada West took the ascendancy in both vital sectors – farm and forest – of the economy of the time. In this connection, it must be noted that the economic inferiority of the French Canadians was a result much more of structure than of mentality.[1] Farming was the chief area of economic activity, but poor yields kept it out of the market economy. It remained a subsistence economy, but increasingly forced to retreat before the domination of capital. There were early signs of the disintegration of the petty producers' mode of production. In terms of the processing of products, of course, the lower colony was still at the artisan stage. However, the effects of the industrial revolution were starting to be felt, and in the years between 1850 and 1870, the railways, as well as new textile and paper factories, emerged as indicators of the second phase of capitalist expansion.

The changes that occurred in the trading system had the indirect effect of promoting growth in the new industrial sector of the railways. In the wake of Britain's tariff changes, there was need for stronger connections among the North American colonies, and improved communications emerged as a necessity. While making trade agreements with their competitors to the south, Canadian producers planned to maintain their hold on the Canadian and Maritimes markets for manufactured goods, and if they were going to do this, there had to be a rail link between Halifax and Montreal. Producing coal and fish, the Maritimers could look west for the timber and farm products they lacked. In this period, then, the Canadian economy experienced divergent trends: one created north–south economic relations with the United States, and the other developed an intercolonial trading system on an east-west axis.

The transportation issue would dominate much of Canada's political life. The requirements for expansion of capitalism would shape the spending patterns of government. The mechanism of the state would be at the disposal of 'developers' and financiers to a degree that allows us to see the Canadian federation as largely the creation of capitalist forces needing, if they were to grow, access to markets and the public purse. The development of this unnatural east-west market called for a huge infrastructure investment that was beyond the capacity of private enterprise. Government, then, would be used to wring the necessary funds from the people of the various provinces. And to achieve this, a legal framework on the federal model was put in place.

The policy of transport development had two phases. The first, running until 1848, was canal-based; the second was rail-based. At a time when Canada East was being forced gradually to abandon outside markets, Upper Canadians were set on taking full advantage of the Corn Laws and Navigation Acts so they could tap the demand in the British and St Lawrence Valley markets. Access to external markets, necessary for the accumulation of capital, was impossible without improvement in the means of communication. The sealane of the St Lawrence, leading to the ocean, had to be developed. Part of the objective here was to stop the

Americans from siphoning off western production through the Erie-Hudson canal system: the interests of Montreal's businessmen were at stake.

Yet when at last, in 1848, the canal work was complete, the system was already outmoded. The American rail network was cheaper and more efficient. The colony's commercial class tried to meet the challenge by building a Canadian rail network to support the east-west economy, resist the pull from the south, and bring the economies of the Maritimes into a common market of the British North American colonies. This second phase of transportation development was the one that produced confederation.

Union and responsible government

The new political formation of 1840 responded in general to the economic interests of the Upper Canadians and the Montreal mercantile class. It appears that the banking house of Baring Brothers, which had underwritten virtually all Upper Canada's borrowings, lobbied the imperial cabinet to shift the weight of Upper Canada's bankruptcy, by pooling the provincial debts, to the Lower Canadians.[2] Also, by opening up the markets of Great Britain and Lower Canada to the western businessmen, the union would make possible the completion of the canal system.

No one consulted with the French Canadians on the plans for legislative union. The scheme was approved by a special council, made up overwhelmingly of anglophone bureaucrats and traders, appointed by Colborne. In Upper Canada, the Family Compact and the Toronto merchant community set as the price of their support a smaller representation from Lower Canada, recognition of English as the only official language, and the location of the capital in Upper Canada.

The imperial parliament passed the Act of Union on 23 July 1840; it became the law of the land on 10 February 1841. Making a single province of the two Canadas, it provided for a legislative council whose members were appointed for life, and an elected assembly with forty-two members each from the old Upper and Lower Canadas. To be elected, assembly candidates had to own property worth £500, and the official parliamentary language was to be English.

The assembly was to have control of supply, except for a reserve of £45,000 to pay the governor and the judiciary, and another of £30,000 for senior civil servants. The governor had the power to veto legislation, the Crown could block any bill for up to two years, and the power to create constituencies as well as to appoint their representatives was reserved to Government House.

This new constitution was not remarkably democratic. It was democracy adjusted to the aims of an imperial power bent on the domination of a colonized people. It obliged the French Canadians to pay the debts of the English Canadians. It gave proportionately greater representation to the less populated western section: the old Lower Canada received forty-two seats for its 650,000 inhabitants, while Upper Canada was given the same number for 450,000. And it was imposed without consultation on the people of Lower Canada, despite a petition opposing legislative union. Expressing the Durham *Report*'s call for assimilation, the new union constitution shelved the earl's other proposals: responsible government, the creation of local government, and representation by population. Since these were the chief objectives of Upper Canada's reformers, that group would continue to oppose the power of a legislative council answering to the governor. The struggle for responsible government resumed under Union.

That the new regime did not bring about French-Canadian assimilation is due to the fact that ideological ties proved stronger in the political arena than ethnic ones. In theory, the English had an absolute majority in the assembly; in practice, however, this majority could not be effective, since the campaign for responsible government cut into it, and parties coalesced around ideological, not ethnic, loyalties. The English of Upper and Lower Canada could not form a homogeneous bloc: they were divided, reformers against conservatives, on the issue of responsible government.

In a sense, this division amongst English Canadians made it possible for the French-Canadian minority to play a political role, yet at the same time reduced them to a state of permanent subordination, powerless to work out their own goals. The balance of power was theirs, but they were denied real power. It was now necessary to obtain an ethnic majority if one was to get a political majority and lead a party into office. The reform leaders Baldwin and Hincks turned down the ethnic alliance offered by the English party of Lower Canada. Instead, they pressed the Lower Canadian liberals – the former moderate Patriote group that included Lafontaine – to go along with the union, and co-operation with the western

reformers, in their fight for local autonomy through responsible government. Baldwin used these words to reassure Lafontaine: 'Your brother
reformers of Upper Canada will recognize you and your co-patriots as
Canadians – there will be no national enmity – we desire friendship, mutual respect, and co-operation, if they can be had without yielding our
principles.'[3]

The plan was to rally all progressive forces and swing the political
pendulum towards democratic principles. In this new power sharing,
however, the French Canadians had to content themselves with a supporting role. There was no point in their dreaming of ascendancy and
leadership. They would achieve survival by peddling their political support
in the fight between English tories and reformers; and, reacting to political currents and chances of patronage, they would split internally.

In the shadows around the battle of principle lurked conflicts of interest. The issue of responsible government was inseparable from that of
patronage. Entry to the public purse was vital for the French-Canadian
petty bourgeois; for him, public life was the only avenue to social advancement. This explains his determination in the wars over supply, and his
forced common cause with the Baldwin party. Control of government
expenditure and budget, with the government responsible to the house of
assembly, also meant the allocation of offices, contracts, and subsidies.

Like all French Canadians, Lafontaine opposed the Union Act; yet he
rejected the route of abstention. He condemned the new arrangement in
these words:

It is an act of injustice and despotism, in that it is imposed on us without our
consent; in that it denies Lower Canada her legitimate number of representatives;
in that it denies us the use of our language in the proceedings of the Legislature, against the faith of the treaties and the word of the governor general; in that
it makes us pay, without our consent, a debt which we have not incurred; in
that it allows the executive to seize illegally, in the name of the civil list, and without the vote of the representatives of the people, an enormous part of the
country's revenue.[4]

If they wanted to see it repealed, French Canadians had to participate
in the union, and they had to co-operate with the western reformers. It
was also an opportunity for these moderates to assume the political
leadership, vacant since the radical chieftain's collapse, of French-

Canadian society. Lafontaine presented himself for election and issued a manifesto on the new policy of co-operation, asking his countrymen to accept the democratic play of forces within union and turn out to the polls. (Another former Patriote, Etienne Parent, who generally supported the Union Act and saw assimilation as tolerable under responsible government, was also arguing for co-operation.) At election time, Sydenham's intimidation tactics drove Lafontaine from the contest. He had his eyes opened to the virtues of democracy as practised by a colonizer.

The Act brought no change to the relations between executive and legislature. The government remained answerable to London, not to the assembly. The governor general could be a veritable dictator: he could make public appointments and, through the legislative council whose members he appointed, veto legislation proposed by the assembly. It was harder for him to control the complexion of the elected body, though he could interfere in elections and procure the success of candidates favourable to his policies by gerrymandering constituencies, causing polling places to be set up in areas of strong government support, or by winking at voter intimidation.[5] Moreover, the composition of the executive council was completely up to the governor; he could ignore the balance of power in the assembly, where opposition reformers campaigned to remove this executive power from the royal representative, so that the council members would be chosen from the ranks of the elected majority and majority popular support would become the condition of a government's existence.

The personalities of the various governors determined how the provisions of the Act were applied. Sydenham automatically blocked any reform measure, practised ethnic discrimination in distributing public offices, and gave himself the function of prime minister. Bagot, his successor, took the opposite approach refusing the identification of his regime with a single party. Appointing Morin, Huot, and Mondelet to the magistracy in an attempt to get French support, Bagot broke with his predecessor's discriminatory practices. He also gave offices to the Upper Canadian reformers.

By this time, the shifting balance of power had put reformers in the majority in the assembly. Although the French province had returned twenty-five reformers, it was still represented on the executive council by two tories. Bagot broke with tradition and tried to remedy this sorry situation by bringing French Canadians into government. At the same time Baldwin was named to the post of Attorney General West, Lafontaine was made Attorney General for Canada East; he used the debate on these appointments to make his first speech in his own language, decrying the new constitution's injustice to French Canadians. With Morin and Parent joining Lafontaine as, respectively, commissioner of crown lands and clerk of the executive council, French Canadians had access to executive power and patronage for the first time since the conquest. To a degree, Bagot's administration was at variance with British colonial policy, and, in backing the supporters of common cause between the two reform groups, opened the way for closer east-west co-operation.

Bagot's death and his replacement by James Metcalfe, however, threw these advances into jeopardy. The new governor returned to the Sydenham style, organizing a party to support his administration. Rejecting his patronage policy, Baldwin and Lafontaine resigned with the approval of the assembly, which Metcalfe promptly dissolved; and when, nine months later, the voters returned only eleven reformers from Canada West to join a strong contingent of twenty-eight from the east, the governor's party had a six-member majority. This tory assembly passed some noteworthy legislation: it produced in final form Sydenham's plan for local government, set up the Lower Canadian school system on a basis of voluntary contribution, gave clergymen the vote; it approved compensation for property damage suffered in the 1837 rebellion – although for Upper Canada only – and requested repeal of the Union Act provisions against the use of French.

By the time Lord Elgin succeeded Metcalfe in 1846, the Whigs had taken office in Britain. The earl was instructed to grant responsible government. When, in 1847, the reform group won a substantial majority, he invited Baldwin and Lafontaine to form the new government. From now on, the majority party in the assembly would govern the colony: the governor became simply the royal representative and go-between for colony and mother country. Canadian autonomy applied to matters of internal administration, with the British government retaining all powers having to do with external trade, foreign affairs, defence, and the constitution.

This change in the political system was connected with the imperial government's changing attitude towards the colonies. Britain was less and less willing to bear the old colonial burden. There was a rising feeling against colonies, according to which the colonies cost dear

and returned little, and it was high time they bore the costs of their administration. The mother country wanted to rid itself of colonial responsibilities and gain a free hand for the overhaul of its economic policies. In no
sense was responsible government the fruit of British magnanimity.
Colonialism was a hindrance to imperialism; it had to be sacrificed to the
necessities of free trade and the export of capital.

Other factors influenced the release of responsible government by the
imperial authorities. The influx of 100,000 Irish immigrants swelled
the ranks of the Canadian proletariat and strengthened radical reform.
There was also fear among colonial authorities of the ripple effect of the
revolutionary movement in Europe. In the words of Lord Elgin: 'France
and Ireland are in flames, and almost half the population of the colony
is French, while the other half is almost entirely Irish.'[6] Papineau's people
and the Irish workmen had to be prevented from joining forces. There
was need of a concession to banish the nightmare of revolution. It was
strictly in a context that ruled out any potential political ascendancy
for the French Canadians that the colony was granted internal autonomy
through responsible government.

The chief ideological movements after 1840

No society can emerge unscathed from the experience of military repression. Among the French Canadians, who considered that they
had been defeated by forces and economic interests alien to their society,
the overriding feeling was one of pessimism. The past assumed values
that compensated for the powerlessness of the present. The lessons
of the past were used to counter radical politics and the spirit of
revolution. History became an ideological club to beat back progressive
thinking and discredit anyone who supported it. Distress about what
was to come found expression, in our young literature, in glorification of the
colony's early days. Facing assimilation and fearing oblivion, we
began to write our 'epic.' We were not writing history, but dreaming of the
good old days.

This period was an important turning point in the development of
ideologies in Quebec. The collapse of 1837–38 strengthened certain
structural tendencies that were bound up with the stratification of Quebec
society. Collective introversion, rigidity in social relations, and clerical
domination, all followed the destruction of the Patriote movement. Pre-

viously, within its own specific nature, the rhythm of Quebec's evolution was very much the same as that of other societies. Colonial domination meant imbalance, obviously, but the situation was not impossible to correct. The year 1840 brought a temporary end to hopes of national liberation and political radicalism; it marked the beginning of real clerical supremacy, conservative nationalism, and the ideology of survival, co-operation, moderation, repression, and collective powerlessness. The three chief elements of the reigning ideology would be agriculturism, messianism, and anti-statism. Traditional Quebec society managed to gain the ascendancy only after the collapse of rebellion.

We can distinguish three main ideological streams in the period 1840 to 67. Their representatives were the liberal moderates, the Rouges, and the Ultramontanists.

Liberals

The liberal moderate group was made up of former Patriotes, some of whom, like Etienne Parent, desired reform without going to the length of cutting the colonial tie, and others, like Louis-Hippolyte Lafontaine, rejected the violence of arms and radical positions, putting their faith in change amid peace, harmony, and mutual understanding. Immediately after 1840, this group was a minority in the reform movement, as the radicals continued to receive the bulk of popular support. Gradually, however, the experience of co-operation shifted to this group a relative power that opened the way to political ascendancy.

The arrival of responsible government, opening the gates of patronage to the elected representatives of the people, also opened the way for an increasing liberal sway in political life. The petty bourgeoisie shed its 1830s style of aggressiveness. Ideological disputes turned into mere differences of opinion, open to compromise; such questions subsided in importance as a new, profitable pragmatism advanced. For that element of the middle class embracing the British model of liberalism in politics, national awareness now had no higher aim than the procurement of government jobs for French Canadians and the defence of the language. The cultural aspect edged out the political aspect of nationalism.

In Lafontaine's view, the future of the French Canadians lay in the full employment of the British constitution. Against Patriote radicalism, he offered patience, moderation, temporizing, co-operativeness; reforms were to be achieved in peace, and within the framework of British parliamentary institutions. Lafontaine's political philosophy was moulded by the trauma of 1837–38, and the inability of French Canada on its own to flourish as a community. Here, his thinking betrays the ideological limits of the petty bourgeoisie, which, owing to its vulnerable economic position, felt unable to give political leadership on its own – hence the need to work together with the English-Canadian reformers, form the majority, and get the responsible government by means of which French Canadians might be able to recover what they had lost under union. In this, Lafontaine achieved one of the goals of the middle class: access to the civil service through responsible government. To his credit can also be added reforms in land settlement, seigniorial tenure, and education, the civil code, and the reinforcement of cultural life through government patronage.

On the whole, however, it can be said that Lafontaine's thinking marked the beginning of a lengthy period of collective surrender. Discretion became the liberals' political watchword. We had to bow to the fait accompli since the cause of union was ourselves; if there was union, it was the fault of the extremists. In this respect, Lafontaine faithfully expresses the national guilt feeling typical of colonized peoples. His appeals to realism simply reflected the minority status of the collectivity he wanted to lead. Dorion's verdict, in the 15 April 1848 issue of *L'Avenir*, was a hard one:

It [nationality] was seen as an acknowledged obstacle to our obtaining political rights: it had to be cast out, disregarded, even sacrificed: we must think of ourselves as French Canadians no more if we wish to count for anything in this social system: and so, on the pretext that it was being integrated, it was swallowed up in liberalism. As the principle of nationality was honoured no more, but repudiated through self-interest, it necessarily grew weak, lost its moral strength, and will soon perish utterly ... The union, whose drawbacks and unhappy consequences we exhausted ourselves mitigating in the hope of advantages yet to come, required our national demise in return for political liberty under the constitution: it has been a costly bargain.[7]

Thus did the liberal moderates replace a dynamic, liberating nationalism with a nationalism of survival, based on the preservation of the culture.

After 1848, then, we see a majority element in the élite that was well

satisfied with the acquisition of places in the country's administration
for French Canadians, and the abandonment of the policy of assimilation.
Led by Lafontaine, this majority was identified with the political and
social traditions of Great Britain. It had made the fate of French Canada
dependent on the goodwill of the Upper Canadian reformers. It had
agreed to co-operate in building a Canadian economy that was based on
industrial growth in the west and the inflow of British capital. This
majority rejected the republican, democratic ideals of the United States
and France, preferring instead peace and stability. The Lafontaine
party enjoyed the support of the clergy. It styled itself reform or liberal
because it had campaigned for responsible government and favoured
colonial autonomy in internal affairs. To anyone hoping for overall social
reform, however, its liberalism seemed feeble indeed.

The Rouges

There remained a minority radical liberalism to defend French and
American democratic and republican ideas. The doctrinaire, anticlerical
liberals of the Institut canadien era, together with the heirs of Patriote
radicalism, are known collectively as the Rouge party. It was a group
that kept up the old alliance with the farming folk, and indeed, we can
account for the antagonism of Rouges and liberal moderates on the
basis of a divergence in their notions of the class alliance: the Rouges
refused alliance with the English bourgeoisie, while the moderates
upheld it. Characterized by Joseph Cauchon in his *Journal de Québec* as
'mouthpieces of socialism ... enemies of order and all moral restraint
... [and] foes of God and country,'[8] the Rouges were active only in the
years 1848 to 1867.

Broadcast by the newspapers *L'Avenir* and *Le Pays*, the Rouge ideology had as its chief elements liberalism, nationalism, and anticlericalism. As opponents of Ultramontanist doctrine, the Rouges crossed
swords in the war of ideas with Bishops Bourget and Laflèche. Unlike the
moderates, these radicals rejected the union and called for a Lower
Canada that would remain separate, inhabited and governed by the
French Canadians. Refusing the British political model, they preached
radical democratization. Their announced economic priority was the
improvement of agriculture, a sector that was to be integrated with the
economy of the United States. They even advocated annexation. The

planks of the Rouge platform were universal suffrage, reform of the
courts, abolition of the tithe and the seigniorial system, public education, settlement of the lands, and annexation to the United States.
The main figures in the party were Antoine-Aimé Dorion, Louis-Joseph
Papineau, Louis-Antoine Dessaulles, Jean-Baptiste-Eric Dorion – the
admirer of European socialism – Joseph Doutre, and Charles Laberge.

Lord Durham's *Report* had characterized the French Canadians as
an ignorant people, lacking culture, literature, or history. Young French
Canadians were not insensitive to this contemptuous racism, and they
would make a priority of launching a school system. It was a priority that
said much about changing strategies in the young radical group. It
meant a new scene of conflict. Following the defeat of 1837, education
and culture replaced politics as avenues of collective affirmation. According to the Rousseauesque approach of these young people, social
change was more likely to result from an enlightened educational
system than from the conflict of politics. The more strictly political combinations, geared to positive action, were to be succeeded by activities
of a religious, literary, and cultural nature.

The intention of the Rouges, then, seemed to be a return to politics
by way of educational and cultural institutions. This was the spirit of the
1844 founding of the Institut canadien. For a population hitherto without a library, the institute would function as a popular university and meeting place for young French Canada. Only after 1847, under Papineau's
influence, did the institute abandon its political neutrality to become the
headquarters of radical thinking. It was the centre of a bitter controversy
with Bishop Bourget and the Ultramontanists who wanted to extend
the rules of the Index to secular institutions, including censorship of
the Institut library and a ban on the circulation of proscribed materials. The
Rouges fought against this ecclesiastical meddling in matters of public interest, and they fought for the establishment of a secular school
system. [9] *L'Avenir*, founded in July 1847, took up this theme,[10] presenting education as a means to prosperity for a people of admitted back-
wardness in farming techniques and business. In the Institut elections
of May 1848, members of the *L'Avenir* group took all the important
offices, freezing out the tory *La Minerve* supporters, who accused the
winners of trying to turn an association that was originally intended as
literary and scientific into a political club. The Rouges replied with the
classic articles of liberalism: freedom of thought and religion, freedom of

conscience, and civil and political freedom. They were determined to use the Institut canadien to put these into action.

In addition to maintaining its radical stance politically, the Institut revolutionized its rules when, in 1850, a basic clause excluding non-French Canadians from membership was struck from the constitution. This move was prompted by the ideological principle of universal fraternity. Xenophobia in Quebec, the fear and rejection of the outsider, has always originated with the conservative nationalists: in the opposing, progressive nationalist tradition, the nation was seen as uniting all people living in a country. The Canadian nation, then, must embrace Protestants and Jews,[11] the English as well as the Catholic French. The radicals rejected the religious test of nationality: 'In Canada, it is vain to hope that nationality will be made up entirely of Catholics on one hand and Protestants on the other.'[12] The Institut's new direction led to schism. Under the aegis of Bishop Bourget, a dissident group went off to start the Institut national. This did not, however, stop the Institut canadien from thriving: membership in 1854 had grown to six hundred.

The feud between clerics and radicals was primed by *L'Avenir*'s position on two non-religious issues: union and the 1848 revolutions. Rouge attacks on union began with Papineau's return to active politics. In his manifesto to the voters of Huntingdon and St Maurice, the radical leader condemned the Act of Union as an odious and unacceptable compromise. His nephew Louis-Antoine Dessaulles echoed the manifesto in a letter to *L'Avenir* demanding the repeal of an arrangement that was 'beyond question the most glaring act of injustice, the shoddiest assault on our natural and political rights that could be committed.'[13] The Rouges sought support in the principle of national self-determination that was part of the liberal theory of nationality. Popular at this time in Europe, the principle of self-determination inspired various movements of national liberation, Italy's among them.

The clergy held on to Lafontaine's moderate arguments and gave union their support. They opposed the principle of nationality for two reasons: one, it enshrined the people, and not God, as the source of all law and authority, and two, in concrete terms, it represented the contemporary challenge by Italian revolutionaries to the church's temporal power in the papal states. Such ideological conflict was expressed in provincial politics as solid clerical backing for the Lafontaine-Baldwin party

against the radical liberal group. Bishop Bourget defined the strategy
in these words:

How can we recommend that you avoid the calamities bringing devastation to so
many great and powerful nations? In a word, put your faith in God and be respectful of all lawfully constituted authority. Such is the will of the Lord. Do not
listen to treasonable speeches, for those who make them could not be your
true friends. Do not read those books and papers that breathe the spirit of
revolt ...[14]

The moral influence of the hierarchy was put to work for a political party,
and government candidates had open clergy support against the democrats. In exasperation, the radicals intensified their attacks on church-state
collusion and clamoured for secular institutions.

L'Avenir's annexationist campaign would further inflame antagonism
between Rouges and Ultramontanists, for annexation was a threat to the
privileged status of the clergy. Jean-Paul Bernard[15] notes the paradox in
this Rouge position:

At first glance, it is a surprising revolution that prompted L'Avenir, in April of 1848,
to set itself up as champion of the nationality threatened by union with Upper
Canada, and then, when a year had gone by, appear as the defender of the notion
of annexing Lower Canada to the United States. This development clearly seems
to show a true conversion: the abandonment of the national viewpoint as the
first priority.

It would certainly appear that the radicals' desperate solution placed prosperity, and the savouring of republican freedoms, ahead of national self-
determination. At all events, nationality was bound for extinction through
annexation to English Canada; L'Avenir preferred that it be extinguished
through annexation to the United States.[16]

In choosing annexation by the United States over a confederation
with the other colonies, the radicals argued that French Canadians had nothing to lose with the American plan. They pointed to Louisiana, where
French language and laws had been preserved. They stressed the financial
benefits of annexation. They made much of the autonomy of the states
in the American union. Annexation was the key to the creation of a St

Lawrence republic, and it would achieve the Rouge goal of ending the colonial relationship with Great Britain. Above all, these democrats wanted liberty, equality, and fraternity for everyone.

The Rouge ideology was well summed up in the *L'Avenir* platform of January 1851: education as widespread as possible; improvement of farming techniques; settlement lands within the means of the poorer classes; free navigation of the St Lawrence; reform of the judiciary, decentralization of the courts, and codification of the law; postal reform and free circulation for newspapers; reduction of civil service salaries; decentralization of power and parish-based municipal government; extension of the elective principal to governors, legislative councillors, the magistracy, and the secretaries of government departments; electoral reform to ensure universal suffrage and representation in proportion to population; abolition of seigniorial tenure, of the tithe, of the Protestant Clergy Reserves, and of the system of government pensions; abolition of the special status of lawyers, with freedom for every man to plead his own case – equal rights and equal justice for all citizens.

The radical liberals carried on the Patriote tradition in their continued defence of the democratic and republican ideal. By the influence of patronage, however, their social base was gradually eroded. They would not achieve their desired political and ideological ascendancy. Three paradoxes further explain the Rouge decline: their ideology was the expression of an increasingly limited element of the petty bourgeoisie; it was anticlerical while conceding that the clergy played an essential role in society; and Rouge ideology, working in the institutional environment of a union where French Canadians formed a minority, never managed to reconcile nationalism with democracy.

Ultramontanism

The chief voices of Ultramontanist doctrine in Canada were those of Bishops Bourget and Laflèche. Opposing the Gallicans, the Ultramontanists identified themselves as Catholics without qualification. They rejected all compromise with modern freedoms, any reconciliation with liberalism. They hurled anathema at all political parties and individuals whose ideas differed from those of the church. They told the faithful whom to vote for. For the Ultramontanist, the religious sphere was bound to the secular as intimately as the soul to the human body: it was not possible to build

a society without religion, and moreover, the temporal had to bow to
the spiritual, politics to religion, so that social legislation rested on the precepts of the church.

It was an ideological eddy that had first surfaced in France, the scene in
the mid-nineteenth century of what might be termed a religious revival –
a renewal of Catholic fervour speaking to the unease created by the
industrial revolution, and spawning new religious orders whose members
came to swell the ranks of the Canadian church.[17] Partly responsible
for the success of the movement was the journalist Louis Veuillot, who,
according to Philippe Sylvain,[18] did more to mould the mentality of French
Canada than any other French writer. Veuillot and his Ultramontanist
school had as their political ideal an officially Catholic state that was subject to the pressure of public opinion. Their objective was the return of
theocracy; the pope would exercise worldwide jurisdiction in the social and
political spheres. All modern freedoms, the principles of nationality and the
sovereignty of the people, as well as science, Naturalism, and Rationalism,
were roundly condemned by the Ultramontanists. They wanted some-
how to restore the church to its twelfth-century eminence. Their arguments pointed to universal dictatorship by Rome and the papacy. They
rejected everything that had come out of the French Revolution: for them,
revolution was absolute evil, the target of their unceasing fight. French
Ultramontanism was antinationalist as well: the nationalist movements
of the day were republican, threatening in Italy the temporal power of
the pope.

In this respect, things were different in Canada. Here, in confronting
liberalism, the Ultramontanist ideology had to turn nationalist. It was
only by being nationalist that the clergy could regain control of the situation
and oust the radical middle class. Bishop Bourget was not slow to grasp
the possible advantages for his church, after 1837, of launching a counter-
revolution in which nationalist arguments would be used to win the
people's confidence and 'gently, discreetly, tell them their duty.' The
nationalism of the Ultramontanists was a special hybrid in which nation
and faith were one. In the words of Bishop Laflèche: 'The faith will be the
cement of the nation.' Bourget's strategy lay in counteracting the liberals' radical, aggressive nationalism with a cultural nationalism that was
conservative and defensive, purged of any overall visions of the future,
and marching to the three-step of 'our institutions, our language, our
rights.' The Ultramontanist convictions and conservative sympathies of the

bishop of Montreal emerge clearly in Sylvain's summary of three pastoral letters from early 1858:

In the first, the bishop described the pernicious effects of the revolution, which he ascribed to the dissemination of bad books; in the second, he explained how to stop revolutionary propaganda in Canada by applying the rules of the Index; and the third anathematized those whom he saw as the armourers of 'revolution' in this country, the liberals of the Institut canadien.[19]

This was the bishop's campaign against the spread of the spirit of revolution. In promulgating the rules of the index – something the bishop of Quebec had refused to do – Bourget aimed to ruin the Institut by obliging all Catholics to pull out. In his third pastoral, he condemned not only that 'seat of pestilence,' but also the political party with which the Institut was associated, and the newspaper *Le Pays* which had succeeded *L'Avenir* as the official Rouge organ. In line with its principles, the institute refused to obey the prelate's commands, denying that anyone had the right of censorship or supervision over books or lectures; liberalism upheld the right of everyone to decide what was good for him.

In his political philosophy, Bourget drew on the encyclical *Mirari vos*, which rejected the principles of popular sovereignty, freedom of opinion, and the separation of church and state, proclaiming instead the principle of uncritical obedience to church and established government. The Catholic Church should become involved in politics when the interests of faith and morality were at stake, for her mission was to teach rulers wise government and subjects joyful obedience.

Italy, where the first great success of the principle of nationality was unfurling, provided the backdrop for an epistolary duel between Rouge and Ultramontanists. *Le Courrier de Québec* and *L'Ordre* faced *Le Pays*, in which Dessaulles declared the solidarity of the Canadian liberals with the Italian liberals and the unification of their country at the expense of the papal states, whose administration he criticized. Bourget retorted with a demand that the directors of *Le Pays* publish a series of seven letters debunking Dessaulles' arguments. He lashed out at the newspaper for sneaking in the spirit of revolution condemned by holy writ:

The columns of *Le Pays* ... are filled with contempt, insult, and outrage. For the paper takes a malicious pleasure in picking apart the papal circle, i.e. what there is that is most deserving of respect in the world. It is accused of having misled its people, promising reforms that have not been carried out, even though this is proven to be false. *Le Pays* exposes in its financial administration horrible abuses that do not exist. The paper wants to pass off as cruel and tyrannical a government that is the most paternal in the world. Finally, its courts are portrayed as a ruin to be hacked down and cast into the fire, when no system is more equitable ...[20]

Bourget accused *Le Pays* of being anti-Christian, anti-Catholic, antisocial, slanderous, and hence dangerous for the country's youth. He required from its directors a change of ideological position. The gentlemen did not obey the prelate's summons. They refused to publish his letters in the name of the freedom of the press and the principle of the separation of church and state.

Another Canadian spokesman for the Ultramontanist ideology was Bishop Laflèche of Trois-Rivières. Presenting his ideas in the essay 'Some Considerations on the Relations of Secular Society with Religion and the Family,' Laflèche opposed secularization and tried to prove the paramountcy of the spiritual over the temporal power. His thinking proceeded from two basic assumptions: one, nations and societies are built and guided by Providence, and two, the family is inherently divine. These equipped him to challenge the liberal theory of the separation of church and state, because, as he declared, 'The family is but the nation in the seed, writ small, and the nation is the family writ large.'[21] Given the divinity of the family, and given that the nation was only its enlargement, the temporal powers were therefore subordinate to the Creator's decrees as conveyed by the church. Since the authority of government came from God, government had responsibilities toward the church and could not, as liberals were claiming, be neutral in religion. Quite the reverse: 'The mission given to our forefathers was to convert and civilize the savages of this country ... and the goal assigned by Providence is nothing less than the settlement of a deeply Christian people on these lands it gave them as their heritage.'[22] Laflèche condemned the 'errors' of modern society: civil marriage, divorce, state education of the children. Under his ideological system, the government must pass laws to ensure respect for divine law, the sole interpreter of which would be the church. The state must be Catholic.

This right-wing ideology offered little by way of analysis or explanation, tending instead to the bald assertion. Ultramontanism idealized the colony's feudal past. An apologia for no change, it was not after novel solutions for the stagnation of French-Canadian society; rather, it extolled that society as a model of civilization. Agriculture, a preferred theme in this ideology, was held up as the guarantee of prosperity. Ultramontanism damned industrialization and the cash economy along with their materialistic and cosmopolitan consequences. It preached a rapture of harmony and concord, focused on family and church.

The ideological ascendancy of the church came largely after 1850. Before that time, there were too few clerics to challenge the local politicians. After the collapse of the rebellion, however, the priesthood joined the liberal professions as another outlet for young people. The aim of its swelling ranks was the creation of a clerical society anchored in a Catholic nationality: 'We will be Catholic above all things, yet not Catholic only by conviction, but Catholic also by nationality.'[23] This clerical ascendancy and sidetracking of nationalism were made possible by a degree of depoliticization in the country, a widening gap between public men and people, that was itself a consequence of the rise of political parties, the requirements of the parliamentary system, and the collapse of democratic revolution.

Intellectual and cultural life

The mid-century saw unprecedented strides in Quebec's intellectual production. Imaginations had been fired by events; action gave place to nostalgic dreamings. In the space of two years, there were ten or so new novels with national and historical themes.

Elementary education was put on a fresh footing by the new religious orders from France. Laval University was founded in 1852. The Institut canadien spread out with sixty or so provincial chapters, study centres to guide discussion and foster an awareness of history. There, the Quebec public looked at issues of national interest, debated religious and political freedom, philosophy, and education; their examination of history stressed their French roots.

The recurrent themes of this literary movement were the glorious past, the mystique of nationhood, and the church as patroness of nationality. Abbé Casgrain described the movement in these words:

If, as is beyond question, literature is the mirror of a nation's manners, character, talents, and spirit ... ours will be solemn, meditative, spiritualistic, religious and evangelistic like our missionaries ... But above all else it will be a literature of faith. Religious: such will be its typical form, its expression; otherwise it will not live, it will die by its own hand. This is the sole condition of its being; it has no other reason for existing, any more than our people's lives have an anchor without religion, without faith – the day they stop believing, they will stop existing.[24]

The anti-materialist credo and religious nationalism preached by the Quebec school would set the standards for French-Canadian literature from 1860 to 1930. In addition to its rejection of realism and materialism, it was typified by a closing in of vision and hope, a narrowing in the view of the French-Canadian world. They were to be content with making models of what others had done, as, in Montreal, Bishop Bourget dreamed of building a 'little Rome.' They began to believe themselves fated to small destinies here below, an inferiority that was balanced by a compensating heavenly future. P.-J.-O. Chauveau may have wanted to be a 'nation builder,' but for Charles Guérin, the hero of his novel, building a nation was equated with building a parish north of Montreal. In several other nineteenth-century novels, an example being Antoine Gérin-Lajoie's *Jean Rivard*, the hero's ideal was to found a mini-republic. The ruling ideology made this spiritless, shrivelled universe the very pattern of civilization.

There was, however, another literary stream, one based on commitment and action in society, that emerged in Montreal. Its writers of liberation were looking for new philosophical and political systems; they wanted to loosen the bonds of society, achieve progress through science, and lift the masses out of their wretchedness. The Montreal group proclaimed the principles of justice, progress, and liberty, expressing liberal and socialist influences in the importance they gave to the themes of democracy, political freedom, republicanism, the liberation of the state, and secularization. Lamennais' *Paroles d'un croyant* had a great impact on this generation of Institut canadien reformers headed by names such as Papineau, Gérin-Lajoie, Dorion, Barthe, Dessaulles, Doutre, Laflamme, Buies, Lusignan, and Fréchette. Victor Hugo, he for whom 'romanticism and socialism are the same thing,' was their hero, and they made him honorary president of the institute.

These men were in revolt against the society of their times, and at the heart of their revolutionary awareness was the need for intellectual freedom. They preached tolerance and freedom of thought; they attacked the rule of the clerics that perpetuated the economic inferiority of French Canada. Their movement went under the clerical knife in 1865, and the church proceeded to make strict morality the sole criterion in literature. The Balzacs, Sands, Lamennais, Proudhons, Taines, and Renans were chastised for realism and naturalism by the bards of mossbacked classicism as they tried to shut the gates to the corrupting influence of French literature, the declared foe of God and his Church. The few models Quebec did find in the godless homeland came from the pens of such as De Bonald, DeMaistre, and, most of all, Louis Veuillot, who gave his Canadian disciples the basic philosophy of Ultramontanism.

Conclusion

The period 1840 to 1867 brought major changes of ideological direction for French-Canadian society. Change occurred in the chief elements of the ruling ideology under the influence of the economic, social, and political changes that followed the defeat of 1837–38. The republicanism, secularism, liberalism, and liberationist nationalism of the petty bourgeoisie gave way in these years to the chief ideological themes of the clergy élite: clericalism, Ultramontanism, agriculturism, and the defensive nationalism of survival.

The nationalism that had been active politically before 1840 was now restricted to the cultural realm. It was expressed in the defence of the Catholic religion and French Canada's language and institutions. The key tests of nationality were to be, first, religion and, second, language: 'Here is how we understand French-Canadian nationality: religion – Catholicism – first, country second. Canada without Catholicism is like a flag without colour. Our religion is our primary national characteristic, as it is also the base of our institutions.'[25] So it was that, by the development of a system of confessional schools, the defence of the language became secondary to the defence of the faith.

This redirection of nationalism in line with clerical interests would affect other areas of social and political thought. To begin with, it saddled French Canada's economic life with the ideology defined in these words by Michel Brunet: 'Agriculturism is a general mode of thought, a philosophy of life, which idealizes the past, condemns the present, and is distrustful of the modern social order. It is a rejection of the contemporary industrial age inspired by a static concept of society.'[26] The clerical school banned all contemporary freedoms as well as industrialization, technical development, materialism, and most of the principles of the Age of Enlightenment. For the agriculturists, the race's golden age was that during which the vast majority of people drew subsistence from the soil. Brandishing their nostalgic image of the sower, they were firm in their belief that men would regret abandoning the rural for the factory life. According to them, the true power of nations was based on agriculture and the farming folk.

The idealization of agriculture did not emerge as a national credo until past the mid-century mark. To maintain its socio-economic position, the clerical, lower-middle-class élite attempted to persuade French Canadians to stay on the farm even under poor conditions. George-Etienne Cartier gave as his reason for begging farmers not to sell their land that by doing so they would lead the nation to extinction. Anyone who went into American exile or emigrated to the town was denounced as a traitor or deserter, and the myth of agriculture as the nation's last defence was spread by many a novel and song. The agriculturist thinking of official Quebec circles was summed up nicely in a speech by Bishop Laflèche:

Now, gentlemen, I have no hestitation in stating that the work of the land is the normal work of men in this life and that to which the mass of humanity is called. This work is also the best for the development of men's physical, moral and intellectual faculties; and above all, it is the work that puts men in the most direct relation with God ... Yes: the prosperity and the future of the French Canadian is to be found in the fields and pasturelands of his rich domain. May the Canadian people understand this important truth and never lose sight of it, if they wish to fulfil the high destiny that Providence undoubtedly reserves for them.[27]

Isolated from real conditions, proclaimed by a class whose ascendancy was dependent on its subordination–co-operation to another social tier, this ideology rationalized the chronic powerlessness of a colonized community by lauding and idealizing the very results of that community's exploitation and alienation. In other words, it took as the basic tenets of its world view the results of the colonial situation, and then saddled French-Canadian society as a whole with an unrealistic scheme whose sole purpose was to excuse the ascendancy of a class bereft of real power and without the ability to give leadership to internal economic development. Thus, instead of exposing the economic causes of the exodus from the countryside, they attributed this phenomenon to such psychological factors as love of extravagance and the easy life. In preparing their arguments, these élites forgot the factors of rural overpopulation and Quebec's lack of an economic infrastructure strong enough to host a degree of development that would improve living conditions. This lack of realism reflected the incompleteness of our social structure, and it would become more absolute with the growth of the Canadian economy as a whole.

This quality in the ruling ideology was a result of the national and social domination of French Canada by the British colonizer. The process of industrial and urban growth was, given the economic and political forms imposed by colonialism, carried out almost entirely by English and American capitalists. The alliance of clergy and petty bourgeoisie was unequipped to play such a role and advance its class cause by assuming the leadership in economic growth. Threatened and panicked, this class chose the way of inversion, rejection of the contemporary advances that eluded their countrymen, and sought refuge in a world of heavenly hope. To compensate for economic inferiority, this class foretold a grand destiny for French Canada in North America. Poor though the people were, they were God's choice for a spiritual, moral mission: the conversion of a continent as torch-bearers of civilization. There was a vague feeling that the world of commerce, of factories and cities, belonged to other people; that the French Canadians, deprived of a dynamic, commanding bourgeoisie of their own, had no place in that world.

French Canada's ruling ideology in this period was also anti-statist. This involved it in a vast contradiction: the farm policies called for by the agriculturists required massive support from government, whereas current social thinking assigned government a very limited role. In fact, apart from agriculture, the proponents of this ideology foresaw a situation of total laissez-faire, or rather, the replacement of government by the church and the subordination of state interests to those of religion. Government was to smile on the projects of the clergy while abstaining from any active role. Education, social security, and health services were to be left in the hands of private – that is to say, religious – institutions. This petty-bourgeois social philosophy was agreeable with that of the English-speaking bourgeoisie, whom it left free to manipulate the public purse

for their own benefit and back such undertakings as the building of railways and canals, handouts to private companies, and the military conquest of the Amerindian peoples and lands. As for the French Canadians,
they had cut themselves off from the only instrument that could make
up for the structural weaknesses of their society and promote their collective development.

This phobia of government also blocked the growth of political awareness. Generation after generation since this time has been convinced
that politics were essentially corrupting and undeserving of French
Canada's spiritual quality. The human inventions of democracy, the vote,
and political institutions have been widely discredited. French-Canadian
political cynicism is the result, not of a hereditary defect, but of their
absence from the decision-making arenas and the domination of clerical
ideology. The collapse of democratic revolution weakened and stigma-
tized the secular lower middle class, and it lost social leadership to the
men of the church.

Anti-statism and clericalism come together, for according to the Ultramontanist ideology: 'The church has the duty and the power to chastise
civil governments whenever they act contrary to the law of God, thus
failing to meet the basic conditions of their mission.'[28] It follows from this
that government must bow to the will of the church, which alone can
mediate God's law. According to the terms of the great Victorian compromise, the church left the British commercial class free rein in the economy while she entrenched her control and leadership in French-Canadian
society, leaving the political and honorary offices to the tame petty bourgeoisie.

5

Noonday of Ultramontanism
1867–1896

The second half of the nineteenth century saw important structural changes in Canada's economy, propelled by outside forces increasingly towards industrialization. Internationally, this period coincided with the second phase of capitalist expansion. Canada received large amounts of American and British investment, the latter estimated at $100 million in these years and concentrated in railway enterprises.[1] In Quebec, these broad economic trends were reflected in the shift from square to planked timber for export, and in the submersion of the petty producers' mode of production by capitalist-style farming.

By the 1851 census, with over 80 per cent of its people still on the land, Quebec's was still a rural economy. By 1896, however, the situation had changed dramatically: the value of production in the secondary sector had risen from about $2 million to $153,470,000, an increase of over 7500 per cent as evidence of the arrival of industry.[2] In 1851, the traditional timber trade accounted for 57 per cent by value of the exports of the united province. This trade was being challenged by strong Baltic competition and the switchover from sail to steam in the north Atlantic, and there was a falling-off in demand for Canadian square timber until American markets – markets for processed timber that meant revamping Canada's industry – took up the slack: 'Beginning in the 1850s, two factors prompted entrepreneurs to move into the lumber business – planks and boards: the exhaustion of American forests, generating strong demand for sawn timber, and the urbanization of New England.'[3] In Quebec, according to Albert Faucher,[4] it was the Americans who supplied the much-needed new capital for this sector. These new market and production trends had significant side effects, requiring rail construction, port improvements, and the creation of secondary industry, such as pulp and paper plants, for wood by-products. Moreover, these changes helped open up new land for settlement, plant new towns, and produce the diversified habitant, half lumberjack, half farmer. The industrial picture was rounded out by new enterprises in flour milling, sugar refining, butter and cheese, leather, and textiles.

The National Policy tariff of 1879 stimulated industry by raising duties on manufactured and semi-manufactured goods from 17.5 to 30 per cent. Growth occurred chiefly in Ontario, where there was a developing heavy industry. In Quebec, the process was delayed by a limited market, the absence of iron deposits, and the lack of native capital. The industries that did gain a foothold were connected with the resource sector; secondary industry was light, as in food processing, and employed few workers. In 1871, the 'industrial class' accounted for only 5½ per cent of the population,[5] and 'the main industries one finds in Quebec ... were generally small-scale, geared to local market needs, and produced items required for current consumption. Virtually all industry was concentrated in Montreal and Quebec City.'[6] This first phase of Quebec's industrialization, then, was typified by the leading position of light industry and the dependent, outward-looking nature of economic development. Entrepreneurs, markets, techniques, capital, all came from outside. The economic life of the people of Quebec was based on small business and farming, and neither allowed for sufficient capital accumulation or the growth of a financial and industrial middle class capable of playing a decisive role in the overall process. Quebec could offer only its natural wealth and a docile, cheap labour force.

Industrialization always goes hand in hand with urban growth. From 1851 to 1900, the population of the towns and cities rose from 20 to 40 per cent of the total. The chief factor was the flood of immigrants, mainly Irish, but important as well was the rural exodus of French Canadians who could no longer make a living in the overpopulated countryside. Two other alternatives were available to young French Canadians eager to improve their prospects: a half million chose emigration to the United States, hoping to get rich and return one day to Quebec, while the farm crisis[7] moved others to open up new settlement lands in the Eastern Townships, the Laurentides, and the Saguenay. French Canadians were moving in substantial numbers into the towns of Quebec, however, even though the urban proletariat of the mid-nineteenth century was largely English-speaking Irish. In 1843, for example, 62 per cent of the people in Montreal's Ste Marie district were French Canadian.

As well as breaking down the traditional fabric of society, industrial and urban growth gave rise to new social problems that spurred workers to organize in defence of their own interests. The main difficulties facing the emergent working class were low wages, unemployment, segregation of workers by nationality, the impact of new technology, and the labour of women and children. Their economic situation added new themes to social and political thinking, and prompted the pioneer efforts at unionization.

The transportation revolution

After the 1837 rebellion, the commercial bourgeoisie took over the machine of government with the full intention of turning their influence to profit. Having filled the tory war chest, Quebec's 'lumber lords' took out their licence for barefaced pillage of our natural resources, and got timber concessions for such derisory rates as $11 a square mile. 'From 1851 to 1896,' as Hamelin and Roby tell us,[8] 'Quebec's forest policy was typified by improvising, lack of planning, and favouritism ... The Quebec government served the purposes of trading groups much more than those of the collectivity.' When the 1849 Crown Timber Act, a product of the purest economic liberalism, removed our forests from private exploitation, these same capitalists took advantage of railway policy to profit from public funds in the name of public service.

Depending on an inefficient canal system, unusable in winter and outclassed by the United States rail network, commercial Montreal risked losing its hegemony in western trade to American seaports. To reverse the trend, it joined the politicians in promoting rail construction. Sir Alan MacNab's 'Railways is my politics' admirably sums up this view. Official economic policy was shaped by railway promoters in search of huge capital sums. Federal and provincial governments offered them cash and land subsidies. If the politicians' desire was to pull together a national market and national unity, the financiers wanted to corner western farm surpluses, maximize the value of their land concessions through speculation – for rail development generated land booms – and, by the defence of the St Lawrence, compete with New York.

The railway boom was really a western Canadian phenomenon. Quebec remained on the fringes in this new sector, since the existence of the seigniorial system restricted land speculation. Most of Quebec's rail-building boom would occur in the twentieth century. 'Thus, land speculation and rail development were bound up together. The speculation, however, remained largely a Canada West phenomenon. At least in its seigniorial lands, the east was immunized against this sort of profligacy – useful though it may have been to this capitalist-style economic promotion.'[9] Only the Montreal region and the Eastern Townships, controlled by the British American Land Company, felt the impact of the railway revolution. It was not until after confederation that the St Lawrence north shore was reached by this new means of transport. In 1867, Quebec had 575 miles of steel compared to Ontario's 1393. Adolphe Chapleau commented that the province of Quebec had 'never been favoured as Ontario.'[10] The difference explains in part Quebec's lag in industrial and urban development.

Farming

This period was one of far-reaching change in Quebec's rural economy. After 1867, the traditional small-scale subsistence farm, geared to self-sufficiency, disappeared. Farming fell in with the capitalist system, and the shift was supported by well-organized government propaganda campaigns that encouraged farmers to specialize in accordance with market demands. The cause was taken up by farm associations, schools, and periodicals, all trying to do something about poor crop yields in the province and soften the economic blow of competition from western grain.

The 1873–79 economic slump marked the start of the proletarianization of Quebec farmers, who were in many cases forced to sell their land. Those who stuck it out had to specialize in order to survive. There were plans to build the dairy business into a national industry; it required fewer workers, while its markets were stable and more profitable. Farmers moved into butter and cheese production, and by the century's end their little factories were springing up like mushrooms. Income from dairying paid for the mechanization of agriculture, thus generating a farm labour surplus and underscoring the now irreversible trend towards proletarianization.

As the farm entered the market economy, the farmer became dependent on the capitalist coming and going – for his fertilizer, his machinery, and the marketing of his product. He was also dependent on the market for his and his family's subsistence, since he was moving out of diversified production towards a maximum one-crop yield. In structural terms, these new trends meant the decline of rural society.

The French Canadians and confederation

Before proceeding to analyse French reaction to the fact of confederation, we must consider the economic and political causes of the new system. In economic terms, the union was first seen as a solution to the colonies' problems. In 1864, the Reciprocity Treaty expired, and the Americans would not renew it. New markets were needed for Canada's products. The growth of trade among the British North American colonies was hampered by the existence of different tariffs and trading regulations in each colony. Separately, the colony governments could not finance the transport network and the development of the economic infrastructure required by the commercial bourgeois who were the main instigators of the federal scheme.

Thus, the Act of Union was discarded because it had become incompatible with the growth of the forces of production and capital's need to expand. In fact, according to Stanley Ryerson, the determining factor in the adoption of the federal scheme was the rise of an English-Canadian industrial capitalism dependent on railway development. A united, autonomous state was needed to promote the growth of colonial markets; steel rails were the backbone of the Canadian nation. The greater union of the British North American colonies opened the way to uniform trading regulations and the creation of a market which, given adequate tariff protection, could replace the United States market, absorb some of central Canada's products, and thus stimulate the growth of industry.

The network assembled in this way was also, for the commercial community of central Canada, a route to the outside world. This group needed a year-round seaport; in winter, Canada depended on American companies to export its products to the Maritimes, the West Indies, and Europe. The plan was to build a rail link between Halifax and Rivière-du-Loup, giving Toronto and Montreal a route to the Atlantic that did not pass through the United States. Also, the wheat of the west was to be funnelled into the St Lawrence, and the manufactures of central Canada shipped back to the grain farmers.

The job was handed over to private businessmen – for the eastern road, those of the Grand Trunk – who financed it by dipping into the public treasury. In 1862, rail construction accounted for 60 per cent of the province's debt. On the brink of bankruptcy, the rail entrepreneurs were counting on the other North American colonies, New Brunswick and Nova Scotia, to bail them out. For this purpose, they obtained the politicians' support.

The Grand Trunk's legal advisor happened to be George-Etienne Cartier. He rose in defence of railway interests on several occasions as an MLA, supporting bills that gave guarantees and loans to these private companies. Canadian confederation was inseparably bound to the growth of Canadian capitalism, which sought prosperity by the creation of a state that was equal to its expansionist designs.

In political terms too the 1840 system was obsolete. Under the Act of Union, Upper and Lower Canada were equally represented. At the outset, this provision resulted in proportional over-representation for the upper section, and was regarded as unjust by the French Canadians. Gradually, however, as the western population grew,[11] the situation was reversed, and the principle of equal representation worked in the French Canadians' favour. The majority now found the principle unpalatable, the constitution outdated and undemocratic, and raised lusty voices for the democratic rule of 'Rep. by Pop.' – elected representation in proportion to population. And at the same time, a similar reversal was occurring in government revenues: whereas in the beginning, Lower Canadians were saddled with the debt of Upper Canada, after 1850, the western section contributed the greater share of a total that was, as always, divided equally between the two regions. Here was yet another 'injustice' to be redressed.

Political instability was another factor favouring the new federal scheme. The double majority system in the union resulted in frequent changes of government; in the period 1862 to 1864 alone, there were four. It was very difficult to piece together cohesive majorities to carry out policies.

The colonies were also pushed into federation by the United States threat. It was feared that the victorious north might move against Canada in revenge for British aid to the confederacy. There were also the boundary questions of the west. In the fever of western expansion, some Americans were moving into British territory. They had the support of United States annexationist movements, which were not without followers in Canada.

This fear of the United States finally materialized in the Fenian raids. The

Irish nationalist movement had been making inroads in the United States since 1861. Its members received military training in the civil war. Their plan was to carry their anti-British crusade into Canada, seizing the country and using it in negotiating Ireland's independence. In 1866, Fenians attacked New Brunswick at Campobello, Canada West along the Niagara Peninsula, and Canada East at Frelighsburg. Canadian politicians used these border incidents in arguing for confederation, and improved defence. To achieve the latter, a million dollars were needed. Confederation would spread defence costs over the whole colonial population.

Finally, the federal cause was helped by the consent of the mother country. British politicians and people wanted the colonies to become self-sufficient, to cease being drains on the imperial treasury. British strategy favoured federation as a means of forestalling a United States takeover of the colonies, and of handing over the costs of their defence.

French-Canadian reaction

Jean-Charles Bonenfant tells us that Canadians in general were not especially intrigued by the theory of federalism. Rather, their approach was pragmatic.[12] Everyone was familiar with the example of American federation, but most Canadians rejected that form of democracy, too different from the British tradition. This ignorance of theory was reflected in their ambiguous definition of the Canadian version, with 'confederation' and 'federation' used interchangeably. Canada is not a confederation; it is a federation.[13]

A brief glance at the division of powers between the federal and provincial governments clearly reveals the centralizing quality of Canadian federalism. Under the new constitution that joined the provinces of New Brunswick and Nova Scotia to the Canadas, the central government had jurisdiction over all matters involving the overall interests of the country. Provincial powers were limited to matters of local or special interest. In addition, section 91 of the British North America Act assigns to the federal authority the power to pass laws for the peace, order, and good government of the country. This is a far-reaching section. It goes on to list a number of areas – for example, the regulation of trade, transport, taxes, and defence – where federal jurisdiction would be exclusive. The federal government was also given the power to disallow, and thus control, provincial legislation.[14] Finally, the federal authority was assigned all residual powers, which meant everything not specifically defined in section 92 plus anything for which provision was not made in the Act. An example of the latter would be radio and television.

The provincial powers listed in section 92 are exclusive, limited to areas specified in the constitution: the power to tax and borrow, jurisdiction over hospitals, prisons, asylums, municipal institutions, company charters, public works, marriages, property laws, civil rights, and the provincial justice system. Education was reserved exclusively to the provinces, although the guarantee in section 93 applies only to the rights of the Protestant minority in Quebec. The section reflects only those rights in education that existed in law at the time of federation, when such rights were clearly defined only for that Quebec minority group; no rights, then, are given under this section to the French minorities outside Quebec. And it is equally silent about the language of instruction, referring only to separate school systems on a confessional basis. It allows for dissent on grounds of religion. In case of complaint, the constitution includes a right of appeal to the federal level that is highly problematical for French Catholics, since the federal parliament is controlled by an English Protestant majority.

Section 133 defines the official language policy. Either English or French can be used in debate in the parliaments of Canada and Quebec. Both are obligatory in government publications for these two jurisdictions. Finally, the Act provides for concurrent or shared powers in immigration and agriculture.

It may be said in conclusion that the division of powers is unclear and open to a number of possible interpretations, varying in their centralizing effects according to the political situation of the day. No provision was made in the Act for a mechanism of constitutional change, for Canada remained subject to the overlordship of empire. The BNA Act is a law of the British parliament. It was not an expression of the will of the people of Canada: it expressed the desire of Canada's middle class to lay hold of a state.

Confederation was the embodiment of a list of compromises that conferred special benefits on the people of Canada West and the commercial upper class of Montreal. It opened up the western territories to the former, and it reassured them as to the permanent minority status of the French Canadians; for the latter, confederation offered a road to financial recovery. In Ontario, opposition to the scheme was virtually nonexistent: of sixty-five assemblymen, fifty-seven voted in favour. Things were otherwise, however, in the Atlantic colonies, where Newfoundland and Prince Edward Island backed off, and strong currents of opposition surfaced in Nova Scotia and New Brunswick. In this last province, the supporters of confederation met defeat at the polls. Approval was finally engineered through the office of the governor general.

French Canada was confused and divided on the issue. Of forty-eight French-speaking assemblymen, twenty-six voted for and twenty-two against. Factors working in the scheme's favour were the desire to get out of political instability by settling the Rep. by Pop. question, fear of the United States, clerical influence behind the Conservatives, and the deter-mination of George-Etienne Cartier.

Cartier and Hector Langevin favoured change in the rules of representa-tion even if this change set the seal on French minority status. They argued that there was no need for concern about the safety of French na-tionality, for even if the English did form a strong majority in parliament, there would still be no debate on matters of nationality, language, and religion: these were areas of provincial jurisdiction. As for the Rouges, they were in a poor position to oppose reform in the system of representation, having campaigned for it on numerous occasions. Among others, Pap-ineau had emerged in 1849 as a champion of Rep. by Pop.

The French-Canadian élite supported the scheme too. They worried about United States annexation, and according to Taché, Cartier, and Langevin, it had to be that or confederation. With this background, the conclusion was inescapable. No one believed that the language, religion, and institutions of French Canada could be preserved in the American system.

These arguments were taken up by the church hierarchy. Clerical pressure induced the French Canadians to accept confederation through church support of the Conservatives who were its chief advocates. In a speech, Cartier declared: 'I will say that clergy opinion favours Confed-eration ... The clergy as a whole are the foes of political discord of any kind, and if they support the scheme, it is because they see in Confedera-tion a solution for problems that have existed for so long.'[15] In the first election after the new constitution came into force, most of the bishops declared in its favour. In his episcopal letter of 18 June 1867, Bishop Laroque of Saint-Hyacinthe told his flock: 'Do not heed the treacherous and oft-repeated insinuation that annexation is to be preferred to the confederation that is given us. Be persuaded that for those who use these words, confederation is but a pretext. Annexation is clearly the object of their passion, which they have been stoking for some time.'[16] The hierarchy meddled politically on behalf of confederation as the only key that could open the gates of theocracy. With the creation of a provincial state, the church could hope to carry out the Ultramontanist plan for a French, Catholic society.

But the chief propagandist for this constitutional change was George–Etienne Cartier. He was converted to the scheme because he saw it as the only way to settle the representation problem, and also because he loathed the instability that had typified the political life of the Province of Canada for a decade. Moreover Cartier held republican and democratic institutions in horror, and dreaded United States annexation. He told the Province assembly in February 1865: 'I am opposed to the democratic system that prevails in the United States. In this country, we need a proper form of government, informed with the monarchical spirit.'[17] Conservative, monarchist, authoritarian, Cartier stood against universal suffrage, recommending a voters' list based on property ownership. A man of empire, he saw danger in the customs union and industrial reciprocity with the United States. His political stance was consistent with his financial interest in the Grand Trunk Railway Company.[18]

Finally, the scheme was supported by the lower middle class. By creating a new level of government that this group could then control and use, confederation reinforced its political power and position in the economy. After the collapse of the 1837–38 rebellion, the loyalty and obedience of this class were rewarded. Its legitimacy and ability to run a provincial government – under the watchful eye of a paternalistic federal regime – were recognized. The French-Canadian nation had its mini-state; the ruling class had its civil service.

At the same time, we must point out that Montreal's English-speaking middle class had much influence on the running of the new mechanism of provincial government. Up to 1897, between 40 and 50 per cent of the province's cabinet ministers were drawn from this group. The provincial treasurer was the representative of the Bank of Montreal, the government's recognized creditor.[19] There may have been provincial autonomy, but there was no autonomy for the petty bourgeoisie.

Opponents of confederation

The scheme's opponents accounted for a strong percentage of the population. Twenty-two anti-confederation MLAS were elected. They were supported by such dissident tories as Henri-Etienne Taschereau, Honoré Mercier, and L.-O. David, who left their party in order to stand against confederation.

Motives for opposition were various. There was fear of English domination. There was reluctance to hurry things. Anti-confederationists wanted to place the question before the people, which the Conservatives refused to do. Antoine-Aimé Dorion, their leader, outlined his arguments in a manifesto to the voters of Hochelaga. In his view, the scheme was premature; he was against the creation of a non-elected upper house; he claimed that the real fathers of confederation were railway magnates who wanted to balance their books; and on the marriage and divorce issue, the scheme represented a threat to French-Canadian institutions.

What these liberals wanted more than anything else, however, was an appeal to the people such as had taken place in New Brunswick. The Conservatives retorted that this decision was one for the people's representatives, and that during debate of the scheme, some eighty by-elections had returned a sole anti-confederationist. Once again, then, the voters were not consulted, and according to Jean-Charles Bonenfant, it is by no means certain that if they had been, they would have supported Cartier and Macdonald. It would have been a very close thing. This anti-democratic attitude of the tories means that we have no knowledge of how the people reacted to confederation. In any case, in the last analysis, it was up to the imperial parliament to pass the law establishing the colony's status: the British North America Act.

Pioneer unionism

Before 1850, given the colonial, agricultural nature of Quebec's economy, there was little industry. What industry did exist was small in scale and, except along the Lachine canal, geographically dispersed. Its main base was the province's forest resources. Its work force was unstable, seasonal, and variable. In the few factories, moreover, the division of labour, which occurred on a craft basis, was rudimentary. The fact that the 1851 census listed only 125 occupations is a good indication of the largely undeveloped state of Quebec's economy. In this environment, strikes and trade unions were rare. One finds only such embryonic worker organizations as the Quebec City printers' union (1827), the Montreal shoe workers' combination (1830), and the craft societies in joinery, carpentry, masonry, and stonecutting that in 1834 launched a battle for the ten-hour day.[20] Until 1872, all workers' organizations were unlawful and clandestine.

The dominant social philosophy of the era was based on the liberal principles of individualism and unrestricted competition. The ruling concept in law was individual liberty, the person's right of absolute freedom to bestow his work and his capital as he saw fit. This was the policy of nil restraint. Since the state's role was to watch over the free labour market, it must not attempt to regulate the relations of labour and capital. This being the case, unions were seen as criminal conspiracies against 'natural law.' The labour market must be unrestricted, and the owner of the means of production alone had the right as well as the power to lay down work and wage conditions. The law did not recognize unions, and the church denounced them as threats to its authority, its supreme position in society.

The Irish were the first to challenge the tenets of economic liberalism as, in 1862, they combined in the Quebec Ship Labourers' Benevolent Society. For their part, in 1865, the French-Canadian stevedores founded the French Ship Labourers' Benevolent Society to fight the Irish union's attempt to gain a monopoly in the port of Quebec. From the outset, then, the working class was divided by nationality, and there were numerous conflicts between the two groups. The Irish attacked the practice of the free labour market; they refused to have the price of work set by the laws of supply and demand. Carpenters too waged fierce struggles against employers.

Strikes were frequently accompanied by violence. Police repression was brutal, and as a result some workers died. The worker movement was most aggressive in Quebec City in the mid-nineteenth century, and in August 1869 and June 1878, the capital saw serious clashes between workers and repressive forces. During a riot on 12 June 1878, two workers were killed and several others wounded. They were demanding a wage of a dollar a day. In August 1879, there were mob brawls between Irish and French-Canadian stevedores.

These combinations and strike actions ran up against the dominant ideology. Clergy and press were opposed to them. *La Minerve* made this comment: 'Strikes seem to have become an endemic disease in this country. Here is one of Europe's worst products trying to take root in Canadian soil ... This pestilential plant has been flourishing for a long time in the United States, always anxious to bring in from Europe the evils that are most dangerous to the social system.'[21] The paper went on to state that strikes were always declared on behalf of the lazy, and that they won nothing for the workers, since the employers were the stronger. The collusion between church and capital proceeded from very different ideological principles: the church fought the union movement to entrench a social control that was based on a hierarchical, static idea of society, while if capital refused to let workers combine, it was in the name of liberal individualism and in order to preserve its economic power.

Médéric Lanctot, social reformer

A son of the lower middle class and the radical liberal tradition of thought, Médéric Lanctot rose to the workers' defence and fought to organize them. For him, the questions of nation and society were inseparable, and this was why he committed himself in 1867 to political action as a candidate opposing George-Etienne Cartier and confederation. Lanctot compared Cartier to Durham, for in his opinion confederation would leave French Canadians at the mercy of the English-speaking majority. He also accused Cartier of being against the workers. With the Rouges, he organized a number of public meetings and petitions demanding that the federal scheme be submitted to the people. In his paper *L'Indépendance*, he called for an end to the colonial tie. *Le Nouveau Monde*, which could not be accused of radicalism, recognized the social dimension of Lanctot's fight: 'The election campaign we have just seen in Montreal offered, for the first time in this country, the sad spectacle of severe conflict between the different classes of our society.'[22]

Thus, in addition to being an anti-confederationist, Lanctot can be seen as our first social theorist. He was influenced by the founding of the International Workers' Association by Marx and Engels, as well as by the condition of Montreal's working class, when he recognized the need for a worker's organization. A certain shrewdness must be conceded to a man who grasped the importance of industrialization in the future of the French Canadians at a time when Quebec society was still 80 per cent agricultural. To tie patriotism and the workers' cause together, and to locate solutions for working-class problems, Lanctot promoted the idea of uniting the workers of all the craft groups in a single federation. On 13 February 1867, he wrote in *L'Union Nationale*: 'Now the patriotic press must give these demands space on its pages, so that the whole country can know about them. If strong pressure is brought to bear on public opinion, the government of the land will probably be ashamed to keep the worker in that colonial condition of unrelieved wretchedness and disappointment for the working classes.' In the spring of 1867, he managed to get this workers' federation under way, and launched a campaign for higher wages, organizing a rally that drew 15,000 workers to Montreal's Champ de Mars. His aim in this was to promote labour-capital co-operation, work for the workers' well-being, and, finally, stop immigration.'[23]

It was after a trip to Europe that Lanctot became aware of the contradiction of capitalism: the workers are the main force of production and the creators of social wealth; they are also the ones who suffer the pauperdom that is an effect of industrialization. The more they work, the poorer they become. Lanctot saw a solution: 'Capital and labour in Canada must enter into association, and there will have to be a law obliging every capitalist-industrialist to share the profits of the factory, mill, or workshop, with the workers he employs.'[24] Thus, he thought, the employee would gain in riches and dignity, and society would be protected from the evils inherent in destitution and ignorance. And if capital could associate as it wished with whom it wished, so workers too should have the right to join together and form an association:

It is up to you, my worker friends, to make sure that in the discussions going on, and in the movement getting under way, your choice stresses your rights to control of your labour and ownership of its product jointly with capital. You understand now your need to bestir yourselves in order to save your families from the exile and poverty, the evils and maledictions by which Europe is racked today.[25]

In addition to improving the workers' material conditions, this co-operation of the classes was to reduce strikes and discontent, letting everyone live in peace and order.

Lanctot's utopian schemes did not stop with the organization of the

workers in the workplace. He also wanted to become involved at the consumer end, founding a Montreal chain of food co-operatives that were
known as 'bargain stores.' Reaction was swift. His enterprise was anathematized by the clergy. The bourgeois papers attacked him on the grounds
that he was not a worker. His ventures fell apart: ruined financially, he
was forced to emigrate, first to the United States and later to Ottawa.
Lanctot was probably the first French Canadian to make contact with
European socialist theory and try to use it in analysing his own Quebec
society.

His failure to meld the craft groups together would not mean the
end of the movement. Quebec workers were inspired by their brothers in
the United States and Toronto to launch nineteen unions in the 1880s.
According to a scratch survey by Jean Hamelin and Yves Roby, there
were forty-four strikes in the period 1886 to 1890. The chief concerns of
the workers' movement were better wages, the nine-hour day, the right
of combination, the enactment of labour laws, and consultation of workers
on technological change and mechanization. And worker demands were
not limited to economic issues: the worker organizations of the era also
tried to defend their interests in the political sphere.

The Knights of Labour

The rise of organized labour in Quebec was influenced by the union
movements of Britain and the United States. Yet up to 1870, there was
nothing that one could call class consciousness among the province's
working people. The aim of their solidarity was not to alter the structure of
society, but to satisfy certain demands related to their jobs. These
years also saw an abundance of mutual aid associations, amassing funds
to tide working families through the crises of sickness and death. In
1866, there were forty or so of these. Unions in this era, then, placed
much greater emphasis on identity among workers than opposing the
bosses.

The appearance of American unions in 1872, coinciding with legal
recognition of labour combinations, changed this course and encouraged
workers to draw the line between themselves and the bosses with
their paternalism. With the decline of small-scale craft production and the
rise of industrialization, the labour movement gradually abandoned the
policy of co-operation, was radicalized, and entered the field of active
politics.

The Order of the Knights of Labour, established in Canada in 1881, initiated this change. The order had a membership of ten to twelve thousand members in some twenty-two local assemblies, thirteen of which were French-Canadian.[26] Unlike the craft unions with their corporatist aims, the Knights were looking for changes in the social and economic structure. They wanted to substitute production and distribution co-operatives for the capitalist system founded on monopolism and worker exploitation. They also stressed the need of the working class for education, organization, co-operation, and political action.

Among the Knights' main demands were the reduction of working hours, control of immigration and labour contracts, the establishment of a department of labour and a system of labour statistics, equal wages for equal work, a ban on employment of children under fourteen years of age, and a maximum eight-hour day for older children and women. They wanted bosses to be responsible for the education of their illiterate child employees. They called for night schools and public libraries. They advocated such judicial reforms as the establishment of a court in every town, the abolition of statute labour and the seizing of property for debt, an arbitration tribunal, and a more equitable system of taxation. The Knights wanted to cut out the property requirement for candidates in provincial and municipal elections, broaden the franchise, and abolish the Legislative Council.

The politicization of labour ideology was evident in the demands that issued from the 1891 meeting in Quebec City of the Trade and Labour Congress of Canada: universal suffrage, nationalization of railways and telegraph lines, the takeover by municipalities of gas, electricity, telephone, water, and public transport services, standardization of the country's labour laws, exclusion of Chinese and Jewish immigrants, the nine-hour day, and free education. French- and English-speaking delegates did not, however, agree on every issue. The congress refused to vote on a motion by Thomas Saint-Pierre calling for Canadian independence; the Québécois opposed a motion on compulsory education. In similar fashion the year following, a motion that called for the creation of a socialist state was defeated.

These demands from the Knights and their associates are evidence of the rise of worker class consciousness. Although the order's strength was beginning to fall off by 1894, it had profoundly influenced the Quebec labour movement, most particularly by carrying the conflict into the political and economic arena. It was for this purpose that in 1886 the

Knights founded the Montreal Trades and Labour Council that promoted labour involvement in city politics. The council also supported labour candidates at other levels, such as Adélard Gravel in the federal election of 1883, T.A. Lépine, elected federally in 1888, and in the 1886 Quebec provincial vote, W. Robertson, E. Gravel, and W. Keys. The defeat of most of these labour candidates was traceable to the election practice that made polling hours nine to five when the working man's day began at seven and did not end until six. Other reasons were problems with financing and the lack of an independent labour party.

After 1890, the American unions, relegating political action to a secondary role, concentrated on raising the workers' economic status within the existing capitalist system, and spent itself in the defence of trained workers at the cost of the untrained. The Knights continued to insist on the absolute need for solidarity in the whole working class in the contest with capitalism.

The reaction of churchmen and employers

These pioneer labour experiments were received by the ruling class with 'church-boss' paternalism. Basic to the church's ideology was respect for authority, the fundamental law that ran through all human relations. Employer-employee contacts should mirror the pattern of the family, in which the father holds his authority from God. Also basic was the principle of natural inequality among men, a view that necessitates a social hierarchy and produces a static picture of society: 'The poor will be always with us; therefore hope for nothing in this world, and look to the hereafter.'

The rain of exhortation to obedience, resignation, and respect for established authority was redoubled by clerical repugnance at the European revolutions of 1848 and 1871. In the devout press, socialism and unionism were portrayed as tandem forces of darkness. Panicked by the urban, industrial reality, fearful for their social supremacy, the clergy showed a deep distrust of labour organizations, associating them with the Masonic lodges. The church deployed its spiritual influence to alienate Quebeckers from the labour movement. Bishop Taschereau of Quebec, for example, threatened excommunication to any Catholic attempting to restrict the freedom of labour in order to improve his material circumstances: 'We should all remember that every man is the master of his own labour and may dispose of it at whatever price suits him. He has the same right over his work as the farmer over his land. This is why the workers' associations are guilty of a serious injustice whenever they try to force anyone to join them or work for the wage they have set.'[27]

In general, the clergy's attitude to the innovations that came with the labour movement was a negative one. Moreover, churchmen did not have a very clear understanding of the phenomenon of industrialization and its consequences: in their interpretations, they used a rural model, as, for example, in the comparison of the ownership of labour with the ownership of land. The most favourable, such as Monsignor Fabre, would support only those associations of workers and craftsmen 'established under the patronage of religion' and the employers – that 'literate, wealthy class that can devote itself to these Catholic workers' associations.' The purpose of such bodies was to make members happy with, and re-signed to, their lot in life. Confronting the problems of industrialization and the working class, the church elected to support the bosses. It adop-ted a policy of co-operation with the middle class, leaving to the members of this class their problems concerning the accumulation of wealth and the things of the flesh, while preaching humility and heavenly hope to the workers.

Bishop Taschereau waged all-out aggression on the Knights of La-bour. On his own authority, without any firm direction from the Holy See,[28] he identified the order with those secret societies, membership in which was a grave sin. Even when his interdict on the Knights was lifted by Rome, Monsignor Taschereau was reluctant to retreat. He told the priests of Quebec archdiocese in his letter of 6 January 1888: 'Anyone who comes to consult you is to be told on my behalf that I strongly advise all Catholics of the archdiocese not to enrol in this society, which is dan-gerous to say the least, and to get out as soon as possible if they do be-long.'[29]

The church, then, used every means at its command to smash the first attempts at union organization. It did so in the name of religion and na-tionality, and to maintain its social ascendancy. Not even the breach made by the encyclical *Rerum Novarum* and the more liberal attitudes of some American bishops would divert the reactionary approach of Quebec's clergy to social change brought about by industrialization. The Quebec church shut its eyes and fell back on its organic, patriarchal concept of so-ciety; it allowed the capitalists to exploit the workers in peace, and attempted to disarm the latter into respect for the liberal economic system.

It was also in the name of liberty and individualism that Quebec employers opposed the organization of the workers. A speech by Judge Tessier is an accurate indication of the thinking of the business world: 'There seems to be a belief that the workers have the right to dictate the price of their labour to the employers. This is wrong. The workers have the right to work for whom they wish and at any price whatsoever: equally, the employer can hire whom he pleases and at any price whatsoever. All claims to the contrary are false, antireligious, anti-social, and illegal.'[30] Similarly, in the purest liberal tradition, Le Moniteur du Commerce held that 'labour is an article bought and sold like any other kind of merchandise, its price being determined by quality, supply, and demand ... Unite who will, work who will, abstain who will.'[31] Naturally, in this view, the strike was not accepted as the worker's means of self-defence. Quite to the contrary, all freedoms belonged to the employers: lockouts, instant dismissals, hiring at low wages, police protection, strike breakers, and so forth. They approached labour with the carrot-and-stick of paternalism and authoritarianism.

It can be said in conclusion that five factors slowed the growth of the labour movement in late nineteenth-century Quebec: the traditional individualism of the newly industrialized habitant, the tradition of trade associations, anti-labour legislation, ideological repression by the clergy, and finally, the division of the labour movement that occurred with the emergence of Catholic unions.

Nationalism and Ultramontanism

The concession of responsible government, followed in 1867 by the re-emergence of a political unit that was French-Canadian, obliged the church to change its political strategy. It could not now rely, as it had in the past, on a 'natural' common cause with the lords of officialdom. The establishment of liberal democracy meant the shift of power to the middle and lower middle classes; political power depended now on the expert handling of public opinion.

This new environment brought the Catholic hierarchy, anxious to preserve the church's privileged status and acquire a new base for dealing with political parties, down into the arena of politics. They were behaving like a party without party structure. They tried to dominate the voters, and through them control French Canada's politicians, who would then be bound to uphold, at the federal and provincial levels, the church's interests and idea of society. They also attempted to influence public opinion by using the press to broadcast their ideology. In converting press to pulpit, they founded several newspapers: *Mélanges religieux*, *Le Nouveau Monde*, *Le Journal des Trois-Rivières*, *Le Courrier du Canada*, and *La Vérité*. Their overall position had been strengthened by the failure of the rebellion; the ascendancy of their Ultramontanist ideology was encouraged by the establishment of parliamentary democracy; the 1867 constitution opened the way for the fulfilment of their theocratic vision – a French and Catholic state on the banks of the St Lawrence. 'States,' commented *Le Nouveau Monde*, 'are like individuals: they all must proceed from the authority of the church.'[32]

Backed by the 1870 Vatican Council's proclamation of papal infallibility, the force of Ultramontanism took shape at the time of the Riel affair and the federal Conservatives' refusal to throw out the New Brunswick law abolishing separate schools. The church sought to increase its power in political life through direct involvement in elections. Exemplifying this attempt to hitch politics to religion is the Catholic platform that appeared in the 20 April 1871 issue of *Le Journal des Trois-Rivières*.[33] According to this document, Quebec was to become a theocracy mediated by elected MLAS. Ideological obedience to the hierarchy would be required of all public men. There was no doubt about Bishop Bourget's intentions:

I will add that I consider this platform to be the strongest possible protection for the Conservative party and the firmest possible support for the good principles that should govern a Christian society. I hold fast to this principle because I see in it the salvation of my beloved country, which will be truly free only in so far as the freedom of the church is respected, with all the rights to be ensured and guaranteed.[34]

The church platform asked electors to make sure that the candidates who got their votes guaranteed to protect the interests of religion:

This counsel, which wisdom dictates, will, we hope, be understood by all Catholic voters of the province of Quebec. It cannot be denied that politics are closely connected with religion, and that separation of church and state is an absurd, impious doctrine. This is especially true of the constitutional system that confers all law-making power on Parliament, thus placing in its members' hands a double-edged sword that could be dreadful.[35]

Le Nouveau Monde, another Ultramontanist paper, issued precise instructions: 'A vote for a Liberal or a Gallican means sending to the House a man who will work against the Church. This is not allowed.'[36] Evident here, beyond the clerical idea of politics, is the church's attitude towards democratic political institutions: the system was valid and acceptable only in so far as it was directed by Catholic principles, and thus, those with law-making power must agree with church teaching. 'Full and complete acceptance of Roman Catholic doctrine in religion, politics and social economy must be the first and the main qualification Catholic voters should require of the Catholic candidate.'[37]

While proclaiming their loyalty to the Conservatives, the Ultramontanists wanted to use their religious influence to get the members of this party to change laws that ran counter to church interests. Obviously, their leverage was small at the federal level, where the French-Canadian contingent had no real power and had to manoeuvre in a complex system of alliances. In Quebec, however, the effectiveness of the Ultramontanist strategy won the clergy a genuine political hegemony. This is not to say that all political decisions were inspired by the bishops: rather, the clergy had the power to oppose any decision that ran contrary to their interests and idea of society.

The Ultramontanist ideology was not restricted to the priesthood. It had supporters and defenders among laymen who shared the church's world view and, out of either principle or opportunism, accepted religious tutelage in political and social life. In the final analysis, however, we may say that its success came chiefly from the use of nationalism as its justification. Thus, the church became the main line of defence for French-Canadian nationality. It was a line that also protected the Quebec lower middle class.

Tardivel

One well-known Quebec figure in whom the strains of Ultramontanism and nationalism met was Jules-Paul Tardivel. Born in the United States to a French father and an English mother, Tardivel did not know the French language at all until he was seventeen. Yet this American who came to Quebec in 1869 became, in the later years of the century, the fiercest of the French-Canadian nation's defenders.

His schooling completed, he wrote for *Le Courrier de Saint-Hyacinthe*, *La Minerve*, and *Le Canadien*. In 1881, he started his own paper, *La Vérité*. For a quarter of a century, Tardivel was at the centre of polemic and controversy. His supporters dubbed him the 'Canadian Louis Veuillot,' while his adversaries, not bothering to mince words, reviled him as a rabble-rouser and a scoundrel ripe for a horsewhipping.

Tardivel was an Ultramontanist before all things: as he himself defined it, an unqualified Catholic who professed unquestioningly the entire doctrine of his church and attempted, circumstances permitting, to carry it into action.[38] The Ultramontanist, according to Tardivel, was he who rejected any form of compromise with the modern world, and above all with liberalism. The Ultramontanist's first rule was to eschew moderation and conciliation. These were, wrote Tardivel, nothing but cowardice:

Where we are ruined is in this mania for conciliation, putting up with the petty encroachments of the wicked, accepting mongrel agreements that, in the end, are invariably fatal to the cause of justice. Let us put up with what cannot be avoided, but protesting firmly, not merely remarking that it falls short of the ideal. It is because we do not bother to show men the principles that error carries the day. That is all liberalism, the most dangerous of all ...[39]

For the Ultramontanist, intransigeance was the road to truth. With this philosophy, it is not surprising that Tardivel exasperated opponents committed to the politics of compromise, most of them liberal Catholics trying to reconcile their faith with contemporary freedoms. Wilfrid Laurier was an object of merciless attack: 'Those who hate the priest love Laurier.'[40] Mercier did scarcely better, given the laws on teachers and the poor compensation for the Jesuit estates that betrayed his liberalism: Tardivel was pitiless at the time of the Baie des Chaleurs railway scandal. Deeply anti-liberal, he was convinced that a true Catholic had to be a conservative, and vice versa.

The great cause of the nineteenth-century Ultramontanists was the crusade against the Gallicans and their tendency to place the church under civil authority. Unlike liberal ideology, which assumed in the joint names

of rationalism and individualism that people were autonomous in relation to their social surroundings and secular society was similarly autonomous of religion, Ultramontanist ideology argued a necessary dependence of men on the church and of the temporal upon the spiritual order.
God being the fount of all things, including men and their society and
their government, and since men worked and lived in order to return to
the godhead, it was therefore logical that the church representing him
in the world should have exclusive authority in the interpretation of his will
and deciding whether or not secular laws corresponded to the spiritual
goals of humanity. Moreover, it followed that there could be no separation of politics from religion, and that the state must be subject to direction and control by the church, that infallible watchdog of morality, firmly
astride the road to paradise. Moreover, if the hierarchy of powers set
the church at its pinnacle, the family too, in which the father's power was
holy, possessed authority exceeding that of the state, the only reason for
whose existence was the protection of the freedom of family and church.

Tardivel saw Gallicanism, working for the omnipotence of government,
as a serious threat to French Canada, especially in education. For in
his view the civil authority was not to get involved in education except to
help the system function in accordance with Christian principles and
the commands of the church, which must have total control in these matters. Tardivel therefore opposed compulsory schooling, which replaced
the father's authority with the government's,[41] and rejected free education as well.

Tardivel's distrust of government involvement determined his attitude
to social problems. He shared the most conservative views of strikes
and worker demands. Since God was the fount of harmony, the interests
of employers and employees simply could not be opposed. It was not
up to men to question the places in society assigned them by divine Providence. Moreover, wage increases were unreasonable and in conflict
with Christian morality: men were born to work and earn eternal life, and
poverty was thus a step towards sanctity. Why were there classes,
rich and poor? Because it was the will of divine Providence, the Christian
does not have to ask such questions: he should rely on the teachings of
the church. When workers tried to improve their circumstances by asking the government to become involved in their education and fight
the trusts, Tardivel was extremely cautious. This was a challenge to the
social hierarchy willed by God, in which the worker is subject to his

employer, the parishioner to his priest, the son to his father, the government to the church, and the church to God. In all things, the fundamental law was respect for authority.

The Ultramontanists also disapproved of science. Material progress was one of their bugbears. Tardivel was famous for his anti-railway tirades. Certain happenings drew his sarcasm: when, for example, a ship blew up in a Spanish harbour, he commented that 'dynamite is a product of modern progress, and like many similar products, seems more harmful than useful to mankind.'[42] Scientific developments and technical discoveries made little impression on Tardivel, since for him, they turned men from their supreme goal of moral and spiritual perfection. Equally, according to Tardivel, novels and plays and alcohol were harmful to society. They were symbols of moral decadence: 'As a general rule, the novel to be seen in our papers is nothing more nor less than a soapbox for Satan. There, the devil preaches every sin and sullies every virtue.'[43] Tardivel called for an impregnable moral strictness.

The same broad ideological concerns lay behind Jules-Paul Tardivel's more strictly political contribution to the intellectual life of Quebec. The importance of this contribution is not to be gauged by its effectiveness in the short term. Tardivel kept his distance from active politics, and made no attempt to carry out his own proposals. Yet his political ideas had a far-reaching influence on the development of French-Canadian nationalism: 'Tardivel can be considered the father of separatist thinking in Quebec. In fact Jules-Paul Tardivel was the first French Canadian under the federal regime to develop the idea of separatism and argue the ideal of a distinct nation, separate from English Canada.'[44] Mathieu Girard sees Tardivel as the dominant figure in the nationalism of French Canada during the years 1867 to 1896. Before him, the notion of independence had much more to do with separation from the mother country. The nationalism of the Patriotes was based on a pluralistic concept of a chiefly French-Canadian nation: it was the yoke of colonialism that prevented their liberation. As Union was followed by Confederation, these views changed. Canada was supreme in terms of its internal administration, and despite the survival of some of the formalities of British colonialism, the country was run less by London than by Ottawa and the commercial middle class. Moreover, for the first time since 1760, the French Canadians occupied a level of political power, the government of the province of Quebec: state and nation could now coincide.

In developing his ideas, Tardivel was conditioned by the political environment of the age: the Riel affair, the rise of Mercier's National Party, its election to office and its autonomist policies, and the Manitoba Schools Question.

What became Manitoba was the scene of Métis and French-Canadian resistance to the arbitrary rule of the Hudson's Bay Company and the federal government of Canada. Louis Riel emerged as the leader of the defence of Métis rights. He demanded that these people be consulted as their lands were absorbed by the Canadian federation, and formed a provisional government which was refused recognition by the federal authorities. Tough negotiations resulted in the creation of the province of Manitoba, with land concessions for the Métis: there were guarantees for Catholic and Protestant separate schools, and the official languages were French and English. These legal accommodations did not quell the imperialism of Ontario, however. Settlers from that province drove the Métis off the land. There were summary executions and a racist reign of terror. The federal government turned a blind eye. Riel won a federal seat in the 1871 election, but with an Ontario price of $5,000 on his head, he could not take his place in the House. He was forced into exile.

Gradually, the Métis people were pushed back to the north and west. On the eve of the creation of Alberta and Saskatchewan, Riel returned once more to lead the defence of their rights. He envisioned the rise in the west of a society without exploitation, in which poverty and destitution would be no more, and people would love one another, work together to build an ideal world. Alarmed by this outbreak of utopianism, the clergy condemned all 'illegal' activities. Riel set up the provisional government of Saskatchewan, and hostilities began. To squash the rebellion, Ontario launched a holy war. A caricature trial preceded Riel's hanging.

Feelings ran high in Quebec. Beyond the repression of the Métis people lay the larger issue: English ambition to control western Canada, with the accompanying threat to French and Catholic rights. Most of the population rose up against Macdonald. His ministers were burned in effigy, and on 22 November 1885, a giant rally drew a crowd of more than 50,000 to the Champ de Mars in Montreal. The Liberals attempted to use this popular movement as a means of loosening the Conservative hold on the French Canadians and the clergy.[45] *La Presse* gave the rallying cry for the national cause: 'From now on, Conservatives, Liberals, Castors are no more. There are only Patriots and Traitors.'[46] Honoré Mercier founded his National Party to bring all French Canadians under one banner. Gaining office in 1887, he evoked the gibbet of Regina. All this widened the rift between English and French, shaking the very foundations of peaceful coexistence between the 'two founding peoples.'

With provisional support from the Ultramontanist press, Mercier loudly proclaimed the national, French, and Catholic qualities of his government, which he described as 'embracing all classes, all nationalities, and all the highest aspirations of the people.'[47] The definition is eloquent of the lower-middle-class view of politics and government. Mercier gave official status and impetus to the idea that the province of Quebec was the French-Canadian national state. He attempted in his legislation to entrench the principle of provincial autonomy. In his view, it was the provinces that brought about Confederation, and therefore the provinces had the power to amend the constitution. With this in mind, he called an interprovincial conference, acting as its chairman. He also made Fr Labelle, much to the indignation of English Canadians, his minister for agriculture and settlement. And, although not to Tardivel's satisfaction, he settled the Jesuit estates question. Mercier was the first political leader since Papineau to found his power on public opinion and hold audiences spellbound by his oratory, returning again and again to his favourite themes of Quebec's Frenchness and Catholicism and the urgent need for unity among French Canadians. 'Let us end our fratricidal fighting and unite' was Mercier's motto.

Against this autonomist and exclusively French-Canadian concept of nationalism, Wilfrid Laurier set a pan-Canadian idea:

We are French Canadians, but our country is not limited to those lands that lie in the shadow of the Citadel of Quebec. Our country is Canada, wherever the British flag flies on the American continent ... What I ask for us is an equal share of the benefits of justice and freedom: this full share we have, and what we ask for ourselves we are eager to confer on others ... This is the idea that inspired Confederation.[48]

The two ideas of nationalism would stand in opposition throughout the history of the French Canadians. One attempted to bind together state and nation; the other wanted to place the state above nationalities.

In his paper *La Vérité* which reached most of Quebec's presbyteries and theology schools for a quarter of a century, Tardivel advertised his hope for a completely independent French society on the banks of the St Lawrence: 'My only reason for starting *La Vérité* was to fan the spark of French-Canadian patriotism. When that spark has become a flame, warming every heart; when the leaders of French Canada are speaking openly to the people of our providential destiny to become an autonomous nation, then there will be no more reason for *La Vérité*'s existence, and *La Vérité* will disappear.'[44] Independence was a religious necessity for Tardivel: above all else, French Canada was a Catholic fact, and this fact had been selected by Providence to evangelize America: 'God has planted a "flower of hope" in the heart of every patriotic French Canadian: a yearning to build on the banks of the St Lawrence a New France, whose mission shall be to continue on this American soil the work of Christian civilization that has given such glory, over so many centuries, to the Old.'[50] To be separatist was to be Catholic. This was why Tardivel damned the stupidity of the 1837–38 rebellion in being revolutionary and anticlerical. He was critical too of Confederation, which he saw as a legislative union carrying on Lord Durham's programme of assimilation. He also detected in Confederation the hand of free-masonry and the Orange Lodge. If French Canada were to check assimilation and achieve independence, it must meet three essential conditions: keep faith with God, come together and abandon the partisan spirit, and eschew emigration and annexation to the United States.

It was only in 1886, following the Riel crisis, that Tardivel became a separatist. He summed up his thinking in his novel *Pour la patrie* (1895) in which the adventures of his hero, as he tries to unravel a secret, anti-Catholic conspiracy to seize federal power and wipe out the French Canadians, becomes a vehicle for Quebec's sense of isolation in the wake of rapid western expansion and the hanging of Riel. The work offers us three essential elements of Tardivel's nationalism: the sacred mission of French Canada, the distrust of all external influence, and the desire for a separate French-Canadian state.[51] In *La Vérité*, he wrote:

My own nationalism is the nationalism of French Canada. For twenty-three years, I have laboured to promote French-Canadian national feeling: my people are the French Canadians; my country, I shall not say it coincides exactly with the province of Quebec, but it is French Canada; the nation I wish to see arise, whenever divine Providence shall so decide, is the French-Canadian nation.[52]

Like Mercier, Tardivel saw political parties and the partisan spirit as endangering the survival of the French-Canadian nation. French Canada should seek its salvation in the defence of the Catholic religion: 'The Catholic spirit comes from God: it is lifegiving and unifying. The party spirit comes from men and the Devil: it is divisive and murderous.'[53] In Tardivel's view, political parties were invented by the colonizers, the better to rule French Canadians by dividing them. This theme of the struggle against the partisan mentality would turn up regularly as nationalists denounced the waste of energy and the family feuds that were inseparable from the partisan approach. They called repeatedly for a single, homogeneous French-Canadian party, which would then be able to offer effective defence for the interests of the nation. In this respect, Tardivel's thinking comes close to that of Henri Bourassa, who tried to maintain his own independence from the Liberal party and spoke against the wrongs of partisan thinking. If there was tactical agreement between the two, however, there was disagreement on strategy: Tardivel attacked Bourassa and the Nationalist League because of their goal to work towards a feeling of Canadian-ness that was free of ethnic origin, language, or religion, within the federal context.

In Tardivel's opinion, Canada was a geographical absurdity, and it was a waste of time to try to build a Canadian patriotism, using strength on behalf of other nationalities who, Tardivel scolded, were perfectly well able to take care of themselves:

Would it not be more fruitful, more useful, to devote our energies to fostering and strengthening the national feeling of French Canada, so that come the day of reckoning for the great Canadian system – something we and our contemporaries may not see – those who come after us will have materials at hand for the rebuilding of a new structure – less huge, but more scaled to the national aspirations of our race?[54]

For Tardivel, Canadian nationalism based on ethnic duality was nothing but a hoax, whose long-term result would be anglicization. His arguments with Bourassa illuminate the two streams in the nationalism of

French Canada, differing as to the political environment giving the best chance of survival: one began with the French-Canadian nation, while the other set its hopes on participation in the federal state of Canada, and believed in the theory of the pact between the two founding peoples.

Conclusion

The pronouncements of the Ultramontanists were based on denigration and the assertion of absolutes. Doubt was forbidden in this environment; there was no analysis of new circumstances; it was pointless to innovate, for official dogma provided a ready-made interpretation of reality. Church doctrine had all the answers. The individual had only to surrender, throw his reason to the winds. He was not to reflect on things. He was to follow and mechanically carry out the teachings of the Church Fathers.

The Ultramontanist ideological programme may be summed up in these words: there must be no change. If the French Canadians were to preserve the features of their nationality as they confronted the dangers of Americanization and the social changes that came with industrial growth, they had to unite in a monolithic group and keep faith with the church, which by the grace of God was able to lead its flock to national (and heavenly) salvation. This approach supposes a church-nation equation as expressed in these words of Bishop Laflèche: 'The elements of nationhood are unity of language, unity of faith, and uniformity of manners, customs, and institutions. The French Canadians have all these and are indeed a nation. Providence has given each nation a mission to accomplish. The mission of the French-Canadian people is to serve as a centre of Catholicism in the New World.'[55]

As a dominant sub-group of the petty bourgeoisie, the clergy defined society in terms of their own desires and special interests. As an institution, the church was trying to establish its supremacy in this national society by appearing as the only agency that could reconcile the various conflicting interests. In so doing, the church was putting itself in the place of the state, the agency of cohesion in liberal societies; it put nation and secular power below its own material and spiritual interests, and made absolute values of resistance to progress, loyalty to tradition, defence of the status quo, and social and political conservatism. The world view of the Ultramontanists ended in an ideological monolithism which, in its intolerance, squelching any impulse to dissent, froze all development in ideology. 'There was no salvation outside the Church.'

Underpinning the ideology of the Ultramontanists was a theological view of history according to which all happenings were the work of divine Providence. Beyond fatalism, this Manichean approach generated a view of the opposition forces as none other than the fiends of hell. Anything that differed from or challenged the established order was a thing of evil, and had to be erased; by reason of its absolutism, this ideology was incapable of tolerating difference, let alone dissidence. Whether its perceived opponents were Rouges, Masons, Jews, labour unions, or later on, Communists, they were identified as enemies of God and the church. Compromise was impossible.

This ideological monolithism would never be complete; it would never manage to block totally the welling of new ideological streams through the growth of the forces of production – the labour movement being one example. It was powerful enough, however, to absorb new movements in society and oblige the forces of change to accept its overall frame of reference. If they were to survive, opponents had to respect the precepts of the clerical ideology, and water down their demands. One problem in studying this era, in fact, is to decide on the relative importance of dissent and its expression as against the unquestionably dominant group that accepted the ideological ascendancy of the church and the nation-church identification.

It also strikes me that Ultramontanism was an ideology of fear. It arose, not through analysis of the real situation, but in reaction to outside occurrences whose possible duplication in Quebec was viewed with alarm. It was essentially an import: Canadian liberalism and its proposed reforms were assessed in terms of the question of compulsory schooling in France and the demands of the liberals of Italy. This alarmist strategy, exaggerating the enemy's size and strength by the yardstick of foreign experience, distracted public attention from the real problems and, in addition, actually built up the monolithism and popular appeal of the ruling ideology. Thus cornered, its opponents became responsible for all the outside confrontations and were constantly having to justify themselves in relation to these events. By shifting the scene of debate, the dominant group drew the public's attention away from its own reform proposals, avoided any real ideological challenge, any genuine test of its strength in terms of the environment in which it existed.

We can understand this externally conditioned and abstract aspect of Ultramontanist ideology only by returning to the internal conditions of its growth and ascendancy. These were a result of colonial domination and its superimposing of two social structures. Since the power of the dominant class – clerical and petty bourgeois – in Quebec was dependent on another social structure, it could not work on the whole society. It was not based on ownership of the means of production and control of economic development, but rather on the responsibility for social control and local management delegated to it by the commercial bourgeoisie. Its special sphere was limited to the superstructures of society, politics, and ideology; it had no control over the development of economic structures, which proceeded from an outside body of ideas. Its ideology was not called upon to justify the material, economic, and social ascendancy of the middle class; it did not have to define itself in terms of the growth of the forces of production. Rather, it was defined in terms of the entrenchment of its class role as official intermediary in the structure of dependence, and it could justify this role only if it continued to exercise a hegemony in politics and ideology. Nationalism, in so far as it was conservative, made it possible for this class to secure its power within the structure of the dominated class, while at the same time reinforcing its power to negotiate with the structure of the ruling class. The church-nation equation, while identifying the specificity of the dominated social structure, also allowed the clergy to preponderate and portray themselves as the authentic champions of the nation. The cause of Catholicism became the cause of French-Canadian society.

In its appeals to the divine and spiritual mission of French Canada, this ideology had the effect of veiling the material reality and the situation of economic and social dependence. Cut off from economic power and the changes accompanying the growth of capitalism, the Ultramontanist ideology could not correspond to reality. Its relative autonomy could only result in a widening rift between the way the world was presented and reality. Powerless to define and control this development, it was content with a programme of rejection: rejection of materialism, wealth, industrialization, and urban growth. The gap between pronouncement and reality would take on its full meaning in the first half of the twentieth century, as the ruling ideology evolved at clear odds with the forces of production.

6

The Ideology of Self-preservation
1896–1929

We are not merely a civilized race, but pioneers of civilization. We are not
merely a religious people, but messengers of the idea of religion. Our mission is
less the management of capital than the movement of ideas, less the light-
ing of the factory flame than caring for and broadcasting afar the radiance of
religion and thought. While our rivals, doubtless in courteous engagements,
claim hegemony in finance and industry, our prime ambition will be the honour of
doctrine and the reward of the apostle.[1]

This messianic social prospectus outlined by Msgr L.-A. Paquet is expressive of the clash between the reality of a Quebec in the process of
industrialization by outside interests and the dominant ideology of Québécois society, holding fast to traditional values and the delusion of continuity in order to combat the view of the future inspired by those innovations. Paquet's words also show how ideologies can be autonomous of
the structural changes taking place in their societies. A few economic
facts will serve to indicate the trends of this period, which is seen by Jean
Hamelin and Jean-Paul Montmigny as the second phase of Quebec's
industrialization.

It was a time of prosperity and rapid economic growth: 'The gross
value of production rose by 74.9 per cent from 1900 to 1910 at an annual
rate of 5.79 per cent, and value added rose by 81.6 per cent, a rate of
6.14 per cent annually.'[2] The fast-developing pulp and paper industry was
the most dynamic growth centre in the economy. Fixed capital soared in
this sector from $7.2 million in 1901 to $284.9 million in 1929; three years
later, Quebec was supplying 62 per cent of United States newsprint
needs. The province was attracting foreign investors by its enormous forest and energy resources, its transportation network, its ample supply

of cheap manpower, and also by the absence of a local bourgeoisie that could put up any resistance to the newcomers.

The most important fact in this period is the surrender of Quebec's economy to foreign capital: 'In the years 1901–29, the capital invested in the manufacturing sector rose from $142 million to $1,246,209,000.'[3] The British were still the main source at the beginning of the period, but massive American participation began with the First World War and soon turned things around. The 85 per cent of foreign investment in Canada that was British in 1900 dropped to 36 per cent in 1930, while the American 14 per cent rose in the same years to 61 per cent.[4] There were new names such as Alcan, the International Paper Company, the Consolidated Paper Corporation. Quebec looked like an appanage of London or New York. And the penetration of foreign capital was made easier by the absence of investment competition from a local bourgeoisie which, in the circumstances, was not in a position to preside over economic development in the province. Lacking accumulated capital, the Québécois dominant class would fall back on its subsistence revenue, which came chiefly from political sources.

War contributed to the launching of the boom in the economy by cutting out Scandinavian competition in forest products, opening up an immense market for agricultural products, and increasing demand for manufactured goods. It was a prosperity inflated artificially by new business practices such as credit and instalment payments. Continuous growth in the Quebec economy of this period is evidenced by more rapid growth in the working than in the general population, 99.3 as against 74.3 per cent, a phenomenon attributable in part to the slowing of emigration to the United States and the 'active proletarianization' of Quebec women.

Change was also wrought by industrialization in the assignment of manpower among the primary, secondary, and tertiary sectors of the economy:[5]

Sector	1901	1911	1921	1931
	percentages			
Primary	48.32	46.51	42.36	38.28
(farming)	(38.5)	(31.2)	(28.2)	(22.4)
Secondary	25.20	22.67	21.77	21.42
Tertiary	26.48	30.75	35.86	40.30

As can be seen from the table, the primary sector yielded pride of place to the tertiary. Whereas in 1900 agriculture accounted for 65 per cent of total production, by 1935 this sector represented only 12.4 per cent and employed only one worker in four. Mining turns up as a growth area in the primary sector, but this economic activity concentrated on extraction; the raw ore was exported. And despite the falling percentages in the secondary sector, employment there rose by a hundred thousand over the period. The economy we see in Quebec is one in the process of industrialization. Manufactured goods were coming in, and raw material and more or less finished goods were going out. Light industry was in the ascendancy. Most enterprises had an annual turnover worth less than $25,000. Heavy industry had not yet emerged in the lead.

It was also a time of urban growth. This part of the population rose from 39.6 per cent of the total in 1901 to 63 per cent in 1929.[6] Between 1891 and 1921, rural Quebec lost 172,000 people. There was urbanization, if we use this term to refer to concentrations of people in limited geographical areas. In terms of attitudes, however, a rural view of the world continued to predominate. Growth in the towns and cities did not prompt the abandonment of traditional values: 'A continuity of attitudes was maintained between rural folk and proletarians.'[7] The French-speaking towndweller was a hybrid, the product of a town-country symbiosis. He had no clear awareness of the changes taking place, or of the ways in which these challenged the dominant mentality. This offers at least a partial explanation of the persistence of an ideology which was out of step with reality.

By its strangeness, its being the foreigner's place, the town reinforced the habitant's loyalty to the traditional values, as well as his mistrust and withdrawal. A worker with few qualifications, occupying a dominated economic position in the lower reaches of the business community, the French-speaking Québécois felt the threat of his other neighbours and competitors. This comes through in Charles Gill's 1911 description of Rue Saint-Laurent:

The sun was setting. The cosmopolitan throng passed by in a cloud of golden dust. This setting sun, this street I had seen completely French twenty years before, and now this crowd of races hostile to our fate, with its babel of tongues, and our own race represented mainly by its prostitutes of 12 and its young drunkards ... how I was struck by it all! We were still by the window. I showed it to Ferland – 'Look, Ferland,' I said: 'Watch French Canada dying.'[8]

For this same Québécois worker, troubled in identity and held down economically, the city and the factory were daily evidence of the superiority of others. This is how the economic position of such people was described in a report by the Association catholique de la jeunesse canadienne-française:

Our natural wealth is monopolized by foreigners; our work force is exploited by the development of artificial industries, four-fifths foreign-owned; production is organized in lopsided and irrational ways for the benefit of big business rather than the immediate needs of the consumer. These are but a few of the problems of our industrial system. We have to face the question of our industrial future. Should we continue to let the Americans and English take the best of what we have, and gradually reduce us to menials?[9]

Here, then, are the essential characteristics of Quebec's economic development in the first decades of the twentieth century. This economy was not autonomous, but integrated into the North American economy. Industrial growth occurred, not in terms of the needs of the local market, but in terms of the province's natural wealth and the demand for it on the world market. Economic expansion was mediated by large-scale industry of a monopolistic type such as pulp and paper and aluminum. This industrialization was not engineered by the majority ethnic group in Quebec, for French-Canadian owners and entrepreneurs were few, and even administration at the local level was handed to a largely English-speaking management group: 'Quebec's economic development was financed, managed and controlled from outside.'[10]

These economic indicators also throw some light on the social forces of the time. The bourgeoisie of industry and high finance was made up chiefly of Americans and Anglo-Saxons, with a small minority of French-Canadian capitalists. Its political representatives were the Liberals of Taschereau. Another bourgeois group, that of the owners of the means of production, was clustered in small and medium-sized enterprises. It was typified by weak capital concentration, location in small towns, and intensive employment of a largely unqualified work force. Closely connected with the petty bourgeoisie of the professions, it would express its class interests politically in support of Duplessis. Meanwhile, the traditional Quebec petty bourgeoisie, represented by the politicians, continued to manage the state apparatus and serve two masters, the church and capital. The church, represented by the clergy, maintained its starring role of intermediary between the people and the various levels of power. Quebec's working class developed with industry. In the beginning, its members were unskilled workers who maintained close contacts with the rural areas from which they came. And of course, there were the farmers and agricultural workers, still accounting for a substantial percentage of the province's active manpower, and strong in their support of the traditional élites. In this social structure the church held the ideological hegemony, and arranged the relations among these social classes, which tended to co-operate and associate rather than emerge in opposition to one another.

Politically, the period was dominated by liberalism at both federal and provincial levels. One may assume from this some ideological adjustment on the parts both of the Liberals themselves and also of the church hierarchy. In earlier times, as we have seen, the Roman authorities considered it impossible – doctrinally – to ally Catholicism with liberalism. For the bishops, any such association would be 'an unrealistic reconciliation of truth and error.' Then, conservatives were cashing in on the 'undue influence' of the clergy, and liberals found themselves invariably in opposition. Their success depended on managing to neutralize the church's influence in politics. To achieve this, moving from one compromise to another under Laurier's leadership, they were to abandon the unabridged liberalism and the old radicalism of their Rouge ancestors.

Co-opted by Edward Blake in 1887 as the new Liberal leader, Laurier was to develop the party's electoral base and attract support from the French Canadians, who had been voting Conservative since Confederation. Moderate and pragmatic in his approach, Laurier wanted to restore national unity, reconcile English and French, and do away with the usual political recourse to race and religion. He used these words to describe himself: 'As you know, I am not a doctrinaire. I am always ready to be practical on the tariff as well as on any other question.'[11] His political strategy consisted in sidestepping controversy and supporting solutions that offended the smallest possible number.

To court the churchmen and get his party into office, Laurier tried to make the distinction between the English style of political liberalism and the social liberalism of the European continent. This was the subject of his speech on 26 June 1877 entitled 'Political Liberalism,' a response to Ultramontanist propaganda about republican, irreligious, and radical lib-

eralism in which he cited his English brethren, whose aim was to reform political abuse and not to destroy society. Laurier asked Liberals to
'prove to the world that Catholicism is compatible with the enjoyment
of freedom in the broadest sense of the word.'[12]

On its own, however, this policy of compromise and moderation
would not succeed in shaking the Quebec clergy's Ultramontanist faith
and ingratiating liberalism with the church authorities. Finally, Rome had
to intervene, and sent Bishop Conroy to coax the clergy to greater neutrality at election time. In fact, they continued placing Liberal supporters
under notice of mortal sin. The feud did not really subside until after the
publication of Pope Leo XIII's encyclical *Affari vos*, which charged the
Canadian church to call off its 'holy war.' In the end, the conflict had
dulled the cutting edge of liberal ideology; French-Canadian liberalism, at
any rate, was by this time not much different from conservatism.

Laurier slid past the potential unpleasantness of the Manitoba Schools
Question, and he placated western farmers by calling for reciprocity
with the United States. He caressed the loyalist and imperialist sensitiv-
ities of Ontario while at the same time bringing reassurance to French
Canada by his autonomist stands. Thus, he put together a Canadian
nationalism. He even reconciled Catholics with Protestants, and played on
the pride and nationalist feeling of his fellow French Canadians. This
was the factor that got his party into power in the 1896 general election,
and it was Quebec support that kept it there for fifteen years. 'Liberalism had been restored to health in Catholic Quebec, but the operation had
largely purged it of its traditional anticlericalism.'[13]

Provincial supremacy for the party began with F.-G. Marchand's victory
in 1897 and continued through the reigns of S.-N. Parent, Lomer Gouin,
and L.-A. Taschereau until 1936. Its accession coincided with the industrial boom in Quebec. The Liberals backed private enterprise and encouraged foreign investment. On the last question, Taschereau made this
reply in 1928 to Camilien Houde: 'Yes, there is American money in the
province and it is welcome here. As long as I and my colleagues are in
office, we will invite foreign investment to help us to develop our
province.'[14] The premier was also a supporter of economic laissez-faire.
The Liberal press supported the government in its extroverted industrialization policy, and loyally opposed social legislation.

The period was also one of extensive co-operation between the federal
administration and the government of the province, which began to

look like local management, bound to the powerful big brother in Ottawa. Shortly after his election, Premier Marchand declared: 'Our flag will fly by our leader who governs in Ottawa. Laurier can now command every province; his words will be listened to and his desires carried out.'[15] This confusion between the federal and provincial parties provoked autonomist reaction from opposition groups and nationalists.

Three great ideological streams dominate the political life of this period: imperialism, the nationalism of Canada, and the nationalism of the French Canadians. After the First World War and the disappearance of Laurier, Quebec attention moved from the federal back to the provincial scene. In my analysis, I have chosen leaders of opinion as representative of ideological movements in the petty bourgeois class, and of the reactions of this class to far-reaching change in Quebec society.

Henri Bourassa: Canadian nationalist

We can see in Bourassa's fate how this apparently uneventful period also knew distress. He was Papineau's grandson and an Ultramontanist, Laurier's friend and an opponent of empire, nationalist and Catholic at the same time. That is a lot of variables for one man.[16]

The liberal Papineau, consistent with his ideology, had been anticlerical. Henri Bourassa turned out to be something of a freak, a mass of contradictions: a *castor rouge*, who tried to reconcile liberalism with Ultramontanism. While remaining a Rouge, he was also a deeply religious man who obeyed faithfully the commands of church and pope. He was complex, idealistic, and independent.

It is extremely difficult to put together a coherent précis of Bourassa's thinking. He wrote copiously, on varied topics, and frequently in the midst of controversy. Many schools of thought have tried to recruit him for prestige value. He preferred ambiguity himself, objecting to no interpretation that remained more or less consistent with his thinking. Some, like M.P. O'Connell, have seen him as a radical nationalist; others, like Claude Ryan, as the god of the nationalist movement, or, like R. Desrosiers, as an idealist who was the antithesis of a radical, and gulled his fellow countrymen.

Bourassa's interest in politics was stirred in 1885 by the Riel affair. In 1887, he campaigned with Mercier for the National Party. At the age of twenty-one he was elected mayor of Montebello. First returned to the Commons in 1896, he would represent Labelle riding for a total of twenty-one years, from 1896 to 1907 and 1925 to 1935. From 1908 to 1912, he sat as an MLA in the Quebec legislature. Independence and duty were the twin banners of his whole political career. He rejected party discipline and the party spirit. Although he was a Liberal and supported Laurier, he would not bind himself too closely to the machine. In 1900, when he was at odds with Laurier about relations with Britain, he resigned from the party to be returned by acclamation on an anti-imperialist platform. In 1911 he deserted Laurier again on the same issue, and contributed to the Liberal defeat in the election of that year. His motto was: 'Do what must be done.'

The two factors behind this anti-party stance were Bourassa's personal understanding of democracy and his Ultramontanist loyalties. For he was no believer in the sovereignty of the people: 'All lawful authority, whatever the form of government, comes from God ... As the son of a liberal and parliamentary family, I believed for a time in democracy and parliamentary government. Not in the sovereignty of the people as a source of authority. That is absurd, as unworkable in practice as it is wrong in theory.'[17] This is why he saw church involvement in matters temporal as perfectly justified. Rule by parliament he rejected because of the party system: 'Our parties are nothing but herds of ignorant or venal slaves that go where their leaders please. Deadening party discipline, and even more, the payment of their election expenses, turn most candidates and members into docile flunkies, beasts of burden for the masters who buy them and lead them to the slaughter ...'[18] The party spirit, Bourassa argued, shackled freedom and encouraged corruption. He was critical of democracy as a system based on the right of the majority to oppress the minority. He was against universal suffrage, and most particularly against the vote for women.

The owner of the former Petite Nation seigniory was an admirer of the seigniorial system. He admired aristocratic systems in general, and lamented the fact that such a system had not managed to develop in Canada. It was in the spirit of making the best of a bad job that he used the rule of parliament imposed by the English. The drawbacks of this political system were to be offset by the mobilization of an alert and informed public opinion and the sampling of it by referendum – an approach that was not entirely consistent with his concept of lawful authority. He founded *Le Devoir* in 1910 as a corrective to the rule of parliament.

Bourassa opposed increase in the power of the state on the grounds that it led to religious neutrality and challenged the natural rights of parents. He would virtually have limited its role to law and order. It should certainly be kept out of education: 'I view the state as an incompetent schoolmaster.' Its only active role should be to encourage new settlement on the land. For all else Bourassa put his trust in the benevolence of the church.

His notions about economics and society were banal and superficial; in these matters, he merely passed on the doctrine of the church. Religious beliefs came before anything else: 'To the Catholic, Apostolic and Roman Church we have vowed boundless love, inviolate fidelity, and complete obedience.'[18] His scale of values was clear:

We must sometimes recall – the whole hierarchy of duties is upside down these days – that religion comes before patriotism, that the preservation of the faith and morality is more important than that of our tongue; that the maintenance of our national traditions, and above all, of our family virtues, takes precedence over the requirements of higher education or the production of literary works.[19]

He opposed compulsory education because it was an inalienable right of the family to make the decisions about schooling. The family, and not the individual, was the basis of society. Bourassa vigorously opposed any change that might reduce paternal authority and the role of the family. Divorce, civil marriage, the feminist movement, working women, female suffrage, were all absolutely unacceptable. For the suffragettes, he had these withering words in *Le Devoir*: 'The woman's chief function is and will always be – whatever the suffragettes say or do, or don't do – motherhood, that holy and fertile motherhood that makes her the true equal of the man ... [Women] are not able to take on the most demanding positions in society; they are not qualified to carry out public duties.'[20] More serious still, working women meant promiscuity and libertinism in the factories. In all this, Bourassa expressed an antifeminism that was general in the nationalist circles of the period. Women were expected to stay at home, breed prodigiously, and transmit the national values to their offspring. The nationalists were unable to accept the emancipation of women; it ran straight up against their revenge-of-the-cradles strategy that compensated for their powerlessness in politics.

With respect to the world of work and money, Bourassa started from the principles that spiritual good was more important than material goods, and that the workings of the mind and the needs of the soul took precedence over bodily appetites and the demands of vanity. His economic thinking was also closely bound up with his nationalism and the crusade against British imperialism. He warned against the invasion of American capital, and seized every opportunity to condemn the foreign-controlled trusts and monopolies. For moral reasons, he opposed industrial development. He saw the English-dominated business world as a vehicle of assimilation: 'The wild passion for business is the most active agent in French Canada of the Anglo-Saxon, Protestant conquest; it is the surest sign of the dominion of materialism, devoid of faith or ideals and without nationality, over the whole social and political life of this continent.'[21]

He condemned liberal economic doctrine along with the sins of profit, competition, banks, and credit. Businessmen, bankers, financiers, and industrialists aroused his ire. He was violent in his attacks on capitalism, 'the concentration of wealth in the hands of special groups that dominate economic activity, private and public credit, and to a great degree the social and political order, and thus tyrannize individuals, the family, and the state.'[22] Yet his thunderbolts were directed equally at socialism. Loyal to the church's social doctrine, he adopted the corporatist model in which capital and labour were seen as complementary and interdependent, and social relations were founded on justice, charity, and co-operation among classes. Ideally, he would have taken things back to feudalism, the system that kept family and property together, and offered a stable social hierarchy filled with harmony and understanding. The nearest thing to this ideal in the Quebec of Bourassa's time was the government's back-to-the-land colonization programme.

Another expression of Bourassa's deeply conservative philosophy was his opposition to the strong imperialist movement that developed in the closing years of the nineteenth century. Britain's supremacy in world trade was being challenged by Germany and the United States. France was a strong competitor in the drive for African colonies. In an attempt to preserve the empire on which the sun never set, British leaders changed their free trade policy and applied pressure on colonies to help build a

'Greater Britain,' an imperial federation in which all the 'British' dominions would unite for defence and have common policies in external relations and trade. They saw the South African war as a chance to put these ideas into practice.

In Canada, this imperialist pressure had the effect of reviving ethnic conflict. The Canadian imperialist movement was anti-French. Its aim was to make Canada a country of a single language and culture. In the wake of the Riel affair and the savaging of French minority rights in Manitoba and Ontario, it stimulated the growth of a group awareness in French Canada that was personified by Bourassa.

The request for a Canadian contingent to fight the Boers brought to the surface the old differences between the militaristic, pro-imperial English Canadians and the antimilitaristic, anti-imperial French Canadians. *La Presse* made this distinction: 'We French Canadians belong to only one country ... For us, Canada is the whole world. The English, however, have two native lands – this one and the one across the sea.'[23] Laurier's ruling Liberals found a compromise. There would be no official contingent, but the government would pay for a force of volunteers.[24] Bourassa resigned in protest on 18 October 1899. To his demand whether Quebec's opinion had been weighed in making the decision, Laurier made the famous reply: 'My dear Henri, the province of Quebec has no opinion, only feelings.' Sent back to parliament by acclamation, the anti-imperialist asked the Commons to rule that the government's action did not constitute a precedent for participation in future conflicts. He was determined that any change in the relations between Britain and Canada must be approved by the sovereign will of parliament and the Canadian people. His motion was buried by an avalanche of pro-British fanaticism.

In 1903, a group led by Bourassa founded the Ligue Nationaliste to combat imperial entanglements, and announced a platform with these three main planks: for Canada in its relations with Britain, the highest degree of autonomy consistent with colonial status; for the provinces of Canada in their relations with the federal state, the highest degree of autonomy consistent with the maintenance of the federal bond; by the federal and provincial governments, implementation of a policy of Canadian economic and intellectual development.[25] In detail, the nationalist demands for Canada were an independent immigration policy, the right to representation at international congresses, a procedure by which Canadian courts could become the courts of last resort, independence in trade, the right to sign its own commercial treaties and appoint its own consuls, and, lastly, Canadian non-participation in imperial wars outside the territory of Canada.

The issue of Canadian involvement in Britain's imperial policies arose again in 1909, when the mother country resolved to increase her war fleet to offset the German challenge to her naval supremacy. Laurier brought in a bill to establish a Canadian navy that would be at Britain's disposal. The Conservatives and English Canada in general were not satisfied with this, preferring instead a straight levy of some millions of dollars. The measure was also opposed by the French-Canadian nationalists, who viewed it as one more expression of British imperialism. It was at this time that Bourassa founded his newspaper *Le Devoir*, from which he launched a full-scale attack on the naval bill. He argued that since Britain had total responsibility for her foreign policy, she should pay the whole cost. Canada's only obligation for imperial defence was the defence of Canada itself. Bourassa's stand found wide support among the basically antimilitaristic and pacifist population of French Canada. Laurier managed to steer his bill through, but it was a pyrrhic victory; his party went down to defeat in the 1911 election at the hands of a tory-nationalist alliance. The same nationalists then had to watch the new prime minister, Robert Borden, embrace the empire with greater fervour than his predecessor had.[26]

The broad lines of Bourassa's nationalism emerge through these issues in the vicissitudes of Canadian public life. Basically, he was arguing for a medieval model, a golden age in which the church presided over the peaceful coexistence of the European nations, each developing its special culture and capacities. The particular was contained in the universal, for these nations were bound together by a common faith and a general morality; they welcomed the leadership of what Bourassa called a 'Father of all the faithful, infallible director of the Faith, unwavering guardian of morality.'[27] In modern times, the church could no longer be the unifying factor. The state replaced the pontiff as the representative of universality above the nations. And in fact this is why Bourassa remained a federalist. In spite of the evidence to the contrary, he had an unshakable belief in the virtues of federalism.

His chief objectives as a nationalist were, first, the regular, gradual growth of Canadian nationality to its full expression in independence, and second, the simultaneous and balanced development of two basic cultures.[28] It was in the light of these that he always made much of the question of Canada's immigration policy, criticizing it as working against this dual development by its partiality to English speakers.

He believed that the French-Canadian culture could flourish in Confederation. His idealism in this matter set him at odds with Jules-Paul Tardivel, who saw disaster in Confederation for the French Canadians, their rights trampled in the west. Bourassa refused to draw the logical conclusions from this obvious fact. He confessed disillusionment with the nation, but kept hoping and acting as if it could work. Indeed, his federalism had a messianic, evangelical tinge to it. Only within the federation could French Canada accomplish its civilizing mission of the spirit. Bourassa emerged as a fierce defender of French minority rights in Ontario and western Canada: there had to be a continental dimension corresponding to the providential vocation of his people. To Quebec fell the responsibility of helping the French-speaking minorities of other provinces.

Bourassa defined himself as a Canadian first and foremost. He dreamed of a Canada in which there would be a stable balance between the two founding peoples, and spoke for an all-Canada nationalism based on the mutual respect of these groups. The nationalism of French Canada could and must develop within a more general patriotism: 'I consider all Canada as my native land, belonging to us on the same basis as to the other races.'[29]

The only possible basis for the solution of our national problems is one of mutual respect for our racial characters and exclusive devotion to our common land. There are no masters or servants here, not victors or vanquished, but rather two allies whose association has been built on foundations that are equitable and clearly defined. We are not asking our neighbours of English extraction to help us develop a political reconciliation with France, and they have no right to use their strength of numbers to break the rules of the alliance, forcing us to shoulder new obligations towards England, even if these were completely voluntary and spontaneous.[30]

Bourassa did not accept the democratic inevitability of majority rule. In his view of the world, relations of power had no place. He condemned imperialist feeling and the race prejudice that lay behind it. He wanted peace, freedom, and grandeur in Canada before any other nation.

This overall nationalism, then, rested upon the two cultural national-isms, which must remain outside politics and never attempt involvement with the state. The state, for its part, must remain neutral, above the component nationalities, and tend the balance between the parties:

My own nationalism is Canadian nationalism, based on racial duality along with the special traditions this duality brings. I work for the emergence of Canadian patriotism, which I see as the best surety for the existence of two races and the respect these owe to one another. My *own* people, for me as for Monsieur Tardivel, are the French Canadians, but the English Canadians are not foreigners, and I regard as our allies all those among them who respect us and desire as we do to preserve undiminished the autonomy of Canada. My native land is all of Canada, a federation of separate races and autonomous provinces. The nation I wish to see grow up is the Canadian nation, made up of French Canadians and English Canadians.[31]

Bourassa was in favour of cultural separatism and yet, unlike Tardivel, he rejected political separatism. He damned it as foolhardy, and danger-ous, just as he did the extremist nationalism of the chauvinist English, with its deliberate campaigns of assimilation and violation of minority rights. In spite of the blighted hopes of Confederation and the wrongs suffered by the French Canadians, Bourassa still hoped that the English would one day come to understand his case for the two founding peoples and their mutual interdependence.

On the one hand, in Bourassa's view, the survival of the French Canadians was the essential precondition of the survival of the Canadian nation, which must escape melting-pot Americanization. On the other, he saw Canadian nationalism as the precondition for the survival of French Canada. As for Quebec itself, its continued health depended on the struggle for minority rights and the preservation of the French-speaking enclaves scattered across the country. In opposing the idea of Que-bec's independence, he argued that it could exist only in so far as it was tolerated by the hundred million and more Anglophones surrounding it. In this reasoning by numbers, it is not especially clear how non-separation would have altered the power patterns, or how the federal bond held out a surer future for the francophones in America than would the creation of an independent Quebec, unless one focuses on the rather hypotheti-cal survival of the French minorities; and the odds would not seem to be enhanced by such statistics as an overall increase in the French-Canadian population over the years 1911 to 1921 of 19 per cent, as against an English increase in the same period of 25 per cent. Bourassa's argument, in fact, was tailored to his own thesis. His nationalism needed strong admixtures of optimism and utopianism to sustain it, and his thinking was not without its paradoxes and inconsistencies.

In the first place, he failed to see that development in the economy requires change in the social structure. He panicked at the danger of demographic and industrial change, but he ignored the facts and preached the land as the basis of French-Canadian economic life. Nor did he note the connection between economic infrastructure and political superstructure. He fought to cement Confederation, but he also fought against the interests of finance and industry that promoted that same political arrangement. His nationalism reveals a paradox: he did all he could to ensure Canada's independence of Britain through the growth of Canadian nationalism, but he denied the validity of the same approach to the French Canadians calling for the independence of Quebec. He cheered for Irish independence but categorically rejected that of his own Quebec. Of Canadian independence, he wrote: 'This is also the solution that is most perfectly in harmony with the order of human societies; the only one to be sought by a people worthy of God's blessings and man's respect.'[32] It we accept this, the French Canadians were clearly unworthy of God's blessings, even though they were the honour guard of Christian civilization. What this incongruity tells us, in fact, is that the key element in Bourassa's nationalism was messianism. Quebec was simply too small a stage for God's plan.

Clearly too, Bourassa suffered from the French-Canadian complex of hereditary powerlessness.[33] In this respect, he shares a certain family resemblance with Lafontaine and Trudeau, with the peculiarity that the main cause of incongruity in his reasoning was its mystic dimension. It was a dimension that increased after 1929, when Pius xi spoke to him in Rome: 'The first duty of a Catholic journalist is to stand up for God and the Church. Other causes, however legitimate they may be, are secondary, and must be subordinated ... At the present time, the main obstacle to the work of the Papacy and the Church in the world is the prevalence of racial passions in all countries, the substitution of nationalism for Catholicism.'[34] From that time forward, the religious spirit ruled his thinking. The focus changed: the campaign for French language and culture became secondary to the struggle for the faith. His nationalist ardour cooled. Now, language and tradition were to be maintained above all for the support they gave to the Catholic social order. In 1912, he had proclaimed the defence of the language as the sacred duty of French Canadians; in 1935, it was the defence of the faith. The language as watchdog of religion Bourassa dismissed as a mistaken approach. The church, being universal, could never be the property of any particular race of men. Here, he was reacting to the new French-Canadian national-ism inspired by Lionel Groulx's separatist tendencies.

Lionel Groulx: French-Canadian nationalist

For Bourassa and Olivar Asselin, the nationalism of French Canada should limit itself to culture and stay out of politics, an attitude that explains their passion for the defence and revitalization of the French language. As-selin, a notorious francophile, tried to build a nationalism based on pride of tongue and the connection with the culture of France.[35]

In fact, that country was again becoming a magnet for these early twen-tieth-century nationalists. Asselin's nationalism was original in the sense that he was one of the few since the 1837–38 rebellion to take adher-ence to the culture and intellectual tradition of France as the prime ele-ment of French-Canadian nationality. For the new intellectuals, clerical an-athema of that wayward daughter of the church was losing its thunder. Asselin himself tried to keep language separate from faith in his nation-alist creed, and placed his emphasis on the former. This sets him off sharply from Groulx, the Ultramontanist who saw these two defining ele-ments as very closely linked. Asselin's nationalism was Canadian and French-Canadian at the same time. Like Bourassa, whom he followed in this respect, he believed in the thesis of cultural duality.

Abbé Lionel Groulx was the first intellectual to attempt a structural anal-ysis of nationalist ideology and work consciously towards a nationalist doctrine. He viewed the nation as a community of culture, faith, history, territory, and race, of which the moving force was a collective will to live. His concept was based on homogeneity. He rejected the existence of social heterogeneity, of social classes, in French Canada. The guid-ing element of his social homogeneity was Catholicism, which he saw as immanent in the French-Canadian nation. The French language was the keeper of the faith: 'We have remained Catholic because we have re-

mained French.'[36] His personal commitment and indeed his entire nationalist doctrine were anchored to this solidarity, which puts him in the
Ultramontanist stream running from Tardivel to Msgr Paquet: the national
and the religious became identical.

Against the 'more Canadian' nationalism of Bourassa and Asselin,
Groulx offered one that was 'more Québécois': 'On the scale of patriotic
feeling, our first and noblest love as French Canadians must be directed at our province of Quebec, the historic French territory, the former
New France, that more than any other part of Canada has been for us the
fount of our life, the pre-eminent productive environment.'[37] In the 1920s,
the attention of the French-Canadian élite was turning away from the
federal scene to become fixed firmly on Quebec. The effects of political
and demographic minority status were beginning to make themselves
felt. Under the federal Conservatives, French-Canadian influence in the
administration of the country waned. There were the successive failures
of attempts to protect the francophone minorities outside Quebec. Relations between Quebec and the rest of Canada had so deteriorated in
the wake of the conscription crisis, when Ottawa's policy was imposed
on French Canada by armed force and the weight of numbers, that MLA
Napoléon Francoeur rose in the provincial assembly to propose withdrawal from Confederation.

Groulx came to epitomize this emerging collective consciousness.
Like many of his contemporaries and followers, he was an idealist, rejecting political involvement and confining himself to work at the intellectual, educational level. He despised parties and politicians, believing rather
in the need for a national doctrine to guide the French-Canadian people:

Action moves as the spirit dictates ... Do you desire to raise a state again, re-establish a nation? Turn to the powers of the spirit ... The truth of this is painfully obvious, when our collective action, lacking a doctrine that would have co-ordinated
from above and so long abandoned to false guides, has spent itself with no definite goal, anarchically.[38]

It was the great ambition of Groulx's life to give this doctrine to his people.
To achieve this, he became a historian: for him, intellectual movements
could guide action and change the world. He made his special field the
education of the young: 'The school is either the citadel or the tomb

of beliefs or nationalities.'[39] He tried to endow it with nationalist objectives.

He was attempting to give legitimacy to the French-Canadian nationality, to dig for its destiny in its past. The situation of his people was to be rectified under the banner of history, the proof and guarantee of national unity, cohesiveness, and identity: 'What we need is a mystique ... There can be no French state, no French people, without a French mystique.'[40] To supply this need, and to legitimize French-Canadian nationalism, he found a mythic vision of the French regime in Canada: 'To our nationalism, I have brought the argument of history, the revelation that we had a past and a culture. At that time, history was what we wanted. From Garneau, I gained the impression that one found oneself through one's past. I was aware of the people, their want and need for history.'[41] The historian's role in revealing the grandeur of the past was to read its lessons and mould the future. In Groulx's mind, we must make the past our master; it must decide our present and our future. Anchored in the time of French rule, this past distilled the essence of the French-Canadian people and defined the values that must be preserved. For Groulx, the settlers who came from France did not form a society of trappers and adventurers, but one primarily of farmers: 'The first we is the rural we.'[42] The models in this society were the clearers of the land, the missionaries and, as in the Dollard des Ormeaux cult, its defenders. Also glorified was the protective role of the church: in Groulx's mystique, the civil and political authority was played down, and the church presided over the destinies and the continuity of this people, this race chosen by God. As André Bélanger has noted: 'Groulx saw the determining factors for the French-Canadian race as being the imperatives of its birth and early childhood. One could even speak in a broad sense of an almost genetic determinism. He returns constantly to the notions of "heredities," patrimony, and cultural heritage.'[43]

What we get from this is a nationalism of preservation. The fundamental element of the doctrine of the stirrer of French Canada's consciousness was Catholicism, which must be preserved at all costs. Groulx searched his vision for proofs of the beneficent role of the church and her bishops in the story of French Canada. He rejected the separation of church and state as he rejected liberalism and democracy, for all power came from God: 'The church charged with the care of souls and our eternal interests is independent of states, and superior to them in the fulfil-

ment of her purpose. The states of this world must subordinate themselves to her, for she is the fount of all power; she has been given all
authority in heaven and earth; she is the mistress of peoples and kings.'[44]
Groulx's political and social thinking was derived from the French right
wing, and more particularly from the theorists of counter-revolution – Joseph de Maistre, Louis de Bonald, Louis Veuillot, and, to some degree,
Charles Maurras. He also inherited a Jansenist disdain for material
possessions, and placed morality above economic issues: the economy
must be the servant of faith and culture. Groulx attacked modern society and condemned economic liberalism, industrialization, proletarianization, urbanization, and their consequence – the depopulation of the countryside – as the causes of the national collapse of French Canada. These
trends were to be reversed by the return of moral strictness.

The clerical élite of this period, anxious to check the workings of material progress in Quebec society, put moral laxity at the top of their list
of contemporary errors. According to the periodical *Action catholique*,
alcohol had to be banned, and the cinema, which whisked us into worlds
of barbarity and moral decay, was an invention of the devil. Movies
warped the mind, corrupted the emotions, promoted lewdness, and
abetted criminality and prostitution. Dancing, especially the foxtrot and
tango, was another of the sins of American materialism. Dance halls were
places of libertinism and schools of scandal: 'They ... scamper around
in frocks that are cut low at the top and high at the bottom, a display of bare
flesh that recalls the butcher's window.'[45] The perversion of industrial
society had even tainted Sunday, a day that was now given over to
games, walks, and noisy entertainments that were the antithesis of sabbath rest and observance. For the traditional ideologues, this moral crisis
was caused by the materialism of modern life, that evil of evils. The
'foreigners,' English and Jewish, were the ones responsible for the decadence sapping the nation and making menials of the French Canadians:
'The economic malaise among us is affecting not only our society, as
everyone knows, but also our nationality.'[46] The attitude to foreign capitalists of Quebec's clergy and nationalists was ambivalent: they were to
be tolerated because they created jobs and slowed immigration, but they
were to be condemned as carriers of outside values that endangered
the very personality of the local order.[47] Groulx's solution was a wholesale
economic nationalism based on possession of the province's three sources
of capital accumulation: 'A national patrimony, and by this I mean the

land and its subsurface working chiefly for our nationals. A labour force managed chiefly by nationals and working mainly for them. Of the fruit of this labour, that is the wages, savings that remain chiefly in the hands of nationals and work for their benefit.'[48] Neither capitalism nor socialism met Groulx's criteria. He chose instead an agricultural and craft society founded on small-scale trade and production, based on occupational guilds. Unless industrialization were to bring about the decay of French Canada's civilization, it had to be controlled and retooled to local scale; this meant limiting heavy industry and promoting small family enterprise that was accessible to a people with small amounts of capital.

In his thinking on constitutional matters, in spite of a brief fling in the 1920s with the notion of La Laurentie, an independent francophone state, Groulx kept the faith with the old nationalist dogma of Quebec within Confederation. The Canadian federation was in his mind equivalent to the 'rebirth of French Canada' because it had resurrected Quebec as a political entity. According to Bélanger: 'His entire thinking revolved around the autonomy accorded Quebec with the end of Union – "Confederation is what we ourselves wanted, what we insisted upon" ... There could be no doubt as to its legitimacy.'[49] In *Notre avenir politique*, consistently with the spirit of the times, Groulx predicted the collapse of the federation, but he did not want to rush the matter, believing instead that Quebec's role lay in vigilant defence of its provincial autonomy on the economic as well as the political plane. He had no time for politicians who were more devoted to the defence of party than they were to the interests of their French-Canadian nation. In his view, the political parties were etiolating that nation, and Taschereau's regime was cast in the role of Trojan horse for industry as it acquiesced in the penetration of foreign capital. The 1921 economic crisis had the effect of whetting national suffering over the arrival of American capital.

Finally, Groulx contributed the mystique of the French-Canadian hero: 'No great thing happens in history unless someone of greatness is involved.'[50] It was the good fortune of New France to be governed by bishops. The ancestors of the Québécois were heroes. The conquest and English domination, carriers as these events were of liberalism, mercantilism, and individualism, caused the downfall of the French Canadians. What was needed now was a doctrine and a leader who would rebuild national unity. Groulx was evidently waiting for a saviour despatched by divine Providence. The words messiah, saviour, salvation, redemption, and resurrection recur frequently in his vocabulary, and stand as evidence of the religious cast he gave this potential leader: 'Let there come a rallyer of minds and wills, who will lead us back to ourselves over all the things that divide us.'[51] He saw the nation of French Canada as an extended family, its potential leader as a father – a liberator who would be able to recreate a doctrinal communion and give meaning to the collectivity that had been so sadly changed by the adversary, the Protestant English.

It was an essential part of his nationalism. Under their messiah, it would be the providential mission of the French Canadians to develop their agriculture, represent the spiritual values in America, and spread the Catholic faith. This chosen people was to be Christ's missionary. Despite all rebuffs, French Canada must never despair: God, its protector, would save it. Messianism seems to be a refuge for cultures under fire, expressing their hopes of emancipation in the form of delusion.

Groulx's main contribution was to raise the idea of the French-Canadian national state to a level of grandeur in the collective consciousness of the province of Quebec. The nationalism of the 1920s generally, like that of the next decade described in chapter 7, came as an expression of self-defence against the externally controlled growth of industrial capitalism. The national issue was confined no more to the protection of the French language and the Catholic religion; it was taking on an economic dimension.

Organized labour: socialism and unionism

In their desperation, the intelligentsia of French Canada clung to the traditional values of a rural society based on family, parish, and priest. It was a social model that generally offered no space for factories, wage earners, cosmopolitan cities, and the reality of large-scale labour forces. However, the submersion of the real world in the dominant ideological stream did not stifle the emergence in Quebec of a critical social awareness that was more in tune with the industrial reality and the structural changes this reality was bringing to pass. The opening of this century, then, saw the growth of an authentic working-class consciousness. It remained a marginal phenomenon, failing to pry loose the ideological grasp of the petty bourgeoisie. Yet some note must be paid to these class stirrings among Québécois workers, the first real milestones of the socialist tradition in Quebec.

A socialist cell had existed in Montreal since the 1890s. It was the product of the deplorable living conditions of local workers, the way the international unions had foisted themselves on the local situation, and also the massive arrivals at this time of immigrants from countries in central Europe with powerful socialist movements. In fact, however, the formal influence came from the United States as, towards 1894–95, R.J. Kerrigan and W. Darlington founded the Montreal cell of the Socialist Labour Party of the United States. The first political workers' organization was founded a few years later, on 17 March 1899, by J.-A. Rodier, a man with long union experience. His Workers' Party reflected the failure of the old parties to enact the promised social reforms, and their identification with the capitalist class. 'In a word,' declared one speaker, 'if the worker wants to better his lot, he will have to seize political power and govern for himself.'[52]

The main planks of the Parti ouvrier platform were free and compulsory education, government old age and health insurance, nationalization of all industries and public utilities liable to coalesce into monopolies, universal suffrage, popularly elected magistrates, the abolition of the Senate of Canada and the Legislative Council of Quebec, and finally, a progressive income tax. Also contested by the workers was the principle of the property qualification for public office, which made workers ineligible for municipal elections and so protected the interests of the bourgeoisie. According to Rodier, compulsory free schooling would bring about the emancipation of the working class, as the ruling class 'has much to gain by keeping us in ignorance; this is the only basis for their power, and the day when we shall have enough education, their reign will be over and ours will begin.'[53] Protest extended to church interference in the choice of textbooks. Finally, the party supported the idea of a department of public instruction.

Its first experiences at the polls were discouraging. In the federal election of November 1900, Roberge, the Parti ouvrier candidate in Ste Marie, the riding with the biggest working-class concentration in the country, collected only 184 suffrages as against 3,188 for the incumbent, the minister of public works Israël Tarte. In 1906, however, Partie ouvrier candidate Verville was elected with a 1,000-plus majority. Once in the Commons, he sat with the Liberals, and Rodier accused him of being the 'toady of the old Liberal party.' The episode occasioned some disillusionment as to the potential for reform within the parliamentary system, though the party itself was active until 1911, with some six hundred paid-up members.

From 1906 the party came to some extent under the influence of the social wing led by Albert St-Martin and Gustave Franck, who in 1916 began publication of *Le Monde ouvrier*, the first workers' weekly in the province. They were insisting on nationalization of all industry; in their opinion, the capitalist system had to be utterly wiped out, and the means of production handed to the workers. Less radical, the Parti ouvrier would have limited nationalization to publicly useful enterprises, and wanted labour to join with honest capitalists to work against the monopolies.[54] Opponents were excluded from the party.

St-Martin emerged as the leader of Montreal's socialists, organizing a number of demonstrations and broadcasting socialist philosophy to French Canadians. In October 1904, a worker delegation from France made a stopover in Quebec on the way to St Louis. A Montreal meeting heard delegates explain socialist principles, and concluded with a chorus of the *Internationale* by the three hundred workers present. On 1 May 1906, St-Martin led a socialist parade some six hundred strong and bearing such slogans as 'Down with the Crows,' 'Long Live Anarchy,' and 'Workers of the World, Unite!' 'This flag,' called out St-Martin, 'will break the shackles of the oppressed and destroy the tyrants!'[55]

Next year, Montreal's city fathers wanted to stop the parade. Bishop Bruchési forbade Catholic participation. The students of Laval University were against the event because 'the mere existence of a socialist revolutionary demonstration is a serious attack on the established civil and religious authority, tending to discredit it among the working classes and foment hostile feelings.'[56] Mounted police broke up the parade and arrested the demonstators for handing out their pamphlets.

This sort of thing did not put an end to Quebec socialism. In 1912, for example, the socialist *Cotton's Weekly* had some twelve hundred subscribers in the province. Meanwhile, the labour movement continued strong and growing. In mode of action, it took much from the British labour movement, with an emphasis on educating the workers. Its internal disputes and the use of the English language in its propaganda help explain its limited influence in Quebec. Finally, the church's campaign against it did much to reduce its reach: 'Realizing that the rise of the workers' movement was an irreversible phenomenon,' Jacques Rouillard concluded, 'the Church attempted less ... to stop it than to stem it, or better still, to give it direction.'[57]

Church interest in labour questions in general reflected a rise in union membership as well as persistent socialist activity. In 1911, Quebec had 276 union locals with some fifteen thousand members; after the First World War, the numbers of unionized workers in the province had risen to 43,514, and in 1931, the movement included 11.9 per cent of Quebec's active manpower. Throughout this period, the international unions were highly active, intensifying their efforts to recruit French Canadians. At times, these unions had socialists as leaders, and they were reasonably aggressive, calling for collective bargaining, collective agreements, and when necessary, strike action to get higher wages or reduce hours. However, they were far from being revolutionary.

The growth of this new social force, in Quebec as in all the industrialized countries, gave much pause to the authorities of the church, who detected a threat to their supremacy in society. The main reason for Catholic unionism was to counter the increasing influence of the neutral unions affiliated with United States based internationals:

The CTCC [Confédération des travailleurs catholiques du Canada] expressed a largely negative, antisocialist, anti-Communist, anti-international, anti-American, anti-English, anti-Protestant, and anti-foreign-capital point of view. In a positive sense, the CTCC supported the nationalist ideas of the time: corporativism, the return to the land, and provincial autonomy.[58]

The clergy asked the Catholic workers to shun the unions where their faith was in danger through encouragement of class conflict rather than respect for the established order, property rights, and Christian charity. As was later evident, the ideology of the Confédération des travailleurs catholiques du Canada founded at Hull in 1921 was a by-product of the traditional social philosophy that dominated Quebec society at the time, one moulded by clerical-nationalist values. While it was used by Catholic labour in the struggle against industrial capitalism, Catholic unionism was above all the creation of a force outside the working class, a force whose control over social development was challenged by industrialization.

This new approach to the union movement by the church in Quebec was drawn from official social doctrine as expressed in various encyclicals by

Popes Leo xiii, Pius x, Benedict xv, and Pius xi, which set out to define the Vatican position on employer-employee relations, and accepted unions as a means of slowing the advance of socialism. The doctrine can be summed up in this way: the church recognized the right to unionize, on condition that the unions be guided by Christian morality and faith; workers were asked to form Catholic unions and strive against neutral unions, socialism, and communism; relations in society were to be conducted on the basis of co-operation among classes, charity, and justice. From this viewpoint, capital and labour are complementary, and must exist in harmony. This, at least, is Leo xiii's prescription in *Rerum Novarum*: 'The capitalist error is to believe that the two classes are the born enemies of one another, as if Nature had armed the poor and the rich in order that they should contend with one another in a stubborn duel. In society, the two classes are destined by Nature to unite in harmony and offer mutual support in perfect balance.'[59] All social questions were to be resolved according to the dictates of morality and religion, as Pius x stressed in his 24 September 1912 encyclical, *Singulari Quodam*: 'These same trade unions must eschew any theory and any action that is not in accordance with the teachings and the orders of the Church, or of the competent religious authority.'[60] The church of Quebec changed nothing in this approach, as can be read in the ctcc's constitution: 'The ctcc rejects in principle and in practice the theory of those who claim that capital, capitalists and employers are the born enemies of labour, labourers, and wage earners. It claims, on the contrary, that employers and employees should live in mutual agreement, help and love.'[61] There were three compulsory qualifications for prospective ctcc members: wage earner, Catholic, and Canadian national. For in addition to defining itself as Catholic, this union described itself as possessing a national character:

One of the reasons for its existence is that the majority of Canadian workers are opposed to the domination of Canadian organized labour by American organized labour. The ctcc believes that it is nonsensical, an economic error, a national abdication and a political danger to have unions in Canada that are answerable to a foreign centre which does not have our laws, or our customs, or our attitudes, or the same problems as ourselves.[62]

Quebec workers were supposed to organize, then, in line with the 'genius of their own race,' and not fall prey to the false fraternity offered by the international unions. What these workers should fight against was not the capitalist economic system, but the presence of foreigners, whether labour or capital.

The church's idea of industrial democracy had its origins in the search for industrial peace. This involved rejection of strike action and class conflict as weapons with which the workers could defend their interests. The church opted for capital-labour co-operation, arbitration, and conciliation, and it is noteworthy in this connection that of over five hundred strikes in the province in the years 1915 to 1936, only nine were declared by Catholic unions. Showing the way, the church worked with employers to throw out workers affiliated with internationals at Thetford Mines and Lauzon in order to promote good relations between social classes. Fr Hébert offered this reassurance to employers in 1919 as to the intentions of Catholic unionism: 'The union that is based on the principles of Catholic morality poses no threat, for by its advocacy of conciliation and arbitration as the normal route to the resolution of difficulties and conflicts, it reduces the employer's risk to the minimum and confers on his industry a character of permanence and stability that is a pledge of prosperity.'[63] In this way, the worker would make a reasonable wage and the employer would realize his due profit; the union and employer became partners.

The CTCC also called for a sort of planned economy in which the state would monitor and adjudicate economic returns. The state was seen here as a juridical apparatus for the defence of the interests of all citizens taken separately, in isolation from their class affiliations. Believing in the need for social legislation, the CTCC none the less opposed nationalization. It did not accept the need for an autonomous workers' political organization, and withdrew into a seemingly apolitical stance. In general, what the Catholic organization was calling for was a labour movement that would integrate with the existing economic and political system. Its mission was to stand for the traditional values preached by the French-Canadian élite to those known enemies, industrialization and neutral unions.

The Catholic labour movement, then, was not generated by aware members of the Québécois working class. It was the child of a clerical and intellectual group within the province's petty bourgeoisie, whose ambition was to take over the ideological leadership of the emergent working class. Most of the CTCC's documents were actually written by priests. This tells us why its guiding principle was not defence of, but defence against

– against another form of union organization, the neutral and material-istic internationals. It was silent about the real enemy, the bourgeoisie. Altar-based unionism was designed to expunge all notion of revolution from the worker's mind, and secure his allegiance to the established order. [64] It proclaimed a status quo ideology of the precapitalist variety, that accepted the existence of class distinctions in society while justifying them as 'natural' or 'holy.' Catholic labour ideology, then, had an aim of integration that ignored the chief anomaly, the relations of capital and labour, in the capitalist mode of production. And the church social doctrine that lay behind the movement was a hoax: its picture of the world was the opposite of reality. It presented an upside-down universe as the truth. Here was ideological alienation pushed to the limit.

Conclusion

The articulation of the contradictions in capitalist society was complex in Quebec. Other contradictions were superimposed on the basic capital-labour opposition. These were contradictions between various elements in the social whole, contradictions between the economic and the ideological-political aspects which brought about distortion in the superstructures with respect to the structures. This distortion was a consequence of the colonial situation and the dependent character of Quebec's economy. The ruling Québécois class was involved with a precapitalist social model just when the dominant economic forces, mainly foreign to Quebec, were entering the monopoly phase of capitalism. This distortion of the social structure was made possible by the existence of a double class structure and a double political apparatus.

What gave Quebec society its ideological specificity in the first decades of the twentieth century was the fact that the struggle for the control and direction of economic development did not, as happened in most in-dustrialized countries, feature a capitalist model plus a counterplan of the socialist type, aiming to use the process of industrialization for the bene-fit of the working class. Instead, a process of capitalist industrialization is found in conflict with a dominant ideology that was produced and broadcast by the church and its lay ideologues, who worked from a traditional, agriculture-based social model and rejected, in public if not always in poli-tics, the consequences of capitalist growth. It is this retarded dominant ideology, then, underdeveloped in relation to the structural changes that were then occurring, that is the peculiarity of ideological development in Quebec.

There is another, non-antagonistic, inconsistency to be pointed out between this dominant ideology and the effective role of the state. On the one hand, the state's role was minimized in favour of an all-powerful church. On the other, capital used the state cheerfully to make its job easier and get cheap labour and resources. The absence of an indigenous bourgeoisie worked in favour of the relative autonomy of the state apparatus, and its enlistment by foreign economic interests whose objectives were in contradiction with the ideology supported by the local dominant class. This class subscribed to a precapitalist social model as a means of its own affirmation and defence against the arrival of an industrial society installed by forces from outside Québécois society.

The special ways in which these contraditions were articulated made possible the ascendancy of corporatism and nationalism in this period. The former was promoted by the church as a basis for the direction of organized labour and employer groups. The latter was promoted by the petty bourgeoisie, who by this means polarized the contemporary growth in Québécois self-awareness and the resultant action around the issues of race, religion, and the struggle for survival. The effect of these two ideological orientations, to be developed in the next chapter, was to disguise those class relations which have to do with the basic contradiction between capital and labour, and thus impede the development of class consciousness.

It must be stressed that the anticapitalism that was inherent in corporatism did not attack the capitalist system as such, but rather the fact that it was brought in by forces from outside Québécois society which were inimical to the hegemonic position of the Québécois élite. It was as a form of resistance to American imperialism that anticapitalism had meaning in French Canada. And thus, corporatism fastened itself on nationalism. Together, these two movements called for a lessening of class antagonism between the bourgeoisie and the French-Canadian proletariat, and for a united front against foreign economic interests. These trends would assume their full significance after the Crash of 1929.

7

Petty-bourgeois Economists

1929 – 1945

In these years of trade disintegration and overseas conflict, changes in the internal structure combined with the external economic situation to generate powerful social tensions in Quebec. The chief triggering events were the Crash of 1929, followed by depression and unemployment, and the intensive penetration of United States capital that took advantage of the economic crisis to displace British investment leadership, achieve capital concentration, and propel the province from the manufacturing to the heavy industry stage. Thus, Quebec entered the monopoly phase of capitalism.

The general causes of the worldwide crisis were intense competition, overextended credit, and rampant speculation. In Canada, it meant sagging exports, reduced national revenue, lowered consumption, and inadequate supplies of capital to support the country's rate of growth. The Canadian economy was dependent on a few major exports such as wheat and flour, minerals, and pulp and paper. This made the country extremely vulnerable to cyclical movements in the American and British economies that brought about a falling-off in investment, the loss of manufacturing jobs, and lower prices for exports. In the period from July 1929 to January 1931, the export price index, based on 100 for the year 1926, fell from 101.9 to 52.4. This in turn caused a significant reduction, 12.5 per cent by gross value, in industrial activity. The percentages of union unemployed moved from 7.7 in 1929 to 14 in 1930, 19.3 in 1931, and 26.4 in 1932. Proletarianized for the space of only one generation and still more or less unskilled, the French-Canadian worker was the first to feel the chill of crisis and experience the humiliation of dependence and destitution.

The French Canadians were still the underlings in Quebec's economy.

In every important economic sector, those of British origin were over-represented in terms of their share of the working population. This was particularly the case in commerce and manufacturing. French-speaking Québécois represented the majority in the timber, construction, and mining sectors, but they were excluded from big business. Of 22,108 businesses in the province, 47 per cent were English-speaking, 40 per cent French-speaking, and the remaining 13 per cent undifferentiated between the two principal languages. When we come to the financial power, however, we find the English-speaking enterprises holding 86.6 per cent and the French-speaking, typically small trade and family businesses, only 12 per cent.[1] In banking, the two French-Canadian institutions accounted for only 6 per cent of Canadian bank assets and 7.5 per cent of profits. Compared with the other ethnic groups, then, the French Canadians were coming a poor last as owners of the means of production. Even in the service sector, the British group was overrepresented. In 1931, 43.6 of office workers were British, while French Canadians, with 75 per cent of Quebec's population, supplied only 49 per cent of the white collar group. Among skilled workers, French Canadians were again underrepresented, with 73.1 per cent of the total; they were overrepresented in the forest worker and unskilled labour categories.

In his monograph on Drummondville, Everett Hughes has shown clearly how class distinctions were paralleled by ethnic ones. In a 91 per cent French-speaking town, the biggest textile mill had only one of its 2,300 French-Canadian employees in a job higher than foreman, and he was the company doctor. Hughes had this to say about the social division of labour at the mill: 'French Canadians form a strong majority among the industry's employees overall. They occur in the largest numbers at the worker level; their ranks thin out on the way from the shops to the offices, and disappear altogether as one moves higher up the ladder.'[2] There was also a French-Canadian majority among small tradesmen and in the professions and public services. The English, a very small minority in Drummondville's population, ran the factories and held the jobs requiring advanced technical education, and Hughes added: 'The same applies from one end of the province of Quebec to the other.'[3] Given their precarious economic situation, the French-Canadian workers were the hardest hit by the Depression. The class struggle turned into a French-English battleground.

The economic disaster, and the privations it brought the workers, obliged governments to intervene, resulting in a series of social reforms. The central government handed Canada's provinces and municipalities $20 million to help the unemployed, and the federal old age pension scheme was in effect as well. Help was needed: in 1932, one hundred thousand were on the Montreal relief rolls. In 1930, the Quebec government passed the Unemployment Relief Act, followed the next year by workmen's compensation. In 1931, Quebec also created a department of labour, and set in motion a series of social programmes to ease labour-capital tensions: assistance for the blind and for needy mothers, unemployment insurance, and so on. Organized labour was far from satisfied with these anodynes, however. The year 1937 saw two militant strike actions. In the first of these, against the 'Simard gang' of Sorel, strikers denounced the capitalist system and claimed the right to collective bargain ing. The priest of the parish of St Pierre avowed on this occasion that capitalism was 'irrevocable.' The second of the 1937 strikes affected the textile industry, where workers demanded a collective agreement with better wages and fewer working hours.

Politically, the Depression came as a shot in the arm to the Taschereau government's opponents. In 1934, Paul Gouin founded the Action Libérale Nationale party whose general aim was the economic and social emancipation of the Québécois. Its platform included a revival of agriculture and a labour policy that featured social insurance, the principle of the collective agreement, and a declaration of war on those 'money powers' the trusts. Gouin went on to form an alliance with the conservatives led by Maurice Duplessis, who got into office by exposing the corruption of the Taschereau regime. Among the ample evidence used in the 1936 election campaign was the sale by that government of eight million cords of wood to the big paper companies in the years 1930 to 1935. The price received was $9,876,000. As it happened, the cost of government forest management in the same period was $9,748,000. This meant that the people of Quebec had made only $86,000 out of their forests in 1930–35, or one and one quarter cents per cord. In a more positive vein, the Union Nationale campaigned as the champion of the little people and the unemployed. It would defend small French-Canadian private enterprise against the almighty trusts. This was no more than a smokescreen, for once he was in office, Duplessis ditched Gouin, and in a fit of absence of mind left the province's wealth of natural resources in the hands of the United States corporate giants. He also forgot to nationalize the electric power companies.

Before the election, the province had seen some new political movements and a radicalization of the opposition press. *La Relève* was boosting a personalist, spiritual revolution, while *La Nation* called for separation. Italian-style corporatism was extolled as the socio-economic system that could put paid to anarchy and laissez-faire. A new constellation of newspapers appeared: *La Province, L'Ordre nouveau, Relations, L'Ere nouvelle,* and *L'Unité nationale.* All this social, political, and ideological rustling had helped sweep Duplessis and his Union Nationale into power.

With this as background, let us look at the contemporary trauma that afflicted that key class, the Quebec petty bourgeoisie, and how it responded to the ideological fragmentation of this troubled period. As we have seen, the élite of French Canada felt threatened and alienated by the socio-economic changes that came with monopoly capitalism. Industrialization and urbanization hit hard at the members of this class who lived outside the towns and cities; with the exodus from the countryside, they saw their economic base slide progressively away. The smaller the farm population became, the less business there was for the store-owner, the doctor, and the notary public. At the same time, the owners of small commercial and industrial enterprises in the larger Quebec communities faced possible extinction by the trend to ever greater capital concentrations. The transport concerns, textile and pulp and paper companies, financial houses, tanneries, and shoe factories were passing into foreign ownership. Realizing the weakness of its economic position, the dominant class turned on the Taschereau government that was dancing attendance on the Americans as they took over the Quebec economy.

The French-Canadian industrialists and businessmen lacked adequate weapons to meet this competition from foreign capitalists. The Union Nationale opposition attracted the support of an entire petty bourgeois group anxious about its income and profits: the small grocer who saw the food chains coming, the retailer who lost his trade in alcohol, the small industrialist who was stuck at the cottage stage because he could not win government contracts, and the professional whose career bogged down because he was not a card-carrying Liberal. The main ideological trends in this class were expressive of its confusion in the face of an eco-

nomic situation over which it had no control. The petty bourgeoisie refused to acknowledge industrialization, fought the foreign monopoly takeover, and lined up behind the economic nationalism of the 'buy Quebec'
campaign and the co-operative movement. Their nationalism reflected
the worries of weakness and inability to rise to the challenges of evolving
capitalism. Their ideology was largely one of rejection. Their presence
was felt mainly in politics.

Traditionally hostile to the state, they now wanted the state to move
in and save them from ruin and proletarianization. They expected lucrative contracts from government; they expected the state to mediate
their conflicts with big business and curb the monopolies. Specifically, they
called for the nationalization of the province's hydro-electric system: the
power trust was preventing the growth of small industry. They were
supporters of corporatism as a 'new order,' a third way that ran between
communism and capitalism. Their attacks on foreign big business and
high finance were not intended as challenges to capitalism; their purpose
was simply to save a piece of the pie for the French-Canadian petty
bourgeoisie. Anticommunism was another constant in their ideology; they
praised the fascism of Franco and Mussolini, and welcomed the Padlock
Law of 1937 which, by its ban on communist propaganda, severely limited
freedom of expression.

In the petty bourgeois view of the world, the national interest was their
own class interest. They accused the foreign capitalists of reducing
their nation to slavery. Foreigner and exploiter were synonymous. 'Our
emancipation,' according to their ideology, was to come from the corporatist state: 'As the representative of the collective interest, the state will
be obliged to play an increasingly strong role in the management of
the national economy.'[4] Instead of toadying to foreign monopolies, government would have to support and promote French-Canadian businessmen.
'National salvation' lay in the fostering of a class of French-Canadian
capitalists who would stand up to the outsiders and thus bring about 'our
economic liberation.'

The dominant ideology in French Canada faced two great economic problems: the economic inferiority of the French Canadians themselves,
and the broader crisis in the capitalist economy. To solve the first problem,
they advocated an agriculturalist economic philosophy, improvement of
the educational system with the aim of developing a competent business
élite, and the practical steps of 'buy Quebec' and the co-operative move-

ment. To remove some of the warts from capitalism, they turned to corporatism. This was the period, then, that saw the awakening of French Canada's interest in issues of the economy.[5] The church's social supremacy was no longer an adequate guarantee of national survival. Survival was also dependent upon the emergence of a national bourgeoisie that could control economic development.

The ideologies of the 1930s

With the exceptions of Bourassa and the *Relève* group, the nationalism of the 1920s and 1930s was focused on the state of Quebec. The main concern of the members of Action Française and Action Nationale, of Jeune-Canada and Jeunesses Patriotes, of *La Nation* and the Action Libérale Nationale party, was the provincial autonomy of the French-Canadian state. Nationalists envisaged the creation of a French Catholic country on the banks of the St Lawrence. Some went so far as to call for separation. There must be an end to English-Canadian and foreign domination of French-Canadian society. But how could this happen as long as 'the sons of our race were in bondage to the alien capitalists'? The economic predicament of French Canada was described in these words by Joseph Bruchard:

It will not seem natural to the coming generation, because 'it's always been this way,' that our streets and highways have an English aspect, that big money speaks English and poverty speaks French ... that all the big industries and business houses are English and only the little ships, headed for petty affairs or ruin, are French – or rather, bilingual; that foreigners take the profits and the good jobs from the exploitation of our forests, our mines, our fisheries, our waterfalls, etc, while our people do the dirty work and get paid next to nothing.[6]

This is eloquent of the distress of a petty bourgeois class that felt its future threatened by foreign monopolists and looked to the power of nationalist feeling and the provincial state to displace the alien bourgeoisie. Its goal of hegemony was frustrated by more than structural inadequacies: it was feeling its lack of the economic skills it needed to reach the class objective that it was attempting to portray as the objective of the entire society. The young were encouraged to study economics, finance, business, and administration. It was for the development of this élite that Edouard Montpetit had founded the Ecole des Hautes Etudes Commerciales in 1907.

These petty bourgeois nationalists denounced the economic dictatorship of the monopolies, but refused to accept the existence of class differences. Their target was not the capitalist class and its mode of production, but the other nationality. Monopolies were to be abolished, not in order to put paid to the class that created them and lived off them, but simply to displace that class in favour of an indigenous version of it. What we see in the anti-capitalist campaign of French Canada's petty bourgeoisie is really this élite's frustrated ambition to become a national bourgeoisie, an ambition that was concealed by the substitution of animosity between nationalities for that between classes. The nationalists' main economic argument was that French Canadians should replace foreigners as the masters of trade and industry. Their aim was not to change capitalism, but to switch the capitalists. Their view was consistent, moreover, with the social teachings of the church, which had explained the Depression, in the encyclical *Quadragesimo Anno*, as the result of excessive accumulation by a tiny minority: 'Everything must be done, therefore, to ensure that in future, at least, the share of wealth which is gathered in the hands of the capitalists shall be reduced to a more equitable proportion.'[7] There was nothing wrong with the capitalist system itself; simply, the capitalists had misused it. Indeed, the encyclical had this to say about the basis of the system: 'Theologians have maintained unanimously that men received the right of private property from nature, and hence from the Creator.'[8] The church's message was that capitalism must be humanized by love, Christian charity, and co-operation among the classes of society.

Fear of communism was an added reason for church support of capitalism. During the 1936 Semaines Sociales, Cardinal Villeneuve told an audience that the system must be improved, but that it was not to be confused with people's misuse of it: 'The doctrine of reasonable, generous, just and charitable capitalism is the only thing that can get the world rolling again.'[9] A newspaper like *La Croix* could t   ware of capitalist exploitation in the sense that foreigners were helping themselves to Quebec's natural resources, but that was as far as its editors were prepared to go:

Some time ago, capitalists came from the United States and England to take over areas of our forests, which they quickly turn into pulp that is sent in its raw state to their own countries, where it is finally made into paper. Thus, we are supplying the American and English factories when by wise legislation we could force these capitalists to build their paper mills right here in Canada, providing lucrative employment for our workers.[10]

Private ownership, even foreign private ownership, of the means of production was not the issue. Nor was the exploitation of the work force. Criticism was aimed simply at some of the side effects of these things. The main goal of the anti-trust nationalists was to increase the French-Canadian share of the capitalist pie. Blame was rarely cast on the basis of the system, private ownership. Criticism stopped at the immediate effects of the system.

It was also frequently couched in Manichean language. In looking at the inherent social anarchy of the laissez-faire system that was highlighted by the Depression, nationalist critics generally left worker exploitation alone and concentrated on moral decadence. Captalism was described as inhuman, irresponsible, self-seeking, greedy. It was a breeding ground for materialism and the love of that 'excrement of the Devil,' money. French Canadians were enjoined to arm themselves against the spirit of extravagance and pleasure that was undermining the peace of society. Business was the black magic of the foreigners, whose aim was the destruction of French-Canadian society. As with politics, so it was with economics: the intelligentsia could not see it as an end in itself, for it had to be subordinated to certain higher values. According to Lionel Groulx, a good representative of this school of thought: 'As I said at the beginning, a plan of economic action is intimately connected with problems of a moral nature. Since it is not an end in itself, economic activity cannot absorb all a people's energies, or claim pride of place in their thoughts.'[11] Ultimately, Groulx decided, the economy must be the handmaiden of the faith.

The plan for rehabilitating Quebec society based on corporatism looked like a plausible solution for the bad effects of capitalism. It was the background for short-term efforts to deal with the crisis of the system. The state was asked to end the economic dictatorship of the monopolies and stop immigration. It was also up to the state to support farming, encourage local industry, and develop a policy to regulate hours of work, wages, social insurance, and so on. Some of the theorists of social reform stressed agriculturism, while others put their faith in the co-operative movement as the most likely antidote to capitalism, or called for a 'buy Quebec' policy to support the French-Canadian businessman. The nationalist ideology as expressed in the plan had the dual objective of preserving Quebec's agricultural vocation and of entering the stream of industrialization at the same time. In giving the plan its support, the church was attempting to maintain the ascendancy of religious power in French-Canadian society. The petty bourgeoisie hoped to hold on to its political power: this required state control of economic development, which would have the long-term result of involving the petty bourgeois class in capital accumulation.

In this process, the petty bourgeoisie enlisted the support of various ideological elements, and one that was endemic in their environment, agriculturism, continued to be more influential than the more contemporary corporatism that inspired their dream of the planned economy. The farming vocation of Quebec remained the main feature of French-Canadian economic philosophy. There was really no challenge to this view: the more audacious writers went no farther than to relativize the importance of agriculture and stress the need for parallel growth in industry. The economic nationalism of Asselin, Montpetit, and Esdras Minville include control of natural resources, economic solidarity for French Canadians, accumulation of capital in family businesses and co-operatives, the updating of economics and management education in the province, and support for the farmers. Asselin considered the work of these latter as 'the most vital and essential of all our industries.'[12] It was seen as the basis of French Canada's economy. Industrialization should proceed as a function of agricultural growth:

In the nationalist thinking of the day, it was a waste of time to attack the giant on his own ground: abundant capital resources and the most advanced knowhow in the world. Nationalists would look instead at a way of rebuilding an entire society from its basic elements: agriculture, the trades, small and medium-sized regional industry, and the control of internal buying power by co-operative action.[13]

Finally, there was the realization that economic development should be guided for the benefit of French Canadians, especially the lower middle and middle class, and that industrial overdevelopment, which would result in increased dependence on American and English-Canadian capital, was to be avoided. What was really involved was a plan to take industrialization to the countryside.

With high unemployment and the resulting social tensions, the return to the soil gained impetus. In the decade 1931 to 1941, inhabited farms rose in number by 13.9 per cent. The ideologues argued from this that citydwellers were breaking away from the meretricious charms of the large communities, and realizing the happiness and well-being that were to be had from clearing unfarmable land. In fact, they invited the state to help stem the exodus of rural people discouraged by the poor incomes they derived from working the land, and keep the process of industrialization in check, by giving financial support to land colonization and devising a parallel policy of forest development that would tide farmers over their first few years. These were the aims of the Vautrin plan for the settlement of the Abitibi region, which turned out to be a colossal failure. The lack of realism in the agriculturists' thinking became painfully obvious at the end of the 1930s, when war drew Quebec irrevocably into the industrial age. It was the last gasp for one of the most cherished dreams of the traditional Quebec nationalists.

The shortage of capital and credit sources was a major cause of French-Canadian economic inferiority and the chronic weakness of the petty bourgeoisie, incapable of competing with outside capitalists or effectively countering the trends towards concentration and monopoly. Some theorists looked to the state as an instrument at the service of all Québécois, while others hoped to refloat the petty bourgeoisie economically through appeals to the public to support French-Canadian enterprises. Since hoarding on a family or individual basis was insufficient, it was then a question of creating a genuine economic force by uniting the small savers.

Thus, co-operativism emerged as an attempt to work within the capitalist system for the economic emancipation of the French Canadians, and for the development of a national bourgeoisie. At the outset, however, the Desjardins movement came out of a moral objection to capitalism, according to which the little people had to be protected from unscrupulous moneylenders. The existing economic system offered no credit facilities within the reach of the farmer and the worker, a deficiency that was paralysing agriculture and land colonization and dooming the Québécois to a futureless dependence. Alphonse Desjardins saw his 'caisses populaires,' his people's savings banks, as a bulwark against greed.

It was his intention to do something to counter the economic disarray of the ordinary people of Quebec by encouraging the habit of saving money, getting it out from underneath the mattress and working for the community. The caisses would give the people borrowing power.

Desjardins' movement was deeply influenced by the other elements of the ruling ideology of the day. The co-operative was seen as a peculiarly rural institution, serving farmers and small businessmen. For the farm organizations, the caisses represented a beginning, a point of departure for a continuing, once-for-all return to the land of Quebec, away from the tinsel of the towns. They held out a hope that was not merely material, but, and above all, moral and intellectual. It was declared by Rosario Tremblay: 'Economic life is appropriately seen as a means of reaching a higher goal. It would be wrong and contrary to the Church's social teaching to see it as an end in itself ... Catholic French Canadians will make use of economic forces in accordance with divine and moral law, so that they will always be at the service of human individuals.'[14] The ultimate deciding factor was religion, above politics as well as economics. And from its very beginnings, the co-operative movement was under church guardianship; its leaders deliberately sought the patronage of Leo XIII's social teaching and thus the support of the Quebec clergy by opening their offices right in the church basement. The gesture was eloquent of the movement's scale of values. Within it, savings and credit activities acquired qualities of Christian charity and morality, for unvarnished personal greed was purified, humanized, and ennobled by its new community orientation. Education was a prime element in the co-operative ideology as it tried to adapt capitalist values to the traditional ones of the church. By persuading its membership, and especially the young, to save and sacrifice, by socializing them to the idea of co-operation, the Desjardins and the Tremblays hoped to give concrete expression to Christian morality and the church's social doctrine.

The co-operative movement had national goals as well. It had a mission to accomplish in the economy of French Canada. By making capital available, and by developing an administrative and financial élite, the caisses would promote the survival of nationality; by supplying the French Canadians with a means of emancipation that might one day make them masters of their own economic destiny, the caisses would strengthen their self-confidence. It was a petty-bourgeois economic vision based on the development of small-scale industry and trade linked to the farm, and leaving large-scale production and heavy industry to the foreign capitalists.

At the same time, nationalists in Quebec were seeing the progressive collapse of a system built on the false principles of economic liberalism. They were concerned to stem the spread of communism. They wanted to restore order and balance in the situation. They were looking for a new philosophy. It was in this frame of mind that *L'Action Nationale* conducted its investigation of European corporatism and concluded: 'Corporatism: our hope and salvation.'[15] Its editors painted a picture of failure and chaos: nothing seemed to be working, there was depression and unemployment, and there was an unequal distribution of wealth. The unemployed thousands who thronged the streets were seen as a threat to the established order of things. Quebec's panicked and powerless traditional élite were prepared to pay any price to prevent social change and sidestep the confrontations that marred the European horizon. The main foe for these people was not fascism, but communism. The Francos and the Salazars and the Mussolinis of Europe would have found a welcome in Quebec, especially among the clergy, who were warm in their support of the corporatist philosophy.

'The existence of classes is a natural thing, and so it is absurd to want to abolish them,'[16] wrote Victor Barbeau in *L'Action Nationale*, who followed up this profession of faith with a diatribe against the social injustice that produces disorder and class conflict. Barbeau then turned his guns on the state non-intervention of the liberals, which had backhandedly inspired the idea of strong government of the welfare state or communist type. Thus, he saw liberalism as the way to bolshevism. Both were heresy. A third way had to be found, one that guided the economy without harm to private enterprise, and that would replace the inherent class conflict of capitalism with co-operation among the classes.

In fact, the corporatist credo had been broadcast in French Canada by the papacy, and in particular by the encyclicals *Rerum Novarum* from Leo XIII and *Quadregisimo Anno* from Pius XI. Both popes stressed the legitimacy of the concept of private ownership, and defined the state's role in these general terms:

the state should not only be the guardian of law and order, but also work with energy to the end that, through the system of laws and institutions, the constitution and administration of society cause a natural flourishing of property, public as well as private ... It is the part of governments to protect communities and their members; as regards the protection of individual rights, they should pay special attention to the weak and indigent ... Let states show particular care and concern for the labourers who belong to the poor class.[17]

Societies would protect themselves from violence by basing themselves on professional bodies or guilds and not on classes in unending conflict. Men should not be grouped according to their position in the labour market, but according to the social activity to which they belong.

In Quebec, the Ecole Sociale Populaire drew on this church doctrine to become the main propagandist for corporatism. It looked back to feudalism, when individuals were integrated through their guilds into a well-ordered, organic social whole. This route clearly excluded liberalism and individualism. There were also social thinkers who detected the corporatist ideal in Thomistic philosophy. One of these was Fr Desrosiers:

Men need society, and society needs a leader who inspires in everyone respect for the rights of others. However this leader cannot govern individuals directly. Secular society is not the sum of its individuals, but the synthesis of its various component parts. The liberals' mistake is in having done away with these components of secular society. The liberal economists succeeded in avoiding too much government intervention and caused the abolition of the medieval guilds, thus opening the way for the anarchy of absolute competition in trade and industry – the law of the strongest, the most self-seeking; society's manpower – the entire wage-earning class – was abandoned to the law of supply and demand.[18]

The labour movement and state intervention were the results of all this. They were disastrous for social order, because they increased disorganization without curing the malady.

In society as in the human body each component part has its own functions to fulfil, said the corporatists. The head could not make its influence felt directly, but must work through the guilds. 'In every occupation, as in every family, every community and every locality,' Desrosiers continued, 'there must be an immediate authority, which works under the eye of the supreme authority to pass laws for that occupation and see that these laws are enforced.'[19] In this social model, the key unit is not the individual but the group, family, and guild: 'Starting from this principle of true social philosophy, that men need multiple societies in order to lead satisfactory lives, the church asks now as she has in the past for the founding of professional societies, in other words that all the labourers, workers and bosses in a given occupation be grouped together.'[20] All men have things in common; they are brothers, and should love one another. There could be no irreconcilable differences between workers and bosses. The classes of society must co-operate in a spirit of Christian charity.

Esdras Minville was another who came out in favour of this concept of a new order, with the state as the impartial arbiter watching over the organic interrelation of the various guilds.[21] In his view, the system mitigated the problems of capitalism, in which the organization of production was anarchic and brought about the concentration of wealth. The corporative model provided for class co-operation, profit-sharing by workers, and harmony among people who were producing the same things. This was a promising vehicle for the fight against the materialistic philosophy of communism, unjust in denying the right of private property ownership and harmful because it opposed religion, family, and society. Though the state had a necessary role to play in the corporative system, however, it should not take the place of private enterprise: 'Our corporatism is exclusively a social thing.' The state's main job was to restore order in a society damaged by economic liberalism.

In fact, as Roger Duhamel pointed out with some pleasure, corporatism had actually been useful to capitalism. It had diverted the labour movement from the real contradictions of the system: 'It cannot be denied that corporatism has been the salvation of private property, based on natural law. By consolidating capitalism, it has rescued the idea of profit, the psychological basis of human labour. It has also brought about a renewal of public-spiritedness; social confict has been reduced by the suppression of strikes and lockouts.'[22] Their phobia about materialism led the supporters of corporatism to reject marxism and indeed all socialist reforms. They would spell the end of private property. It was as if the defence of private property had become the badge of antimaterialism.

Corporatism was also promoted as a means of countering the centralizing tendency of the state as well as the decline of rural society dictated by externally managed economic development. In this respect, the new doctrine can be seen partly as the reaction of the petty bourgeoisie to the economic crisis of the 1930s and to federal economic and social policies that blew the old provincial autonomy out of the water. Given the anti-state aspect of the ruling ideology, it was not possible to support stronger government as a solution for the country's economic problems. Corporatism, then, was on the agenda as a temporary remedy. As an ideology, imprecise and utopian as it was, the philosophy had fewer concrete results than in Europe. Its main achievements were to reinforce authoritarian politics, sabotage the work of the unions and the emergence of class awareness, and give some respite to a capitalist system in the midst of crisis. Its natural affinity was with the nationalism of self-preservation, for its guilds offered a unifying bridge between society and nation. By rejecting the labour-capital and class contradictions and proclaiming the homogeneity of the nation, corporatism worked in favour of the small French-Canadian family business whose survival frequently hinged on a low wage bill and inactive trade unions. Its new economic order was also greeted as a means of mobilizing French Canadians against foreign enterprises – unions as well as industries – in the campaign to get control of Quebec's economic development in the hands of the petty bourgeoisie.

We have been considering some contemporary movements, arriving with or in reaction to the crisis of the 1930s, that took very specific forms in Quebec. In a somewhat more general sense, the ripples of European ideologies had their effect in the province. Bolshevism, the rise of Italian fascism and German Nazism, the French Popular Front, and the Spanish Civil War were subjects of debate and helped define, more often than not in right-wing terms, Québécois ideologies. The traditional ideologues were moved to adopt three bogeymen: the Jew, the freemason, and the Bolshevik, joined together in a vast conspiracy to destroy the temporal influence of the church. By presenting these bogeymen as revolutionary agitators and sons of the devil, the clergy tried to implant a fear of all change.

Contrary to what some right-thinking individuals would have us believe, xenophobia is not a cultural atavism with the French Canadians. It is not an inseparable expression of their mentality, and was certainly not present in Patriote relations with the Jews and the Irish before 1840. Xenophobia was an ideological reflex: it has to be seen in its socio-economic context and understood as one of the vicious side effects of colonialism. Antisemitism emerged as a reaction to power and class structures in which French Canadians were dominated. Fearing their own extinction, they sought reassurance, not by going after the real causes of their situation, but by attacking groups that were weaker than themselves. They were compensating for their own feelings of inferiority.

It was a reaction sustained by keenly felt material interests. The Jews were a threat to the economic position of the urban petty bourgeoisie because they made their way up the social ladder in much the same way as the French Canadians, through small trade and the liberal professions. In this sense, antisemitism was taken up by the petty bourgeoisie as a weapon in the economic struggle. Moreover, the arrival of this relatively new community had been swift, along with that of other immigrant groups encouraged by federal policy to aid the industrialization process. Their arrival jeopardized the linguistic balance of the province. The Jewish population rose from 2,703 in 1891 to 60,087 in 1931, most of it concentrated in Montreal. This was a period when French Canada was experiencing externally dictated and wrenching change in its economic structure. Its rural-based social structure could protect it no longer. French Canadians had the uneasy feeling that the world of cities and factories was an alien place. They did not feel at home there. They were afraid, and their fear soon turned to xenophobia.

The Jews were cast as scapegoats for all the misfortunes of French Canada. Antisemitism lent a meretricious logic to the ruling ideology, which was as usual completely out of step with objective reality. *La Croix* harangued its readers:

Rejected by God, this people is the scourge of the human race, Satan's right arm upon Earth ... The Jew is vicious, wily, and scheming ... He is forever a Jew, whether he lives in Germany, England, France, or Canada. He does not assimilate. He does not change ... They overrun everything – finance, trade, the lucrative jobs ... They are getting rich at our expense ... Well, armed with the Cross, we shall try to bar their way. To begin, we are asking our fellow countrymen to have nothing to do with the Jews, not sell to them, not rent them houses, and not buy anything from them. They must be boycotted, forced out.[23]

Religious teaching gave things of this kind credibility by making the Jews responsible for the death of Christ. The nationalists criticized them for not assimilating, but at the same time they had business reasons for not wanting them. In an article, Gratien Gélinas expressed his revulsion at the thought of Jews learning 'the language of Dollard des

Ormeaux' to corrupt the French Canadians.[24] In 1934 *Le Devoir* was critical of the Jews of France for taking French names.[25]

The Jews were blamed for the First World War and then for the Second. They were held responsible for the Russian Revolution, modernism, materialism, liberalism, communism, and the emigration of French Canadians. If we were to believe *L'Action Catholique*, there was 'no race that can more artfully insinuate itself in a people's economy and appropriate a considerable portion of that economy's vitality and wealth.'[26] It was the aim of the Jews to rule the world and destroy Christian society:

What we have against the Jews is not the blood that courses in their veins, not the shape of their noses, [but rather] the violent hatred they tend to have, their profound contempt for everything Christian. The Jews ... as a race, are our born enemies. Their objective is to obliterate the very name of Christian, even if to do so they have to wade through seas of blood.[27]

Jews were permanent conspirators. They were behind most of the revolutionary movements of the world.[28] They were the partners of freemasonry in a programme of universal subversion. Dostaler O'Leary, the leader of the Jeune-Canada separatist group, made the connection between antisemitism and anticommunism perfectly obvious in his definition of communism as 'that monster with an Asiatic face, bred by a disgusting and sickly Jew from the ideas of 1789.'[29] Even a newspaper like *Le Devoir* was found in the antisemitic camp with Georges Pelletier's editorials. In the list of the enemies of French Canada, the Jews came second only to the monopolies. They were gaining in the professions; they were a menace to trade with such dishonest practices as Sunday opening; they were a threat to the Catholic religion; they were anti-nationalist.

I should not paint too black a picture, for this same antisemitism was denounced by such contemporary newspapers as *Le Jour*, *Le Canada*, and *L'Autorité*, as well as the *Relève* group and such public figures as Bourassa, Asselin, and André Laurendeau. Finally, for many, distrust and ostracism of the Jewish community was accompanied by a sneaking admiration for a group that had survived and prospered through solidarity. Except for Adrien Arcand and his National Social Christian party, the antisemitism of French Canada in the 1930s, though admittedly virulent, was non-violent. I must also expose certain myths according to which antisemitism in Canada was a monopoly of the Quebec nationalists, proof positive of the antidemocratic quality of their society. The recent book by Lita-Rose Betcherman has shown that antisemites were even more numerous and well organized in English Canada, and that liberal circles gave them no trouble at all.[30]

The inventory of French Canada's bad dreams must also include the fear of communism that was endemic in the clerical petty-bourgeois élite In their Manichean world view, the church was civilization's champion against socialism and its barbarous, anarchical, inherently destructive system. In a number of signed editorials for *L'Action Catholique*, Bishop Paquet portrayed communism as a philosophy of assassination, terrorism, theft, and pillage, whose objective was nothing less than the destruction of the entire universe:

Every socialist is calling for the removal of the employers, but all lawful authorities are supportive of one another. One could do nothing to damage the rights of the employers without at the same time damaging the rights of all the duly constituted powers: heads of families, leaders of the Church, civil governments, military commanders ... The socialist targets include all institutions and all organizations that have some sort of share in maintaining our political or religious sovereignty.[31]

Msgr Paquet concluded that the only way of blocking the spread of communism was to re-establish society in accordance with Christian principles and on the basis of the union of church and state.

Similar outbursts of hysteria were to be found in most of the nationalist papers and the pamphlets published by the Ecole Sociale Populaire: 'From March 1931 to August 1936,' as André Bélanger has noted of the latter, '25 issues of the 56 devoted to social and economic issues were completely dominated by anticommunism.'[32] According to the *Manuel Antibolchévique*, being a communist meant being against private property, the family, and religion; it was an attempt to smear the CCF among Quebec workers. There was also a psychotic tendency to label as Bolshevik everything that failed to conform to the established order. If anyone dared criticize that order and call for more social justice, he was ostracized. The aim was more to silence opposition than to stop any real marxist group, for the Quebec wing of the Canadian communist party, though it was very active, had only thirty or so French-Canadian members. It was a tactic used regularly by Duplessis to stir up the animosity of the masses towards intellectuals, union leaders, and liberal reformers fighting for social progress and democracy. Every time there was a strike, the spectre of communism was trotted out. Duplessis used his anticommunism as a screen for his alliance with the United States trusts and English-Canadian business circles, whom he supplied with a docile, cheap labour force.

The antisemitism and anticommunism spread by Quebec's clerical, intellectual, and political élites made the province a fertile ground for the fascism of the day. Quebec nationalists were openly impressed by the authoritarian regimes of Europe. Groulx even wrote, in *L'Action Nationale*: 'Happy the peoples that have found their dictators.'[33] In *La Nation*, Paul Bouchard sang the praises of the Italian example and argued for its use in an independent Quebec. The intellectual climate and economic situation bred such fascist groups as the Fédération des Clubs Ouvriers and the Ordre Patriotique des Goglus, and periodicals like *Le Patriote*, *Le Fasciste Canadien*, *Le Miroir*, *Le Chameau*, and *Le Goglu* – the last three published by Arcand with Conservative financing. In 1934, Arcand turned Nazi propagandist and founded his National Social Christian party. Totalling around seven hundred in 1937, its membership rose to some four thousand in 1938–39. It aped its German big brother with the clenched-fist salute, its blue shirts and paramilitary training, venomous anti-Jewish hate literature, and so on. Its crest was a swastika in a wreath of maple leaves. Its targets included free speech, the elective principle, and parliamentary institutions; it reeked of racism, loved violence, and was rabid for the demise of the trade unions. Its extremism lost it potential mass support to the more level-headed, old-style nationalists. With the coming of war, the federal authorities dismantled the organization by locking up its leaders.

War and conscription

Like its ancestor of 1917, the 1942 conscription crisis came as evidence of the problems of federal cohabitation for English and French Canadians. The squabbling of the period lent credibility to autonomist and even separatist options in Quebec.

The series of European shocks that began with Mussolini's invasion of

Ethiopia and culminated with the German occupation of supposedly safe Czechoslovakia had created a war mentality. In the winter of 1937, the Canadian defence budget was raised from an annual $20 million to $34 million. Under nationalist pressure, the King Liberals who had ruled in Ottawa since 1935 asserted that the country would stay out of wars beyond its own borders. After the lightning invasion of Poland, however, when Britain declared war on Germany, Canada meekly and spontaneously followed suit. Political promises were short-lived in the face of the loyalism of the British majority. Having given their game away, the politicians had no choice but to come out selling national unity.

French Canada was in a state of uneasy indecision about the war. Memories were still green of the crisis of 1917. A replay was to be avoided at any price. English-Canadian loyalism, on the other hand, wanted total commitment. Until the entry of the United States two years later, Canada was the only nation in the hemisphere to take part in the European war.

The war brought a federal invasion of provincial jurisdiction. Duplessis launched his own offensive on behalf of provincial autonomy, and called an election. Their aim of centralization brought the federal Liberals out in support of Adélard Godbout, their provincial brother. They secured his victory over the Union Nationale, and Godbout paid the price with docile acceptance of a new tax-sharing agreement that worked for the benefit of the federal authorities. The 'no-conscription' promises of Godbout and Ernest Lapointe were to evaporate in the face of loyalism and the process of federal politics in which the majority always wins.

Up to this point, the federal government had gone along with voluntary enlistment, which was more than adequate to man the war effort. The economic upswing had not yet reabsorbed the armies of unemployed, and for many jobless enlistment came as a solution, grim though it might be, to their material predicament. Having given his sweat, the working man would now contribute his gore.

The King government took advantage of the emotions aroused in French Canada by the fall of France to take its war policy one step farther. The prime minister asked parliament to approve a general mobilization. After some political manoeuvring, Camillien Houde raised his voice for civil disobedience; the Montreal mayor's attack on forced registration and conscription won him four years in a concentration camp. On behalf of the church, Cardinal Villeneuve preached obedience to the law and the civil authorities. He remained faithful to the pro-British tradition of the hierarchy.

Canada's warmongers were still not satisfied with the way mobilization of the country's human and material resources was proceeding. On 22 January 1942, pressured by 'British' feeling and business circles such as the Toronto 200, the government announced a plebiscite in which it would ask the Canadian people to free it from its promises. It was now to be 'conscription if necessary, but not necessarily conscription.' With Maxime Raymond as their spokesman, the Quebec nationalists opposed the very principle of a plebiscite asking the majority to withdraw a promise given to the minority. Their retort to 'conscription if necessary' was 'separation if necessary.' To get their movement going and bring together the little mutinies that were occurring naturally, they organized the League for the Defence of Canada under Georges Pelletier and André Laurendeau. The league argued the right of any free citizen to vote as he pleased, according to his own judgment and conscience, without being accused of cowardice or lack of patriotism. In their 'No' campaign, they borrowed a leaf from Bourassa's book and asked Canadians to put country ahead of race.

Despite their shaky finances and an opposition dirty-tricks campaign, the league managed to galvanize popular feeling with effective propaganda. In the plebiscite, 85 per cent of francophone Quebeckers voted 'No.' It was a confrontation of two solid phalanxes. The French Canadians had expressed their spirit of resistance and lack of confidence in their traditional élites. The Canadian majority, however, voted in favour of conscription for overseas service. The die was cast. Resistance became desertion. Quebec became an occupied country. In September 1942, the anticonscriptionists founded the Bloc Populaire Canadien as a political vehicle for the public support attracted by the league.

What the bloc did was take the reform ideas of its predecessor, the Action Libérale Nationale, and clothe them with the philosophy of personalism. Its aims were to refurbish provincial autonomy and check the economic dictatorship of the trusts. It charged all governments over the years with having stood up for Quebec's autonomy only to turn it into the playground of the trusts, the kingdom of low wages, and the home of the hovel. The bloc platform was a mixture of traditional concerns and plans for modernization.[34] Defining the family as the cornerstone of society, it called for a family assistance programme that would get rid of the hovels and raise wages so that Quebec mothers would not have to leave the home to take factory jobs. While announcing its opposition to state-controlled medicine, it proposed a health insurance scheme. It claimed absolute sovereignty for the provinces in social and labour legislation. It was insistent about the return of provincial taxing powers seized in wartime by Ottawa. In terms of the economy, the bloc supported agriculturist policy and the co-operative movement, which it wanted to extend to housing, construction, food, transportation, and other new sectors. It went on to attack the trusts that monopolized Quebec's natural resources, exploited the consumers, built up disgraceful profits, and speculated in commodities necessary to human life. To stop these abuses, 'The convention is of the opinion that there must be nationalization in the worst cases and either state control or state competition in the others.'[35] The expression 'state of Quebec' was a recurrent one in the party language. In defining the state's role, the bloc 'took the middle way between the capitalist state in bondage to the money trusts and the socialist state in bondage to the bureaucracy.'[36] It described itself as a pro-Canadian party in Ottawa and a pro-French-Canadian party in Quebec City.

Weakened by internal squabbling, its party image too strongly associated with the war and the conscription crisis that brought it into being, the bloc failed to cut into the old loyalties of the Québécois, which swung back to the traditional parties with the return of prosperity. All the excitement, however, had increased autonomist feeling in the province. In the end it was Maurice Duplessis who once more pulled the chestnuts out of the fire.

Conclusion

French Canada's social and political thought may have been conservative and monolithic in this period, but this does not mean that it was static. There was an attempt by the ruling ideology to adapt to the changes occurring in Quebec society, but it was made on the traditional premises. The desire for continuity produced new orientations that were really responses to external pressure. The salient feature of this change in people's thinking was the realization that the church alone could no longer be the bulwark of the French-Canadian nation, and that if they were to survive, French Canadians had to improve their economic situation, with control of Quebec's economic development as their first priority.

The renewal in ideology was circumscribed, however, by the interests of its sponsoring class. By economic emancipation, they did not mean the end of exploitation and a collective takeover of the means of production. They used it in the sense of mobilizing the resources of French Canada, putting the brakes on the power of foreign economic interests, and encouraging the emergence of a national bourgeois class, which would exploit the working class under the national banner. The specific concerns of the working class, the strength of the nation, were ignored. The labour movement was drawn into practices and principles that were alien to its own interests and the very reason for its existence. The national mobilization against the enemy at the gate obscured the reality of internal conflicts.

The central element in this ruling ideology was still the nationalism of survival that kept its vigil over the church, the language, and the established rights of the French Canadians. The new ideological elements were attempting to reinforce the traditional view of Quebec society. For the élite, survival as a collectivity meant, first and foremost, its own survival as a dominant class. To resist the forces of change, it relied on the durable old values of sacrifice, resignation, and obedience to authority. The national ideal came out as an organic society run by the church and the petty bourgeoisie, and founded on the supremacy of the spirit, the primacy of farming and petty production, the permanence of traditions, social peace through class co-operation, family-style social relations, and a general movement of withdrawal that was expressed in rejection and fear – rejection of material wealth, industrialization, and urban growth, and fear of the other, of Englishman and Jew and anything new. The recurrent themes of this ideology were that Heaven was the essential thing, that the people were poor, Catholic, and French; that the English held French Canada in their economic grip, and that they were responsible for the subordinate status and the national collapse of the French Canadians. It was an essentially negative nationalism, looking always backwards. Its sole ambition was to preserve the established order, which meant the preferred position of the clerical and petty bourgeois élite of Quebec.

8

Catching up with the Modern Age
since 1945

With the postwar material environment changing rapidly under external pressures, Quebec maintained its image as a monolithic, tradition-bound, country-based, and clerical society. The class with political and ideological power clung frantically to the values of the past, sadly powerless to see where its real interests lay. Without realizing it, they were preparing their own destruction as a hegemonic group through blind support for their great man's delusions of grandeur. By his archaic laissez-faire economics and his barren autonomism, Maurice Duplessis was delaying the entry of Quebec's state and society into the contemporary age.

Economic crisis and world war had created the conditions for increasing federal interference in areas 'reserved' for provinces. This advance had the constitutional cover of the BNA national interest provision, the federal spending power, and the assignment of residual powers to the central government. The federal old-age pension scheme had begun in 1927; unemployment insurance arrived in 1941, and family allowances in 1944. Meanwhile, Ottawa was monopolizing the country's tax fields. This centralized federalism was supported by the 1940 report of the Rowell-Sirois Commission on Federal-Provincial Relations. The urgencies of wartime, combined in Quebec with Godbout's branch-management regime, abetted the emergence of the federal state apparatus that was required to minimize the inherent contradictions of capitalism and allow that system to survive. With the economy picking up again, Duplessis returned to office in August 1944. He was uncontaminated by the politics of wartime, and he was wearing all the medals from his campaign for provincial autonomy. That Duplessis hobbyhorse would divert French-Canadian attention away from the real issues of social and economic underdevelopment, the result of structural deformities peculiar to dependent societies.

Quebec's economic development in the 1950s was distinguished by a wave of prosperity and the accelerated growth of monopoly capitalism. The average wage index went from 69.3 in 1945 to 127.7 in 1952 and 168.9 in 1959, steadily outdistancing the cost of living. Although Quebec wages were still lower and unemployment levels higher than in the rest of Canada, living standards showed relative improvement over the preceding period: the province was entering the age of the consumer society. These years also saw heavy capital concentrations in the financial and industrial sectors of the economy. John Porter's study has revealed how extreme this trend had become: in 1956, fifty-four large corporations controlled 44 per cent of Canada's economy.[1] American capital was flowing into Quebec's natural resource sector and especially the rich iron-ore reserves of Ungava, which replaced the exhausted deposits of the Americans' own Mesabi Range.[2] In the period 1953 to 1961, the total American investment in Quebec nearly doubled from $2,305 million to $4,320 million, or 74 per cent of direct capital investment. Claude St Onge has described the effects of United States imperialism in these terms:

In 1961, 42 per cent of manufacturing was foreign-owned. Only 15 per cent of the surplus value in the manufacturing sector was generated by French-Canadian businesses. Foreign concerns, chiefly American, were dominant in the key sectors, with 59 per cent of iron and steel, 77 per cent of chemicals and pharmaceuticals, 72 per cent of precision instruments, 65 per cent of machinery, 80 per cent of transportation equipment, and 100 per cent of oil and petroleum. In other industries, foreigners owned 68 per cent of tobacco, 55 per cent of rubber, and 85 per cent of non-ferrous metals. As for the French Canadians, they were to be found in the traditional industries. The only one where they dominated was wood, where they held 84 per cent; they had 49 per cent of the leather business and 39 per cent of furniture.[3]

It is generally estimated that the Québécois share in the ownership of the means of production varied between 10 and 15 per cent.

Shaped by foreign interests in league with the province's willing and corrupt political élites, the Quebec economy displayed certain structural anomalies such as a weakness in the secondary sector that is typical of dependent, export-oriented economies. Quebec specialized in the extraction of raw materials that left the country without processing, and also in the tertiary sector. This was reflected in its relative concentrations of active manpower:[4]

Sector	1941	1961
	percentages	
Primary	26.5	11.4
Secondary	35.0	34.5
Tertiary	38.4	51.1

The rapid manpower decrease in the primary sector was the result of improved productivity accompanied by small increases in demand. Farm labour in these years, for example, dropped from 21.7 per cent to 7.6 per cent of the provincial total. The secondary sector remained stable, although there were some significant shifts within it that were prompted by the flow of United States investment into fast-developing, resource-based industries such as pulp and paper, iron and steel, and aluminum. At the same time, the trend towards heavier capital concentration, combined with foreign competition, meant a manpower loss in such light industries as food and drink, tobacco, rubber, leather, textiles, and clothing. Relative decline in these industries also meant the gradual elimination of French-Canadian capital in manufacturing, trade, and finance. The French Canadians could not ward off the intense competition, aided by the federal government, of the English-Canadian and United States monopolies. They were tolerated as sub-contractors or, at best, second-rate allies.

The relative economic position of the Québécois is documented in the third report of the Royal Commission on Bilingualism and Biculturalism, which shows them as consistently at the bottom of the ladder in terms both of income and occupational status, while the position of the English-speaking minority was even better than in the rest of Canada, with incomes ranging 30 per cent above the national average. Francophone incomes in Quebec averaged 35 per cent lower than those of English speakers. In Canada as a whole, French Canadians were the twelfth ranked wage earners, sliding in just ahead of the Italians and Natives. The commission also confirmed that French Canadians were underrepre-

sented in high-status and lucrative occupations. One third of the management jobs in Quebec manufacturing, rising to 80 per cent in the top
jobs, were held by anglophones, who accounted for seven per cent of the
provincial work force. French Canadians, on the other hand, held only
17 per cent of the administrative jobs in Montreal. Three quarters of the
administrative positions paying over $15,000 a year were occupied by
English speakers. The commission report went on to note that foreign-
owned and English-Canadian businesses were, respectively, seven and
four times greater in numbers than those owned by French Canadians,
which in any case were usually small ones. Only 26 of the 165 Quebec
concerns with annual turnovers in excess of $10 million were owned by
French Canadians. Moreover:

Taking manufacturing as a whole, the average worker in a foreign-owned
establishment generated $12,000, while in an English-Canadian establishment the
figure was $8,400, and in one owned by French Canadians, $6,500. As far as
markets were concerned, French-Canadian enterprises tended to cater to local
clienteles. Their contribution to the province's 1961 export total was only 4.5
per cent, while foreign-owned businesses accounted for some 51.5 per cent.[5]

The commission study pointed out that a French Canadian's prospects of
finding a good job, particularly in the professional-financial category,
were actually relatively worse in 1961 than they had been in 1930.[6] Here
was evidence of the progressive proletarianization of Quebec's petty
bourgeoisie. French Canadians, then, had made their way up into the
modern, industrial sectors of the postwar economy, but this advance
had not given them the keys to the executive suite. Nor had the modernization of Quebec's economy done much to offset the economic disparity with Ontario and the rest of the country. Since 1926, per capita income
in Quebec had been stuck at 73 per cent of that of Ontario, where industry was more productive and highly developed and wages corres-
pondingly better.

   And so we really cannot talk at this point about Quebec's catching
up. All it had managed to do was maintain a steady state of inferiority. It
showed the classic signs of a dependent, dominated society: the rule
of foreign-owned monopolies, the export of raw materials against the
import of finished products and capital, and lack of diversification in its
external exchanges, which were still chiefly with the United States. How-

ever, Quebec was also part of an advanced capitalist society, and this fact made it special in relation to the countries of the Third World: there was a high degree of concentration, especially in banking, and capitalism had almost entirely eliminated the precapitalist modes of production. We may note one more peculiarity: Quebec was a society with an incomplete state apparatus, too weak in fiscal and monetary terms to have much influence on trends in jobs and investment.

Quebec's class structure in this new era of monopoly capitalism, then, was dominated by American imperialism and its local ally, the English-Canadian bourgeoisie, which was solidly entrenched in the banking system and could use the federal state to promote its common interests with the American companies. A certain French-Canadian element had attached itself to this external ruling class, but it did not amount to a class on its own, or even an autonomous subgroup. By Porter's reckoning, these French Canadians represented 6.7 per cent of the country's economic élite, or only fifty-one individuals.[7] Strictly speaking, therefore, there was no national bourgeoisie in French Quebec. This does not mean, however, with all due respect to the writers who have worked from a dichotomy of bourgeois nation and proletarian nation, that there was no ruling class. The petty bourgeoisie occupied this position, functioning mainly as a political sidekick for American and English-Canadian business interests.

The changing power relations between segments of this petty-bourgeois class reflected the political background of the period and the ideological changes that were on their way. Generally speaking, its members were professionals, farmers, and small commercial and industrial entrepreneurs trying to withstand the social consequences of the trend towards capital concentration and monopoly. The supporters of the Union Nationale, in office during the 1940s and 1950s, were drawn mainly from the rural wing of this class. The Duplessis party was able to maintain a façade of autonomy by the judicious use of patronage, corruption, and the rhetoric of nationalism. The proletarianization of this local élite was therefore delayed. Government contracts and government patronage gave them something to fight with in the unequal contest with the monopolies, backed by the federal state and also, paradoxically enough, by the Union Nationale itself, which supported the interests of the United States against the English Canadians. Gradually, however, the rural group lost its political and ideological hegemony to the urban petty bourgeoisie, made up largely of technocrats and members of the liberal professions who wanted to sell their services to government as a means of avoiding proletarianization and the kinds of career disappointments they encountered in the private sector. They rose to power with the support of elements of the industrial bourgeoisie who had something to gain from the existence of a stronger state apparatus in Quebec. With the coming of the Quiet Revolution, government moved to correct the scarcity of Québécois where economic decisions were made. Making itself a factor in economic growth, the provincial government made it easier for French speakers to enter the economic élite.

In fact this transfer of hegemony, confirmed politically by the Quiet Revolution, was a result of pressure from new elements in Quebec society. Changes in the economic structure had produced a more highly skilled working class. Its members were still overexploited, but modernization of Quebec's economic infrastructure, combined with pressure from organized labour, was raising their standard of living, admitting them to the consumer society of more cars, more televisions, and more single family houses. These changes in material existence produced changes in attitudes: awareness of lagging status and hopes for upward mobility. Ideological change in postwar Quebec society came out of this change in the social structure.

The ideology of Maurice Duplessis

Maurice Duplessis played an exceptional role in Quebec's modern history. His supporters have hailed him as the saviour of his race; his enemies blame him for the obscurantism of the province's mentality in his time, the underdevelopment of Quebec society. For my purposes, he was also the most faithful of messengers for the ruling ideology.[8] He can be said to have been supremely typical of the traditional, rural Quebec. He exemplified the fear of industrialization, urbanization, and all other social change that was the hallmark of the traditional élite, who are at once accomplices and victims in the giveaway of the province's natural wealth.

He appointed himself the champion of provincial autonomy. It was a cult that coloured every aspect of his thinking. And when he came to define the nationality he defended, spiritual and religious values came first: 'The province's strength lies in the depth of its religious feeling ... [It] must be the citadel of Christian civilization in Canada and even the entire North American continent.'[9] His was the triad of language, customs, and faith of the traditional nationalist school: 'Our religious and national traditions are essential. May our acts be inspired by these, for they are the best possible promise of our national growth and survival.'[10]

At the same time, Duplessis' devotion to order made him a supporter of federalism and the constitution: 'No true stability could be founded on the ruin of Confederation ... Only federalism can ensure national harmony and make Canada a nation that is strong and great.'[11] It was not the BNA Act that caused all the problems, but the centralizers in Ottawa who did not obey it: 'I want things to happen according to the constitution, but the [1946] intergovernmental conference has demonstrated Ottawa's bad faith. They want to centralize everything: taxation, pensions, health insurance, even education ... The centralizers and assimilators desire only one parliament, one language and one religion. They want to eliminate our attitudes and our traditions.'[12] He was a believer in the theory of the federal pact between two nations, and indeed argued his defence of provincial autonomy on the basis of the spirit of the Fathers of Confederation: 'Autonomy is the safeguard of provincial freedoms and prerogatives; it is the right to be masters in our own house, the right to make laws as we choose and the power to enforce them ... it means respect for the rights we have won and the constitution confirms.'[13] Ultimately, in Duplessis' eyes, autonomy was the right to maintain the existing social order in Quebec, a base from which to fight change and preserve the role of the religious orders in health care and education. As it happened, his attacks on federal social programmes were helpful to the American monopolists, whom they exempted from any social costs for their already cheap Quebec manpower. Though the premier fought the federal taxing power and federal interference in social legislation, this does not mean that he wanted the tax fields back for the purpose of developing the province's own social services. According to his 'philosophy,' governments should leave these to charity and private enterprise.

Autonomy, then, meant preservation and not innovation. In 1953, to arm himself against Ottawa's ideology of centralism, he set up the Tremblay Commission with the task of canvassing the constitutional issues and writing the book for Quebec's defiant stand on federal-provincial agreements. And he galvanized public opinion around the taxing feud. He refused to renew the fiscal agreements under which Ottawa had been collecting all direct taxes since 1942, on the grounds that these agreements were contrary to the BNA Act: 'For provinces to become the puppets of a power they themselves brought into being would be against the spirit and the letter of Confederation ... The responsible government does not exist that merely administers revenue from taxes imposed and collected by another government.'[14] In 1954 he brought in a provincial income levy and blamed Ottawa for the monster of double taxation.

In reality, his autonomist campaign was a defence of the status quo at a time when the federal state wanted to 'perfect' Confederation by installing the conveniences of centralization. Duplessis was never a separatist. And there were pragmatic, electorally advantageous reasons for his stand: by playing on Quebec nationalist feelings against Ottawa centralizers who also happened to be Liberals, he could discredit the opposition Liberals in his own province, who had been so generous with its sovereign rights in wartime. He did not imagine that Quebec could assume control of its own economic, political, and cultural life. He used the term 'province,' never 'state.' Beyond the practicalities of political life, his autonomist policy came out of his social conservatism and his own negative, defensive attitude in the face of current issues and conditions.

The same conservatism and the same constituency that had spawned Duplessis' drive for provincial autonomy were behind the recurrent theme of respect for law, order, and established authority that was the most prominent one in his thinking. 'The problem is not to reform order, but to re-establish it,' he told the readers of *Le Devoir* in 1949: 'The inventions of modern times have not altered a single great principle. The sun still rises in the east; tradition and morality remain the same.'[15] His notion of political power was almost medieval, and he never missed a chance to remind the people of Quebec of their duty to keep faith with the traditions of hard work and obedience to authority:

We are at a turning point in our history and must confront problems on the industrial and religious fronts. There are those who would destroy religion by attacks on lawfully constituted authority. Both authorities, civil and religious, must receive equal respect, because both come from God ... There can be no new order. The new order is an illusion. The eternal truths are changeless. Do not let yourselves fall prey to this tuberculosis and cancer of the mind ... This province needs economic, social and national stability.[16]

Added to the religious and moral reasons for the poverty and submissiveness of the French Canadians, Duplessis had another: only by so doing could they and their province attract foreign investors.

Obviously, the new theories had to be scotched. In Duplessis' rhetoric, socialism and communism received the same treatment as atheism, anticlericalism, and federal centrism. As Desrosiers has observed:

Duplessis' anticommunism came from his concepts of order and authority. In a static world, social stuctures are unchangeable, and everyone has to accept the lot dealt him by Providence. Happiness is conferred by respect for order; prosperity comes through social status. Evoking the Red menace was a means of hitting at all ideas of change and nipping all seditious movements in the bud.[17]

He was getting at the intellectuals and union leaders who called for social reform. Even *Le Devoir* earned the 'Bolshevik' label from 'the Chief.'[18] Yet the premier rejected the new statism as well; state intervention must be minimal. As Desrosiers put it: 'State paternalism produces idleness, destroys the individual initiative that is the only source of progress, and leads to disorder in society by arousing unrealistic expectations. The unique role of the state was to put an end to social evils and watch over public order and social peace.'[19] Providence and individual initiative were the two main regulators of society, Duplessis announced: ' "God helps those who help themselves." When each has done his duty, the rights of all are completely secure. It is obvious that state paternalism paralyses, invariably and inevitably, all productive and necessary initiative, and leads ultimately to the downfall of individuals and peoples.'[20] State paternalism was ruinous as well as ineffective, for it always resulted in higher taxes. Duplessis, then, did not see the state as an agent of economic growth; it was there to preserve the existing social order.

The same general ideas made him an unqualified supporter of private enterprise, the fount of all prosperity: 'Here is the perfect system: the system of logic, justice, progress, prosperity, the system that generates good administration, healthy initiative, and humanitarian achievements ... the only system consistent with human dignity, profound truth, and lasting progress.'[21] The millions of dollars Quebec needed to meet the needs of its population came from private enterprise. In his mind, it was the capitalists who kept the workers alive. If he had an organized economic policy, it was to leave everything to private enterprise, the only hope for Quebec's industrial development. It was clearly out of the question for the state to assume an active role in the economy. The premier's approach was epitomized in the 1948 speech from the throne: 'It is our opinion that state paternalism is the enemy of true progress. We believe that the province of Quebec will be developed more rationally and more rapidly by well-integrated, that is to say healthy and just-minded, private enterprise.'[22] The role of government was not to control the economy, but to support and co-operate with private enterprise. Duplessis continued the old Taschereau policy of handing off Quebec's natural resources to American big business in the form of 'industrial fiefs' within which the companies had total sovereignty. In fact, this extreme laissez-faire involved Duplessis and the Union Nationale in a paradox that has been pointed out by Herbert Quinn: while the premier proclaimed his Catholicism and the special connections between his government and the church, he seems to have escaped being influenced by the proposals for the reform of capitalism in the papal encyclicals. He quickly forgot their criticisms of economic liberalism, retaining only the barbs aimed at the socialists.[23]

Laws passed by the Union Nationale government were essentially for the benefit of capitalists and farmers. The latter were given special attention. Duplessis was a great supporter of the return to the land, and regarded agriculture as basic to the survival of nationality. Here, he was squarely in the agriculturist tradition: 'Agriculture is truly the fulcrum Archimedes sought to move the Earth. Agriculture is the basic industry; it is the cornerstone of progress, stability and security. The strong peoples are those who assign a prominent role to agriculture.'[24] Such raptures about the countryside did the party no damage at the polls. The basic Union Nationale support came from rural districts, which were overrepresented in the legislature because of an elderly, unreformed electoral map. The Duplessis government's biggest achievements for these areas were rural electrification and farm credit.

The premier was also interested in developing Quebe's natural resources. In his view, however, the only way this could be done was through concessions to American investors. It was his open-door policy: 'We have the resources, you have the money ... Let's work together.'[25] These magnanimous Americans wanted to help Quebec do the job, and in addition, they even brought the province millions of dollars in taxes (without counting what went straight into the Union Nationale war chest) and employment for its people. The state had no need of a dynamic resource-development policy; all it had to do was let things be, maintain peace and order, and this wonderful uncontrolled process would go on and on.

In line with this philosophy, Duplessis granted vast concessions on Crown lands, rich in timber, minerals, and waterpower, at ridiculously low prices. Iron Ore of Canada paid one cent per ton on its shipments from northern Quebec; next door, Newfoundland was insisting on 35 cents a ton. Quebec's mining royalties were kept at minimal levels, and foreign companies received tax exemptions. The premier even opposed a proposal for a steel mill because it would compete with American interests with, in his words, 'enormous plants in the United States which cost them millions.' In terms of the international division of labour, Duplessis saw Quebec as a pool of cheap manpower for the foreigners, with natural resources as the bonus. He rejected the possibility of resource development run by and centred in Quebec. His approach to economic reality was simplistic, demagogic, uncomprehending of the complex industrial world in its monopoly phase, and still seeking salvation through agriculture. This was the attitude of a colonized man.

In Duplessis' reactions to social issues, we always find the same concerns for order, security, and the will of God. It was absurd for workers to want reduced hours and higher wages to boot: 'Labour's first law comes from on high, and the sentence delivered to the first man still holds: "Thou shalt live by the sweat of thy brow".'[26] In this, he was faithful to the church's social doctrine. Labour relations were a variant of Christian charity: there must be understanding – 'capital and labour must shake hands'[27] – and co-operation. He supported unions that had 'honest leadership' and were 'respectful of the law.' They also had to be 'purged of their communist elements.' Workers had to lodge their grievances in an orderly and courteous manner. Industrial action must be used only as a last resort, for strikes were 'harmful to the public interest,' as well as being 'one of the causes of unemployment.' His attitude to organized labour emerged clearly in this statement from the days of the asbestos strike: 'The present strike is basically unlawful because the strike leaders have refused arbitration ... Contempt for the law produces anarchy and disorder. Contempt for the laws of society engenders contempt for all other laws ... If the laws are violated with impunity, it is a disaster from the points of view of the worker, the economy, and the nation.'[28] Basically, Duplessis saw no real value in the labour movement or the right to strike. For him, the role of the unions was a negative one, the prevention of vicious employer practices. If they actually tried to better the workers' lot, they were meddling with the dispositions of divine Providence. Accordingly, the premier asked employers to take moderate profits, and workers to make moderate wage demands. There were no social problems, really, just a handful of communist agitators out to wreck the country. Fatherly understanding and good relations between capital and labour were necessary for progress; industrial peace was the precondition for the prosperity of Quebec.

Duplessis used every means to oppose the irruption of labour activism caused when the Catholic unions went radical. Bills 19 and 20 gave the government the power to change collective agreements, including wage settlements, that had been freely concluded between employers and unions. To keep wages as low as possible, Duplessis arrogated to himself the power to set wage scales in any region or sector of industry. In 1949, his government's Bill 5 contained a provision for the decertification of any union tolerating the presence of communists or communist sympathizers in its midst. What this meant, in fact, was any unionist who was critical of the government. And as if this legislative repression were not enough, the state had to use police repression to protect employers. The provincial police were sent to break strikes at Asbestos in 1949, Louiseville in 1952, and Murdochville in 1956. It was an employer's government whenever it came to union confrontation.

The same conservative beliefs dictated Duplessis' position on welfare and social security. In his canny mind, 'There can be no social security without stability, and there can be no stability if a man's neighbour is asked to pay the whole time and gets nothing in return.'[29] The role of the state in health care must stop with the construction of hospitals and sanatoria, for hospitals were themselves a form of health insurance, and anyway: 'The best kind of insurance is health itself.'[30] Besides, Quebec's hospital system, like its school system, was the best in the world: it was run by the church.

'The Chief' used personal responsibility as his main argument for opposing state involvement in social matters: 'For a genuine social policy, one that does not appeal to the baser instincts, the people must first help themselves.'[31] He was against universal health insurance on the grounds that individuals should be left to solve their own problems, and that in any case such programmes should be carried out in the private sector. When he rejected the proposed federal health insurance scheme in the name of provincial autonomy and the age-old traditions of French Canada, he was in fact condoning the exploitation of illness by the insurance companies. The same reliance on individual responsibility surfaced when Duplessis considered education. The system was not in need of reform, for it was 'as good if not better than in the rest of the country.'[32] Besides, the rights of parents were inalienable; it was their duty to pay for the education of their children. The idea of government grants at the secondary level was unthinkable.

Education, in the premier's view, should aim at helping to maintain order in society. Schools were ideological broadcasters of the dominant social values. They must train young people to accept the existing socio–political order. He wrote in *Le Devoir* in 1948: 'I consider respect for the law and authority to be one of the basic qualities of a good teacher. We will see to it that salaries and pensions are paid only to good teachers. Teachers do not have the right to strike, either by human or by natural law.'[33] Though according to his theory the state should leave schooling to the clergy and stay right out of it, Duplessis did make an exception. He reserved the right to purge Quebec universities of undesirables who were critical of his government, and he was prepared to influence post-secondary education from a political viewpoint. He was also convinced that good politics in teaching were not enough: 'No school system can be good without religion,' and 'A school without God would be like a world without sunlight, a body without a soul, or an eagle without wings. Let us be thankful that our teaching is still carried out on a religious basis in this province. The school is a citadel reminding us of the primacy of things spiritual in a world that inclines us to forget.'[34] His autonomist game was also played in the exclusively provincial field of education, where he angrily refused federal attempts to put funds into the universities. It was a gesture that seriously hampered the growth and modernization of these institutions. Apart from his constitutional fundamentalism, Duplessis had no positive suggestion to make about doing something to correct the underdevelopment of the province's educational system. The government had done its work when the schools were built, the school board deficits covered, and bursaries dealt out to the brighter students. There was no overall policy aiming to bring Quebec education into line with the needs of an industrial society.

Authoritarian, dogmatic, and simplistic in its expression, the ideology of Maurice Duplessis can be summed up under a few rubrics. First and foremost, there were the changeless, eternal goods of stability and order, established for the province by the same Providence that assigned everyone a place in society. From that point on, there was no interfering with the social hierarchy: there were no labour problems, no social problems, and in fact, as far as a Duplessis state was concerned, no problems. Individuals and private institutions were supposed to solve them.

Cracks in the monolith

Still under the sway of the traditional ideology, postwar Quebec was none the less a field for forces that cracked the old monolith and produced an ideological pluralism that bore fruit in the Quiet Revolution. The vehicles for this impetus to modernize were three movements that stood in opposition to the Union Nationale. The radical nationalist group of Action Libérale Nationale, the Bloc Populaire, and the paper *Action nationale*, while they generally supported the government's autonomist policy, attacked its conservative economics. Among other papers, *Le Devoir* went after the Union Nationale for election fraud, the pork-barrelling of public money, and shocking parliamentary procedure. Growing radical, the unions came out against the social legislation and labour policy of the Union Nationale. Even some elements of the church began withdrawing support, the two main examples being *Relation* magazine and Fr Lévesque's social science faculty at Laval. Drawing on the new Catholic social thinking of postwar Europe, these clerical opponents called for the democratization of Quebec institutions and a social policy that could better accommodate the desires of the working class. The attitude of Msgr Charbonneau and the junior clergy at the time of the asbestos strike expressed this fresh mood among churchmen.

With the onset of war, the complete disparity between their view of the world and what was really going on forced the Québécois élite to ask some questions, and make some comparisons with the ways other societies were run. Later on, television boosted awareness by providing a wider range of cultural reference. Quebec's old social concept was revealed as hopelessly out of date in a world where industrialization and advancing technology would not go away, and in a province that had to deal with a booming economy and an authentic, increasingly aware proletariat. The modernization of Quebec was taken up as the cause of a whole generation, which looked for guidance to the experiences of other countries. They wanted to make up for lost time, bring in true liberal democracy, and adjust the province's superstructures to the realities of the industrial age. Their first steps were unsteady and often hard to understand: there was general agreement on what they did not want, but not always on what they did want. Yet there were clear indications that the ruling class was beginning to break apart, and a process of ideological diversification was at work. The old ruling ideology of self-preservation was losing credibility all over the province, and it was under heavy attack by a minority of intellectuals, unionists, journalists, artists, and students. Ideology was in crisis in Quebec.

The cracks in the ideological monolith began to show at the end of the 1940s. The year 1948 was an important one in the thawing of Quebec, for it saw the publication of the *Refus global*, a cry of defiance from a group of poets and artists who wanted to throw off the constraints of their claustrophobic society. It was a ringing affirmation of the rights to dissent, create, be original, and a blanket rejection of the old traditions and the old conservatism. This challenge from the intellectuals was soon carried into a broader social and economic arena by the asbestos strike of 1949. The spectacular fight put up by an increasingly radical labour movement attracted the first left-wing coalition in the province's history. It was a turning point.

During the Second World War, Catholic union membership had actually declined. In 1935, the movement sponsored by the church had accounted for 74 per cent of all unionized labour; by 1943, this percentage had dropped to 28.[35] It must be pointed out that the decline was general, affecting the neutral unions as well; in wartime, it was virtually impossible to do any organizing. The result for the CTCC was a shift to the left and a new ideological position. Besides the membership problem, three factors were at work: the increasing role of big corporations in the economic structure, the new drift in social thinking that began with the rejection of now-tainted corporatism, and finally, the influence of new leadership, as Gérard Picard moved in as president of the confederation and Jean Marchand as general secretary. Moreover, wartime production pressures and manpower shortages had given unions greater bargaining power, better odds for putting their economic and professional programmes into effect. Quebec labour sought to free itself from the church, the politicians, and the employers. It became more militant and aggressive.

The CTCC still remained loyal to the autonomist, nationalist ideology, and continued to look to *Quadragesimo Anno* for its humanitarian and spiritual attitudes: the rejection of communism, a critical attitude towards capitalism, and the aims of joint management and profit-sharing for workers. Gradually, however, the moral and general values that came from the church were pushed aside by the desire to improve the economic status of the working class. The asbestos strike disenchanted not a few Catholic unionists, and killed any spirit of employer-employee togetherness. The employer was no longer a father; he was an adversary, a factory dictator who exploited the workers. The CTCC also came out openly against the collusion between employers and the Quebec government. It launched its first timid programme of worker education, and began dissolving the religious connection. Louis-Marie Tremblay has summed up the changes in Catholic labour during the 1950s:

The CTCC defined itself as a union movement first and a social and national movement second. Economic and labour concerns were put ahead of social and cultural ones. The employers, and not industrialization itself, were identified as the main adversaries ...The CTCC stopped being an altar boy and turned decisively to aggressive unionism to protect and promote the workers' interests.[36]

Throughout this period, organized labour was the main opponent of the Duplessis government. Its most advanced element in this sense was the Fédération des Unions Industrielles du Québec. It was affiliated with the CIO, which encouraged militancy, with direct political involvement and an active recruitment programme. Picking out the Union National as an enemy, the FUIQ attacked it as backward, antidemocratic, and anti-labour. It supported the CCF as the political arm of organized labour. With the amalgamation of the AFL and CIO internationally, the FUIQ found itself in bed with the Fédération Provinciale des Travailleurs du Québec, a trade union group whose policy towards Duplessis was one of co-operativeness. The 1957 appearance of the combined FTQ meant that long-term ideological commitments were shelved along with the idea of union solidarity exemplified by the CTCC-FUIQ alliances in the Asbestos, Louiseville, and Murdochville strikes and the passage of Bills 19 and 20. The internationals were turning back to the American union speculator model and, for a time at least, abandoning their radical thinking and political activism.

The ideology of *Cité Libre*

The magazine was a vehicle for intellectual comment as cracks widened in the ideological monolith and the movement of modernization began to take shape. The break with the ruling ideology was not complete, however; there was a certain thematic continuity between the progressivism of these postwar thinkers and the old beleaguered ideology. Religion was one thing they had in common. In fact, the *Cité Libre* group announced it as one of their basic values: 'These pages have consistently aired concerns about religion or culture that are more keenly felt than those about politics.'[37]

This devout atmosphere can be accounted for by the fact that most of the group had come out of Catholic action movements. For them, there could be no challenging the church's authority in spiritual life, or in composite issues where the interests of the immortal soul were involved. However, the magazine was willing to criticize certain aspects of French-Canadian Catholicism: it carried attacks on clericalism, although protesting tht its aims were constructive, and on the traditional relations of spiritual and temporal power in Quebec. And although it proclaimed its submission in matters of dogma and morality, it tried to make an intelligent contribution to the Catholic renewal. *Cité Libre* joined issue with dogmatism, intolerance, and the big stick of 'Believe, or die.' It was critical of Catholicism for having degenerated into a practice of blind obedience, and for being divorced from the daily existence of the faithful. Observance had become a bloodless routine; it had to be modernized, cleansed of its morbidness and social conservatism. The hereafter was not the only issue any more.

The church, said *Cité Libre*, should not be immune from questioning. Lay people must be brought fully into its life, and to do this the church would have to ban its own intolerance, open all subjects up for free discussion. The magazine called for secularization in the sense of renewing the lay role in religion. It was referring, not to the secular state, but to a kind of religious pluralism. The state itself had the task of protecting the freedom of all religions; its laws must not discriminate against non-Catholics. *Cité Libre* opposed the temporal power of the church: politically, its influence worked against democracy and individual freedom. The magazine's goals were to enthrone the principles of individual freedom and worth, put a stop to intolerance, and promote pluralism in religion.

It was this theme of liberty that permeated the publication and bound together the other elements of its ideology. And it was from the viewpoint of individual freedom that the magazine looked critically at the ruling ideology. The trouble with the Duplessis regime and French-Canadian society in general was that they were authoritarian, conformist, dogmatic, conservative, and demanded uncritical obedience. *Cité Libre* sailed into the whole system of petty élites, institutions, structures, and dehumanizing, set patterns of behaviour that stifled individual existence in the province. In the contemporary personalist philosophy of Edouard Mounier and the publication *Esprit*, the magazine's editors found inspiration for their insistence on the freedom of the individual, personal autonomy in the social environment. And for this to come to pass, freedom must enter the city: Quebec had to be brought into line with the modern liberal democracies. 'First, democracy,' was the watchword of the magazine, and its priority was to revitalize political democracy in Quebec, and enforce the basic freedoms. This was the route that must be taken, for the French Canadians were antidemocratic. They were anti-democratic because they had skipped a stage in their development; they had come to democracy in its established form wihout first experiencing democracy in its striving, incomplete form. Pierrre-Elliott Trudeau argued for this analysis:

The French Canadians' lack of civic and electoral morality, their authoritarian tendencies, the antidemocratic opinions they absorb in school, the juvenile settings of their university debates, the petty role accorded them as laymen in the Quebec church, their narrow societies in the countryside, their unimportant jobs in the authoritarian structures of capitalism, their fear of turning to the state, even though only the state possesses the means by which they can get out of their stagnation, their relative indifference to attacks on freedom of speech, of the press, of association – all these are.the characteristics of a people that has not yet learned how to govern itself, a people among whom democracy cannot be taken for granted.[38]

Clearly, the most urgent item of business for the progressive movement in Quebec was to get a democracy set up. It was to be set up within the Canadian federation, for left to themselves, these atavistic French Canadians could not function democratically. *Cité Libre*'s federalist analysis lacked a historical and dialectical perspective; its members disregarded the fact of colonial domination, and themselves displayed the mentality of colonized men, who accept the value assigned them by their oppressors.

To sum up, the prime objective of the *Cité Libre* group was to mend the holes in existing parliamentary democracy, so that citizens would enjoy truly effective participation in the state, with political decisions accurately translating the popular will. Formal parliamentary democracy was not a bad thing in itself, but its machinery needed to be modernized and political practice made healthy. And in the process, the Québécois had to change their attitudes and receive a political education. Social democracy would thus be an extension of political democracy.

Quebec's ruling ideology had always been mistrustful of the role of the state in society. To preserve the social hegemony of the church, the traditional élites tried to cut back government activity as much as possible. They saw its basic job as maintaining order and handing out honours and favours. The *Cité Libre* group rejected this idea. Their revitalization of the democratic process was to be followed by a revitalization of the role of the state. They took a neo-liberal view of state intervention. The state should protect its citizens not only by the administration of justice, but also socially and economically, so that they could enjoy the benefits of prosperity and technological progress. The state, therefore, did have a social role – to offset social inequalities by welfare and social security programmes, and to take charge of health and education services since by its very nature, private enterprise could not deliver these effectively and equally to all citizens.

Unconsciously influenced by monopoly capitalism, the *Cité Libre* group also called for state intervention in the economy. It must clearly not displace private enterprise from every sector, for 'capitalism is not all bad.' Intervention should occur where private enterprise has proven its incompetence. In general, the state should play a supporting role, orchestrating harmonious development in the economy: 'Between the minimal activity of the liberal state and the massive appetite of the totalitarian state, *Cité Libre* offers the vigilant state, quick to intervene when chaos poses any threat to individual freedom.'[39] With this in view, the state mechanisms for economic prediction had to be brought up to date and it should devise policies to regulate the economy. Without imposing total planned control, the vigilant, regulatory state would pay the social costs of capitalist development, working to reduce the contradictions of the system by reducing the disparities between individuals and groups. The kind of planning *Cité Libre* supported was indicative planning: planning in social policy, in the various departments, and in the activity of the provincial as well as of the federal state. Through its overall policy for growth, and its regulation of purchasing and investment, the state would establish priorities for social and economic development.

Nevertheless, this greening of the state of Quebec was to occur within the federal system. This meant that its activity would be subject to the federal division of powers as well as the rule of the capitalist economy. Overall planning would be an impossibility for the Quebec state. What *Cité Libre* was proposing was a neo-liberal vigilant state with roles as a pinch hitter and monitor; it would tailor social policy to ensure that the benefits of prosperity were spread more equally throughout the population, and thus assume the social burdens of the capitalist economy.

What we are seeing in all this is an ideological hybrid. *Cité Libre* refused, in fact, to accept or condemn any system as a complete entity – to assess capitalism, for instance, condemn it root and branch, and substitute socialism. The group preferred to look at each problem separately and then provide a separate solution; change would be achieved bit by bit, by a series of partial reforms. With their so-called 'functional' approach, they could never have been revolutionary socialists, and indeed *Cité Libre* found socialism wanting as a potential solution for the economic inferiority of Quebec.[40] Capitalism may have been wanting too, but in the end both were cast in the shade by a weightier issue, the issue of industrial society. 'Our immediate task,' announced a 1958 article,' is much more to adapt small Quebec industry of the paternalistic, family type so that it can be integrated into the worldwide capitalist economy.'[41] The priority for Quebec, then, was to get its economy modernized and master the arts of capitalism. The troublesome by-products of industrialization – unemployment, automation, pollution, inflation, regional disparity, and so on – had to be dealt with. *Cité Libre* believed social justice was possible under capitalism as long as a functional, welfare-state mechanism was created to carry it out. As for the social problems spun off by industrialization, the best solution was a mixed economy in which the public and private sectors worked together for the general good. 'The state takes the responsibility of shielding citizens from inflation, unemployment, and sickness ... Industry has to maintain an adequate margin so that it can function with a minimum of restrictions.'[42] The idea was to have the state increase its social role within the capitalist economy. Reforms such as nationalization were compatible with such a system, although given our closeness to the United States, said *Cité Libre*, it would be unwise to call for collective ownership of the means of production and the end of competition. The important thing was to focus directly on the problems arising from the growth of industry and technology, and work out solutions that embody the principles of social justice and respect for the individual.

Cité Libre saw the labour movement as the only progressive force that could, through its various demands, bring about social change in Quebec. This movement, however, though it had managed to penetrate many of the province's industries in the early 1950s, was still fighting for its existence, and lived with the constant threat of political mayhem. *Cité Libre* broke with the ruling ideology by opposing political interference in labour disputes and advocating an end to church control in Quebec unions. The magazine was critical of Duplessis' social legislation and attacked Bills 19 and 20, which, by limiting freedom of association, severely hindered the progress of organized labour. Other articles fulminated against the unholy alliance of capitalists and politicians to muzzle worker demands. As far as the church was concerned, its role had been beneficial at one time, but *Cité Libre* thought it had outlived its usefulness. The magazine was also concerned about the way spiritual and temporal considerations became confused in labour disputes, one such occasion being when the teachers' alliance was pitted against the Catholic school board of Montreal. *Cité Libre*'s editors advised the unions to declare their independence from the church by secularizing their structures and personnel.

For the intellectuals of the postwar generation, to be against Duplessis meant being against nationalism. The left of the 1950s, traumatized by the type of French-Canadian conservatism represented by the premier, laughed at the mere idea of a progressive, independentist nationalism that would sweep away the cobwebs of colonialism. *Cité Libre* had an obvious interest in the decolonization process then occurring in the Third World, and pronounced itself in favour of self-determination for colonized peoples. The only trouble was that the group never accepted that Quebec might itself be a colonized country. Quebec was industrialized, they said by way of refutation: Quebec was an exporter of capital. It was not under the domination of a mother country, nor was it in a state of political and economic dependence.[43] Believing this, they were bound to see independentism as so much reactionary nonsense, a diversionary tactic that had to be scotched.

They advanced other and more basic reasons for opposing Quebec independence. Quebec was not capable of independence because it was not like the other modern nations. Culturally, economically, intellectually, and spiritually, the French-Canadian nation was too impoverished to meet the challenges of separate existence.[44] The assumption behind all this was that French Canadians were congenitally weak and inferior: 'The French Canadians are not able to form a complete society.'[45] Their only hope for development and modernization was a close association with English Canada, whose institutions and political tradition made it the very model of a complete secular society. Left to its own devices, 'shut up inside its borders,' Quebec could never overcome its hereditary conservatism on its own. Hence, Quebec independence could not be a progressive move.

Although *Cité Libre* was critical of the established order within French-Canadian society, its position on constitutional matters was conformist and conservative. The division of powers should be left as it was: the provinces already had the powers they needed for the cultural and political health of their societies, and the federal state, supreme in all issues that had no ethnic dimension, could act for the good of Canadian society as a whole. All the French Canadians had to do in this pluralistic and multicultural Canadian state was use the powers they already possessed, become competent as a participating society, and thus make themselves indispensable to English Canada. Based on reasoning that was ahistorical and fatalistic, this was the plan the 'three doves' of *Cité Libre* tried to sell to French Canada. The rest had to share their own failure of authentic existence.

Pierre Vadeboncoeur understood the spirit of that generation when he described it as the generation of immediacy, intent on shedding the myths, confronting things as they were, and then proceeding to change them on a basis of pragmatism: 'Pelletier, Trudeau, and Marchand wanted the society they were studying to develop an awareness of its own times. ... There was nothing very daring in what they outlined for this society. Their aim was simply to bring it up to date ... The *Cité Libre* group was not particularly attempting to introduce new ideas, but merely point out some old ones.'[46]

The Quiet Revolution

'In the land of Quebec, nothing ever changes.' The old tag from *Maria Chapdelaine* came up whenever English Canadians, looking for a liberal lift, made the comparison with the reactionary, 'priest-ridden' French province in their midst. And then, suddenly, there was movement. Americans, Europeans, and English Canadians looked on in astonishment: 'Things are happening in Quebec!'

If we use the word 'revolution' to describe the changes occurring in the Quebec of the 1960s, it is much more because of the ground that had to be made up than the actual substance of this change. The fact is that there was a great deal more imitation than innovation going on, as new leaders tried to remedy the old structural imbalances and the dependence of Quebec's economy and society. The ideology of replacement was a borrower. The incoming power élite adopted American and European management models; their emphasis was quantitative, on profits and efficiency. The new opposition groups looked to African decolonization, the Cuban revolution, and the rights campaign of the American blacks.

The rapid pace of change, coming after a long period of stagnation, is what lent a revolutionary tinge to these years of boisterous evolution in Quebec. The changes were by no means unheralded, as various fringe groups had been promoting them for some time. These groups had been unable to bring their plans to term, however; they were defeated by the ideological monolith of a Quebec dedicated to the soil, seamlessly Catholic, messianic, and ruled by the clergy.

The death of Duplessis in 1959, therefore, simply meant that an already detectable modernization process could now begin to gain speed. What was new after 1960 was that the minority proposals rejected in the 1950s were accepted as valid by a majority of Quebec's citizens, and began to coalesce into a new ruling ideology. It is in this sense that we can say that the Liberal victory of 22 June 1960 was a turning point in the ideological development of Quebec, the moment when 'respect for tradition' gave way to the 'challenge of progress.' The era of clerical and political conservatism was succeeded by the era of progress, social and cultural change, and the revitalization of politics and nationalist philosophy. The new buoyancy that emerged with the end of the long Duplessis night came out in such slogans as Paul Sauvé's 'From now on,' Jean Lesage's 'A hell of a team,' 'It's time for a change,' René Lévesque's

'Masters in our own house,' the RIN's 'We can do it,' and the 'Equality or independence' and 'Quebec knows how' of Daniel Johnson and Jean-Jacques Bertrand.

The expression 'Quiet Revolution,' then, encompasses the reforms carried out under Liberal administrations in the years 1960 to 1966. It was a clean-up and catch-up operation that affected Quebec's institutions, politics, and ideology; in other words, a renovation of the superstructure. An attempt was made to adapt the superstructural elements so that they would reflect the far-reaching structural transformation of economy and society in postwar Quebec. The revolution went beyond the politics of the party in power, but it did express new power relations in the class structure, and the arrival of a new political élite. This élite was backed by an alliance between the neo-capitalist elements in the Canadian bourgeoisie and the technocrats – planners, administrators, and so on, carrying out the new functions of monopoly capitalism – of the Quebec petty bourgeois class, hoping for career advancement that would turn their knowledge into power. Finally, the Quiet Revolution was a response to the Canadian economy's first big crisis of growth, which began with the 1957 recession and did not end until early in 1961. The winter of 1960, for example, saw unemployment levels rise above 14 per cent; there was no increase in real income, and regional disparities were painfully apparent. People expected the state to move in to revive economic growth without attempting to impose too much qualitative change on that growth, except, of course, for the priority of handing economic power back to the French Canadians. By means of modernization and its accompanying ideology, the petty bourgeoisie hoped for acceptance of a significant state role in boosting the French-Canadian share of the economy. It enlisted Quebec nationalism in its campaign for hegemony. I might add that this drive to modernize the state services necessary to the smooth operation of the capitalist economy also had the support of the English-Canadian bourgeoisie.

Clearly, the Quiet Revolution generated a dynamic of change that came to affect every aspect of Quebec: political, economic, social, unionist, cultural, religious, and national. What, in concrete terms, did it achieve?

According to Bourque and Frenette,[47] the Quiet Revolution comes down to a successful manoeuvre by the new Québécois petty bourgeois class in which it laid hold of the state apparatus and strengthened its economic and political position. Daniel Latouche has tested this hypothe-

sis against the province's public accounts, and concluded: 'To the extent that the volume of government expenditure is a reliable and valid
indicator of the ruling class's efforts to entrench its position, we can
say that the Quiet Revolution was indeed characterized by a strong increase in the Quebec state's potential ability to intervene in the economic system.'[48] Quebec's public expenditure rose from a total of $91.1
million in 1945 to $3,145 million in 1970; the 1970 cost of debt servic-
ing was greater than the total figure of 1945. Whereas expenditure increased by only 11.4 per cent between 1954 and 1959, Latouche noted
that the average annual increase from 1960 to 1965 was 20.9 per cent,
falling to eight per cent in 1966–70. In the years of the Quiet Revolution, government priorities were health, social welfare, and education,
which together accounted for 67.6 per cent of all the money Quebec
spent. It was also a period of rapid government expansion, with twenty-
seven new administrative institutions and an increase of 53 per cent in
the civil service. All this growth in the government's financial and institutional resources found expression in an intensified state economic role.
And the government's petty-bourgeois constituency, whose members
were rarely promoted above foreman in industry, looked to political
power as the route to satisfactory entry into the economy.

The Liberals aimed to democratize politics and revitalize the state.
They attacked the corruption and patronage by setting up the Salvas Commission, which was instructed to investigate the former Union Nationale administration and propose measures to clean up political practices in
Quebec. It was also a useful political move for the Liberals: the commission stood as evidence of their integrity, discredited the Union Nationale, and threw the old influence networks into disarray so that they could
then be replaced by new ones. Work also began on reform of election
legislation and redistribution of the provincial ridings; rural over-
representation had favoured the Union Nationale and partly disen-
franchised the demographically and economically more important urban
districts. Except for a few minor adjustments, however, the project
never got beyond the research stage. This circumstance gave the Union
Nationale a final chance; in 1966, the party returned to office with 41
per cent of the popular vote as compared to 46.5 per cent for the outgoing
Liberals.

It was also an aim of government to attract more citizen participation in
public life. Québécois heard how their votes and pressure tactics could

influence political decisions. Special use was made of this participatory ideology at the time of the debate on Bill 60, when Paul Gérin-Lajoie toured the province as the government's representative to consult the public at large as well as groups closely affected by educational reform.[49] Everywhere in Quebec, citizens were beginning to speak up, and openly challenge the political authorities; things got even more disputatious after 1966, with the proliferation of citizens' groups. And in the same spirit of liberal democratization, the civil service was reformed to remove its members from political pressure. Open competition replaced service to the party, or a note from the local MLA, as the criterion for hiring and promotion. The public employee's status was reinforced by higher salary scales and official encouragement to unionize. The objective was to get Quebec's ministries as competently staffed as those of Ottawa. The government also lured back some senior federal officials and a number of intellectuals, who had been driven either to Ottawa or to apolitical distraction by the unwelcoming Duplessis dictatorship, and now wanted to share in Quebec's new thrust.

The Quebec state itself shared in this renewal of vitality. The old laissez-fare was dropped in favour of a policy of state interventionism that was more consistent with the needs of growing monopoly capitalism. It was not an impartial role, for the state's discretion did not extend beyond policies that were consistent with the existing economic order. In advanced capitalist societies, the state acted as regulator. It nationalized risk. Its buying and spending were organized in such a way as to absorb surpluses and guarantee economic growth. It took over investments that were too expensive for the private sector. It took the place of private enterprise in sectors where profits were too low or too long in coming. The state also underwrote the costs of new technology. It regulated economic progress as defined by capitalism.

Planning was presented as a natural state activity in support of the economy, but, just as naturally, the approved form was indicative planning. In 1962, to carry out this function, the government created the Council of Economic Orientation which became the Bureau de Planification in 1969. A similar initiative was the Eastern Quebec Development Office which opened in 1963.

The 1960s also saw the launching of a number of Crown corporations and joint ventures with the private sector that gave institutional form to the state's role as pinch hitter in the monopoly phase of capitalism.[50] In

1962, the Société Générale de Financement was given the mandate of
capitalizing new small enterprises and assisting existing ones in difficulty.
The definition of the SGF as 'a private enterprise of public interest' said a
good deal about the neocapitalist notion of the state, and also about the
strength of the government's determination to get into the economy.
Even if the state did turn entrepreneur, it must not compete with business;
instead, the state should actively support business by making public
resources available. As indicated by these ventures, the state's role in the
monopoly phase of capitalism was to be a supplier of capital and a
creator of jobs.

In an effort to deliver even better service to private business, the
government undertook to improve the province's transportation system by the construction of superhighways. This was also the reason
behind the nationalization of the power companies, followed by massive new public investment to develop Quebec's energy resources. Private concerns were pulling out of the energy sector, protesting purely for
the sake of form, because profit levels were falling and they could
not pay for needed expansion on their own. In the process, these companies filled their pockets with public money which they reinvested in
more profitable sectors. The whole operation was dignified by a fanfare
of economic nationalism as an advance in the reconquest of the
Quebec economy. Another effect of the hydro-electric takeover was to
give the petty bourgeois technocrats a chance to show that they were
as good as English Canadians at developing and running the big corporations that had always been monopolized by the others. Finally, state-run
economic activity held out bounty for Quebec's architects and con-
tractors, businessmen and industrialists, and engineers. There was no
move to spread into other sectors of the economy, such as iron and
steel.

This rationalizing, modernizing impetus, spurred on by economic
imperatives, carried through into the area of social policy. There, it
spelled the end of Quebec's social services as works of private charity
under the wing of the Catholic Church. The province's religious institutions were simply not capable of responding to the needs of the new
industrial society. God the Father and the insurance companies could no
longer give adequate protection against illness. The state-run hospital insurance scheme that came into effect in 1961 increased public access to treatment and led to the socialization of medicine nine years

later. The Quebec government also strengthened the social security system by increasing family benefits and old age pensions. In 1964, the creation of the Quebec Pension Plan repelled the federal invaders and gave the state increased financial flexibility as well as a source of funds for its Deposit and Investment Bank.

Developing capitalism also required rationalized education; industry needed a better-educated and more highly skilled work force. Quebec's clergy-run school system was so anachronistic and disorganized that it could not provide an effective response. In 1960, the satirical *Insolences* by 'Brother So-and-So' suggested closing down the Department of Public Instruction on charges of incompetence and irresponsible behaviour. Following the recommendations of the Parent Commission, the Lesage government, led in this matter by Paul Gérin-Lajoie, brought in Bill 60 to set up a fully fledged education ministry. Despite dogged resistance from the clerical lobby, the ministry was created in 1964. It was the first step towards declericalization.

If it was going to accommodate the aspirations of the urban masses and the needs of the economy, the educational system had to be democratized as well; it had to be free as well as available. The process began with grants for secondary-level studies in privately run collegiate institutions. Then the government considered how to respond to the Parent recommendations about classical colleges and the integration of educational levels; the CEGEPs were ultimately set up by the Johnson government, in 1967. These changes were paralleled by the adjustment in courses of study to scientific, technical, and professional priorities, at the expense of religion and the humanities. No move was made, however, to include universities in the state-run sector. The net effect of the Quiet Revolution in education was to make it a top national priority: in ten years, enrolment in secondary schools rose by 101 per cent, in colleges by 82 per cent, and in universities by 169 per cent. A whole nation was going back to school.

The cultural dimension of the Quiet Revolution was a general strengthening of Québécois identity. The process of defining this identity attracted ideological controversy, with one side insisting that the aim was 'good' French and the other, more radical side wanting to dignify 'joual,' the language spoken by the ordinary people. Identity emerged as the theme in plays, books, films, and popular songs that took Québécois back to their roots. This cultural renaissance paralleled the revitalizing and spread of education. It was presided over from 1961 on by a ministry of cultural affairs. And it was reinforced by the mutual rediscovery of France and French Canada that occurred during this period. The secular and republican traditions of the Europeans were no longer a barrier. The new élites in Quebec were enthusiastic about building a sense of shared identity and culture with the old mother country, and support came at the official level with the opening of the Quebec Délégation Générale in Paris in 1961, various cultural agreements, and the France-Québec Office de la Jeunesse. More and more university students were going over to France to complete their studies, and this in turn stimulated ideological variety in Quebec.

These years also brought new developments in personal and social morality. Change was now a good in itself. A general infatuation with whatever was new opened the way for the cultural flood from the United States. Personal freedom was uppermost in people's minds, and its expressions were frequently borrowed. In their daily lives, the Québécois wanted to be up to date with the most advanced, capitalist consumer societies. They threw out the old strict morality and embraced the pleasures of immediate consumption. Young people cheerfully shattered the old taboos on sex and drugs, and joined the various liberation movements that were sweeping through Western societies. Quebec entered the world cultural revolution proclaiming its own national specificity. Its people no longer defined themselves as French Canadian, but as Québécois.

Language problems took up centre stage in these years, and assumed great economic and political importance. The alarm was sounded by the 1961 census figures along with demographic studies that showed the accelerated assimilation of francophones in Canada and Quebec. The French-Canadian birthrate was falling ominously: from 28.3 per thousand in 1959, it had reached 15.3 per thousand by 1970. The francophone share of Quebec's population was falling too, from 81.2 per cent in 1961 to 80.7 per cent ten years later. The three issues that contributed most to arouse national feeling and stimulate the pro-French-Quebec movements of these years were the Québécois' economically dependent situation, immigrant identification with the English group, and the attendance of English schools by children from French-speaking families. Demands ranged from simple signs and labels in French to French unilingualism and integration of the school system.

People would no longer be appeased by the bilingual cheques and endless litanies about their cultural rights. They wanted dynamic state intervention, for the situation was urgent and the Quebec state was the servant of the majority. The fight in 1969 over Bill 63, which gave parents the right to choose their children's language of instruction, was the culmination of this unresolved language conflict.

The fresh air the Quiet Revolution was letting into Quebec's institutions, coupled with the strong assertions of dynamic nationalism and identity, stimulated an unprecedented upsurge in Quebec's intellectual and cultural life. Gradually, shame and self-contempt, those old habits of the colonized, grew less common. And what the foolish, self-defeating universalism of the élite culture used to dismiss as provincial or folkloric now became, under the impetus of the search for identity and self knowledge, the ruling cultural forms.

As far as the church and all its works were concerned, the sky was falling in Quebec. Announcements of the demise of the French-Canadian deity may possibly not have been premature. The old Catholic Quebec took up religious toleration and slid quietly towards a mass exit from the churches. There were numerous parish bankruptcies. More and more workers and young people were rejecting religion. The bottom literally fell out of recruitment, as the 2,000 new priestly vocations of 1946 became a bare one hundred in 1970. Being French was clearly no longer synonymous with being Catholic. As it collapsed as a temporal power and was replaced by the state as the central institution of the Quebec collectivity, the church's moral influence ebbed as well, a wave of secularization swept through Quebec's institutions and society generally. In the ruling ideology, the age-old focus on spirituality was giving way to a more rationalist, materialistic social philosophy.

These changes all went deep into Quebec society, and they would have decisive effects on its future. It should not be imagined, however, that they occurred in an atmosphere of perfect progressive unanimity. The forces of conservatism did not melt away with the arrival of the 1960s. There was still no socialist party making headway with the masses. There was a strong movement of objection to the secularization of the schools. The right-wing populism of the new Créditiste group harvested the protest votes of the rural petty bourgeois and the disadvantaged folk who disapproved of the changes. The alliance of the neo-capitalists and petty-bourgeois technocrats fell apart, and as a result, the dynamic of change was contained after 1965 in order to reassure foreign investors and stabilize things for the Canadian bourgeois and the French-Canadian capitalist. Stabilization set in when the Union National-ale, using these contradictions and the rural disaffection to its advan-tage, got back into office in 1966.

However, neither Daniel Johnson nor his successor Jean-Jacques Bertrand would succeed in stifling the spirit of challenge and ideological experimentation that arose in the Quiet Revolution. Reform had given people a taste for revolution, and this taste was only whetted the more when the ruling class decided that enough was enough. Under the Union Nationale, the economic and political situation deteriorated. Social antagonisms increased. Terrorism persisted. The left and the labour movement grew more radical and not less. There were more demonstrations in the streets. Citizens' groups were outspoken in their criticism of the authorities. The legitimacy of existing liberal demo-cracy and its formal participatory structures was not being accepted with-out question. Challenges reached out to the social system in its entirety. The students took mobilization and politicization to the limit. And the independentist movement was noticeably strengthened after the visit of General de Gaulle and the founding of the Parti Québécois as a plausible alternative to the old parties. The Québécois had been con-vinced that they could make many changes. They had put away the fatalism and submissiveness of a conquered minority.

Ottawa was being pressured by the English-Canadian bourgeoisie and political élite, upset by all this liberation in Quebec, to launch a counter-attack on the quiet but not soundless revolution. To achieve this, they were prepared to hand power to Pierre-Elliott Trudeau, to-gether with instructions to neutralize Quebec's demands and deal appropriately with the irritating progressives in that province.

BNA revisionism

The vagueness of the federal-provincial division of powers has been a cause of perennial debate in Canada, and especially in Quebec. With the coming of the Quiet Revolution, these debates heated up to the point where they began to look like a constitutional shoot-out. Moderniz-ing Quebec society was bound to mean challenge for the constitutional

division of power, because modernization, nationalization, new institutions, and new social responsibilities for the Quebec state required
improved revenue sources. Merely increasing taxes was not enough.
And the existing political parties were being pushed into taking more
radical positions by the growing forces of Quebec nationalism and independence. The inevitable confrontation took place, not only over the
division of powers but also over Quebec's aggressive international role
and, later, immigration policy, communications, and social legislation.
In this confrontation, the new Quebec ruling class, wanting to entrench
its position, came up with a new concept of federalism for tabling in
the process of constitutional review. The representatives of the ruling
ideology offered three revisionist choices.

The first of these was based on the ideas of equality between the
two founding peoples and the absolute need to decentralize Canada.
From the time he came into office, Jean Lesage, who still remained
a staunch federalist, was skirmishing with the federal authorities. In the
course of his fight, he developed the notion of special status for
Quebec as the 'point d'appui,' the necessary prop for French Canadians
everywhere. According to Lesage, Canada was made up of two nations, two majorities, with unequal distribution in the country. The English minority in Quebec and the French minorities in the rest of
Canada were simply extensions of their majorities. These majorities
should have identical rights in the federation.

According to the second of these alternatives, the real battle to get
political power for Quebec was being fought far away from such resonant
declarations of principle. The point of the real battle was to force a
better division of powers, an improved tax share, and increased equalization payments. Quebec must have special powers in a renewed
federation. Supporters of this proposal ranged from members of the
Liberal and Union Nationale parties to Le Devoir and the Montreal
St-Jean-Baptiste Society.

The third position was the one expressed rhetorically by opposition Union Nationale leader Daniel Johnson as 'equality or independence.' Lesage had sent Ottawa his ultimatum demanding a Quebec
share of 25 per cent of personal income tax, 25 per cent of corporate
income tax, and all succession duties paid in the province; Johnson
countered with an opposition demand for all personal income tax, the
same amount of succession duties, and 100 per cent of all corporate

income tax paid by companies taking natural resources out of Quebec. He told the Quebec assembly on 17 January 1963: 'We are left with two possible options, and we have to choose one of them before 1967: either we become masters of our own destinies in Quebec and equal partners in the running of the whole country, or it is going to be total separation.' This made it possible for him to attack Liberal pliancy and attract separatist support at the same time. But though words flew between the two old parties, and there was some haggling with the Ottawa Liberals, very little actually happened.

René Lévesque's proposal for associated states was really a subset of the first of these three. It went farther, however, and was in this sense more logical than the idea of special status in suggesting a new federal concept in which each of the two nations had its own state, and shared the federal structures with the other. This was the thesis of absolute decentralization that would emerge later on as Lévesque's proposal for sovereignty-association.

Special status drew little support in English Canada, where people failed to understand why Quebec was challenging national unity. Most English Canadians simply reaffirmed their faith in federalism and their wish that Canada continue to be run by their own majority. The publication of the first report of the Royal Commission on Bilingualism and Bicul-turalism drew this comment from the Winnipeg *Free Press*: 'The basic truth is that we have no association between two equal communities. We are equal before the law, we have equal rights in our respective languages, we are equal as individuals, but we are not equal politically. Our problem will not be solved by making one province the equal on all these questions with the rest of the country.'[51] English Canada was generally cool on the theory of the two-nations pact with special status for Quebec. The same theory was rejected by Pelletier, Marchand, and Trudeau in their campaign to stop the autonomist rumblings in Quebec and sell their own rigid, uncompromising brand of federalism. Separat-ist pressure was threatening to turn the crisis of Canadian unity into a bloodbath for the federalists. The trio had the blessing of Canadian and American capitalists in their bid to renovate the constitution. For the domi-nant interests in Quebec, the crisis in the capitalist economy, as evi-denced by inflation and looming recession, was not compatible with de-centralization. Expanding capitalism could not tolerate the official recogni-tion of differences; it required centralization and uniformity. Nor could

Quebec's unconditional federalists agree to any form of compromise; they fought back at the ideas of special status and independence by establishing bilingualism in the civil service and massive public investments that were supposed to be dedicated to regional development, and 'make the national reality so attractive that it will make the separatist group uninteresting.'[52] They were trying to build a federalist nationalism. Naturally, in this scheme of things, Quebec had to become a province like the others. Indeed, in some respects, the 'three wise men' who went to Ottawa thought like the old-style nationalists: they rejected Quebec nationalism and viewed Quebec as a culture, an ethnic group among all the others. Ignoring the economic and political dimensions of the issue of nationality, they reduced it to one of culture only. They expected bilingualism and multiculturalism to solve the crisis of Canadian unity and silence the claims of Quebec.

Their concept of federalism, in fact, turns up prominently in the political ideology of Quebec's ruling class. After the departure of René Lévesque, the provincial Liberals reasserted their confidence in Confederation, and exchanged special status for 'profitable' federalism. The party's new leader, Robert Bourassa, set out to prove that Quebec could get more funds from the federal connection than it had in the past. Here are the commandments of this new crusade: be competent, have good documentation, and above all, re-establish the foreign investor's confidence by generous money grants and unconditional support for federalism. This puts the priority in the economy; Quebec must buckle down to work, and not keep bickering with Ottawa. Dialogue and consultation were to replace ultimatums and threats. Illusions die hard with colonized people.

Since the Liberal big brothers in Ottawa thought unconditional federalism meant provincial obedience to central decisions, the constitutional review process was blocked. In Victoria, the federal government refused to accept Quebec's primacy in social legislation, and made no secret of its overall centrist aims. Even profitable federalism was too much for Ottawa. In order to escape this dilemma and disguise his own lack of real power, Bourassa tried to refurbish his party's image with cultural sovereignty. He refrained, however, from disclosing what he actually meant by cultural sovereignty.

To sum up, while the balance of powers between Ottawa and the provinces was altered in the 1960s in favour of the latter, and especially

Quebec, it all changed when power passed to the hard-line federalists in Ottawa and their disciples in Quebec City. They reduced the Quebec state to a simple local government, responsible for maintaining order and the capitalist economy.

The rise of separatism

The arrival of new elites and the revitalizing of the provincial state in the early 1960s renewed national awareness, driving out the old French-Canadian nationalism of self-preservation and ushering in a nationalism that was Québécois in its focus. The old defensive stasis gave way to a frankly political, progressive, decolonizing drive that owed something to the African experience of Berque, Fanon, and Memmi. Gradually, the inferiority complexes were weeded out. There was a fierce new pride in being Québécois. National self-assertiveness became less negative, less 'against the others,' and more positive: 'We can do it.' Out of the Quiet Revolution came a new national identity based on control of the collective destiny through joint action by nation and state.

A branch of the general stream of decolonization in the countries of the Third World, this new nationalism spawned a variety of independentist movements: the Alliance Laurentienne (1957), the Action Socialiste pour l'Indépendance du Québec (1960), the Rassemblement pour l'Indépendance Nationale or RIN (1960), the Parti Républicain du Québec (1962), the Ralliement Nationale (1964), the Mouvement Souveraineté-association (1967), and, from 1968, the Parti Québécois. This ideological element was recruited from a recently visible petty-bourgeois group that included students, teachers, various types of professionals, workers from the service sector and unionists, all of them technocrats with a certain amount of education who had dissolved the alliance with the neo-capitalists and were trying to turn their knowledge into power, using the state as a lever for the advancement of the collective cause and hence their own. There was no national bourgeoisie to drive Quebec's economic development. The sole means of national liberation, and of the social advancement of this petty-bourgeois class, was the Quebec state. Their aim was to carry to its conclusion the process of change that had begun with the Quiet Revolution, and turn Quebec into a complete society, one that could decide its own political future.

Let us begin with a look at the Rassemblement pour l'Indépendance

Nationale or RIN, which emerged as a political party in 1963. In the context of the day, it was well to the left. As defined by the first article of its constitution: 'The RIN is the Quebec political party that is pledged to decolonize Quebec by the creation of a sovereign, democratic and secular state that fully represents all the workers.' Even more than its platform, however, what put this group on the left was the way it operated. Unlike the traditional parties, the RIN ran street demonstrations, took its literature from door to door, depended on personal donations, and was otherwise financed democratically by its own membership. And these methods had their effect. In the June 1966 election, the RIN and Ralliement National together captured ten per cent of the vote, contributing to the Liberal defeat.

The RIN ideology was based on the necessity of Quebec independence. Their argument ran as follows: we are outsiders in our own country. Our economy and our natural wealth are being developed to suit foreign interests, and not our own. This economic dependence reflects our culture, and will lead ineluctably to the assimilation and permanent minority status of the French-speaking population. Within Confederation, Quebec is a dominated society, lacking the powers by which it could control its own destiny. Until we gain our political independence, economic independence and Québécois culture will always be myths; if we do not separate, we will simply be repeating the weakness and negligence of past generations, and bequeathing our colonized attitudes and inferior economic status to the generations to come. For the RIN, then, independence was more a means than an end. It was seen as the only route to a truly healthy society for French Quebec. And it was to be won not by violence, but by votes.

In excising religion from the national identity, the RIN was departing sharply from traditional nationalist practice. The solidarity of Catholicism was replaced by that of language and culture: 'The Québécois identity stems from a culture of French descent and French expression, which everybody wishing to belong to the collectivity must make their own. The RIN rejects minority status and believes that the Québécois are, or must become, an assimilating majority.'[53] Once elected, the RIN would make French the only official language and the working language of Quebec. The party's economic and social ideas too, without being revolutionary, went beyond what the Liberal reformers were proposing. The RIN programme stressed overall economic planning, generalized state intervention, a more equal distribution of income, the secularization of Quebec society, and nationalization of natural resources and other economic sectors vulnerable to monopolism.

Describing all this as moderate socialism, party president Pierre Bourgault argued that Quebec could not be independent without being socialist as well.[54] A careful reading of the 1966 election platform of the RIN helps define just what this socialism consisted of. It promised to encourage 'worker participation in business profits and ownership,' and expressed approval of the idea of joint management; it went on to make a commitment to nationalize the monopolies. Yet the platform also clearly stated that the RIN's interest in setting up state corporations was limited to cases of 'the failure of private enterprise to meet obvious needs,' and that it would welcome foreign investors 'in so far as they will agree to consider the objectives of the [economic] plan.' There was nothing about socializing the means of production or making basic changes to the structures of Quebec society. According to the platform, 'economic production and the distribution of wealth are two separate functions, and must be dissociated from one another,' with the first taking a capitalist and the second a socialist form. The term 'social-democratic' is much more appropriate to describe a party that, while assigning the dominant economic role to the state, never envisaged an independent Quebec without private enterprise. It was also, as we have seen, an approach that made political independence a necessary precondition for Quebec's economic liberation.

In its eight years of existence, the RIN acted as a catalyst for Quebec national feeling. During the Quiet Revolution, its active campaign of public education forced the old parties to define where they stood on the constitution, and speak to the question of Quebec independence. The RIN managed to raise democratic consciousness in the people of the province. Its ideas had their influence on the men and parties then in power, and they were later taken up by the Parti Québécois. Despite its limitations, the role of the RIN as a source of ideological innovation was decisive for the future of Quebec.

It was in November 1967 that René Lévesque resigned from the Liberal opposition to found the sovereignty-association movement that became the Parti Québécois one year later. The Lévesque group managed to get the various separatist elements working together and give the notion of independence a moderate, respectable image. In the space of a few years, the party had a hundred thousand members, the majority of whom came from the petty bourgeoisie: teachers and students, civil servants, and highly trained professionals of various kinds. About ten per cent of the Parti Québécois membership came from the working class. It was the party of the new generation, the under-forties who believed in education as a means of social advancement and had acquired a good deal of it themselves.

Taking up the firebrand of separatism, the PQ projected mildness and competence, and overlaid the early movement's wild purity with the practical considerations of politics. The point was not so much to persuade the ordinary Québécois of the need for independence as it was to get them to vote for the party. This change of approach meant that the PQ varied somewhat from the earlier separatist ideology. The PQ's version was subtler than that of the RIN in softening the effects of the proposed break with Canada. Independence was still basic, for without it, Quebec could not set its own economic, social, and cultural priorities. And the obsolete constitution of Canada was in the way of a truly flourishing Québécois collectivity: 'The federal structures are depriving us of the fiscal resources and the legislative powers we need, not only to set our own social policy but also, and especially, to make the social decisions that give a society a personality of its own.'[55] In order to exist as a nation, Quebec needed control of political decision making. The PQ accent was on sovereignty rather than independence and liberation, terms of decolonization that implied a unilateral move. 'Québec libre' was downplayed in the Lévesque phrasebook. The moderate image was reinforced by the idea of association or an agreed economic interdependence with Canada, and later by putting a referendum in the sovereignty process. It was a strategy that would allow the party to take office without immediately achieving its basic objective. Also, since secession had ceased to be a political aim and become a solution of last resort, it gave the central government a chance to do some highly visible revamping of Canada's political structures.

On the language issue, the position of the PQ was again less radical than that of its predecessors, promising 'the English-speaking minority its own institutions of public education at all levels.'[56] The party did undertake, however, to make French the language of the workplace, and to slow the assimilation process by seeing that immigrant groups were integrated into the French-language school system. Here again, the PQ's intention was clearly to deradicalize separatism in order to increase its constituency, win office, and work out the transition in a stable atmosphere. With independence or without it, therefore, the technocratic petty bourgeoisie could satisfy its class aspirations.

The PQ proposals did not call for sweeping changes in Quebec's economic structure and external economic relations. The party did not define itself in terms of either anticapitalism or anti-imperialism. Its first care was to bring humanity into the capitalist system. At the same time, it called for a Quebec-Canada economic association based on a common monetary and customs policy. Wrongly assuming a dichotomy between the economic and political realms, the association proposal worked as a sweetener for the idea of sovereignty, but failed to resolve the problem of economic dependence. The PQ was claiming to have broadened the area of discussion by assuming economic powers in the Quebec state that equalled those of the federal government. They were idealizing politics.

For Quebec itself, the PQ suggested a mixed economy that would preserve private enterprise and the spirit of competition, while still asking the state to co-ordinate and drive the economy. The state had at its disposal the taxes returned by Ottawa, its own law-making and planning power, its purchasing policy, and added leverage in the expansion of the public sector. A sovereign Quebec would still be receptive to foreign capitalists, especially American, providing always that they accepted the association-participation of the state – something that was routine already – that they reinvest at least half their profits in Quebec, and employ skilled Quebec labour.

This was a quite moderate set of proposals. The PQ platform carefully avoided reference to social classes or the capitalist system, using instead such soothing expressions as post-industrial society and consumerism, expressions that were redolent of the technocrat ideology. 'In the final analysis,' wrote Jean Meynaud of the party's economic platform, 'it is based on strengthening and expanding a Québécois capitalism.'[57] Its aim was to harmonize a capitalist mode of production with a socialist programme of redistribution. In fact, the PQ emerged as most progressive in its social policy: among proposed measures to ensure a more equal distribution of wealth were a guaranteed annual income, compensation for housewives, state-run daycare, an increased minimum wage indexed to the cost of living, lowering the retirement age to fifty-five, and broadening the health insurance scheme. In labour relations, the PQ was in favour of the generalization of democratic unions 'that rise above their defensive and purely protest role to work for responsible worker participation, at all levels, in making the decisions that affect them.'[58]

Two ideological streams are intermingled in the politics of the Parti Québécois. There is the technocrat stream that emphasizes rational, functional, and efficient management of society by the state, and a powerful, streamlined state becomes a basic party objective. At the same time, this centralized state must undergo a great deal of deconcentration if it is to reconcile efficiency with participatory democracy, which is the party's second great political objective. In PQ philosophy, the state is seen in abstract terms as a neutral, objective arbiter, above interests of class; the centre for demands to be lodged and regulations meted out; a device to serve the common good.

Democratization is understood by the PQ in a functionalist sense: a greater spread of information reaching the base of society and integrated citizen participation in dialogue with administrative bodies through consultation early in the decision-making process. At the same time, the PQ imposes limits on participatory democracy by supporting the principle of the delegation of power at the level where decisions are actually taken. Their intention has evidently been to develop modes of delegation and representation that are more equitable and consistent with the interests of the Québécois citizen: 'There will be democracy in Quebec on the day when MNAS and parties truly reflect the will of the people.'[59] And although the PQ has been an advocate of participatory democracy in political and social life, coming up with specific reform proposals in this area, the party has been much less specific about how the same principle is to be applied to labour and the economy. It has announced its intention 'of establishing an economic system that eliminates worker exploitation in all forms, and responds to the real needs of all Québécois rather than the requirements of a privileged economic minority,' with worker participation in decision making as part of this process.[60] However, the PQ has also been committed to maintaining the private enterprise profit system, and this places it in a problematical, if not a contradictory, position. It is not at all clear that political democracy can humanize capitalism all on its own. In general, then, the PQ's nationalist and social-democratic ideology expresses, in the name of the entire Québécois collectivity, the particular interests of a new sub-class attempting to win control of the political apparatus and become the state bourgeoisie, the managers of Quebec's capitalist interests.

According to a certain number of militant separatists, these parties have been too timid; their electoral strategies were unrealistic, and they were content to tinker with social reform. These critics have chosen secrecy and violence as their strategy for national liberation in Quebec. The Fédération de Libération du Québec, or FLQ, used bombs, arms, thefts, and kidnappings against the symbols of colonialism, hoping by these violent tactics to startle the national and social consciousness of the people into action. In the ideology of this group, revolution was inseparable from liberation. As its first manifesto stated: 'Quebec's independence is possible only through social revolution.' And Pierre Vallières wrote, in 'Revolutionary Strategy and the Role of the Avant-garde': 'Independence is understood here as meaning something other than a paper sovereignty such as we are promised by René Lévesque, supported by the parasitical petty bourgeoisie of Quebec, whose aim is simply to displace the English as managers of United States imperialist interests in Quebec.'[61]

This FLQ ideology was certainly not a homogeneous system. It changed as Quebec's internal circumstances and the international revolutionary movement changed. But beyond ideological variations and nuances of terminology, certain principles were held in common by the different FLQ cells. One was that Quebec workers were being oppressed and exploited by the English-Canadian bourgeoisie and the American imperialists. Another was that the Québécois ruling class was in bondage to foreign interests, and a third, that an independent, socialist Quebec simply could not be built by lawful, democratic means. Some of the variations on these themes have been pointed out for us by Marc Laurendeau. There was, for example, the purely nationalist element represented by *La Cognée*, which rejected the communist connection and attacked its representatives, the Vallières-Gagnon group, made up of the Maoist-leaning Marxist-Leninists of Charles Gagnon, the anarchist strain that was typified by the Chénier cell of 1970, and the eclectic Marxism of Vallières himself. One also noted variations in the FLQ manifestos over the years. The first of these, issued in 1963, was couched in 'academic' language, while the second was written in the down-to-earth French of the people. The 1970 manifesto was specific about the nature of the FLQ social revolution: it proclaimed solidarity with the workers' struggles, announced worker management as part of its revolutionary philosophy, and was savagely anticlerical. These were all things that had been muted in the early manifestos. Also noted by Laurendeau was a contradiction between the FLQ's Marxist-Leninism and what the group actually did: 'They reasoned as orthodox Marxists and acted as anarchists.'[62] The armed struggle had not been integrated with the party philosophy. In fact, the FLQ revolutionary strategy rated action higher than ideological warfare or the politicization of the masses. This mistake necessitated a thorough revamping of the Quebec revolutionary movement after the 1970 October crisis. The competing philosophies that emerged from this crisis were represented in the Vallières-Gagnon debate.

As far as Charles Gagnon was concerned; 'The petty-bourgeois nationalists are the most dangerous ideological element we have.'[63] The PQ's built-in class interests, and its willingness to settle for formal independence, meant that the party could never take the axe to exploiting capitalism and foreign domination. The nationalist, social-democratic ideology espoused by the PQ and Quebec's union leaders obscured the true interests of the working class, and was delaying its liberation. In Gagnon's opinion, the leaders in the national liberation struggle should be the working class and its advance guard, the proletarian party, for only they could, through the process of class conflict, bring socialism to Quebec. Nationality became a secondary contradiction in the system. Moreover for Gagnon, armed violence was premature. The priorities of the young Marxist-Leninist movement must be ideological warfare and the building of their revolutionary party.

Vallières, on the other hand, was not working from orthodox Marxism. He rejected the concept of spontaneous action and the classical notion of the dictatorship of the proletariat through its own avant-garde party, calling instead for an egalitarian, self-governing, and democratic socialism that would free men from constraint. In 1971, he issued a critique of his own strategy, *L'Urgence de choisir*, in which he admitted that Quebec was not in a revolutionary situation; armed violence was not justified, and ultimately played into the hands of the established order, for it became a pretext for repression: 'The army of the existing power is not to be goaded in the people's name when there is no army the people can recognize as their own and consciously identify with.'[64] Vallières saw violence as having become the unconscious but real ally of official repression. This being the case, he opted for the democratic route and gave his support to the Parti Québécois. In so far as decolonization remained a revolutionary means of liberation, the FLQ had no more reason for existing.

The socialist movement

The ideological thaw of the Quiet Revolution years and the contradictions inherent in the modernization drive created a favourable atmosphere for the growth of socialism. The movement was first noticeable as a ferment of ideas. Quebec saw the proliferation of such periodicals as *Revue socialiste*, which supported separation as well as a proletarian national liberation, *Parti pris*, *Socialisme*, and *Révolution québécoise*. They were run mainly by academics and other intellectuals, with a gradual influx of activists. The next stage brought into being such groups as the Mouvement de Libération Populaire, the Parti Socialiste du Québec, and the Front de Libération Populaire, which tried to put the thinkers' theories and strategies into practice. Up to now, if we exclude the union organizations themselves, socialism has not managed to penetrate the working class to any great extent, and has not inspired the founding of any working-class political group. Its main influence has been among the educated members of the lower middle class.

My own analysis will be based on the ideological content of *Parti pris*. It was the main vehicle for the radical left and progressive separatism in the mid-1960s, and performed a demystifying, critical function in Quebec society. *Parti pris* is important also because it clearly stated the two dilemmas that prompted the founding of a Quebec socialist movement in the first place: how to combine nationalism with a strategy based on class conflict, and how to bring the working class and revolutionary avant-garde together.

A Marxist-inspired organ of the radical left, *Parti pris* wanted to be practical as well as theoretical, a fighting journal as well as an analytical one. Its objectives of independence, socialism, and secularization were announced in the first issue:

We are struggling for Quebec's political independence because it is a necessary condition of our liberation. We believe that political independence will be nothing but a hoax unless Quebec gains economic independence at the same time. Finally, we believe that there can be no real control of the economy and the means of production unless this control is shared by every Québécois, through a complete transformation of our economic system. The essential thing is for us to liberate ourselves from those inside as well as outside Quebec who dominate us economically and ideologically and benefit from our alienation. Independence is only one aspect of the revolutionary liberation of the Québécois. We are fighting for a free, secular and socialist state.

Turning to Marxist theory and to Berque, Fanon, and Memmi, the philosophers of decolonization, the editors of *Parti pris* tried to apply the concepts of dispossession, alienation, colonialism, and class conflict to Quebec society. They wanted to unmask and destroy the structures of the existing order, and to describe the various phases of revolution, from initial awareness to final achievement. They attempted to make the connection between national liberation and the liberation of the working class from capitalist exploitation and imperialist oppression. To do so, they began with the assumption that national liberation can come only from the working class, since only this class has a deeply rooted motive for doing away with all forms of oppression, including the oppression of the Quebec nation by the Canadian state.

First, *Parti pris* went on the attack against the signs of colonialism in Quebec. It pointed out that the Québécois were economically dispossessed. Their natural resources were controlled by foreign interests; their industries belonged to American and Canadian capitalists; their standard of living was lower than that of Ontario, and the majority language was not the language of the workplace. Living within the capitalist system, Quebec was dispossessed of its own wealth, and its workers were dominated and exploited by American imperialists, Canadian capitalists, and the petty bourgeoisie of Quebec itself. Quebec was dominated and alienated politically as well: its power was only partial, and it lacked control of its own destiny. Under the federal system, the decisions were made by an outside majority on behalf of the ruling class and against the minority nation. Thus, the Québécois underwent an extreme cultural alienation, for in his deepest self he was colonized and dehumanized. The result of this critique of colonialism was a genuinely progressive nationalism, since this was one of the rare occasions in the history of social thinking in Quebec that the Québécois were defined in relation to the others, not nationally, but socially. And the others were denounced not as a nation but as an exploiting class. Similarly, the attack by *Parti pris* on the Québécois élite was wholesale, and not an enumeration of individual misdeeds as such attacks had been in the past.

The magazine's analysis of clericalism may serve as an example of this highly original approach. In contrast to the representatives of the ruling Quebec ideology, *Parti pris* was savagely anticlerical. The priest was always a favourite target in its attacks on the French-Canadian élite. He and his confreres were held responsible for the political, economic, and cultural alienation of the Québécois. By preaching obedience, the church had thwarted the genuine political forces of Quebec. By its support for the ruling class, the church had implanted the idea in people's minds that political authority was changeless, unchallengeable because of the interdiction of an authority that was greater still. The clergy were agents of economic alienation as well, not merely by their approval of the foreign economic interest that dominated Quebec, but also by their active participation in the exploitation of the working class. They were also guilty of Quebec's cultural alienation: slipping into the political vacuum after 1840, they had established a cultural monopoly, controlling the educational system and filtering out the ideological currents coming from outside.

Clericalism followed from colonialism: 'Clericalism is internalized colonialism.'[65] Clericalism could not be treated in isolation, for what Quebec was suffering from was 'the neocolonial-clerical-capitalist order.'[66] The power of the church could not be eliminated without the elimination of the colonialists and capitalists upon which it ultimately depended. This being the case, the entrenchment of religious tolerance and the removal of all direct religious authority outside the church walls would still not have satisfied *Parti pris*. Only a complete policy of secularism could stop the social influence of the church and make religion what it should be, an exclusively private matter. The editors of *Parti pris* were calling, not for a neutral state that would support all forms of education, but for a secular state that would see religion as irrelevant in the schools. Secularism was an extremely important aspect of the Québécois revolution, for it offered the possibility of a renewal that would take culture back to the people.

For *Parti pris*, Quebec's colonial situation was an all-inclusive one requiring an all-inclusive, revolutionary solution. And this solution was decolonizing socialism: 'For us, decolonization means the first phase of the true liberation drive of the Quebec collectivity; it means access to political sovereignty, and the applying of the mechanisms of economic democracy, the ultimate effect of which will be to remove the Quebec collectivity from English-Canadian colonial domination and American imperialist exploitation.'[67] Decolonization was a precondition for any popular revolution in Quebec. Class consciousness could not be expressed in the revolutionary struggle of the working class until this national lien was removed. According to the revolutionary strategy of *Parti pris*, independence was a preliminary step in the building of a socialist society. And this independence had to be economic and cultural as well as political. If it were achieved by the bourgeoisie, Quebec's independence would be incomplete, and it would have to be followed by class struggle and the establishment of socialism. As theorists, the magazine's editors did not think much of this bourgeois independence; as strategists, however, they were prepared to be more flexible and admit that it would achieve a great deal politically: 'it causes us to conquer, in Marx's phrase, the ground of conflict.'[68] They suggested a policy of tactical support: its hopes aroused by the Quiet Revolution, 'the bourgeoisie has as much to gain as the proletariat from breaking the chains that bind us to Confederation.'[69] This position would vary according to their analysis of the political situation. It was also the subject of an ideological disagreement that ultimately made the magazine cease publication.

It was the liberation of the Québécois people from double domination, capitalist as well as colonial, which meant that independence needed socialism, and vice versa. The one created the conditions for the other: 'Though independence does not necessarily lead to socialism, it makes socialism possible; we had also forgotten in joining the Parti Socialiste that although it is true that socialism would lead to independence, this socialism was not possible without independence.'[70] By the phrase 'decolonizing socialism,' *Parti pris* was attempting to express the double dimension of the national liberation struggle, and the close connections between the two elements of the solution. Ultimately, of course, socialism was seen as the necessary precondition for total liberation.

In their Marxist critique of capitalism, the editors of *Parti pris* argued from their own analysis of exploitation and the class structure in Quebec. Capitalist exploitation was characterized by private ownership of the means of production, the accumulation of capital, and the extortion of surplus value. The product of the workers' labour was taken away, becoming foreign to them, even antagonistic. Under the capitalist system, the worker was alienated: he had no control over his own life; he took no part in decisions affecting his own work; and he was exploited because he was dispossessed of the products of his labour. *Parti pris* also went on the attack against modern capitalist forms that feature domination by monopolies, mass production, and state intervention in necessary but low-profit sectors of the economy. Its editors had harsh words for the post-1960 revitalization of the Quebec state, which in their opinion had ultimately served only the bourgeois interest. According to them, the Quiet Revolution had soon run up against its own contradictions, and its powerlessness against imperialism of the United States.

What made capitalist exploitation in Quebec even worse was that the profits squeezed from the workers were pocketed by the foreigners who controlled the economy. The capitalist system was responsible for this foreign domination, and the Québécois were being exploited, not only as workers, but as a people. The exploiters were the American and English-Canadian capitalists and their local lackeys. The aim of *Parti pris* was to overturn the whole existing system: 'Our goal, the revolution, is to free from this tutelage the toiling masses of Quebec; to achieve this, we must overthrow the ruling bourgeoisie and thus basically overthrow the very structures of colonial and capitalist power.'[71] The revolution was to be the people's struggle, the workers' struggle, against the arrayed forces of the French-Canadian bourgeoisie, the dominant English-Canadian colonialists, and the exploitive American imperialists. To prepare the way, the priorities of the left were to organize a revolutionary avant-garde and found a workers' party. As to the likelihood of armed violence, *Parti pris* thought that the revolution might very well be carried through without loss of life, but the magazine did not rule out the possibility of turning to violence in order to oust the social enemy, who did not hesitate even now to use force and police repression against workers. And in this revolution, the largely proletarian Québécois people would be facing a neo-capitalist bourgeoisie whose members were recruited largely outside the borders of Quebec.

The magazine did not want to import a ready-made socialist model for Quebec: 'The socialism we have to build will be neither Russian, nor Chinese, nor Cuban; it must not and cannot be anything but Québécois.'[72] Above all else, this Quebec socialism would be a force of decolonization, procuring the workers' economic and political liberation in the same process. After the political liberation of Quebec, a workers' party would come to power and nationalize all foreign-controlled businesses of any size, set up manufacturing industries as required for Quebec's economic development, encourage the setting up of key industries, and build a planned, autonomous economy that would respond to the economic, social, and cultural needs of the people of Quebec. Socialism for the editors of *Parti pris*, however, was more than a simple technique of organizing society in a rational way. It involved a revolution in the forces of production and a corresponding revolution in the forces of society, which resulted in the gradual suspension of class struggle and the transformation of the modes of existence: work, leisure, and consumption. Theirs was not to be a totalitarian form of socialism. The aim of their socialism was to define and fulfil the Québécois.

Thus, *Parti pris* socialism was very different from state capitalism or the neo-capitalist experiments of social democracy. The magazine was critical of state capitalism for giving control of the means of production to government, and not to the workers, who really had very little to say about the planning and management of their workplaces. In neo-capitalist societies, on the other hand, the state was only an executive committee for monopolistic private interests, which were the determining factors in the state's indicative planning. According to *Parti pris*, these modified forms of socialism and their reforms allowed the capitalist system to survive and did nothing to improve the lot of the workers. And state socialism was acceptable only as a transition: 'The state obviously has an important part to play in altering the property structures before self-management is brought in, but it must surrender its power to the workers of the communes and enterprises that have substantial economic powers.'[73] The magazine recommended a form of worker-managed socialism: 'There is true self-management when the producers, those who work in a factory or other enterprise, own and manage it democratically.'[74] The means of production, then, were not to pass directly from private to public ownership; these would be socialized, given back to the workers themselves. *Parti pris* thought that a self-managing structure could be installed first in the public and near-public sectors, then, through 'increasing interventions by the Quebec state as economic planner,' involving nationalization, expropriation, or the creation of new industries, move into the old realm of private enterprise. Once self-management was general, the state would become obsolete. A free Quebec would be a society in which the real power belonged to the workers.

Parti pris was not of one mind in its socialist politics or revolutionary strategy. It harboured two schools of thought. The first of these argued for socialist tactical support of the bourgeoisie, apparently inspired by the Quiet Revolution to a degree of self-affirmation that would work to the detriment of the federal state. This school proposed a two-step strategy: independence first, and socialism second. The second group were insistent that the revolutionary struggle be waged directly by the working class, and aim at achieving both socialism and independence at the same time. With the founding of the Mouvement de Libération Populaire, this second school emerged on top. Evidence of this change of direction came with the publication of *Manifeste 65-66*, which announced that the Quebec bourgeoisie was incapable of achieving anything against the colossus of American and Canadian capital. Coincidentally, the Quiet Revolution was running down, its limits and fantasies now known. It was generally realized that Quebec's embryonic national bourgeois class could not drive the fight for national liberation.

In addition to dismissing the ideas of a bourgeois alliance and outlining the revolutionary struggle that would occur under working-class hegemony, the *Manifeste* pointed out the Mouvement's crucial role in the workers' struggle and the worker rule to follow, as well as the distinctions between the party and the revolutionary avant-garde of Marxist doctrine. Nationalist thinking must now begin with the workers' interests. There remained the problem of cementing relations with the labour movement. Militant socialists rejected the ideas of joining forces with labour. The unions had grown bourgeois, and they were now part of neo-capitalist society. Organized labour stopped at economic demands; it was doing nothing for the development of class consciousness and solidarity, and could therefore not revolutionize Quebec's social, economic, and political structures unaided. *Parti pris* hoped that its criticisms would arouse the unions sufficiently to give their workers a political education, equipping them to make choices in accordance with their own class interests. The MLP militants would not accept a union connection; they thought they could develop a bond with the labour movement by joining the PSQ. Because of the economist, social-democratic, reformist, and federalist programme of the PSQ, however, the liaison with the socialists was short-lived. Thereafter, the socialists moved quickly back to separatism, and affiliated themselves with the RIN so that independent Quebec would be as far to the left as possible. Experience proved this new venture to be as impossible as the first. In the end, when the question came up of tactical support for the Parti Québécois, the differences within the *Parti pris* group became acute, and the magazine collapsed.

The failure of *Parti pris'* measured strategy meant the end of the idea of independence as a preliminary stage before the coming class struggle. From 1968 on, the basic topics of left-wing discussion were the building of a revolutionary avant-garde and the problem of integrating with the labour movement. The Front de Libération Populaire came up with the idea of building the avant-garde as an element in worker and student confrontations. The FLQ's approach had been for its members to put themselves in the place of the masses in order to decide how the party should develop; the FLP wanted to do the opposite, to go to the masses and apprentice to the workers, develop mutual relations, and become directly involved in their struggles. Community- and politically-oriented citizens' groups would actually carry out this strategy of spontaneity, which was certainly influenced by world student agitation and China's Cultural Revolution.

Beginning in 1965, the rise of citizens' committees was a response to general disappointment in the wake of the high hopes for a society of abundance that were aroused by the Quiet Revolution. The political authorities were revealed as incompetent to deal with the immediate problems of the workers: insanitary accommodation, and lack of green space, community services, urban renewal, and so on.[75] Led by community organizers, these groups were especially active in underprivileged districts, but they were also isolated, organizationally unstable, and narrow in their perspective.

The CAPS or political action committees arrived to fill the gap, if only partially and superficially. They came out of the citizens' movement and the politicization of the unions, especially the Confédération des Syndicats Nationaux. Looking at a deteriorating economy and the levelling-off of the citizens' movement, the CSN decided that there had to be a 'second front,' which would take the economic struggle on to political ground, but outside the workplace, in neighbourhoods or shopping areas. The old citizens' committees should therefore reorganize into a political action movement for wage earners (FRAP). The prime target for this movement was the Montreal civic administration.

FRAP decided to set out to raise the workers' class consciousness and in so doing, shatter the isolation of the intellectual cliques that had so far failed to make headway with the working class. The idea was to set aside the daily worker problems and discuss a realistic, progressive political programme. It was assumed that the political situation was not ripe for an attempt at the national level, and so the first stage had to be a municipal strategy. This refusal to become involved in nationalist questions reflected a tacit alliance with the PQ, some of whose local organizations were identical in membership with those of FRAP. Combining opportunism with a recognition of the unevenness of its membership, FRAP also avoided discussion of such issues as the labour movement and the bases in capitalism and imperialism for worker exploitation. Given its internal contradictions and its infancy as an organization, FRAP could not survive the October 1970 wave of repression. The movement broke down into its various elements – reformist, socialist, and unionist – and some CAPS went off on their own to discuss questions that were still unresolved and school themselves in Marxist-Leninism.

In the wake of this brief period of activism, then, socialist militants retired to carry on intense ideological debates. These debates may well have resulted in clarification, but they also had the short-term result of making the left a politically powerless marginal force. It had gone back into hiding. And today, the Quebec left is still divided on the issues of nationalism and an autonomous workers' party. The socialist movement has been paralysed by fragmentation, sectarianism, and bad temper. The alliance between the socialists and the working class remains no more than an objective.

Labour to the left

The area of labour relations was another in which the Quiet Revolution broke with the past. Two pieces of legislation stand as evidence of this: the Quebec Labour Code and the Civil Service Act that encouraged unionization and collective bargaining in the public sector. This modernization of labour law was followed by the reorganization of the labour department, changes in the minimum wage law, a new system of union certification, and legislation providing manpower training and certification. The state was asked to play a new role, both as employer and as regulator and lawmaker in labour relations. This new state role was to have a far-reaching effect on the Quebec labour movement.

In this connection, we should note that the growth of organized labour is paced by the development of capitalism and industrialization. This is what accounts for labour's arrival on the political scene. The politicization of the unions was not a mere matter of the revolutionary fervour of their leaders; nor was it, as the establishment propaganda would have us believe, the product of a general plan to subvert society. The plain fact is that the political involvement of the unions was a result of the move from competitive capitalism to state monopoly capitalism, the phase in which the state intervenes in the economy to make sure the capitalist system survives. In this role, the state is not neutral, working for the common good. It does not treat everyone equally, and to persuade ourselves of the truth of this we have only to look at the trends in state economic priorities, the Trudeau measures, wage control, the limitation of the right to strike, and repression of organized labour by the courts and the police. The state has become an important element in the process of worker exploitation, for it is present in the economy as the regulator of growth, trying to mitigate the contradictions of capitalism. To this end, the state backs private ventures, finances research and new technology, and controls the distribution of goods and services. And beyond these functions as surrogate and support for private business, the state is itself one of the country's biggest employers, with a roster of 180,000 in Quebec.

This big employer is the same state that regulated wages and working conditions, not only for its own employees, but for those in every sector of the economy. Given this, it is perfectly natural for unions to be taking political positions that go far beyond mere wage demands to express criticisms of the state and its branches: that is, where working conditions and the sale of the labour force are negotiated. The workers are not now struggling against isolated capitalists, but against a cartel of the state and the employers. Their economic demands inevitably become politicized. Here is the origin of the ideological radicalization and the functional politicization of the Quebec labour movement, which the aggravated contradictions of their local environment have pushed to the forefront of the North American movement.

With the Quiet Revolution, then, organized labour experienced unprecedented growth and made significant gains. As was not the case in the Duplessis years, the movement's right to exist was not only recognized, but also institutionalized, as unions were seen as valid mediators and spokesmen. Because of its secular character, its homogeneous membership, the prestige that surrounded its opposition to Duplessis, and its

Liberal sympathies, the csn benefited the most from the Quiet Revolution. In the years 1960 to 1966, its membership more than doubled from 94,114 to 204,361. The expansion occurred chiefly in the public and mixed sectors of the economy, which accounted for 40 per cent of its membership in 1966, up from 15 per cent in 1960. This change was not without its problems of integration and orientation for a group that had represented mainly blue-collar workers. Overall, in the same period, the percentage of unionized workers in the Quebec labour force rose from 28 to 33 per cent, with the latter figure including the teachers. At this time, union ideology was still holding to its 1950s course and supporting the drive to modernize the economy. At the 1964 convention, csn president Jean Marchand followed this line as he spoke about participation and planning, which was seen as a key to get Quebec's economy out of stagnation and provide harmonious economic development. It is true that union leaders criticized the free-enterprise system that led ineluctably to monopolism, economic and social inequalities, inflation, and unemployment, but it was believed that the state could solve these problems. They criticized government inactivity, especially at the federal level, for they thought that only the state, as regulator of the economy, could offset the chronic problems of capitalism and correct its structural imbalances: the weakness of the secondary sector, the bad policy on the exploitation of natural resources, and dependence on American economic imperialism. In these years, union strategy was based on collective bargaining and co-operation with government.

After 1966, however, there was an ideological renewal in organized labour, prompted by the start of an economic recession and the cyclical crisis of capitalism, the mounting aggressiveness of the workers, and critical pressure from the young socialist movement:

The state's social and economic thrust, the broad agreement among union leaders with the ideology of the technocratic and political ruling class, the revolt of the little people against all forms of oppression, and the political and social involvements of young students and workers forced the labour movement to realize that it had no monopoly in the matter of disputes, that it had lost the special, avant-garde quality that it seemed to have had in the years of the long night, and that it had in a sense become bourgeois.[76]

The union movement wanted to be a force for change once more. The catch-up ideology went on the shelf and was replaced by an 'ideology of socio-economic democratization' that involved a partial redefinition of the role of organized labour and its relations with the other elements of society. The two main characteristics of this ideological renewal were its humanism and a certain growth in class consciousness that generated the desire to expand union activity into the social and political realms, while remaining in the tradition of profit-oriented unionism. In fact, this expansion was a response to the state's increasing activity in these areas in the monopoly phase of capitalism. This change in organized labour's approach to economic and social problems was also a reaction to a hardening of attitudes towards unions on the part of government. Union people found out what the state was really about at the time of the laws that forced striking teachers, transport workers, and construction workers back to their jobs.

The principal spokesman for the renewal was CSN president Marcel Pépin. His annual reports bore such titles as 'A Society Made for Mankind' in 1966, 'The Second Front' in 1968, and in 1970, 'A Party of Freedom.' Further signals of this new direction in union ideology and action came with manifestos entitled 'Let's Only Count on our Own Resources,' and reports such as the FTQ's 'The State as the Machine of our Exploitation,' and from the CEQ, the teachers' union, 'The School as Servant of the Ruling Class.' The new ideology came out of an all-inclusive critique of capitalist society, which was seen as anarchic, and responsible for poverty, the economic instability of inflation, chronic unemployment and factory closings. In 'A Society Made for Mankind,' Pépin challenged the free-enterprise system because of the excessive power it gave a small number of large corporations and its lack of social responsibility in the exploitation of worker and consumers. Having believed that the state could make up for capitalism's deficiencies and bring the system's power relations into balance, unionists now realized that a problem with liberal democracy was the control of the economy by the money powers and the subordination of public interest to their private interests by the state. The liberal delusions about unending progress could not stand up to the reality of a steadily deteriorating situation, as evidenced by growing unemployment, loss of buying power by the worker, and the aggravation of socio-economic inequalities. Pépin called for company books to be opened for the worker, and he stressed the ineffectiveness of collective bargaining without action by the wage earners. The objective indicated by all this was one of humanizing and democratizing society by union participation, the key word in the new CSN ideology.

It was a critique and an objective that challenged the very nature of the labour movement, which had until that time been locked into the profit-seeking model of collective bargaining and the defence of workers' strictly economic interests, with no consideration for the underprivileged or the working class as a whole. And in fact, organized labour did try to move beyond its wage-demand function, which levelled off in any case with the coming of the North American recession, and which could do nothing about the problems of unemployment, education, and social security. Workers were not included in decision-making in these areas. There must therefore be a second front by which the labour movement could expand its activity and defend the cause of workers without collective agreements. It must be remembered, however, that the second front was not something completely new for the CSN, which had always had a social and para-professional dimension.

In his 1968 moral report 'The Second Front,' Pépin elaborated on a trade-unionist or social-democratic concept of the connections between the economic and political struggles of the workers. He kept the former for the unions, and for the latter he recommended forming citizens' committees or political action groups. The result of this was to divide worker organization in terms of workplace and spending place. It was a position that avoided any radical challenge to the profit-seeking tradition of the unions, for it left politics at the factory door. The CSN remained apolitical in the sense of party affiliation, although this did not prevent its union professionals or members from getting involved in politics. The confederation rejected the idea of a revolutionary party or avant-garde. It wanted to avoid organic ties with any political party. The freedom of the labour movement was to be preserved at all costs.

Despite its ambiguities, this redefinition of its role by the CSN was a first step in the direction of a class ideology, based on an antagonistic view of the social forces that put the workers in opposition to a minority of capitalists, and also based on the beliefs that the working class should play an active and preponderant role in changing society, and that there must be solidarity of the unionized with other workers. There was always a difference, however, between the revolutionary claims made by union leaders and the actual practice, which stuck to bourgeois legality with a flavour of liberal reformism. While declaring a constant desire to expand into social and political activity, when they reached the bargaining table the unionists invariably fell back on the profit motive. Their general criticism of the capitalist system was not accompanied by a general solution, or an overall proposal to go beyond capitalism. The CSN refused to accept any ready-made model. In the cause of man's liberation by man, the confederation stuck to participatory democracy. The union masses were to control the structures and the ideological and strategic directions of their labour movement.

As the 1970s opened, recession not only ate away at the declining sectors of the economy such as leather, clothing, and textiles, but also affected the key sectors and those that were usually stable, such as iron and steel, the aeronautics industry, pulp and paper, and petrochemicals. These industries had the highest wages and the best job security in Quebec. They were also organized labour's most solid base of support. There were disputes followed by more disputes, lasting longer and getting rougher: General Motors, the pulp and paper companies, and then the public and mixed sectors. The strikes at *La Presse*, Soma, United Aircraft, and others, revealed the inadequacy of the old union strategies against multinationals or the state employer. They spurred on the ideological radicalization of the labour movement, which came out in such manifestos as the CSN's 'Quebec has no Future under the Present Economic System,' and 'Let's Only Count on our own Resources.' These documents were both a reaction to the offensive of big business and an indication of the deficiencies of profit-seeking unionism; if the labour movement was to become effective again, it needed new strategies. They clearly identified the workers' enemies: in the lead was United States imperialism, whose power caused distortions on Quebec's economic structure as well as unemployment and the worker's loss of buying power. Under the existing economic system, the state, Canadian as well as Québécois, was not on the side of the workers, but on the side of the foreign investors who controlled priorities in the allocation of public money. In this sense, the state was an enemy of the working class.[77] Similarly, the FTQ saw the state as an agent for economic power that was for the most part American, for a small part English-Canadian, and for a tiny part Québécois. It had become one of the essential elements in the exploitation of the workers. Under capitalism, then, Quebec's economic liberation was impossible, just as it was impossible to free the state from its bondage to private interests. There was no question of replacing foreign economic domination by Québécois economic domination: 'Quebec's economic liberation must be sought elsewhere than in capitalism, for a Québécois capitalism, whether private or state, would have no alternative but to submit to the will of the American giant.'[78] And 'the ground on which the working class can neutralize the American giant is socialism.'[79] The socialist choice raised the problem of nationalism.

At the beginning of the 1960s, the Quebec labour movement subscribed to the ideology of the two-nation pact and the policy of bilingualism. At the level of the province the csn, faithful to its own history, was in favour of reinforcing Quebec autonomy in the areas of housing, manpower, unemployment insurance, and social security. After 1966, however, this constitutional conformism became incompatible with the union's critique of the capitalist state, especially since the balance of the old political forces was being shaken by the rise of a new social-democratic nationalism in the form of the Parti Québécois. On the language question, for example, the ceq and the ftq were insisting that French should become the language of the workplace, while the csn went so far as to call for French unilingualism. Although the labour movement refused to get openly involved in debate on the national issue, it was still moved to rethink its federalist policy, and to drop hints about a possible alternative that stopped just short of separation.[80]

Reporting on political action to the csn executive in January 1976, André L'Heureux stated: 'Independence and socialism cannot be set up against one another: they are inseparable ... An eventual declaration in favour of independence would not automatically acquire a party-political colouring. The csn has taken a federalist position and no one saw it as party-political.'[81] There was disagreement on the correct line to take with the main representative of separatism. One group in the labour movement was tempted by the proposal of tactical support for the pq to pave the way for a far-reaching transformation of Quebec society. Other unionists, already critical of the state's role, asked themselves what kind of society they would get from the pq. They called for the creation of a workers' party that would combine the national liberation struggle with the fight for socialism, and ensure the workers' political hegemony and their ideological autonomy on the question of socialism in the new state. Finally, a third and extremely small union group were trying to start a non-separatist workers' party. These differences tied into a deeper discussion about the nature of organized labour and the autonomous political action of the working class that led back to the ambiguity of union politics in the Front Commun of 1972.

The research indicates[82] that the labour movement had been on the defensive since 1967. Its evolution was governed by the political moment when it seemed the only force of opposition in Quebec, and by the negotiating strategy used by the state, which reflected the employers' interests. In this light, the Front Commun was more a momentary tactic than a sign of general strategy. Contrary to what the bourgeois ideologues have claimed, the Front did not represent a wholesale challenge to the existing political system; nor did it represent a radical break with the traditional unionism of the crafts and liberal reform, whose basic approach was a routine, mechanical separation of the economic from the political elements in the workers' struggle. Rather, the Front indicated a hardening of union attitudes against a background of worsening contradictions between the capital-state cartel and the working class, determined to stop the state from solving the crisis of capitalism on the backs of labour. The Front also had positive things about it: it called for a $100 minimum weekly wage, a central negotiating table, and a move to strengthen the union spirit of solidarity, aggressiveness, and unity among the membership. Its relative failure can be explained by a variety of problems: in terms of theory and strategy, it concentrated on the nature and role of the state, and on the political dimension of the union struggle, with no talk of working-class democracy and thus no mobilization of the worker vote; in organizational terms, there was the separation of the support and negotiating structures, a shortage of money, a virtual lack of communication with the unionists in the private sector and the working class as a whole, and conflicts of interest in terms of the Front's objectives, and finally, tactical disagreements about the strike and how it proceeded. Division among the union groups, contrast between radical words and traditional practice, and the lack of solid communications with the membership combined to make the unions an easy target for government, which let loose a whole arsenal of demagoguery, laws, fines, and prison sentences. The Front Commun was followed by a period of exhaustion in the labour movement, with the dispersal of the union activists and a scission in the CSN. And yet the battle of the Front Commun had exposed the collusion between the Quebec state and the capitalists. It had also heightened class consciousness, and convinced some people of the need for an autonomous workers' party.

In conclusion, I must emphasize the special direction taken by this inevitable politicization in the Quebec labour movement. Advocated up to now has been a defensive politicization; the unions are not directly raising the question of power. They obey the rules of the bourgeois democratic system, in which they function as negotiators of the sale of labour and pressure groups on issues arising out of collective bargaining. Their politicization is not revolutionary, but reformist. They refuse to affiliate with any political party, and do very little to educate their memberships politically. And finally, the bureaucratized union apparatus often stifles new movements coming from the membership to rock the old profit-seeking unionism. A union-based workers' party is still only a question mark.

Conclusion

In Quebec, ideological development has been distorted by the special nature of a society with a double class structure, the classes being differentiated by nationality and, temporarily, by mode of production. The ruling ideology, then, would not be that of the economically dominant class. There was relative distortion. Economic relations between classes would be mediated by political relations which, in the colonial environment, gave substantial weight and relative power to the petty bourgeoisie, whose political and ideological positions swung, depending on the circumstances, between bourgeois interests and the interests of the ordinary people.

Whereas the European bourgeoisie was nationalistic, democratic, and progressive, the Canadian bourgeoisie in Quebec, consisting largely of British merchants, was unable, from the conquest to the mid-nineteenth century, to play this role. Because of the colonial situation, and the English minority's domination of the French majority, the commercial middle class was prevented from imposing political hegemony on its own, and was thus obliged to seek an alliance with the British bureaucratic aristocracy. There was a contradiction between the aspirations of this class to democracy and control of the state apparatus, and the material basis – colonial oppression – of its class status. So long as the French Canadians formed the majority, the British commercial middle class supported the reactionary party and did what it could to keep out liberal democracy.

In this situation, the French-Canadian petty bourgeoisie of the professions moved in to raise the standard of nationalism and liberal ideology. The members of this class had their roots in the common people; they were the sons of peasants who went into the professions because the other avenues of advancement were closed to them. This petty-bourgeois group was in conflict with the commercial bourgeoisie, the collaborationist clergy, and the government oligarchy. It campaigned for democratic, republic institutions, responsible government, independence for Lower Canada, and the abolition of clerical and seigniorial privilege. The nationalism of this class had as its aim the liberation of French Canada from British colonial domination, and the consequent entrenchment of its own political hegemony. Economically, it opposed the growth of commercial capitalism, calling for growth based on agriculture. It was democratic, anticlerical, progressive, and nationalistic. Its hopes and endeavours were wiped out by the military repression of the 1837–38 rebellion.

In the wake of this failure it fell to another petty-bourgeois group, made up of moderate Patriote elements and the clerical élite, to define French-Canadian nationalism and take the leadership in society. For over a century, the nationalism of French Canada, which had been dynamic and progressive, became defensive and conservative. The political face of nationalism gave way to its cultural face, which became all-pervasive. The ideas of liberation and independence were replaced by the idea of survival. The objective was not now to build an independent nation and a democratic state, but to rely on a French and Catholic provincial government for the preservation of faith, language, and traditional institutions. The petty bourgeoisie co-operated willingly with the English, and later the American, bourgeois class. Granted responsible government and the resulting access to government jobs, this class exchanged its radicalism for a lucrative pragmatism. It gave political support to the industrial bourgeoisie, which replied with honorific posts and marginal revenues. With the clergy in the ascendant, Quebec withdrew into itself, and lay still under the domination of a conservative ideology whose main themes were anti-statism – in this case, the substitution of church for state – the worship of agriculture and the French colonial past, the rejection of industrialization, progress, and all the modern freedoms; and finally, a messianic vision according to which French Canada, poor but chosen, was the vessel of a great moral and spiritual destiny, no less than the conversion of America. The century from 1850 to 1950 was the time of the nationalism of submission and powerlessness that defined Quebec as a rural, clerical society.

This abdication gave the British and American capitalists free and profitable reign over the exploitation of our natural wealth, our work force, and the growth of industry, so that beginning with the Second World War, the rift between reality and the official ideology was gaping dangerously, and the traditional nationalism began falling apart. The political power of the rural petty bourgeois was challenged by a new petty bourgeoisie, urban, educated, and eager for modernization and change.

The defensive, cultural nationalism of the French Canadians became positive, progressive, and political. We defined ourselves now more as Québécois than as French Canadians. The recurring theme of 'our religion, our language, our laws' gave way to 'our state, our language, our natural resources.' The state replaced the church as the main institution of the collectivity. The issue of the nation became an issue of political power. Quebec's new nationalism placed supreme emphasis on the collective will to find a source of power, a device by which to control and decide its own destiny.

Of course, this ambition was nothing new. But it had been repressed by an increasing minority status in Canada and the clericalization of Quebec society. The rebirth and development of this society coincided with a structural change that was inherent in the transition from competitive capitalism to monopoly state capitalism.

The revitalized Quebec state and its increasing interventionism, required to maintain the rate of economic growth, were seen at the outset as a threat to collective survival, for these things came as challenges to the traditional institutions of Quebec society, and they responded to externally imposed economic imperatives. At the same time, however, the increase in the socio-economic functions of the state fanned hopes of liberation. People found that the state could also be a means of collective advancement, providing it was controlled by Québécois and used for their own benefit. All that had to be done was to retrieve the powers of a normal state, with the capacity for self-determination in a movement of liberation from the federal power. Such was the message of the new nationalist ideology. It particularly attracted the new technocratic petty bourgeoisie. Taking advantage of the change in the political function, it could legitimize its claims to hegemony against the traditional petty bourgeoisie and the Canadian grand-bourgeois class.

This involved making up for lost time in every area: democratizing Quebec's political institutions, secularizing the educational system, and adapting Quebec's state and society to the requirements of rising monopoly capitalism. The revitalization of the Quebec state, and the implementation of such huge projects as the nationalization of electric power and the massive Manic dam, gave a new impetus to nationalism. The renewal of Quebec's political and social structures require more power for the Quebec state. To get it, Quebec had to challenge the federal state and demand a new division of powers. These contradictions bred a new awareness: the Quebec state could become a means of collective advancement, and so why not make state and nation coincide? Why not have a sovereign state and an independent Quebec? 'We can do it,' was the RIN slogan in 1966.

The new élite that took the political leadership of Quebec society in 1960 was not homogeneous. One of its components was a traditional group tied to English and American capitalism, which supported the process of modernization but wanted to control its direction, keeping it within the federal political structure. The Quebec state should be strengthened, but not to the point of becoming too powerful and threatening to the dominant economic system. The other part of this élite consisted of intellectuals, engineers, economists, sociologists, and union leaders, all of them from the public and private technocracy. This élite put its faith in planning and more vigorous state intervention in the economy. It showed great intransigence towards the federal power. Its aim was to complete the process of the Quiet Revolution, and it became more and more wedded to the concept of a sovereign Quebec state, controlled by the technocratic petty bourgeoisie, which would then turn its skills into power.

On the fringe of this struggle was another path of nationalism. Just as the Quiet Revolution was running down, young academics and students drew on Marxism and the decolonization movements to present an analysis of Quebec society that linked liberation with socialism. For this group, the Québécois were oppressed, both as workers and as Québécois. From this viewpoint, political independence was not enough. The exchange of English bosses for French ones would in no way solve the exploitation and oppression felt by the workers. Hence, they wanted to pair national liberation with the liberation of the working class. The enemy was no longer just the federal power, or even English-Canadian capitalism: the enemy was capitalism itself, whether American, English, or French. They developed a plan of liberation that took into account all the dimensions of Quebec society. They offered a revolutionary alternative that would replace the imperialist, colonialist bourgeois with the power of the workers and the establishment of socialism. To this group, the fact that they put political independence ahead of economic liberation meant that the Parti Québécois and other nationalist reform movements were incapable of solving the national question in terms of worker interests. These parties could only create a national state bourgeoisie that would ultimately be the servant of United States imperialism and the multinational corporations.

Evidently, Quebec society had now reached the crossroads. The traditional ideological monolithism, disintegrating, gave way to three new streams of thought. The first of these, the bourgeois ideology that was represented politically by the Liberals, has again in the 1970s taken up the banner of the nationalism of cultural survival, clutching at a futile cultural sovereignty and willingly forgoing the economic and political sovereignty of Quebec. Economically, then, this ideology was in favour of maintaining capitalism, opening Quebec unconditionally to foreign investment, the looting of our natural resources, and the use of public funds to heap profits on American multinationals. This ideology's political representative, the Quebec Liberal party, defends federalism, accepts Ottawa's centralizing approach, and wallows in lucrative subordination. In social terms, it has attempted to justify cutting down on services in order to give impetus back to capitalist accumulation, and it has imposed such restrictive measures on Quebec workers as wage control and reductions in public spending. It also displays a savage anti-union bias. In the area of lawmaking, it has codified the needs of capitalist exploitation and adapted the repressive judicial machine to launch an offensive against the labour movement and the progressives. On a grander scale, the planned provocation of the October crisis in 1970 demonstrated the willingness of the English-Canadian bourgeoisie to mobilize the state against the people, using public security and Canadian unity as a cover for the establishment of universal manipulation and repression as a form of government.

A second stream of thought, opposing the ideology of the ruling class and yet in its own way participating in that ideology, is represented by the technocratic petty bourgeoisie, with the Parti Québécois as its political arm. This does not mean that the PQ is made up essentially of technocrats; it does indicate, however, that the working class and progressive elements that form the party's base take their political and ideological direction from the technocrats, who would be well pleased to see power handed out as a reward for education. Contrary to the first, this second ideology advocates political sovereignty and the creation of a social-democratic Quebec state. Essentially reformist, it refuses to challenge radically the existing economic relations – capitalist internally and imperialist externally – preferring to civilize them instead. Its supporters believe that capitalism can be humanized through state controls, with the state as the meeting place of the many and fragmented interests of society. This technocratic ideology defines social conflicts as imbalances, devoid of fundamental antagonisms. Thus, it misconstrues the structural nature of the crisis of capitalism, and the irreconcilable character of the conflict between capital and labour. It aspires to act as arbitrator in the class struggle, and thus seeks support on both sides of the barricades, lecturing the exploiters while asking the workers to be patient and reasonable.

The adherents of this ideology oppose the ruling class because they believe that class to be backward and incapable, not only of standing up for the interests of the Québécois, but also of managing society. From their viewpoint, the Liberal party is incompetent: it cannot neutralize the crisis in Quebec society, and it aggravates rather than smooths the relations of capital and labour. This group, then, offers its services as mediator and manager to the social forces in conflict, stressing its administrative abilities, objectivity, and honesty.

In the economy, this group proposes to reduce support for private capital and encourage the development of state capitalism. It wants to use the state to guide Quebec's economic development. The primary objective is to rationalize the workings of the state so that it can play a more dynamic and effective role in economic growth. By controlling the state apparatus, this class aspires to become a state bourgeoisie capable of dealing with the forces of modern economic life. This ideological approach on the part of the technocratic petty bourgeoisie represents a further step in the process of capitalistic development, at which the growth of the economy requires the growth of the state. This makes the class a legitimate successor to the liberal élite that has failed to marshal the state to mitigate the contradictions of capitalism.

A change in political authority does not, however, mean change in social relations; nor does it necessarily mean that the plan of national liberation will be carried through. In the history of ideologies in Quebec, we have already seen that although the initiative in resistance to federalist ideology has fallen to the petty bourgeoisie, this class has not been able to mastermind the struggle. Economic weakness has forced it into compromise. It does not realize as a class that any political hegemony it might hold is not a result of its own strength, but rather is conferred on a temporary basis to better disguise its basic contradictions. The petty bourgeoisie cannot hope to lead society as a class; at best, through co-operation, it may be allotted an inferior position, as a political or administrative élite, within the ruling class. Its ideology is not in itself completely false or reactionary, but any good ideas that might come out of it are mired in the delusions – the neutral state, equality before the law, parliamentary democracy, social advancement through education, and so on – that are inseparable from its class situation. This class is incapable of representing a liberation scheme. This is not to say, however, that in a special set of circumstances such as a situation of colonial and imperial domination, the petty bourgeoisie cannot become actively associated with such a scheme and contribute to its implementation.

A third stream of thought has been attempting for some years to offer the Québécois a radical alternative, and to this end has urged a new ideological approach – a change that is not limited to a few reform proposals, but reaches out into all parts of Quebec society. For the moment, in the absence of a working-class organization, this ideology is promoted by the petty-bourgeois subgroup that has its base of support in intellectual and unionist circles as well as in mass organization. This group is made up mainly of workers in public and mixed-sector services. It still finds expression politically through the Parti Québécois, but also finds outlets for its political radicalism in the labour movement, especially in the CEQ and the CSN, as well as in local confrontations. The group is polarized, objectively and subjectively, towards the working class, for its experience of exploitation is a comparable one. As a result, it is trying to join with the workers. Its economic positions are anticapitalist and anti-imperialist. It is not merely after Quebec's political liberation, but also the social and economic liberation of the workers. Its resistance to the ruling ideology is expressed in its plan for a free, socialist Quebec.

This plan can only be carried out by a workers' party. The creation of an autonomous, political working-class organization does seem, in the current circumstances, to be the prime condition for ideological change in Quebec. There is a second and equally necessary condition: this organization must avoid fatal isolation. Nor should it abandon the initiative to the ruling ideology. To prevent the working class from being surrounded and cut off, this organization will have to destroy the ruling class's ideological ascendancy over other classes by supporting the struggles of the people – currently, those of farmers, women, citizens' groups, and so on – which in turn means plugging the revolutionary fight into a mass base. The petty bourgeois are not reactionary as such. Their interests are both common with and contradictory to the interests of the working class. The so-called silent majority becomes manipulable by the ruling class only when it is isolated. And finally, there is a third condition: the individual revolts have to be brought together, so that the contradictions in the Québécois population are not allowed to turn into conflicts, obscuring the really antagonistic contradiction, that between the ruling class and the mass of the people. If this did happen, it would destroy the working class. It should never be forgotten that fascism springs up where revolts have failed, to impose its own brand of counter-revolution.

The PQ and the Test of Power

The Parti Québécois election win of 15 November 1976 came as symbolic revenge for the Patriotes of 1937. On the following day the sky had still not fallen on Quebec, whose French-speaking citizens were already showing a new pride and enthusiasm. Above all, the PQ victory had touched them with hope. Ten years of brooding were coming to their end.

Unless one followed some of federalism's acolytes in holding the Québécois and their blinkered atavism in contempt, it was impossible to doubt the clear desire for self-determination and resistance of national oppression that appeared in the November results. Significantly, the Quebec voters had not let themselves be taken in by the spectre of disaster unleashed by the Liberal demagogues. This was more than throwing out an incompetent and corrupt administration; it was a declaration for social and national renewal.

In fact, the failure of the well-heeled anti-separatist fear campaign of the Liberals was the surprise of the election. Admittedly, it was smart of the PQ strategists to hammer away at down-to-earth problems in the areas of agriculture, housing, and the environment, but no one could seriously argue that the voters had simply decided to oust one administration in favour of another. What they had done was cast their ballots for a 'real government,' one that was identified with the interests of the people and the goal of political sovereignty for Quebec. At the very least, the Québécois wanted to register dissatisfaction with the federal octopus. The crushing defeats suffered by two of Ottawa's three special envoys were certainly eloquent of this. And at most, they were endorsing independence. The majority of French-speaking voters did not support the unequivocally federalist parties. In the Montreal region,

more than 60 per cent of the francophone vote went to the Parti Québécois.

Another important and revealing indicator of this change in the political
behaviour of French Quebec was its rejection of the conservative, anti-
union social policies of the Liberals. The old conditioning, the colonized
reflex, did not work; we seemed to have a more mature electorate. And
significantly, the voter turnout of 85.2 per cent was the highest on
record. Some have seen this, especially when contrasted with falling
turnouts at federal voting time, as an assertion of Québécois national
identity.[1]

The PQ triumph marked a departure in the twentieth-century history
of Quebec. Previously, power had been traded back and forth between
the two old parties. In terms of brains and money, the PQ represented
the biggest effort yet made by the Québécois to develop a democratic
and popularly based political organization. In this sense, the party was
symbolic of Quebec's modernization. And the quality of the new government team was unprecedented. In the PQ, the people of Quebec had
chosen political leadership that expressed their deepest national aspirations and their commitment to social change. They had chosen a government that claimed to be for the worker. Now came the test of power.

The most immediate result of the 1976 election was a revitalization
of the political process for individual Québécois, citizen groups, and organized labour. The PQ purged the sickness in political life and gave the
Quebec state new legitimacy as a social regulating force. This in turn
meant greater participation in the process, with more and better-pre-
pared demands coming from the general public. The PQ leadership welcomed this development, while attempting to contain it in ways that
would avert excessive financial and administrative responsibilities for the
state. They responded to the challenge by changing the structure of
government, appointing deputy ministers and creating the priorities committee that freed five ministers from day-to-day administration. The
party's strong popular base would also help channel pressure to the
places where the decisions were made.

In its first months in office, the PQ tried to establish its political credibility and defuse potential hostility from the United States, the rest of
Canada, and English speaking Quebec. By appeasement and conciliation,
it managed to fend off all baiting attempts. This approach may have
produced an impression that the government was failing to move on its

institutional, social, and economic reforms, but it promised to prove its effectiveness in the longer term, by getting the process of social and political change under way while at the same time eroding the forces of resistance. The party's overall strategy required a delicate balance. Government should not actively inflame opposition hostility, but it had to demonstrate how it proposed to benefit the workers, on whom, after all, it depended for its political survival and the success of Quebec independence. To a great extent, in fact, the government's clout in Ottawa depended on a sound social atmosphere and its ability to mobilize popular support at home.

In its early acts, then, the PQ government seemed to be trying to reconcile the two objectives of defusing opposition and consolidating popular support. It moved quickly to suspend the prosecution of Dr Morgentaler, aid the self-administering Tricofil company, and raise the minimum wage to $3 an hour, indexed semi-annually to the cost of living. The Quebec Anti-Inflation Board was forced to accept new wage settlements in the public sector. Charges laid against Quebec unions in the wake of the last Front Commun were now withdrawn. The government announced its intention of improving job security and adding provisions to the labour code for union certification on a whole-sector basis, which would open the way for unionization of two thirds of the active labour force and thus improve the finances of some union organizations. Another pro-worker measure was Bill 45, brought in by labour minister Pierre-Marc Johnson, which provided for the general application of the Rand formula and made it an offence for employers to use strike breakers against legal strikes or lockouts. These various measures helped to relax tensions in Quebec society and win the confidence of organized labour – but not its unconditional support, since the PQ's desire to be neutral meant that it had formed no intimate ties with the movement.

The government also wanted to cement its nationalist support and solve the vexed language question. Bill 101, shepherded through by Camille Laurin, was a master stroke that stemmed the tide of assimilation in the French and immigrant communities while preserving the traditional privileges of the anglophones. The bill put French on the same footing in Quebec as English in the other provinces. By passing the Quebec clause and proposing reciprocal agreements to the other provincial governments, the government showed the country what sovereignty-association could mean. It also exposed the foolishness of the policy of functional bilingualism and the inequalities between the rights of French-speaking minorities elsewhere in Canada and those enjoyed by the English-speaking minority in Quebec. It was a clever strategy that showed up the bad faith of the bill's opponents and built up francophone confidence in the party.

In the social field, the PQ's first steps were less dramatic. There were free prescriptions for those aged 65 and over, and plans to extend the free children's dental programme gradually to the age of sixteen. To mitigate the regressive effect of the tax on children's clothing in his first budget, finance minister Parizeau announced that the surplus would be given back in family allowances. The budget and the tax, even with mitigation, did nothing for the party's image, which was not so far one of brilliance in social reform. They were followed by a timid proposal for state-run auto insurance that merely reinforced one's impression that this new government would move with caution where the bases of the capitalist economy were at stake.

The PQ also held back on economic matters. It planned to cut unemployment back to three per cent, help farmers and small businessmen, and get government buying 'at home.' In the longer term, for the PQ leaders independence meant state control of businesses in the cultural and financial sectors, and in asbestos. As René Lévesque announced: 'We are not in favour of total state control. We are a social-democratic party that can be compared to those in Scandinavia ... We will tell foreign investors what the rules of the game are in Quebec.' There would be no systematic nationalization policy. The PQ government seemed more inclined to intermittent nationalization, picking up companies at opportunity prices as it did with Quebec Steel. The approach has the advantage of being cheaper and in this sense more expeditious. It can supply leverage to get industrialists to maintain investment levels and modernize in sectors that are falling behind. Yet the weakness of the PQ policy of consultative economic management emerged clearly at the summit meetings in La Malbaie. The government's aim was to reach social harmony through exchange among the main movers in the economy. Few concessions were wrung from big business, however. Business attended mainly to make contact with the new government, and the unions came to stage a confrontation with business. The only actual result of the conference may have been to reinforce the image of the state as mediator in the public mind.

As these lines are written in 1977, many questions remain. Is this confidence going to last? How will the Parti Québécois balance its social reform programme with the imperatives of economic crisis? Will competent, honest management and the repatriation of powers now resident in Ottawa be enough to stifle the conflicts in Quebec society? Such factors as regional under-development, unemployment, the influence of high finance, and possible sabotage by the federal government and the English-Canadian bourgeoisie may well reduce the government's ability to manoeuvre and revive class conflicts, even in the party itself. The PQ leaders would then be forced to do unpopular things that would cut into their popular support and undermine their position in the coming federal offensive.

With the 1976 election, sovereignty and getting it became concrete issues. Constitutional deadlines were suddenly brought forward. Prime Minister Lévesque defined the new provincial attitude to Ottawa in these words: ' We are going to show them that we are ready to play the game as long as Quebec's needs are respected, but we will constantly be reminding them that our ultimate goal is Quebec's independence.' For the moment, then, PQ strategy is clear and effective. It is putting the federal system on trial, demonstrating how the current division of powers prevents the Québécois from satisfying their aspirations and planning the development of their society in accordance with their own needs and their own priorities. Areas of federal jurisdiction are to be challenged and renegotiated one by one.

Theoretically, the referendum should be brought into play to free the government, in case of federal intransigeance, from its commitment to peaceful renegotiation; or else, taking the more optimistic view, to confirm a new agreement or new political pact. In all probability, this referendum will not take place before the next federal election. This gives the PQ more room to manoeuvre than the federal parties. Before we reach that stage, however, we are going to see some fascinating political confrontations. For the PQ is not stuck with pamphlet persuasion these days. It has real power. The strength of its conviction is more than moral and intellectual – it is actual. The PQ has the state on its side. After a scant few months in office, the list of questions raised by the new government is already long. In every area, it has tried to show that without full sovereignty, the state of Quebec cannot assume its full responsibilities, and produce the rounded and coherent policies that are required for Quebec's proper development.

There was the issue of the Olympic deficit and then the government's case that federal policy on dairy production was a disaster for Quebec farmers. After that, we heard about the idea of a duty-free zone around Mirabel to promote economic development in that area, and the federal refusal that came as proof of Quebec's limited power. The same sort of thing happened a little later over the abortion issue, when justice minister Bédard asked his federal counterpart to amend the section of the Criminal Code under which Dr Morgentaler was charged; the law could not be applied, and Quebec lacked the power to change it. The new government also wanted to assert Quebec's constitutional competence in communications and more specifically in cable television. Here once again was the old straitjacket in which federalism has wrapped Quebec. Judge Marceau's ruling in the case of the Gens de l'Air came as further confirmation for the PQ thesis. We may add the government's challenge over the RCMP role in Quebec, and justice minister Bédard's attempt to open discussion about a $500-million federal payment to cover the cost of policing services undertaken by Quebec. To bring the list to an end, the federal proposal to make the Caisses Populaires comply with the Bank Act and place reserves with the Bank of Canada was objected to by the Parti Québécois as indefensible meddling, one more proof, if any were needed, of the way in which Quebec's activities were restricted and its dependence on a foreign power.

The dialectic of social reform and national liberation could not but be muted in a political process whose managers were members of a petty-bourgeois class that routinely chose the moderate over the radical approach, and which was aiming, not to limit the economic power of the bourgeoisie, but to secure its own hegemony by satisfying worker demands. The test of actual power has brought the goals of this class into sharp focus. As I write, it is too soon to reject the progressive qualities the new government does have in the name of a revolutionary vision, and to commit myself to the principle of all or nothing. However it all may end, the PQ victory has reversed the political picture, handed the opposition role to the political right, and left a vacuum on the left. In the days before 15 November 1976, the PQ's role as a relatively weak opposition set against the autocratic and anti-labour propensities of the reigning Liberals had created a tacit solidarity, or at least a watchful support for the PQ, in the Quebec left, with the exception of the Marxist-Leninists. In this fog of obscurantism, appeals for a real workers' party fell on deaf ears. Now that the PQ is in office, however, its limitations will be revealed. The left will have to reconsider its position and hive off as an autonomous political force. One can plausibly envisage the re-emergence of a socialist party in Quebec. There are elements in the union movement who, realizing that political action within organized labour has its own limitations, are anxious to assume the leadership role. Such a political party, like all else in post-1976 Quebec, would develop in an atmosphere into which a dynamism has been released that makes a different future possible. The challenge is there.

On the Referendum of May 1980

In Quebec, the question of nationality arises in a unique form. Our situation is peculiar to ourselves in that it calls for a process of liberation within a developed society; at the same time our nationalist movement has to contend with the conditions imposed by the federal character of the Canadian political system. As far as I am aware, Quebec's is the sole example of a national liberation movement in a federal state that was formed after a gradual, and relative, process of decolonization. So far, this aspect has been disregarded; nationalism has masked the interaction between the sovereignty movement and the federal system. An examination of this dialectic may open the way to a better understanding of the results of the referendum of 20 May 1980 and, beyond the events themselves, of the structural trends determining the evolution of the Québécois community.

This essay makes no claim to completeness, and I do not regard my statements as being in any sense final. It is intended simply as a critical review of Quebec nationalism, not to discredit it, but by removing the weight of confusion, to make it more effective politically.

Throughout their history, francophones in Canada have had a problem of identity. Their sense of belonging to a national community has been an uncertain one – hence their various different ways of describing themselves, as *Canayens*, French Canadians, Québécois, and so on. This ambiguity about belonging has been expressed in two currents of nationalism running side by side and often intermingled, one more Canadian in focus, the other more Québécois. The chronic ambivalence in our feeling of community reflects our minority-nation status and our desire for collective self-assertion in a political structure we do not control, but on which we are dependent.

Forced into a defensive posture by power systems that excluded us, we Québécois have always fiercely resisted any attempt, whether deliberate or unthinking, to put an end to us as a structured community. This collective will to live has been taken as given at various times by our élites, clerical or secular, who suited their approach of co-operation or confrontation to the circumstances in order to protect our continuous existence and their own particular interests.

Placed in a minority position by force of arms and weight of numbers, we have had to bargain for our survival and accept a schizoid loyalty in the process. Each succeeding historical compromise has made us more deeply dependent, for there is a dynamic of compromise that yields benefits while at the same time forcing acceptance of the relative distribution of power and allegiance to the power structure. Where this distribution is unequal, the will of the stronger invariably prevails over the will of the weaker. The latter can negotiate concessions, but in return he must recognize the legitimacy of the existing power system; it is the dominant party in this system, after all, that gives recognition to his rights. He is then drawn into a system of alliances where he lacks the initiative. He has to accept a subordinate, collaborative role, and eventually he comes to value the system that institutionalizes his state of dependence. Docile dependence becomes a function of the concessions it makes possible in a power system that is, or is seen to be, unfavourable. In the process, submissiveness becomes a condition of survival. It ends in an unfair bargain; the dominant party gets the enjoyment of his power, while the dominated can enjoy only his survival.

For more than a century this process was upheld by the traditional nationalism that played an active role in socializing Québécois to the Canadian political system. As Lionel Groulx declared: 'Confederation is what we ourselves wanted, what we insisted upon.'[1] Groulx never doubted the basic legitimacy of our belonging to the Canadian political system, even though the acts of the system could be criticized.

Given this viewpoint, a break was unthinkable. Integration into the power structure by minority participation prevented us from challenging the system itself. In order to spare himself the mortal risk of battle, the minority party accepts his position of inequality on condition that the dominant party accept him as a participating entity, an element necessary to the proper functioning of the whole. All relations of dependence can be said to operate in ambiguity, and this applies as much to relations between peoples as it does to relations between employers and employees and the role of socialist parties in the liberal democracies. It clearly applies to the policy of collaboration used by our traditional élites from Bishop Briand right through to Mr Duplessis. Glossing over the contradictions and the resulting national oppression in Canadian society, this ambiguity has, by its delaying effect, contributed to the stability of federalism.

However, the effectiveness of this approach was reduced by structural changes that came in the wake of the Second World War. And with the Quiet Revolution, Quebec became a storm centre in the Canadian political system.

The modernization of industry, carried out under pressure from external economic forces, required the adaptation of new social and political superstructures that proved to be fertile ground for the emergence of a new national awareness, focused on changing the distribution of economic and political power in Quebec. The new social forces created by modernization put forward a strategy of growth based on the use of political power for the necessary leverage. Occurring in the heady context of general prosperity and unlimited growth, these developments carried with them the seeds of the Canadian political crisis of today. In fact, the rising neo-nationalism of Quebec called for a strengthening of the powers of the Quebec state, which meant challenging the division of powers in the Canadian federation. Two poles of political legitimacy came into conflict because their processes were incompatible. The federal process was moving towards a greater centralization of powers; the response to the needs of increased capital reproduction was to be a concentration of growth centres. Quebec meanwhile, first within the system and then through the drive for political sovereignty, has tried to counter the forces of centralism, and has wanted to see the developmental powers concentrated in the Quebec state, thus ensuring the reproduction of the Québécois nation and also reinforcing the power of the new technocratic élites that went with the new functions of government. This was the process that led to the ideology of sovereignty-association. Nationalism was being called on to justify political change and the yearnings for social advancement of the children of the Quiet Revolution. The direct result of all this was the constitutional crisis.

The rise of neo-nationalism, however, also had some less direct and quite unexpected results. Paradoxically, it opened the way for the arrival of

'French Power' and the Trudeau phenomenon in Ottawa, which in the end helped, as the pendulum swung back, to make the Canadian political system more legitimate in Québécois eyes, block the process of change, and increase the political power of the federal state. The result for the Québécois political system was the splitting of society into two camps and the partial reorientation of our nationalist feeling.

Let us examine just how this recovery process took place. At first, the independentist movement challenged Quebec's very adherence to Confederation. The bombs of the FLQ sounded the alarm and hastened English Canada's awakening to the issue of Québécois nationality. During the 1960s, the Canadian political system was facing a crisis of support that threatened the community, the regime, and the authorities in general. To deal with the crisis and stem the ebbing of its support, the federal government created a commission of inquiry and launched a process of renewal in its political institutions that made federal power accessible to francophones. This ill wind brought in the three Quebec doves and their entourage. Having supported the revitalization and modernization of the political apparatus of Quebec, they now wanted to contain its dynamic and get power back again for the smoother operation of the Canadian political system. There is a dynamic connection between Quebec's political self-assertion and the logical result of this, the emergence of the separatist movement, and the sudden prominence in Ottawa of francophones whose job it was to absorb the crisis without altering the distribution of power between the two national communities.

The aim in the second operation was to use Quebec nationalism to stimulate the growth of a Canadian nationalism. This was to be achieved by generating a new symbolism that incorporated certain elements of Quebec's demands. Trudeau is a product of the same nationalism as Groulx and the others who reduced nationality to culture. French-speaking alienation from the Canadian system would be appeased by changing the image of the federal government, getting the francophones to identify with it. And first and foremost, the policy of functional bilingualism would put an end to the flagrant injustices that fed the flames of separatism, and provide francophones with more adequate representation in the federal state apparatus. There was not much room to manoeuvre, for the dominant forces in the economy and the regions of Canada had a low pain threshhold when it came to this change; hence, the need to shelve the two-nations and special-status theses and, beginning in 1968, strengthen the centralizing propensities of the federal regime in the name of the national interest. When it came to the structural causes of Québécois alienation and national oppression, there was no change. Ottawa continued to concentrate on the systems of equalization and transfer payments to individuals, which did nothing to remedy the problems of unequal development, but did have the advantage of making the existing political system and adherence to the Canadian political community more acceptable to these individuals. Thus, contributing actively to the management of the Canadian state, the 'French Power' group kept up appearances; by symbolic reforms, they led Québécois to believe that their interests were supported in Ottawa. Separatist barbs were to be turned aside by concrete facts. In this sense, the move clearly worked; many francophones came to hold key jobs in the government of Canada, and in spite of rebuffs, the effects of bilingualism were immediately perceivable by the citizens. This strategy was effective and profitable, resulting in a Liberal near-monopoly on federal seats in Quebec, especially in the last two elections. This has helped in turn to increase the credibility of the Canadian political system in Quebec.

In spite of the overwhelming Liberal majority, the power in Quebec City was weak during these years, and the independentist opposition was doing its job. The action shifted to the socio-economic arena where the unions emerged as the new challengers. Paralysed by these internal contradictions, Quebec was unable to counter the federal offensive.

Because nationality was defined in terms of language, Quebec nationalism was sapped from within; the federal structure meant that two levels of government could announce that they were the legitimate representatives of the francophones. This legitimacy conflict had a diversionary effect on national awareness and prevented the sense of Québécois national identity from centring around the Quebec state. Here was nationalism turning on itself and being used to promote the continued existence of the Canadian political community. The Québécois nation was united on the federal scene and split on the provincial scene; this paralysed the dynamic of political liberation.

The paradox comes from our minority situation, for the condition that gets an ethnic minority access to power in a federation is maximum solidarity; yet in the final analysis, this solidarity, itself a product of nationalism, prevents that nationalism from working freely towards liberation. Québécois political behaviour is not inconsistent, then; it is completely determined by the structure of Québécois dependence, a defensive reaction on the part of a threatened minority.

If francophones are to emerge as a political force in the federal system, they must resign themselves to domination by a single party. To gain power, they have to reject pluralism, for if their votes were not channelled towards a single party, their political strength would be divided among the various political groups. In a way, federalism and political pluralism are incompatible for the francophones. In order to exist politically on the federal scene, we are condemned to accept the dictatorship of the Liberal party.

The Liberals have been granted the old dream of the traditional nationalists who distrusted parliamentary democracy because the party system divided and weakened the nation. In turn, the Tardivels, Bourassas, and Groulxs denounced the partisan spirit that divided the French Canadians into tory Bleus and liberal Rouges. Competition between Conservatives and Liberals was very lively at this time, and the even division of strength in the House did not allow Quebec's representatives to play a significant role in decision making. Francophones on the government side were merely extras in a system of alliances where they were powerless, caught up in a dynamic where their·influence was minimal. It was to counteract the inherent divisiveness of the party system that support arose for a national front strategy; Quebec must vote as a monolith to increase its political clout in Ottawa. Paradoxically, it was only with the rise of separatism that this strategy became possible for the federal Liberals, who have now managed to eliminate all political competition in Quebec in favour of single-party representation.

The law of majority rule under the democratic system puts minorities in the position of having to use special political behaviour. It forces them to concentrate their votes in order to be as effective as possible in the party system, and this means accepting a party monopoly. The rule applies to the anglophones of Quebec, and in Canada as a whole, francophones, unable to choose freely from the various alternatives offered on the national political market, discover that a minority has in this respect less freedom than the majority. French-speaking power in the federal political structure, then, is incompatible with the practice of pluralist democracy in Quebec itself. To the degree that Quebec's representatives belong to one political group, they will maximize their influence in the political process. This argument from structure, however, is highly prejudicial to the democratic system, tending as it does to eliminate opposition. When that happens, federalism and democracy no longer go together.

Without the support of the Québécois, the Liberals could not hold office, and francophones would not have access to the political élite. This would mean that the Québécois, ceasing to identify with the federal state, would marshal their forces behind the cause of sovereignty. At the same time, without Quebec nationalism as a foil to English Canada, the Trudeau team would not have gained and kept its power. The threat of Quebec nationalism, in fact, is what gets the Trudeau team its support in Ontario; and this Ontario support, combined with the nationalist electoral behaviour of Quebec where voters want francophones in Ottawa, is what gives 'French Power' its political strength. Here, then, is the vicious circle or unsolvable dialectic that prevents Quebec from attaining sovereignty.

Beyond momentary impressions and short-term benefits, however, 'French Power' is a delusion. The logic of politics is expressed in the decision-making process of the party in power in Ottawa. In this context, 'French Power' is a delusion to the extent that it is at risk, dependent on alliances between regions in which the Quebec representatives play a supporting role, with no structural guarantee that their position in the power system will be maintained. This is subject to the risks of election time, as was clearly demonstrated in the Conservative victory of 1979.

Moreover, in all political systems, choices are made primarily in terms of the interests of the majority and the dominant economic forces. Political decisions correspond to the demands of economic groupings or regions that count for something politically, in other words bargaining with their political support to maximize their gains. The lucky one is he whose support can make the difference between power and defeat for the party in office. Political resources being scant, the ruling group tries to extract the greatest possible profit from its decisions, not only in terms of the results achieved by national policies, but also for their own re-election. The beneficiary in this situation is not the captive supporter, his loyalty assured, but the one whose political favours are up for negotiation. Up to now, the main winner in this process has been Ontario, which, through a combination of political heft and strategic support, has managed to get its demands met. Quebec's interests are subject to the dynamic of a power system in which, for historical, demographic, and economic reasons, our political clout is necessary but not necessarily decisive in the system of alliances on which power in Ottawa depends. In Canadian politics, the political weight of the economically advanced regions is decisive, a situation that allows them to influence decisions to their own advantage. These Ottawa decisions have in fact always aimed to create a maximum national growth rate, and this has resulted in a cumulative growth process centred on Ontario. Despite the francophone presence in government in Ottawa, moreover, the gap of regional disparities has not stopped widening, and industries have continued to leave Quebec. In a political structure where we are a minority, we cannot control the spending of public funds, nor can we guide general policy decisions in accordance with our own priorities, for whatever the ethnic origins of the leaders may be, they have to follow the national interest. This does not mean that Quebec's interests are ignored; what it means is that these interests are not maximized. Even though we participate in power, we do not control the strategic levers of power.

To sum up, in the federal system we are condemned to be nationalists, on the Ottawa scene as we solidify our political support, and on the provincial scene as we favour autonomist or sovereignty-seeking policies that will keep constant pressure on the Canadian political system. In other words, because we are a minority in the power system, we have to think defensively. We must summon our collective energies to resist pressures that will tend to threaten our position in the power structure and such rights as may be included in a new constitution. In this respect, the history of federalism is our guarantee for the future; constitutions have never stopped the movement. Because it is legitimate for a people to want to survive, we shall be constantly on the alert, to defend our rights, regret our demographic shrinkage, and protect our position in the economic and political power structures. Federalism locks up nationalism in the struggle for survival and takes away its potential for development, turning its creative dynamism into sullen withdrawal. In other words, the federal system gives us no choice. We are obliged to mobilize our national solidarity to meet expanding external forces that are chiefly concerned with maximizing their own interests, and view the rights of local minorities as obstacles to be overcome.

Nationalism in a federal system has other unpleasant effects. It gives rise to other types of delusions that prevent it from carrying out its potential for liberation. These delusions have to do with our relation to power on the Quebec scene itself. Here, too, the federal structure, with its division of powers, clouds the issue. The existence of two levels of government makes it possible for us to imagine that we have gained power. We cling desperately to the concessions made by the ruling group, as when at the time of confederation we proclaimed that Quebec had 'conquered' its provincial autonomy. The truth is that Quebec is without real power. The strategic decisions affecting our society elude us; they are made elsewhere. In spite of this, however, our political parties struggle gamely for the privilege of transmitting the wishes of Ottawa, or Washington. This ambiguity reached its height when the PQ gained 'power.' Quebec's intellectuals, among others, fell into the trap of keeping the party at arm's length because it was now in power. They were forgetting that the real power was somewhere else. In relation to the whole, we are still in opposition. We do not have the helm in our own hands. The schemers in Quebec City have only a paddle to guide the ship of state.

Nationalism is a precondition for our collective awareness and guides us in our actions, but at the same time, it can hold us back. We need it as a source of solidarity, but it can distort our view of the world. Its role as a vitalizing agent, a vehicle of self-assertion, can distract us from the real power system. In building up our pride, it tends to understate the power of the forces that dominate us. This can lead us to believe that our dreams are coming true, and to act as if the antagonistic interests did not exist, as if there were no adversary. On the other hand, nationalism can tend to produce self-satisfaction by placing too much value on our collective achievements. During the Quiet Revolution, for example, we thought we had launched a strategy for development when in reality we were barely maintaining our level of inequality.

We must escape the vicious circle in which we alternate between a completely uncritical self-glorification and a collective masochism which, over-compensating for our sense of powerlessness, looks to the dominant forces for its success model and presents subordination as a token of freedom and prosperity. A constructive nationalism must seek a balance between self-assertion and recognition of our real situation. There is no question here of denying the need for nationalism; what I want to do is eliminate its distorting effects on our collective consciousness. We mush learn to recognize true power and to confront reality. Because we feel powerless, we tend to hide from reality. We fondly imagine that there are no real conflicts, and that everything can be arranged by friendly negotiation. Being dispossessed, we overestimate what we have managed to preserve or achieve. We cling to the appearance of power, when the real game is going on elsewhere.

The belief that the PQ is actually in power is a delusion that helps perpetuate our subordination as a society. Let us stop wasting time on a partial power. We are fooling ourselves. Our little political baubles, whether in Ottawa or Quebec City, take away our resolve and lull us in false security. We are the masters only of appearances, and yet for this we are ready to be complaisant, to perform any intellectual contortion that lets us escape reality.

We need a lucid nationalist philosophy if Quebec is to be more than a country of the imagination. We need a nationalism that begins by exposing the patterns of domination. Quebec's political liberation must include a process of generalized autonomy that spreads power into every area of society. The legitimacy of our national liberation will rest on the legitimacy of the liberation of our now dominated social forces, so that each level of the struggle will strengthen the others, thus making our real solidarity, poised for action, possible at last.

Notes

Preface

1 Denis Monière and André Vachet, *Les Idéologies au Québec: bibliographie* (Montreal 1976)

Introduction

1 Karl Marx, *A Contribution to the Critique of Political Economy* (New York 1970) 20–1
2 Karl Marx and Friedrich Engels, *The German Ideology* (Moscow 1968) 37
3 *Ibid.* 62
4 *Ibid.* 61
5 Karl Marx, *The 18th Brumaire of Louis Napoleon*, in Marx and Engels, *Collected Works*, vol. 11 (New York 1978) 103
6 Letter to J. Bloch, Sept 1890, in Marx and Engels, *Selected Correspondence* (Moscow 1965) 417
7 Lucien Goldmann, *Recherches dialectiques* (Paris 1959) 74
8 This is a shortened version of an article that appeared originally in the March 1976 issue of *Canadian Journal of Political Science.*
9 In Marx, *The 18th Brumaire*
10 *The Communist Manifesto*, in Marx and Engels, *Collected Works*, vol. 6 (New York 1976) 503
11 Letter to H. Starkenburg, Jan 1894, in Marx and Engels, *Selected Correspondence* 467
12 Mao Tse-Tung, 'On Contradiction'
13 Samir Amin, *Unequal Development* (New York and London 1976) 294
14 *Ibid.* 296
15 Roberto Schwarz, 'Dépendance nationale, déplacement d'idéologies, littérature,' in *L'Homme et la société*, Oct-Dec 1972, 100

16 *Ibid.* 104
17 *Ibid.* 107
18 Cf. the Malagasy example in G. Althabe, *Oppression et libération dans l'imaginaire* (Paris 1969) 47.
19 Pierre-Philippe Rey, *Golonialisme, néo-colonialisme et transition au capitalisme* (Paris 1971) 457–8

Chapter 1: Nouvelle-France

1 Cf. Louise Déchêne, *Habitants et marchands de Montréal au XVIIe siècle* (Paris 1974) 46.
2 Richelieu, *Maximes d'Etat*, cxxv
3 Quoted in Jean Touchard, *Histoire des idées politiques* (Paris 1967) 1, 343
4 Bossuet, *Politique tirée de l'Ecriture Sainte*, i, ii, art. ii
5 Bossuet, *Les Devoirs du Roi*, quoted in H.-E. Sée, *Les Idées politiques en France au XVIIe siècle* (Paris 1923) 168
6 *Ibid.* 36
7 H. Denis, *Histoire de la pensée économique* (Paris 1971) 100
8 Monchrestien, *Traité de l'économie politique* (Paris 1889) 246, 320
9 This is a shortened version of my article on the petty producers' mode that appeared originally in the March 1976 issue of *Revue d'histoire de l'Amérique française.*
10 Régine Robin, 'La Nature de l'Etat à la fin de l'Ancien régime' in *Dialectiques*, nos 1–2, 1973, 42
11 N. Poulantzas, *Pouvoir politique et classes sociales* (Paris 1968) 168–9
12 C. Mazauric, *Sur la révolution française* (Paris 1970) 93
13 Karl Marx, *Oeuvres* (Pléiade edition) i, 401
14 Guy Dhoquois, *Pour l'histoire* (Paris 1971) 189–90
15 Y. Lamarche, M. Rioux, and R. Sévigny, *Aliénation et idéologie dans la vie quotidienne des Montréalais francophones* (Montreal 1974) 32
16 Larry MacDonald, 'Petty Bourgeois Aspects of Pre-Industrial Canada' (unpublished ms) 15
17 Cameron Nish, *Les Bourgeois-gentilshommes de la Nouvelle-France, 1729–1748* (Montreal 1968) 156
18 Sigmund Diamond, 'Le Canada français au xviie siècle: une société préfabriquée' in *Annales*, March-April 1961, 353
19 Larry MacDonald, 'France and New France: the Internal Contradictions' in *Canadian Historical Review*, June 1971, 130
20 *Ibid.* 124
21 Diamond, *Le Canada français*, 338, 354
22 Déchêne, *Habitants et marchands*, 265

23 Nish, *Les Bourgeois-gentilshommes*, 115
24 Jean-Pierre Wallot, 'Le Régime seigneurial et son abolition au Canada' in *Canadian Historical Review*, Dec 1969, 375
25 Quoted in Diamond, *Le Canada français*, 350
26 Gustave Lanctôt, *Histoire du Canada: du traité d'Utrecht au traité de Paris, 1713–1763* (Montreal 1964) 281
27 Marc Bloch, *Caractères originaux de l'histoire rurale française* (Paris 1952) 82, 84
28 Guy Frégault, *La Civilisation de la Nouvelle-France* (Montreal 1944) 125
29 Déchêne, *Habitants et marchands*, 186–7, 230
30 Jean-Pierre Wallot, *Un Québec qui bougeait* (Montreal 1973) 183
31 Déchêne, *Habitants et marchands*, 476
32 *Ibid.* 452
33 R. L. Séguin, 'L'Esprit d'insubordination en Nouvelle-France et au Québec au xviie et xviiie siècles' in *L'Académie des sciences d'Outre-Mer*, xxxiii, 4, 1973, 576
34 See Guy Frégault, *Le XVIIIe siècle canadien* (Montreal 1968) 125.
35 Lionel Groulx, 'Le Gallicanisme sous Louis xiv' in *Revue d'histoire de l'Amérique française*, June 1947
36 Quoted in Guy Frégault, *La Civilisation de la Nouvelle-France, 1713–1744* (Montreal, 1969) 189–90
37 *Ibid.* 187
38 Frégault, *Le XVIIIe siècle canadien*, 121–39
39 Wallot, in *Un Québec qui bougeait*, 203–10, holds that this continued to be the case until after the middle of the nineteenth century.
40 Instruction to Vaudreuil, quoted in Guy Frégault, *La Civilisation de la Nouvelle-France, 1713–1744*, 105–6
41 *Ibid.* 211–12
42 Charlevoix, *Histoire et description de la Nouvelle-France* (Paris 1744) vol. v, 117
43 Déchêne, *Habitants et marchands*, 96ff
44 Antoine Roy, *Les Lettres et les arts au Canada*, 75
45 Marcel Trudel, *L'Influence de Voltaire au Canada* (Montreal 1945) 19–20
46 *Ibid.* 23
47 *Ibid.* 35

Chapter 2: Under British Rule, 1760–1791

1 Michel Brunet, *La Présence anglaise et les canadiens* (Montreal 1964) 116
2 Gilles Bourque, *Classes sociales et question nationale au Quebec, 1760–1840* (Montreal 1970) 44–5

3 *Ibid.* 43
4 Brunet, *La Présence anglaise*, 66
5 *Ibid.* 58
6 According to a 1778 petition from businessmen in Quebec and Montreal, 80 per cent of the colony trade and half of its wealth in money and real estate were in the hands of the three per cent English minority.
7 Bourque, *Classes sociales*, 55
8 *Ibid.* 56
9 See *ibid.* 64–5
10 This image was still accepted by the traditional Quebec historians; even our historical consciousness was colonized.
11 See *Economie québécoise* (Montreal 1969) 41
12 Cf. Briand's May 1775 mandamus in Bourque, *Classes sociales*, 81–9
13 *Ibid.* 91
14 *Ibid.*
15 Quoted in *ibid.* 60
16 Brunet, *La Présence anglaise*, 89
17 Quoted in Bourque, *Classes sociales*, 112
18 Brunet, *La Présence anglaise*
19 Michel Brunet, *Les Canadiens après la Conquête, 1759–1775* (Montreal 1969) 37
20 Quoted in *ibid.* 46
21 Quoted in *ibid.* 121
22 Bourque, *Classes sociales*, 79
23 Marcel Trudel, *Louis XVI, le Congrès américain et le Canada* (Quebec City 1949) 6
24 Brunet, *Les Canadiens après la Conquête*, 54–5
25 *Ibid.* 63
26 Quoted in Lionel Croteau, 'Les Origines intellectuelles de la rébellion de 1837–38' (1943, thesis for the University of Ottawa) 33
27 See Abbé Verreau, *Invasion du Canada* (Montreal 1873) 5–6
28 See Gustave Lanctôt, *Le Canada et la révolution américaine* (Montreal 1965) 39
29 Religion was no obstacle; the thirteen included Catholic Maryland.
30 Quoted in Trudel, *Louis XVI, le Congrès américain et le Canada*, 59
31 Quoted in Bourque, *Classes sociales*, 144
32 *Ibid.* 81–2
33 Lanctôt, *Le Canada et la Révolution américaine*, 82
34 *Ibid.* 86
35 *Ibid.* 87
36 John Hare and Jean-Pierre Wallot, 'Les Idéologies dans le Bas-Canada au début du XIXe siècle' in *L'Information historique*, Sept-Oct 1969, 183

37 Bourque, *Classes sociales*, 91
38 Hare and Wallot, *Les Idéologies dans le Bas-Canada*, 183
39 Michel Brunet, 'La Révolution française sur les rives du Saint-Laurent' in *Revue d'histoire de l'Amérique française*, Sept 1957, 159
40 *Ibid*. 161
41 *Ibid*. 156
42 Quoted in Mason Wade, *Les Canadiens français de 1760 à nos jours* (Montreal 1963) vol. 1, 117 (ed. note: as Wade is used in these chapters as a source of quotations from contemporary writers in French, the French-language edition of his work has been retained)
43 Quoted in Jean-Pierre Wallot, 'Courants d'idées dans le Bas-Canada à l'époque de la Révolution française' in *L'Information historique*, March-April 1968, 73
44 Jean Pierre Wallot, *Un Québec qui bougeait* (Montreal 1973) 203
45 *Ibid*. 210

Chapter 3: Under British Rule, 1791–1840

1 Fernand Ouellet, *Histoire économique et sociale du Québec, 1760–1850* (Montreal 1966) 193
2 *Ibid*. 163, 202
3 Gilles Bourque, *Classes sociales et question nationale au Québec, 1760–1840* (Montreal 1970) 165
4 Quoted in Jacques Lacoursière *et al*, *A New History of Canada* (Montreal 1972) vol. 5, 473
5 Bourque, *Classes sociales*, 218
6 Ouellet, *Histoire économique*
7 *Ibid*. 147–8
8 *Ibid*. 57
9 Mason Wade, *Les Canadiens français de 1760 à nos jours* (Montréal 1963)
10 *Ibid*. 122–3
11 See T.R. Preston, *Three Years' Residence in Canada from 1837 to 1839* (London 1840) vol. 2, 35–6
12 Bourque, *Classes sociales*, 233
13 *Ibid*. 295–6
14 *Ibid*. 299
15 *Ibid*. 226
16 Stanley Ryerson, *Le Capitalisme et la Confédération* (Montreal 1972) 57
17 Quoted in Bourque, *Classes sociales*, 230
18 Lionel Groulx, *Histoire du Canada français* (Montreal 1962) 166
19 Ryerson, *Le Capitalisme*, 38

20 *Ibid.* 63
21 *Ibid.* 64
22 Wade, *Les Canadiens français*, 183–4
23 Quoted in Fernand Ouellet, *Papineau* (Quebec City 1959) 100–1
24 *Ibid.* 53
25 Bourque, *Classes sociales*, 240
26 Ouellet, *Papineau*, 9
27 Quoted by Ryerson, *Le Capitalisme*, 69–70
28 Bourque, *Classes sociales*, 251
29 Ouellet, *Papineau*, 77
30 Ryerson, *Le Capitalisme*, 59–60
31 Fernand Ouellet, 'Nationalisme et laïcisme au xixe siècle' in J.-P. Bernard (ed.), *Les idéologies québécoises au XIXe siècle* (Montreal 1973) 44
32 Quoted by Wade, *Les Canadiens français*, 181
33 *Ibid.* 190
34 *Ibid.* 189
35 Bourque, *Classes sociales*, 322
36 Fernand Ouellet, 'Le Mandement de Mgr. Lartigue de 1837 et la réaction libérale' in *Bulletin des recherches historiques*, vol. 58, 1952, 104
37 Quoted by Wade, *Les Canadiens français*, 191
38 Quoted by Bourque, *Classes sociales*, 271–2
39 Quoted by Ouellet, *Papineau*, 102
40 Wade, *Les Canadiens français*, 192
41 Richard Chabot, *Le Curé de campagne et la contestation locale au Québec de 1791 aux troubles de 1837–1838* (Montreal 1975) 116
42 Richard Chabot, 'Le Rôle du bas clergé face au mouvement insurrectionnel de 1837' in *Histoire du Canada* (Montreal 1970) 88
43 Chabot, *Le Curé de campagne*, 119–20
44 *Ibid.* 129–30
45 G.M. Craig (ed.), *Lord Durham's Report* (Toronto 1963) 42
46 Quoted by Chabot, *Le Curé de campagne*, 109
47 *Lord Durham's Report*, 20
48 *Ibid.* 148–51
49 Quoted in Groulx, *Histoire du Canada français*, 131–2
50 *Lord Durham's Report*, 23, 146
51 *Ibid.* 26
52 *Ibid.* 146
53 *Ibid.* 147
54 *Ibid.* 146
55 See Gérard Filteau, *Histoire des Patriotes* (Montreal), vol. iii, 243–4

Chapter 4: The Path to Confederation, 1840–1867

1 See Stanley Ryerson, *Unequal Union* (Toronto 1975) 175
2 Upper Canada's revenue at this time was inadequate even to service the provincial debt of £1.2 million, while the public debt of Lower Canada was only £95,000.
3 Mason Wade, *Les Canadiens français de 1760 à nos jours* (Montreal 1963) 256
4 *Ibid.* 257
5 Thus it was that in the spring of 1841, Sydenham procured the election of nineteen tories in the forty-two seat Lower Canada assembly and got a majority.
6 Stanley Ryerson, *Le Capitalisme et la Confédération* (Montreal 1972) 222
7 *L'Avenir*, 15 April 1848
8 Quoted in Jean-Paul Bernard, *Les Rouges: libéralisme, nationalisme et anticléricalisme au milieu du XIXe siècle* (Montreal 1971) 81
9 Cf. Dessaulles's diatribe against regimentation in church-operated schools, quoted by Philippe Sylvain in W.L. Morton (ed.) *The Shield of Achilles* (Toronto 1968) 130.
10 As the paper announced in its issue of 23 Oct 1847: '*L'Avenir* will devote itself more than ever to the interests of Canada's youth, and the priority, in our opinion, is education.'
11 Led by Papineau, the Patriotes recognized the Jewish right to suffrage in 1832.
12 Gonsalve Doutre, 'Le Principe des nationalités' (speech to the Montreal Institut canadien, 1 Dec 1864) 53
13 *L'Avenir*, 8 May 1848
14 Quoted in Sylvain, in *The Shield of Achilles*, 120
15 Bernard, *Les Rouges*, 120
16 The annexationist manifesto was first published in *L'Avenir* on 13 Oct 1849.
17 The Oblates arrived in 1841, then the Jesuits returned in 1852 followed by various other religious communities.
18 Sylvain, in *The Shield of Achilles*, 144
19 *Ibid.* 221
20 *Ibid.* 238
21 Quoted in René Hardy, 'L'Ultramontanisme de Laflèche: génèse et postulats d'une idéologie' in *Recherches sociographiques*, vol. 10, 1969, 168
22 *Ibid.* 202
23 *Les Mélanges religieux*, 7 Sept 1847
24 H.-R. Casgrain, 'Le Mouvement littéraire au Canada' in *Le Foyer canadien*, IV, 1866
25 Quoted in Fernand Dumont (ed.), *Les Idéologies au Canada français, 1850–1900* (Quebec City 1971) 71

26 Michel Brunet, *La Présence anglaise et les Canadiens* (Montreal 1964) 119
27 *Ibid.* 126
28 *Le Nouveau Monde*, 6 Dec. 1873

Chapter 5: Noonday of Ultramontanism, 1867–1896

1 Hartland estimates direct United States investment at $15 million in 1867; see 'Canadian Balance of Payments since 1868' in *Trends in the American Economy in the 19th Century: Studies in Income and Wealth*, vol. 24, 717–55.
2 Jean Hamelin and Yves Roby, *Histoire économique du Québec, 1850–1896* (Montreal 1971) 262
3 *Ibid.* 217
4 *Ibid.* xiv
5 Charles Lipton, *The Trade Union Movement of Canada, 1827–1959* (Montreal 1968) 26
6 Andre Gosselin, 'L'Evolution économique du Québec' in *Economie québécoise* (Montreal 1968) 108
7 Some 44 per cent of the active farm population consisted of wage-earning workers, and with falling prices and the depression of 1874–78, exhausted fields and lagging technology, the Quebec farm could not support this rural proletariat.
8 Hamelin and Roby, *Histoire économique*, 214
9 Albert Faucher, *Québec en Amérique au XIXᵉ siècle* (Montreal 1973) 61, 62, 67
10 *Ibid.* 48
11 The 1861 census showed 1.4 million Upper Canadians as against 1.1 million in Quebec.
12 Jean-Charles Bonenfant, 'L'Idée du fédéralisme en 1864' in *Culture*, Dec. 1964, 314
13 See M. Duverger, *Institutions politiques et droit constitutionnel* (Paris 1966) 72.
14 Some 150 provincial laws were disallowed until the practice fell into disuse after 1945.
15 Quoted in Jean-Charles Bonenfant, 'Les Canadiens français et la naissance de la Confédération' in the C.H.A. *Report*, 1952, 42
16 In Jean-Charles Bonenfant, *La Naissance de la Confédération* (Montreal 1969) 13
17 In Jean-Charles Bonenfant, 'Les Idées politiques de George-Etienne Cartier' in Marcel Hamelin (ed.), *Les Idées politiques des premiers ministres du Canada* (Ottawa 1969) 36
18 It was revealed in the Pacific Railway Scandal of the 1870s that Sir Hugh Allan, representing a consortium based in the United States, had contributed $350,000 to tory election funds at the request of Cartier and

J.A. Macdonald in exchange for their commitment to deliver the construction contract for the transcontinental railroad.

19 Jean-Claude Robert, *Du Canada français au Québec libre* (Paris 1975) 147–8

20 See Charles Lipton, *The Trade Union Movement of Canada, 1827–1959* (Montreal 1968)

21 Quoted by Hamelin and Roby, *Histoire économique*, 311

22 Denis Héroux and Richard Desrosiers, *Les Travailleurs québécois et le syndicalisme* (Montreal 1973) 27

23 Gaétan Gervais, 'Médéric Lanctôt et l'Union nationale' (1968, thesis for the University of Ottawa) 146

24 See Médéric Lanctot, *L'Association du capital et du travail* (Montreal 1872).

25 Quoted by Denis Héroux and Richard Desrosiers, 'Un Adversaire de la Confédération et un théoricien social en 1867' in *Histoire du Canada* (Montreal 1967) 102

26 See Jean Hamelin (ed.), *Les Travailleurs québécois, 1851–1896* (Montreal 1973) to which I am indebted for much of this section.

27 In *Mandements, lettres pastorales et circulaires des évêques du Québec* (Quebec City 1890) vol. 6, 205; see also 576–7.

28 Rome had included the order among its prohibited societies but did not make this dogma.

29 Quoted in *Le Courrier du Canada*, 11 Jan 1888

30 In *La Minerve*, 29 April 1880

31 Hamelin (ed.), *Les Travailleurs québécois*, 171

32 Le Nouveau Monde, 25 Nov 1873

33 André Lavallée, '20 avril 1871. Un programme électoral catholique' in *Histoire du Canada* (Montreal 1967)

34 *Ibid.* 124

35 *Ibid* 117

36 *Le Nouveau Monde*, 26 July 1872

37 Lavallée, '20 avril 1871,' 118

38 *La Vérité*, 31 May 1884

39 *Ibid.* 28 April 1906

40 *Ibid.* 18 July 1896

41 *Ibid.* 28 Jan 1882

42 *Ibid.* 11 Nov 1893

43 *Ibid.* 11 Feb. 1893

44 Mathieu Girard, '*La Pensée politique de Jules-Paul Tardivel*' in *Revue d'histoire de l'Amérique française*, Dec 1967, 397

45 Mason Wade, *Les Canadiens français de 1760 à nos jours* (Montreal 1963) 456

46 Robert Rumilly, *Mercier* (Montreal 1936) p. 319

47 Quoted by Wade, *Les Canadiens français*, 466–7
48 *La Vérité*, quoted in *ibid*. 398
49 Tardivel, *Pour la Patrie* (Montreal 1895; Toronto 1975 in English) 7
50 See John Hare, 'Nationalism in French Canada and Tardivel's Novel *Pour la Patrie*' in *Culture*, Dec 1961, 403–12
51 *La Vérité*, 2 April 1904
52 Quoted by Wade, *Les Canadiens français*, 420
53 Quoted by André Laurendeau, 'Sur une polémique entre Bourassa et Tardivel' in *L'Action nationale*, Feb 1954, 257
54 In 'Quelques considérations sur les rapports de la société civile avec la religion et la famille' quoted by Wade, *Les Canadiens français*, 381

Chapter 6: The Ideology of Self-preservation, 1896–1929

1 Bishop Paquet, quoted by Mason Wade, *Les Canadiens français de 1760 à nos jours* (Montreal 1963) 554
2 Jean Hamelin and Jean-Paul Montmigny, '1896–1929: un deuxième phase d'industrialisation' in Fernard Dumont *et al.*, *Idéologies au Canada français, 1900–1929* (Quebec City 1974) 17
3 *Ibid*. 21
4 See Alfred Dubuc, 'Développement économique et politiques de développement: Canada 1900–1940' in *Economie québécoise*, 196
5 Analysis made by Céline Saint-Pierre in her thesis, 'Le développement de la société québécoise,' submitted in 1973 to the Ecole Pratique des Hautes Etudes
6 Hamelin and Montmigny, '1896–1929: un deuxième phase,' 21
7 Dumont *et al.*, *Idéologies*, 3
8 Charles Gill, *Correspondance* (Montreal 1969) 28
9 Quoted by Saint-Pierre, *Le développement de la société québécoise*, 99
10 *Ibid*. 102
11 Quoted in Blair Neatby, *Laurier and a Liberal Quebec* (Toronto 1973) 137
12 Wade, *Les Canadiens français*, 478
13 *Ibid*. 480
14 *Ibid*. vol. 2., 230
15 Quoted in Jean-Claude Robert, *Du Canada français au Québec libre* (Paris 1975) 163
16 Dumont *et al.*, *Idéologies*, 13
17 *Ibid*. 224
18 *Ibid*. 227
19 *Ibid*. 237, 223
20 Quoted in Michèle Jean, *Québécoises du XXe siècle* (Montreal 1974) 197–201
21 *Ibid*. 242

22 Quoted by Roland Parenteau, 'Les Idées économiques et sociales de Bourassa' in *L'Action nationale* (Montreal 1954) 177–8
23 In Wade, *Les Canadiens français*, 522
24 Canada eventually sent 7,300 men to South Africa at a cost of $2.8 million to the taxpayers.
25 Wade, *Les Canadiens français*, 559
26 Borden's plan to hand the UK $35 million was scuttled by the Liberal-dominated Senate.
27 *Le Devoir*, 24 Nov 1923
28 Dumont *et al.*, *Idéologies*, 233
29 Quoted in André Laurendeau, 'Le Nationalisme de Bourassa' in *L'Action nationale*, Jan 1954, 30
30 *Ibid.* 17
31 *Ibid.* 31
32 Quoted in Dumont *et al.*, *Idéologies*, 249
33 See Robert Rumilly, *Henri Bourassa* (Montreal 1953) 757.
34 *Ibid.* 392
35 See M.A. Gagnon, *La Vie orageuse d'Olivar Asselin* (Montreal 1962) 39
36 Lionel Groulx, *Notre maître le passé* (Montreal 1936) II, 324
37 Lionel Groulx, 'Vers l'avenir' in *L'Action nationale*, Oct 1941, 101–2
38 Lionel Groulx, *Directives* (Montreal 1937) 17–18
39 Lionel Groulx, *La Confédération canadienne, ses origines* (Montreal 1918) 158–9
40 Lionel Groulx, *Orientations* (Montreal 1935) 266
41 Quoted in Jean-Pierre Gaboury, *Le Nationalisme de Lionel Groulx* (Ottawa 1970) 93
42 Quoted in André Bélanger, *L'Apolitisme des idéologies québécoises: le grand tournant de 1934–1936* (Quebec City 1974) 202
43 *Ibid.* 219
44 Quoted in Gaboury, *Le Nationalisme de Lionel Groulx*, 137
45 Dumont *et al.*, *Idéologies*, 330
46 Groulx, *Directives*, 61
47 See Yves Roby, *Les Québécois et les investissements américains (1918–1929)* (Quebec 1976) 45.
48 Groulx, *Directives*, 56
49 Bélanger, *L'Apolitisme* 250
50 Lionel Groulx, *Histoire du Canada français depuis la découverte* (Montreal 1960) vol. 1, 61
51 Quoted in André Bélanger, 'Lionel Groulx et le culte du chef,' in *Le Jour*, 30 Jan 1975, 9
52 *La Presse*, 26 Oct 1898, 5
53 Quoted in Dumont *et al.*, *Idéologies*, 290

54 *Ibid.* 303
55 *Ibid.* 295–6
56 *Ibid.* 305
57 *Ibid.* 309
58 Samuel Barnes, 'The Evolution of Christian Trade Unionism in Quebec,' in *Relations industrielles*, Oct 1958, 571
59 Quoted by Saint-Pierre, *Le développement de la société québécoise*, 242
60 Quoted in *ibid.* 245
61 Quoted by Louis-Marie Tremblay, *Le Syndicalisme québécois: idéologies de la CSN et de la FTQ* (Montreal 1972) 25
62 *Ibid.* 26
63 E. Hébert, *Le Problème social et sa solution* (1919), 9
64 See CTCC Almoner-General Boileau's speech in the minutes of the union congress at Sherbrooke in 1926, page 9.

Chapter 7: Petty-bourgeois Economists, 1929–45

1 Céline Saint-Pierre, 'Le développement de la société québécoise' (Thesis, Ecole Pratique des Hautes Etudes 1973) 114; see also 109
2 E.C. Hughes, *Rencontre de deux mondes, la crise d'industrialisation du Canada français* (Montreal 1972) 88–9 and 93
3 *Ibid.* 98
4 *La Nation*, 5 Aug 1937
5 The awakening began with the publication in 1910 of Errol Bouchette's *L'Indépendance économique du Canada français*.
6 Joseph Bruchard (pseudonym of Alexandre Dugré), 'Le Canada français et les étrangers' in *L'Action française*, Oct 1922, 201
7 Quoted by Saint-Pierre, *Le développement de la société québécoise*, 247
8 *Ibid.*
9 *Comptes-rendus des Semaines sociales du Canada*, vol. 14, 'L'Organisation professionnelle' (Montreal 1936) 335
10 Quoted in Fernand Dumont *et al.*, *Idéologies au Canada français, 1900–1929* (Quebec City 1974)
11 Lionel Groulx, *Directives* (Montreal 1937) 24–5
12 *La Rente*, 1 July 1920
13 François-Albert Angers, 'L'Industrialisation et la pensée nationaliste traditionnelle' in *Economie québécoise*, 424
14 Quoted in Gaston Turcotte, 'De l'idéologie des Caisses populaires' (1971, thesis for Laval University) 108–9
15 *L'Action nationale*, vol. XI, no. 1, 25
16 *Ibid.* 27

17 Saint-Pierre, *Le développement de la société québécois*, 248–9
18 J.-B. Desrosiers, 'Principles et description de l'organisation corporative' in *L'Action nationale*, vol. xi, Jan 1938, 145
19 *Ibid.* 146
20 *Ibid.* 147
21 Esdras Minville, 'Libéralisme, communisme, corporativisme' in *L'Actualité économique*, Dec 1936, 160
22 Roger Duhamel, 'L'Ordre corporatif sous le signe du fascio' in *La Relève*, vol. 1, no. 8, 1935, 202
23 In Dumont *et al.*, *Idéologies*, 71
24 Gratien Gélinas, 'Du patriotisme ça' in *L'Action nationale*, vol. 5, May 1935
25 'Le grincheux' in *Le Devoir*, 30 Nov 1934
26 Dumont *et al.*, *Idéologies*, 335
27 *Ibid.* 336
28 *Ibid.*
29 Dostaler O'Leary, *Séparatisme: doctrine constructive* (Montreal 1937) 210
30 See Lita-Rose Betcherman, *The Swastika and the Maple Leaf* (Toronto 1975) 45.
31 Bishop Paquet, 'Le Bolchévisme' in *Action catholique*, 31 Jan 1920; see also editorials of 21, 24, 31 Jan and 7 Feb 1920
32 André Belanger, *L'Apolitisme des idéologies québécoises: la grand tournant de 1934–1936* (Quebec City 1974) 308
33 Lionel Groulx (writing as J.-J. Brassier) 'Pour qu'on vive' in *L'Action nationale*, Jan 1934
34 Jean-Louis Roy, *Les programmes électoraux du Québec* (Montreal 1971) vol. ii (1931–1966) 322–7
35 *Ibid.* 327
36 *Ibid.*

Chapter 8: Catching up with the Modern Age

1 John Porter, *The Vertical Mosaic* (Toronto 1965) 234
2 As concluded by the Paley Report in 1952
3 Claude Saint-Onge, 'L'Impérialisme U.S. au Québec' (1973, thesis for the University of Paris) 145–7
4 Mario Dumais, 'L'Evolution économique du Québec' in *Economie québécoise*, 222
5 Lysiane Gagnon, 'Les Conclusions du rapport B.B.' in *Economie québécoise*, 244. Evidence that this is still true can be found in *La Presse* of 30 April 1977, 8.

6 See Porter, *The Vertical Mosaic*, 83–9 and 93–4, and the third report of the Royal Commission on Bilingualism and Biculturalism.

7 Porter, *The Vertical Mosaic*

8 In this section, I am making use of Richard Desrosiers' MA thesis, 'L'Idéologie de Maurice Duplessis' (1969, for the University of Montreal).

9 *Le Devoir*, 22 Nov 1946 and 3 Jan 1950

10 *Ibid*. 2 Jan 1951

11 *Ibid*. 3 Jan 1946 and 4 Oct 1955

12 *Ibid*. 17 Oct 1946 and 4 Jan 1946

13 *Ibid*. 19 Sept 1949

14 *Ibid*. 27 Jan 1947 and 27 Jan 1955

15 *Ibid*. 9 June 1949

16 *Ibid*. 14 July and 19 Aug 1949 and 21 June 1948

17 Desrosiers, *L'Idéologie de Maurice Duplessis*, 43

18 *Le Devoir*, 14 Jan 1954

19 Desrosiers, *L'Idéologie de Maurice Duplessis*, 52

20 *Le Devoir*, 2 Jan 1952

21 *Ibid*. 18 Oct 1950

22 H.F. Quinn, *The Union Nationale: A Study in Quebec Nationalism* (Toronto 1963) 81

23 *Ibid*. 76

24 *Le Devoir*, 29 June 1950

25 *Ibid*. 20 July 1953

26 *Ibid*. 3 Jan 1949

27 *Ibid*. 12 June 1952

28 *Ibid*. 28 March 1949

29 *Ibid*. 5 Dec 1950

30 *Ibid*. 25 Oct 1955

31 *Ibid*. 25 Jan 1951

32 *Ibid*. 29 Aug 1946

33 *Ibid*. 12 Nov 1948

34 *Ibid*. 26 Aug 1946 and 11 Sept 1950

35 See Quinn, *The Union Nationale*, 88.

36 Louis-Marie Tremblay, *Le Syndicalisme québécois: idéologies de la CSN et de la FTQ* (Montreal 1972) 36–7

37 Gérard Pelletier, 'Sur les gaietés de l'opposition' in *Cité Libre*, no. 24, 1960, 7

38 P.-E. Trudeau, 'Un Manifeste démocratique' in *Cité Libre*, no. 22, 1958, 18

39 André Carrier, 'L'Idéologie politique de Cité Libre' (1967, thesis for the University of Montreal) 129

40 See P. Charbonneau, 'Défense et illustration de la gauche' in *Cité Libre*, no. 18, 1958, 37.

41 *Ibid.* 39
42 G.J. Wisley, 'La Planification dans une société libre' in *Cité Libre*, no. 53, 1963, 8
43 See P.-E. Trudeau, 'La Nouvelle trahison des clercs' in *Cité Libre*, no. 46, 1961, 4
44 *Ibid.* 12
45 *Ibid.*
46 Pierre Vadeboncoeur, 'Salutations d'usage' in *Parti Pris*, vol. 1 no. 1, Oct 1963, 50–1
47 G. Bourque and N. Frenette, 'La Structure nationale québécoise' in *Socialisme québécois*, nos 21–2, 138ff
48 Daniel Latouche, 'La Vrai nature de ... la Révolution tranquille' in *Canadian Political Science Review*, Sept 1974, 532
49 See Leon Dion, *Le Bill 60 et la société québécoise* (Montreal 1967)
50 Among the most important of these were the Société General de Financement, the Caisse de Dépôt et de Placement, Sidbec-Dosco, SOQUEM, SOQUIP, Programmes d'Aide à l'Industrie, the Centre de Recherches Industrielles, the Ecole Nationale d'Administration Publique, the Institut National d'Administration Publique, and the Institut National de la Recherche Scientifique.
51 Quoted by Gérard Bergeron, *Le Canada français après deux siècles de patience* (Paris 1967) 218
52 P.-E. Trudeau quoted in Marcel Rioux, *La Question du Québec* (Montreal 1976) 146
53 André d'Allemagne, *Le R.I.N. et les débats du mouvement indépendantiste québécois* (Montreal 1974), 42
54 See Réjean Pelletier, *Les Militants du R.I.N.* (Ottawa 1974) 35.
55 Parti Québécois platform, 1975, 19
56 *Ibid.* 26
57 Jean Meynaud, 'Le Programme économique du P.Q.' in *Maintenant*, March 1970, 99
58 Parti Québécois platform, 1975, 21
59 *Ibid.* 6
60 *Ibid.* 11
61 Quoted in Marc Laurendeau, *Les Québécois violents* (Montreal 1974) 40
62 *Ibid.* 49
63 Charles Gagnon, *Pour le parti prolétarien* (Montreal 1972) 9
64 Pierre Vallières, *L'Urgence de Choisir* (Montreal 1971) 111
65 L. Racine, P. Maheu, and G. Tremblay, 'Bilan du cléricalisme' in *Parti Pris*, vol. IV, nos 3–4, 37
66 Pierre Maheu, 'Laïcité 1966' in *Parti Pris*, vol. IV, no. 9, 47
67 R. Beaudin, 'La Stratégie de Parti Pris' in *Parti Pris*, vol. II, no. 9, 47

68 'Manifeste 1964–65,' in *Parti Pris*, vol. II, no. 1, 14
69 R. Beaudin, 'La Stratégie de Parti Pris'
70 'L'Indépendance au plus vite' in *Parti Pris*, vol. IV, nos. 5–6, 3
71 Pierre Maheu, 'Perspectives d'action' in *Parti Pris*, vol. II, no. 3, 10
72 Pierre Maheu, 'Notes pour une politicisation' in *Parti Pris*, vol. II, no. 1, 47
73 G. Gagnon, 'Pour un socialisme décolonisateur 'in *Parti Pris*, vol. IV, no. 1, 51
74 G. Gagnon, 'Les Voies de l'autogestion' in *Parti Pris*, vol. IX, nos 7–8, 62
75 For an exhaustive study of these movements, see *Quelques aspects du début d'un mouvement socialiste à Montréal*: Les Editions Mobilisation, vol. 3, no. 1.
76 Tremblay, *Le Syndicalisme québécois*, 39
77 Marcel Pépin, *Pour vaincre* (Montreal 1972) 24
78 CSN, *Ne comptons que sur nos propres moyens*, 57
79 *Ibid.* 64
80 See Louis Le Borgne, *La CSN et la question nationale depuis 1960* (Montreal 1976.
81 *Le Jour*, 17 May 1976, 18
82 See Diane Ethier, Jean-Marc Piotte, and Jean Reynolds, *Les Travailleurs contre l'Etat bourgeois* (Montreal 1975).

The PQ and the Test of Power

1 See André Bernard, *Québec: élections 1976* (Montreal 1976)

On the Referendum of May 1980

1 Lionel Groulx, *Orientations* (Montreal 1935) 248